Spinoza's Paradoxical C

Books available
Affects, Actions and Passions in Spinoza: The Unity of Body and Mind, Chantal Jaquet,
translated by Tatiana Reznichenko
The Spinoza-Machiavelli Encounter: Time and Occasion, Vittorio Morfino, translated by
Dave Mesing
Politics, Ontology and Knowledge in Spinoza, Alexandre Matheron, translated and edited by
Filippo Del Lucchese, David Maruzzella and Gil Morejón
Spinoza, the Epicurean: Authority and Utility in Materialism, Dimitris Vardoulakis
Experience and Eternity in Spinoza, Pierre-François Moreau, edited and translated by Robert
Boncardo
Spinoza and the Politics of Freedom, Dan Taylor
Spinoza's Political Philosophy: The Factory of Imperium, Riccardo Caporali, translated by
Fabio Gironi
Spinoza's Paradoxical Conservatism, François Zourabichvili, translated by Gil Morejón

Forthcoming
Affirmation and Resistance in Spinoza: Strategy of the Conatus, Laurent Bove, translated and
edited by Émilie Filion-Donato and Hasana Sharp
Spinoza and Contemporary Biology: Lectures on the Philosophy of Biology and Cognitivism,
Henri Atlan, translated by Inja Stracenski
Spinoza's Critique of Hobbes: Law, Power and Freedom, Christian Lazzeri, translated by Nils
F. Schott
Marx with Spinoza: Production, Alienation, History, Franck Fischbach, translated by Jason
Read
Spinoza and the Sign: The Logic of Imagination, Lorenzo Vinciguerra, translated by
Alexander Reynolds

Visit our website at www.edinburghuniversitypress.com/series/SPIN

Spinoza's Paradoxical Conservatism

François Zourabichvili

Translated by Gil Morejón

EDINBURGH
University Press

Edinburgh University Press is one of the leading university presses in the UK. We publish academic books and journals in our selected subject areas across the humanities and social sciences, combining cutting-edge scholarship with high editorial and production values to produce academic works of lasting importance. For more information visit our website: edinburghuniversitypress.com

Edinburgh University Press Ltd
13 Infirmary Street,
Edinburgh, EH1 1LT

Typeset in 10.5/13pt Goudy Old Style
by Cheshire Typesetting Ltd, Cuddington, Cheshire, and
printed and bound by CPI Group (UK) Ltd, Croydon, CR0 4YY

A CIP record for this book is available from the British Library

ISBN 978 1 4744 8904 1 (hardback)
ISBN 978 1 4744 8905 8 (paperback)
ISBN 978 1 4744 8907 2 (webready PDF)
ISBN 978 1 4744 8906 5 (epub)

Published with the support of the University of Edinburgh Scholarly Publishing Initiatives Fund.

For Félix and Timothée

Contents

Reference Conventions

I. Spinoza's Works

All quotations from Spinoza's works in English are taken from Curley's two-volume *Collected Works of Spinoza* (CWS). For each quote, I provide an internal reference to Spinoza's text using the conventions below, as well as a reference to the CWS volume and page number.

CM   *Appendix Containing Metaphysical Thoughts* (*Cogitata Metaphysica*). The first Roman numeral refers to Part number; the second refers to chapter number; Arabic numerals refer to line number.

CWS   *The Collected Works of Spinoza* (Spinoza 1985–2016). Roman numerals refer to volume number; Arabic numerals refer to page number.

Ep.   *Letters* (*Epistolae*). Roman numerals refer to letter number. Spinoza's correspondent is given in square brackets.

Ethics   *Ethics* (*Ethica Ordine Geometrico demonstrata et in quinque Partes distincta*). Roman numerals refer to Part number; Arabic numerals refer to Proposition number; further specifications follow the conventions below.

KV   *Short Treatise on God, Man and His Well-Being* (*Korte Verhandeling*). Roman numerals refer to chapter number; Arabic numerals refer to section number.

PP   *Descartes' Principles of Philosophy* (*Renati des Cartes Principiorum Philosophiae*). Roman numerals refer to Part number; further specifications follow the conventions below.

TdIE   *Treatise on the Emendation of the Intellect* (*Tractatus de Intellectus Emendatione*). Arabic numerals refer to the section numbers added by Bruder.

TP   *Political Treatise* (*Tractatus Politicus*). Roman numerals refer to chapter number; Arabic numerals refer to paragraph number.

TTP   *Theologico-Political Treatise* (*Tractatus Theologico-Politicus*). Roman numerals refer to chapter number; Arabic numerals refer to paragraph number.

Alt. Dem.	Alternative Demonstration
App.	Appendix
Ax.	Axiom
Cap. #	Chapter
Cor.	Corollary
DA #	Definition of the Affects
Def.	Definition
Dem.	Demonstration
Exp.	Explanation
GDA	General Definition of the Affects
Lem.	Lemma
Post.	Postulate
Praef.	Preface
Prol.	Prolegomenon
Schol.	Scholium

II. Other Works

For most major canonical works I have sought to provide references both for internal textual divisions and for the page numbers of the specific edition quoted. I do not think it should be necessary to enumerate these in detail; I trust the reader will be able to determine what the specific schema is in each case. Nevertheless, here are two examples: 'De Cive XII, 8 (Hobbes 1998: 137)' refers to paragraph eight of chapter twelve of Hobbes's *De Cive*, which can be found on page 137 of the 1998 Cambridge edition; '*Dialogues* XIV, 8 (Malebranche 1997a: 273)' refers to section eight of dialogue fourteen of Malebranche's *Dialogues on Metaphysics and on Religion*, which can be found on page 273 in the 1997 Cambridge edition.

For writings by Descartes I provide references to the volume and page number of *Œuvres de Descartes* edited by Adam and Tannery (Descartes 1964–76), abbreviated as *AT*, and to the volume and page number of *The Philosophical Writings of Descartes* edited by Cottingham, Stoothoff, and Murdoch (Descartes 1994–95), abbreviated as CSM.

Zourabichvili regularly refers to Macherey's five-volume *Introduction à l'Éthique de Spinoza*. I cite this work as 'Macherey, *Introduction*', with Roman numerals indicating the volume number and Arabic numerals indicating the page number.

I cite St Thomas Aquinas' *Summa Theologiae* using standard internal references; for instance, 'I-II q.49 a.2' refers to Article 2 of Question 49 from the First Part of the Second Part.

For quotations from Scripture I provide standard references using the name of the Book with chapter and verse numbers, and page numbers from the New Revised Standard Version (Coogan et al. 2018), abbreviated as *NRSV*.

Notes on Translation and Acknowledgements

This translation required more than a few difficult decisions, not only due to the density of Zourabichvili's French prose but also thanks to the complicated relationships between certain terms in English, French, and Latin. I have occasionally left Zourabichvili's French in square brackets, and the text below will sometimes include footnotes where I explain specific linguistic discrepancies and translation choices. Usually these have to do with my choice to modify the English translation of Spinoza's Latin, and I often provide comparisons with the extant translations. Since Zourabichvili also sometimes interpolates Spinoza's Latin directly into the translations he cites, I have adopted the following convention: when these interpolations are Zourabichvili's, they are placed in parentheses; when I add them for additional clarity, they are placed in square brackets. When the reference for a quotation is to a text in the original French or Italian, the quoted translation is my own.

These general considerations aside, two particular sets of translation decisions seem to me to require particular and more extensive justification, namely those having to do with the language of *conservation* and the language of *childhood*.

Conserving Oneself/Conservation/*Conservatisme*

Most importantly, the French terms *se conserver*, *conservation*, and *conservatisme* presented a basically impossible task for the translator. The verb 'se conserver' is the standard French translation of Spinoza's Latin 'perseverare', as in the famous formula of the conatus: a mode's actual essence is its striving to persevere in its being, *in suo esse perseverare conatur*.[1] In speaking of

---

[1] *Ethics* III, 7; CWS I, 499.

Spinoza's *conservatisme*, Zourabichvili is provocatively drawing the reader's attention to the link, manifest at the level of the French language, between the self-preservative activity of modal conatus and the notion of conservatism in a political register: a reader would not fail to immediately note that if a mode essentially strives *à se conserver*, this would seem to establish a metaphysical ground for some version of conservatism. However, Zourabichvili also clearly distinguishes the political conservatism he draws out of Spinoza's metaphysics from the reactionary conservatism with which we are more familiar today (see the end of the Introduction and the book's final chapter).

The difficulty, for the translator, is obviously that there is no such link in the English terms: the standard rendering of 'striving to persevere in its being' is a perfect translation of 'in suo esse perseverare conatur', but has no resonance with 'conservatism', and it would be unhelpful and artificial to attempt to force an ugly neologism like 'preservatism'. I have consequently chosen to translate Zourabichvili's use of the terms *se conserver* and *conservation* as 'conserve' and 'conservation' in order to retain the resonance with 'conservatism', although these should be understood as renderings of Spinoza's *perseverare*, and 'persevere' and 'preservation' would have been more faithful to the original Latin and to the standard English translations. By contrast, when the word 'persevere' appears below, which happens only rarely, it is always a direct translation of 'persévérer', so that this play on words is absent in the original. Readers familiar with standard English translations of Spinoza might balk at formulations such as 'a mode strives to conserve itself in its being', but in order to capture the play of Zourabichvili's language this minor discomfort seemed impossible to avoid.

Childhood: *Infans/Enfance*

Another resonance that was impossible to capture precisely revolves around the language concerning children and childhood, infants and infancy. Zourabichvili himself comments on the complex in/distinction of these terms in Latin and French in the final pages of the Introduction, below. The relevant Latin terms from Spinoza's texts are *infans* and *puer*. As Zourabichvili notes, sometimes the former seems to be distinguished from the latter in the same way that, in English, we distinguish 'infant' from 'child', as specifically marking out the very earliest years of life; thus in the scholium to III, 2: 'Sic *infans* se lac libere appetere credit, *puer* autem iratus vindictam velle, et timidus fugam'; 'So the *infant* believes he freely wants the milk; the angry *child* that he wants vengeance, and the timid, flight.'[2] However, sometimes *infans* is used broadly to encompass all of youth, as in the scholium to V, 39: 'Qui enim ex *infante vel puero* in cadaver transit, infelix dicitur'; 'For he who has passed from being an *infant or child* to being a corpse is called unhappy.'[3]

It is clear to me based on Zourabichvili's argument that when he speaks of *enfance* or *enfant* as a properly philosophical Spinozist concept, he almost always means it in the broader sense, so that it would be misleading to allow the English reader to think that the argument is more narrowly about infants. Accordingly, I have adopted the following protocol: I render 'enfance' and 'enfant' as consistently as possible as 'childhood' and 'child'; when I use the terms 'infant' and 'infancy', it is almost always because Zourabichvili has used the terms 'nourrisson', 'tout-petit', 'petite enfance', or 'jeune enfance'. A bit more flexibly and dependent on context, I translate 'enfantin' and 'puéril' either as 'childish' or 'childlike', and the French 'infantile' either as 'infantile' or 'childish'. Note that I have left the standard English translations mostly unaltered, and Curley tends to render *infans* as 'infant'. The most important exception to this is without question V 39, schol., where Zourabichvili insists that we must read *corpus infantiae* as 'the body of childhood', and not 'the child's body' or 'the infant's body'. I must leave it to the reader to determine whether this set of decisions was appropriate.

As for the 'ambiguous and transitory age'[4] between childhood and adulthood, there was ironically nothing ambiguous about it for the translator: Latin *adolescens*, French *adolescence*, and English *adolescence* have the same semantic value in this context.

I am blessed to have been supported by numerous friends and colleagues during my time working on this project. Let me name only a small handful without whom this would not have been possible: Eric Aldieri, Lillian Cicerchia, Filippo Del Lucchese, Owen Glyn-Williams, Carlie Hughes, David Maruzzella, William Paris, Daniel Pepe, Michael Peterson, and Alejo Stark. I could have named many others, and beg forgiveness that I have kept this list so short. I would also like to extend my gratitude to the wonderful team at Edinburgh University Press, especially Carol Macdonald and Tim Clark, for their tireless efforts. My deepest thanks to everyone.

---

[2] *Ethics* III, 2 Schol.; CWS I, 496. Emphasis added.
[3] *Ethics* V, 39 Schol.; CWS I, 614. Emphasis added.
[4] See below, p. 131.

The Problem of Transformation in Spinoza's Metaphysics according to Zourabichvili

Gil Morejón

Every student of Spinoza's philosophy knows the formula of the conatus: the actual essence of each finite thing is its striving to persevere in its being. But few have recognised with quite so much acuity and sensitivity as François Zourabichvili what profound difficulties this basic notion must inevitably produce for a philosophy that precisely calls itself an *ethics*. The question that serves as the founding insight of this book is disarmingly simple: if all things strive to persevere in their being, how could they ever seek to change in anything other than a superficial way? Could they not merely confirm, and reconfirm each time anew, whatever it is that already pertains to their essential nature? For is not the fundamental feature of any ethics – even one that manages to avoid the traps of a transcendent moralism – that it involves some kind of demand that one change oneself? And is not the task and promise of Spinoza's philosophy to determine how one can leave behind a passive state of ignorance in order to develop the active powers of think-ing? Yet the formula seems to block any such transformation in advance: *Conatus, quo unaquaeque res in suo esse perseverare conatur, nihil est praeter ipsius rei actualem essentiam.*[1]

This apparent puzzle is the first way to understand the *paradoxical* in the title of this remarkable book by François Zourabichvili, one of two he pub-lished in 2002, and a strong candidate for the most creative and unique work of Spinoza scholarship in many decades. Zourabichvili's rigorous fidelity to the letter of the text across the entirety of Spinoza's oeuvre is matched, per-haps even outmatched, by the frequently surprising nature of the concepts and problems that catch his sustained attention, attested to by the seeming disparity of the themes of the three studies that constitute the book: ethical conversion and the notion of one's element; childhood and growing up; and

---

[1] *Ethics* III, 7; CWS I, 499.

political form and revolution. Yet the definite unity of the text is organised around this fundamental problem: how can we hold together this metaphysical claim, that finite things are characterised above all by their striving to persevere in their being, with the continual demand that we become somehow other than what we are – whether in an ethical, personal, or political register? This is what I would like to call the problem of transformation in Spinoza's metaphysics.

In this introduction I begin with a brief biographical sketch of the author and proceed from there to lay out a roadmap of the book, explaining how the three studies it contains hang together and what is at stake in each of their analyses. I believe that each of them individually offer striking and novel insights that can and should make a considerable impact on contemporary Spinoza research. But taken together, synthetically and holistically, they are also exemplary in showing us what it means, as Zourabichvili writes elsewhere, to 'speak Spinozan'.[2] They function according to an entirely new grammar or syntax of thought, in light of which the juxtaposition of the three studies no longer strikes one as idiosyncratic: in the end these problematics clearly belong together, and it is one of the peculiar strengths of Zourabichvili's work that it enables us to understand this adequately.

In 1898, a man named Georges Zourabichvili was born in present-day Georgia in the Russian Empire. He acquired doctorates in philosophy and political economy at the University of Heidelberg before moving to France in the early 1920s. He had two children: Hélène Carrère d'Encausse, born 1929, a historian and member of the Académie française, and Nicolas, born 1936, a composer. In 1957, Hélène gave birth to Emmanuel Carrère, a writer and film director. Emmanuelle's 2007 autobiographical work *Un roman russe* revealed more of his grandfather's story: Georges, it turns out, had collaborated with the Nazis during the Second World War as an interpreter and then vanished without a trace in 1944.[3] In 1965, Nicolas had a son, François, the author of the present work, in Poitiers. He would live only to forty-one years old, tragically taking his own life in Paris in 2006.

François Zourabichvili accomplished a great deal in his short time.[4] He passed the *agrégation* in 1989, teaching at secondary schools until 2001. In 1999 he received his doctorate in philosophy, defending a thesis on Spinoza

---

[2] Zourabichvili 2002, ch. 5.
[3] Carrère 2007.
[4] See Smith and Lambert, 'François Zourabichvili and the Physics of Thought', in Zourabichvili 2012.

directed by Étienne Balibar and Dominique Lecourt. He was *maître de conferences* at University Paul Valéry, Montepelier III, from 2001 onward, and a director at the Collège international de philosophie in Paris from 1998 to 2004. As a student he attended Gilles Deleuze's seminars at Vincennes, and there can be no question both that Deleuze was the thinker who had the greatest impact on his own thought, and that in return Zourabichvili left an indelible mark on our understanding of Deleuze's philosophy. His first book was *Deleuze: Une philosophie de l'événement* (1994), and his last was *Le vocabulaire de Deleuze* (2003), published together in English translation in 2012 as *Deleuze: A Philosophy of the Event*.[5] In 2002, he published two books on Spinoza: *Spinoza: Une physique de la pensée* (*Spinoza: A Physics of Thought*),[6] and the present work, *Le conservatisme paradoxal de Spinoza. Enfance et royauté*. Two years after the latter's publication, in 2004, the book was the focus of a session of Pierre Macherey's weekly study group 'La philosophie au sens large', with a critical exposition of the text by Macherey and a response by Zourabichvili himself; that exchange is included as an appendix to the present volume. In addition, Zourabichvili wrote numerous articles, some on philosophers like Spinoza and Deleuze, as well as Leibniz, Hegel, Nietzsche, and Bergson, but many of which focused on aesthetics, with essays exploring themes such as literality, film, and play. In 2011, Anne Sauvagnargues edited a collection of his writings on art entitled *La littéralité et autres essais sur l'art*.[7]

Spinoza's Paradoxical Conservatism is, as I have suggested, organised around the central problematic of transformation in Spinozist metaphysics, a theme whose variations are explored across the three separate studies. The first concerns what Zourabichvili likes to call 'ethical conversion': the journey by which the ignorant become wise and come to lead a philosophical life. This is, of course, a classical problem in Western philosophy, tracing back to the paradox of learning in Plato's *Meno*: either it is the case that the ignorant already knows what they seek to learn, so that they cannot be said properly to learn anything new; or else, they do not know what they seek to learn, in which case it is not clear how they could seek it at all.[8] In Spinoza, Zourabichvili argues, this dilemma is approached twice: first in the *Short Treatise*, where Spinoza elaborates the image of being out of one's 'element' and reconfigures the Christian image of 'rebirth', and again in the early par-

---

[5] Zourabichvili 2012.
[6] Zourabichvili 2002.
[7] Zourabichvili 2011.
[8] 80d-e (Plato 1997: 879–80).

agraphs of the *Treatise on the Emendation of the Intellect*, where it is a matter of recognising the unsatisfying character of the everyday goods that distract us from our own natures. In both cases, the solution will ultimately be our union with God, our realignment with our own natures, and our belonging to Nature now in an adequate, rather than a merely confused and inadequate way.

This is in fact *not* a transformation, it does not involve a *subjecti transformatio*: to return to one's own proper element, to turn away from the distracting goods of ordinary life and to establish an organisation of one's affectivity oriented toward the union with God or Nature does not amount to a fundamental transformation of the subject at all, but a discovery of one's own nature and a reshaping of one's life in accordance with that discovery. Yet it is a terrible ordeal to redirect one's already-invested striving so profoundly, and one would be forgiven for scarcely recognising oneself after enduring it. Zourabichvili rightly emphasises the panic and despair breathlessly animating the narration of the *Treatise on the Emendation of the Intellect*: philosophy, for Spinoza, begins not in curious wonder nor love of truth, but in a desperate state of affective misery and yawning existential dread, where the things of everyday life are already being experienced as empty and futile, *vana & futilia*. The illusion of this change being a transformation arises from a double misrecognition: our initial misery comes from the fact that we find ourselves living in a foreign and hostile element, which we confusedly think is proper to us, and on whose basis we then misunderstand our own natures. This makes it impossible for us to preserve or conserve ourselves in any lasting or reliable way – indeed, it leads us to strive to undermine the conditions for our own perseverance. Ethical conversion is a matter, then, of instituting a new mode of existence that corresponds to our nature, not a transformation of our conatus but its fundamental reorientation.

The second study focuses on the concept of childhood, and it contains some of Zourabichvili's most creative and unique insights into Spinoza's philosophy. To begin with, let us notice that Spinoza, with his thoroughgoing anti-teleologism, could never have accepted the dominant Aristotelian paradigm according to which the child is understood as an incomplete human being, a human being merely *in potentia* in comparison with the realised human essence of the rational adult, *vir perfectus*. This forces a total re-evaluation of the notion of the child, which must be understood as perfect, just like everything else in nature. But to be a child is also not particularly desirable, any more than it is desirable to be ignorant or distracted. After all, like the biblical Adam, the child is above all characterised by the inadequacy of its knowledge and its relative lack of power to persevere in its being.

Hence the problem to be posed and solved is that of an adequate pedagogy. Here Zourabichvili draws our attention to the paradoxical figure of the *infans adultus*, the grown-up child or the newborn adult, which appears surprisingly often and at crucial moments in Spinoza's writings; and he connects this image, which seems to combine the incommensurable forms of the child and the adult in a disturbing chimera, to the contradictory representations of childhood in Baroque painting and in the new medical science of paedi-atrics in late medieval and early modern Europe. Zourabichvili suggests that this period bore witness to the discovery of childhood as such, freed from the actualisation schema of Aristotelian metaphysics with its final causality, and that Spinoza was perhaps the first to elaborate this discovery in a philosoph-ical register.

Is the process of growing up a transformation or not? The question seems more difficult to answer this time. On the one hand, Spinoza remarks: 'In this life, then, we strive especially that the Body of childhood [*corpus infan-tiae*] may change [*mutetur*] (as much as its nature allows and assists) into another, capable of a great many things and related to a Mind very con-scious of itself, of God, and of things.'[9] The reference to changing *as much as its nature allows* (*quantum ejus natura patitur*) suggests that this too is not a transformation, or a replacement of one nature or essence with another that differs from it in kind, but rather an immanent development of one and the same form in the course of duration. Yet on the other hand, there is clearly a kind of rupture between the child and the adult, one more striking even than that between the ignorant and the wise of the first study: 'A man of advanced years believes their nature to be so different from his own that he could not be persuaded that he was ever an infant, if he did not make this conjecture concerning himself from [the example of] others.'[10] Here again the radical difference in nature between the two is illusory, but for a differ-ent reason than in the previous case: it arises, this time, due to the fact that the infant is without memory, whereas the adult's general tendency to be trapped in inadequate ideas is precisely a function of the overbearing weight of memorial associations formed in the contingency of experience.

Childhood, then, is properly understood not as a stable state – in yet another paradox, that the child is, 'as it were, in a state of equilibrium'[11] is not a marker of stability – but as the very process of development, of

---

[9] *Ethics* V, 39 Schol.; CWS I, 614. Translation modified. See the section on childhood in the Notes on Translation, above.
[10] *Ethics* IV, 39 Schol.; CWS I, 569–70.
[11] *Ethics* III, 32 Schol.; CWS I, 513.

the formation of memory and the progressive institution of the individual human being in its singular form or essence, from which it must nevertheless emancipate itself. In this way childhood may well be, as Zourabichvili provocatively suggests, the image of humanity itself in its becoming, at the same time that Spinoza is perfectly aware that the vast majority of human beings never manage to leave behind the impotence and confusion of childhood. For without any moralisation about the obstinate childishness of most human beings, Spinoza here as always is insistent that all things excellent are as difficult as they are rare. The study concludes with a reflection on the elements of a Spinozist pedagogy, which seeks not to transform but to support the child in its progressive development to the point of rupture, and with a very beautiful and pensive sketch of a fictional retrospective autobiography written by the philosopher Benedictus, born infant and become philosopher.

This finally leads us to the third study, which itself is split into distinct inquiries whose unity is at first glance hard to discern. But the connections become increasingly striking. There is, for instance, the analysis of the Hebrew people after the flight from Egypt, whose continual characterisation by Spinoza as being 'childish' throughout the *Theologico-Political Treatise* must now be understood as having a previously unrecognised philosophical significance. Or again, the question of constitution or political form is raised now from the perspective of memory: the problem with revolutions – Zourabichvili, like Spinoza and moreover Deleuze, is deeply sceptical about their prospects[12] – is that the people who undertake them still have *too much* political memory, that they remain too bound by the habituations

---

[12] This topic deserves a much lengthier digression than would be appropriate here. Still, allow me to provide some references that would help triangulate the problem, which concerns Deleuze's opposition between *becoming* and *history* and which Zourabichvili's work in these chapters can help clarify considerably. 'It is not the historian's reflection which demonstrates a resemblance between Luther and Paul, between the Revolution of 1789 and the Roman Republic, etc. Rather, it is in the first place for themselves that the revolutionaries are determined to lead their lives as "resuscitated Romans", before becoming capable of the act which they have begun by repeating in the mode of a proper past, therefore under conditions such that they necessarily identify with a figure from the historical past' (Deleuze 2001: 90); 'the success of a revolution resides only in itself, precisely in the vibrations, clinches, and openings it gave to men and women at the moment of its making and that composes in itself a monument that is always in the process of becoming, like those tumuli to which each new traveler adds a stone. The victory of a revolution is immanent and consists in the new bonds it installs between people, even if these bonds last no longer than the revolution's fused material and quickly give way to division and betrayal' (Deleuze and Guattari 1994: 177). See Smith 2012, chs. 9 and 20; Nail 2012; Lampert 2006; and Michael-Matsas 2016.

and customs that they hope to leave behind by transforming the political order. As Zourabichvili writes, 'a revolutionary multitude may well aspire to freedom; it so aspires like the ignorant person who believes themselves free while being totally unaware of the causes that determine them'.[13] The freedom of the multitude, by contrast, involves well and truly the forgetting of its previous political form, thematised again as a kind of rebirth or new childhood: the movement of liberation is a liberation from memory as such.[14] All of Spinoza's philosophy is ultimately organised around the problematic of liberation, and just as in the case of ethical conversion there is a need to forget one's former affective constellation, here the political liberatory movement is frustrated in advance insofar as memory persists in determining the orientation of the conatus of the multitude that hopes to preserve itself in accordance with its own nature.

Hence one can say that it is only here in the third study that we finally encounter genuine instances of transformation, or at least of transformative aspirations, and here more than anywhere else we find Zourabichvili and Spinoza working as symptomatologists, diagnosing contradictory and untenable configurations of desire. This is why Zourabichvili says that the desire for revolution is a 'logical monster' for Spinoza: this, indeed, is a case of one's striving to have a nature other than that which one has, of one's remembering what one is and sadly wishing to be otherwise. And we can also now see why Zourabichvili provocatively describes Spinoza's philosophy, in politics as well as for individual striving, as a 'conservatism': the only viable course of action is to seek the conditions under which one may strive to persevere in one's being adequately and effectively, not to seek to transform one's own nature in order to accommodate oneself to fundamentally hostile and inhospitable conditions.[15] This, of course, has little to do with the everyday sense of 'conservatism', and nothing about this conception entails that a Spinozist would need to be 'conservative' on any particular political, social, or cultural issue. But Zourabichvili is surely right that the metaphysics of the conatus should give pause to those who see in Spinoza a simple advocate for revolutionary change. Indeed, a direct transformation of this sort, the replacement of one essential nature with another, whether at the political level of the

---

[13] P. 16, below.

[14] As Spinoza says in the sentence following the line we quoted earlier about our striving to change the body of childhood: 'We strive, that is, that whatever is related to its memory or imagination is of hardly any moment in relation to the intellect' (*Ethics* V, 39 Schol.; CWS I, 614).

[15] See the section on conservation in the Notes on Translation, above.

multitude or the individual level of the person, is best understood simply as a death, and this cannot be desired for itself.

Hence too one of the other objects of the third study, absolute monarchism, which can be properly characterised in these terms as being suicidal by virtue of its obsessional desire for transformation. In Spinoza's political thought, absolute monarchy is the most obviously paradoxical and untenable of all political forms, and this is clearly true even in spite of the fact that the explicit aim of the *Political Treatise* is to determine the conditions of maximal stability for each of them. Truly absolute monarchy, as Zourabichvili emphasises, cannot be what it claims to be, on Spinoza's analysis; it would be wholly impossible as such, and thus must dissimulate its really composite nature – itself chimerical and contradictory – beneath a false appearance of unity. At the same time, it is a political form that would be suitable for the governance of a humanity that is also something other than itself: human beings cannot in the end abide this sovereignty that demands to prescribe for them even what it is permissible to think and to desire. Thus absolute monarchy seeks to transform human beings into something other than what they are, which is as futile as the desire for self-transformation. Spinoza develops this analysis, as Zourabichvili notes, in a historical moment when absolute monarchism, this monstrous and doomed state-form, was in fact on the rise in Europe, and exemplified nowhere better than in the paradoxical person of the Sun King, Louis XIV. For its claim to absoluteness, absolute monarchy encourages and even requires a confusion of the power of God and the power of kings, which even at its maximally conceivable concentration and force remains all-too-human, fundamentally lacking the immutability and necessity that really characterises the power of *Deus sive Natura*. So while on the one hand absolute monarchy strives in vain to transform its subjects into something other than the human beings that they are, on the other hand it does the same for its own monarch, whose essential nature similarly cannot fail to be human. If striving to transform nature, whether that of subjects or leaders, of others or oneself, is futile according to Spinoza, a confused and suicidal undertaking at the level of social organisation, it is appropriate that Zourabichvili closes the third study with a reflection on the concept of the free multitude, which refuses the allure of transformation in favour of, once again, a redirection of desire on the basis of the rediscovery of its own nature, a reorientation of collective conatus within the element proper to it, there to discover and develop its own powers of acting in the memoryless struggle for survival.

All of the three studies that comprise this book, as I have argued, revolve around the problem of transformation, but another way to put this is that they all revolve around the concept of *form*. Spinoza's refusal of classical notions of form – for instance in his rejection of the idea that there is a unitary essence of humanity – does not, as Zourabichvili convincingly demonstrates, mean that he rejects the concept of form outright.[16] Rather, Spinoza reconfigures it on entirely new theoretical bases, most significantly on the notion of the individual as essentially determined as the communication of a certain ratio of motion and rest among the parts that constitute it, and this new concept of form forces re-evaluations of very old practical and philosophical problems, as well as the articulation of new ones. Above all, the new concept of form recasts transformation as essentially fatal and undesirable in itself, and one of the most pressing tasks for Spinoza becomes the explanation of the possibility of its being desired in fact in spite of this. Alongside this, it becomes necessary to explore what kind of change is possible and desirable when transformation is ruled out, since all the real problems of practical life do require that significant changes be made, whether that means a restructuring of our memory and affectivity or of our modes of social and political organisation. In this book, Zourabichvili takes on both of these tasks by focusing on these elements of Spinoza's work that at first glance seem so idiosyncratic and unfamiliar – the notion of one's element, the concept of childhood, absolute monarchism – but which reveal themselves to be focal points where these crucial questions of transformation and change are raised in a rigorous and systematic fashion.

In this introduction I have just barely touched on the complexity and subtlety of the remarkable and innovative ideas that the book so vividly brings to life, and I hope you will find that I have done some justice to the potency and creativity of Zourabichvili's strikingly original work. Zourabichvili once said that philosophy would not escape the Deleuzian adventure unscathed, and I am convinced that similarly no understanding of Spinoza can emerge from the encounter with Zourabichvili's reading without undergoing profound changes.[17] The metaphysics of the conatus does not mean simply remaining what one already was, but striving to become what one is and can be, in order to be able to persevere and thereby to produce whatever effects follow from one's nature actively, as an adequate cause. For, as the final lines of the book's conclusion tell us, conservation is a condition for the possibility of creation.

---

[16] See too Zourabichvili 2002, ch. 1.
[17] Zourabichvili 2012: 41.

Introduction

After the death of my son, from one man I transformed into another, and then into another still. I had nothing to do with it, all of that happened to me and carried me away, suddenly I was another. And you must know all this. You saw it. I do not know what those I used to be had wanted, I do not know what others await me, I do not know whether I myself, here, Spinoza, am not one of the others. (Excerpt from the film *Les Autres*, by Hugo Santiago)[1]

The characteristic peculiarity and tension of Spinozism is most striking when one raises the question of change. Doubtless this question could not remain external to a thought that is defined above all as an ethics, and which, under this heading, is inseparable from an idea of progress (*ad majorem perfectionem transire*), elaborated on the basis of an incessant oscillation (*in continua vivimus variatione*), in relation to a fundamental permanence (*immutabilitas Dei*). Nevertheless, this schema, which after all is only a truism of moral philosophy, tells us nothing of Spinoza's originality. It must be completed, or rather troubled, by what we might call the paradoxical triangle of Spinozism: to progress is ultimately to learn to conserve oneself;[2] and the work of conservation constantly runs up against the question of transformation. The

---

[1] The elegance of the film is that it allows one to believe in a relation of simple homonymy between the principal character, a bookseller by trade, and the philosopher who polished lenses; and consequently in the 'surrealistic' character of the allusions to the latter. In reality, the film unfolds in light and sound what Borges, co-screenwriter, sensed a long time ago, namely that the question of transformation works from within the motif of *perseverare in suo esse*. See the short story 'Borges and I' [Borges 1964: 230], and the last tercet of the sonnet 'Spinoza' [Borges 1981: 285].

[2] [See the section on Conserving Oneself/Conservation/*Conservatisme* in the Notes on Translation, above. – GM.]

key to this triangle, so to speak, is given at the end of the *Ethics*, when – notwithstanding his critique of ideas of chimeras and metamorphosis – Spinoza tosses out the great contradictory image of the *infans adultus*, the 'adult child', which refers back to a whole set of texts whose problematic connections it reveals.

The notion of transformation, in the seventeenth century, still belonged to the domain of mystery: it was of interest to the theologian and alchemist, and one could point out that the theology of mysteries itself required that of alchemy.[3] We know what scorn Spinoza had for the fundamental belief of Christianity, that of the Incarnation, or of God become man.[4] We also know the mechanistic approach that he adopted in his approach to chemical phenomena.[5] Furthermore, transformation was a key motif of baroque aesthetics, and of the taste for mythological marvels on display in the Calvinist Netherlands: there again, we have Spinoza's scorn.[6] Finally, the seventeenth century bore witness in England to the first great modern attempt at political transformation – and Spinoza was pessimistic.[7]

It might seem that a thought resolutely inscribed within the horizon of essence and the principle of non-contradiction would have little to say about transformation, and could only remain limited to the sterile confirmation of its fundamental impossibility, perhaps going on to formulate a moral and political prohibition. Transformation, understood in the strong or strict sense of a change affecting the subject and not its predicates, transformation thus understood as a change of identity means illogic itself, the height of transgression, revealing a collapse of reason.[8]

---

[3] Brunschvicg 1971: 195.

[4] *Ep.* LXXIII [to Oldenburg] (Spinoza has here just emphasised the wisdom of Christ): 'As for what certain Churches add to this – that God assumed a human nature (*naturam humanam assumpserit*) – I warned expressly that I don't know what they mean. Indeed, to confess the truth, they seem to me to speak no less absurdly than if someone were to say that a circle has assumed (*induerit*) the nature of a square' (*CWS* II, 468).

[5] See *Ep.* VI and XIII to Oldenburg, where the latter was just an intermediary between Spinoza and Boyle. See too *Ep.* XL to Jelles and LXXII to Schuller, which reveal a guarded curiosity with regard to alchemy.

[6] *TdIE* 37; *CWS* I, 18–19; and *Ethics* I, 8 Schol. 2; *CWS* I, 412–16.

[7] *TTP* XVIII, 33; *CWS* II, 329–30.

[8] Throughout this work, we will utilise the word 'transformation' in this strict technical sense. This precision is important in order to avoid certain false polemics. For example, we will explain that, for Spinoza, the ethical journey is not a transformation, and that the latter can not really be the object of desire. This in no way implies that we are opposed to Antonio Negri when he writes that Spinoza presents 'the activity of the masses as the foundation of both social and political transformation', or that, for

Moreover, in Spinoza the becoming of each thing is circumscribed by its essence, which corresponds to the form of its individuality. His novelty here is clear, since the traditional notion of form is redefined in a strictly mechanistic sense:

> what constitutes the form of the Individual consists in the union of the bodies (by the preceding definition).[9]

> what constitutes the form of the human Body consists in this, that its Parts communicate their motions to one another in a certain fixed proportion.[10]

Not only is form no longer related to the soul, but it is now individuated, and no longer specific. On the other hand, the essence is actualised in a certain *quantum* of striving by which the form is affirmed and tends to conserve itself (the famous *conatus*).[11] The principle of 'persevering in one's being', which defines existence in duration, implies the maintenance of a form and leads to the ontological disqualification of transformation.

At first glance, then, Spinoza's thought does not seem conducive to a positive or fruitful investigation into transformation, and from this point of view the historian of philosophy might be more inclined to turn to Bacon.[12]

Spinoza, 'Truth is freedom, transformation, liberation' (Negri 1991: xviii and 134); nor that we deny what Foucault says when he underscores that the problem of access to the truth, in the *Treatise on the Emendation of the Intellect*, is tied to the question 'in what aspects and how must I transform my being as subject?' (Foucault 2005: 27). Suffice it to say that these authors do not use the word in its technical and scholastic sense. Later our interest in this verbal ascesis will become apparent.

[9] *Ethics* II, L4 after 13; CWS I, 461.

[10] *Ethics* IV, 39 Dem.; CWS I, 568.

[11] *Ethics* III, 6–7; CWS I, 498–9.

[12] Bacon is the first 'modern' philosopher to update the concept of form. And his critique of chemistry (or of alchemy) is animated by an acute interest in the technical possibilities of transformation: 'But no one can endow a given body with a new nature or successfully and appropriately transmute it into a new body without possessing a good knowledge of modification or transformation of body. He will find himself using useless methods, or at least difficult and cumbersome methods unsuitable for the nature of the body on which he is working. Thus here too the road needs to be opened and constructed' (*The New Organon* II, 7 [Bacon 2000: 107]). The most general programme of metaphysics is thus the 'inquiry after forms', to which there corresponds, on the practical level, a purified 'magic' (*The New Organon* II, 9 [Bacon 2000: 109]). Would it be worthwhile to explore in greater depth a possible relation of filiation between Bacon and Spinoza, for example by way of the following passage? 'The principal advantage which we derive from things outside us – apart from the experience and knowledge we acquire from observing them and changing them from one form into another – lies in

However, there are reasons to believe not only that Spinoza ran into the problem of transformation, but that he confronted it like no philosopher before him.

In numerous texts that invoke a *formae mutatio*, or *in aliam formam mutatio*, the word *forma* can be replaced by an equivalent term, *natura* or *essentia*: 'change of form', 'change from one form into another'.[13] In the same sense, Spinoza also speaks of *aliam naturam induere*, 'taking on a new nature'.[14] In all these cases, it is a matter of a change of form or essence, or, as the only passage where the word *transformatio* appears, of a 'transformation of the subject'.[15]

the preservation of our body' (*Ethics* IV, App. Cap. XXVII; CWS I, 592). Doubtless the rejection of final causes, which implies the physical redefinition of form in terms of 'schematism' or internal laws, was influential for Descartes and Spinoza. Nevertheless Bacon was still far from a truly mechanistic conception: 'But there is a danger in [the "*instances of transition*" that preside over generation and corruption] which requires a caution; they may bring the form too close to the efficient cause, and may soak, or at least dip, the intellect in a false view of the form in relation to the efficient cause. The efficient cause is always defined as nothing other than the vehicle or bearer of the form' (*The New Organon* II, 23 [Bacon 2000: 137]). And form for Bacon remains a species or quality (for example, heat, light, weight) that comes to inform matter, and whose 'pure act' is to be explained by the discovery of the laws that are proper to it (*The New Organon* II, 17 [Bacon 2000: 127–8]). This is why we do not really buy the rapprochement suggested by Koyré, departing from one of Sigwart's claims, between 'particular affirmative essences', namely the 'fixed and eternal things' of the *Treatise on the Emendation of the Intellect*, and forms according to Bacon (see the footnotes by Koyré in his edition of the *Treatise* [Spinoza 1994: 111–12]). Koyré invokes a dynamism supposedly common to the Baconian and Spinozist conceptions; we hardly see a significant filiation here, and certainly not between the former's 'latent schematism' and the latter's 'relation of movement and rest'. Rather, there seems to be a more interesting relationship between Bacon and Leibniz (see Leibniz's letter to Arnauld of 30 April 1687, where he borrows from Bacon the notion of 'metaschematism'). Finally, the passage from the *Ethics* cited above clearly shows the centre of gravity of Spinoza's thought: the 'conservation of the body'. Of course, we here leave aside Spinoza's remarks on the subject of Baconian method.

[13] See, for example, *Ethics* I, 8 Schol. 2; I, 20 cor. 2; II, L4–6 after 13; III, Praef.; IV, Praef; IV, 20 Schol.; IV, 39 Schol.; IV, App. Cap. XXVII; *TTP* XVIII (three times on one page in the original); *TP*, VI, 2; *TP* X, 1; *TP* X, 10. Here we are leaving out the numerous occurrences of the expression *mutare in*.

[14] See, for example, *Ethics* II, A3 after 13; IV, 20 Schol.; IV, 39 Dem.; *TP* IV, 4.

[15] *CM* IV, 4; *CWS* I, 321: *subjecti transformatio*, which defines *transformatio* properly speaking. Spinoza here takes up the scholastic notion of a 'corruption that at the same time includes the generation following corruption', which repeats the traditional axiom: *corruptio unius est generatio alterius*, for matter does not lose a form without receiving a new one. Translation modified.

Spinoza begins by displacing transformation into the domain of fiction, or of superstition. But this is only the beginning: the first Part of the *Ethics*. Already the second Part explores the limits of form: to what extent is an individual capable of variation without being transformed? In this regard, the affective complexity of the human body places it at the apex of the natural hierarchy. Then, the Preface to the third Part invokes perfectly natural or lawful transformations. It is the final two Parts that raise transformation to the level of a problem, like a gnawing and stubborn counterpoint, insofar as these two Parts move in the direction of trying to define the third kind of knowledge. Spinoza there invokes transformations that are surprising, unacceptable, and nevertheless manifest, reviving questions that were thought to have been resolved once and for all, first by Thomist, and then by Cartesian, good sense.

What could justify such an inquiry into a concept that is at first glance secondary, even though its field of application encompasses everything from individual life to politics and metaphysics? We will take as our dual point of departure something surprising and an observation, asking ourselves whether there might be a link between the two.

The surprising thing is as follows: in the middle of a sequence of the *Ethics* concerning the utility of social life,[16] Spinoza very suddenly devotes a scholium to individual death, and to the idea that death does not necessarily designate a *mutatio in cadaver*, but sometimes a *mutatio in aliam naturam*. He had just established the difference between good and bad in matters of physiology, calling bad those things that, altering the relation of movement and rest that the parts of the body have among themselves, lead the latter to 'change into another nature', by which it finds itself 'destroyed':

> In Part V I shall explain how much these things can be harmful to or beneficial to the Mind. But here it should be noted that I understand the Body to die when its parts are so disposed that they acquire a different proportion of motion and rest to one another. For I dare not deny that – even though the circulation of the blood is maintained, as well as the other [signs] on account of which the Body is thought to be alive – the human Body can nevertheless be changed into another nature [*in aliam naturam . . . mutari*] entirely different from its own. For no reason compels me to maintain that the Body does not die unless it is changed into a corpse.
>
> And, indeed, experience seems to urge a different conclusion. Sometimes a man undergoes such changes that I should hardly have said

---

[16] *Ethics* IV, 29–40; CWS I, 560–70.

he was the same man. I have heard stories, for example, of a Spanish Poet who suffered an illness; though he recovered, he was left so oblivious to his past life that he did not believe the tales and tragedies he had written were his own. He could surely have been taken for a grown-up infant (*pro infante adulto*) if he had also forgotten his native language.

If this seems incredible, what shall we say of infants? A man of advanced years believes their nature to be so different from his own that he could not be persuaded that he was ever an infant, if he did not make this conjecture concerning himself from [NS: the example of] others. But rather than provide the superstitious with material for raising new questions, I prefer to leave this discussion unfinished.[17]

We will have occasion to return to this passage; for now, let us limit ourselves to underscoring two of its remarkable formal aspects. First of all there is the rather associative chain of ideas: from the thesis (death = transformation) to the illustration (the convalescent amnesiac) and then to the analogy (infants), and then finally to the sketch of an interrogation into the nature of the second term of the analogy and into the relationship between its terms (what about the nature of infants? and of the relation of the adult to the infant it had been?). In a few lines, we have passed from the end of life to its beginning, by way of a strange, almost 'incredible' phenomenon. And this is the second formal aspect: first, a reticence, rare in Spinoza, to make a straightforward assertion ('I dare not deny', 'No reason compels me': negative turns of phrase, the first even doubly so); second, a slight uncertainty about the status of the assertion ('experience seems to urge', *suadere videtur*; the end of the passage invokes precisely a difficulty in being persuaded: 'he could not be persuaded . . . if', *persuadere non posset, se*; 'I should hardly have said . . .'); third, finally, the combination of hearsay, belief, and conjecture, which as much affects the subject of the statement (the amnesiac, then any given adult) as the subject of enunciation (Spinoza), and which plunges the reader into a climate of oddness and perplexity ('I have heard stories', 'he did not believe', 'He could surely have been taken for', 'If this seems incredible . . .', 'A man of advanced years . . . could not be persuaded . . . if he did not make this conjecture . . .'). Everything ultimately appears uncertain, in a text that, however, began with a sharp thesis; and that which is baroque in the theme of amnesia seems to pass from content to form, contaminating Spinoza's very writing. The apparently definitive anonymity of the poet in

---

[17] *Ethics* IV, 39 Schol.; CWS I, 569–70.

question[18] certainly contributes to this nebulous atmosphere, which is not the philosopher's typical style. This is why he interrupts himself, breaking things off *in medio*, at the point where the reader might be tempted to leave behind reflection for reverie. However, we will see that this scholium can be read otherwise – namely, as an eruption of vivid and distinct traits that clearly outline the configuration of a problem.

Let us turn now to the observation: the same concept of *in aliam formam mutatio* plays a major role in the two political books, since in them there appears the very concept of revolution, or at least of its project (the establishment of a new regime). Each of the two political *Treatises*, as is well known, is haunted by a recent event: the 1648 English revolution and regicide, and the 1672 lynching of the brothers De Witt in Amsterdam, which marked the end of the republican experiment in Holland. In both cases, the possibility and viability of a transformation was at stake: a change of subject in politics, a mutation of the political subject.

Can one seriously believe, then, that it was by chance that the scholium to IV, 39 was placed in the middle of a sequence bearing on politics? Is this a matter of a pure demonstrative tactic, or of an intention of another order? There is nothing preventing Proposition 39 from coming after Proposition 40, which does not rely on it in any way, and which closes the political sequence: the chain of reasoning inaugurated in Propositions 38 and 39 only truly begins with Proposition 41.

Memory and Form: The State and Its Ruin

Let us cast a sweeping eye across the *Theologico-Political Treatise*. The first part has for its object the establishment of a new method of investigating sacred texts, and devotes long passages and numerous remarks to collective habits, whether that means rituals, morals, or the evolution of the meanings of words. Then, in the second part, Spinoza more directly raises the problem

---

[18] Guérinot believed it to be [Miguel de] Cervantès, but this is hardly likely. The name of [Luis de] Góngora is often invoked. For yet another hypothesis we have the name of the dramaturge [Juan Pérez de] Montalbán (1602–38), Lope de Vega's most celebrated disciple. Shortly before his death, in 1635, Montalbán was subject to fainting spells and illnesses, his health rapidly declined, and he ended his life in an asylum in Madrid, considered to be mad. According to Francisco de Quitana (in *Lagrimas Panegyricas*, published in his memory in 1639), a series of attacks 'reduced him, even in his speech, to the state of an infant'. See Parker 1975. Spinoza possessed a piece by Montalbán: *Comedia famosa: El divino nazareno Sanson*, listed as number 65 in the inventory of his library.

of tyranny, expresses doubts about the prospects of revolution, and searches for another strategy (this is different in each of the two *Treatises*). Now, if Spinoza did not believe in political transformation, and still less in the possibility of deliberately changing the meanings of words,[19] it is because revolution boils down to tyrannicide and does not affect the causes of tyranny, which are also of the order of custom or memory (Spinoza does not distinguish between the two).

On the one hand, a people is 'accustomed' (*assuetus*)[20] to the present political form, or 'little accustomed' to the new one, which amounts to the same thing. This was true for Cromwell's recent revolution, as it was for the Hebrew people when they sought to transform the popular regime into a monarchy. It is the memory of a form which is to blame, or in other words an arrangement of 'laws and mores'.[21] For the two go together, and, depending on the circumstances, will decline together. Above all, human beings develop customs (*consuetudines*) and form a civil state (*societatem formare*):[22] these are one and the same process.

---

[19] *TTP* VII, 40–3; CWS II, 179–80.

[20] *TTP* XVIII, 7 and 15; CWS II, 324 and 325. To this must be added *consuevit, consueverat* (*TTP* XVIII, 28 and 35; CWS II, 328 and 330). [The French terms here translated as *custom* and *accustomed* are *habitude* and *habitué*, which is how Zourabichvili renders *assueti*. None of the major English translations are consistent about this Latin term. In the first case, *TTP* XVIII, 7, Spinoza writes that the priests could have no wish to issue new decrees, 'sed tantum assueta, & recepta administrandi, & defendendi'. Curley: 'but only to administer and defend familiar and accepted decrees' (CWS II, 324). Silverthorne and Israel: 'but merely administered and safeguarded the existing edicts' (Spinoza 2007: 231). Elwes: 'but took care, on the contrary, to administer and defend familiar and accepted laws' (Spinoza 1951: 238). Curley and Elwes both render *assueta* as 'familiar', whereas Silverthorne and Israel run together *assueta* and *recepta* as 'existing'. I think 'customary and received' would have been appropriate here. In the second case, *TTP* XVIII, 15, Spinoza's Latin reads as follows: 'At postquam populus regibus minime assuetus'. Curley: 'But after the people, who were by no means accustomed to kings' (CWS II, 325). Silverthorne and Israel: 'But after the people, despite having no experience of kings' (Spinoza 2007: 232). Elwes: 'But after that the people, little accustomed to kings' (Spinoza 1951: 240). Here Curley and Elwes accurately translate *assuetus* as 'accustomed to', whereas Silverthorne and Israel somewhat less strictly render it as 'having experience of'. As for *consuevit* and *consueverit* (*TTP* XVIII, 28 and 35), Curley renders these as '(not) accustomed' in both cases (CWS I, 328 and 330); Silverthorne and Israel as 'accustomed' and as 'having learned (something)' (Spinoza 2007: 235–6); and Elwes as '(un)accustomed' and 'not being used (to something)' (Spinoza 1951: 242 and 244). – GM.]

[21] *TTP*, for example XVII, 93–4; CWS I, 317. Translation modified. [Spinoza writes: 'legum & morum', 'legibus & moribus'.]

[22] *TTP*, III and IV; see also *TP* I, 7.

On the other hand, Spinoza underscores that the power of a new king is precarious insofar as the memory of the previous one remains strong (*memoria praecedentis*).[23] A *fortiori*, if they succeed an assassinated tyrant, they will in turn and by the force of things become a tyrant, since they will be led, in order to establish their own power, to embrace the cause of their predecessor and to follow in their footsteps (*vestigia*).[24] Clearly, Spinoza has Cromwell in mind.

Consequently, if revolutions fail, this is a matter of memory or of what it is impossible to forget: the proximity of the amnesiac poet and the utility of social life already appears less a matter of chance. Moreover, if we read IV, 39, its demonstration and its scholium in light of the preceding propositions, it is obvious that the death invoked concerns society: the surprising thing is rather that the scholium brings us back to individual cases.[25] Death, in the *Ethics*, concerns the political body as much as the individual body.

Like Machiavelli and Hobbes, Spinoza utilises the medieval metaphor of a collective body as a quasi-individual, so that the State falls under the purview of a special medicine.[26] Moreover, the threat of the death of the State, expressed by the terms *ruina, eversio, dissolvi*, hovers over the whole of the *Political Treatise*, and must be interpreted exactly as it is in the scholium to *Ethics* IV, 39: not as a pure and simple cadaveric decomposition, but rather as a transformation. The fundamental claim in each case, the logical content of the two, is identical, as becomes apparent when we place these two passages alongside one another:

> For I dare not deny that – even though the circulation of the blood is maintained, as well as the other [signs] on account of which the Body is thought to be alive – the human Body can nevertheless be changed into another nature entirely different from its own (*in aliam naturam a sua*

---

[23] *TTP* XVII, 110; CWS I, 321.

[24] *TTP* XVIII, 32; CWS I, 329.

[25] H. A. Wolfson suggests the following rapprochement: 'For death, Spinoza adds in the Scholium, does not come when the body "is changed into a corpse"; a man may be called dead if he "undergoes such changes that he cannot very well be said to be the same man," even though physiologically he is still alive. Anything contrary to this is evil. So also in the case of the state. Good is that which makes for complete harmony between the individual members of the state and for the stability of the state as an organic unit' (Wolfson 1934: 249). Our only reservation here would have to do with the 'individual members of the state': Spinozist politics envisages intermediary parts such as the army, families, towns, etc.

[26] *TP* X, 1; CWS II, 596–7.

prorsus diversam mutari). For no reason compels me to maintain that the Body does not die unless it is changed into a corpse (*mutetur in cadaver*). And, indeed, experience seems to urge a different conclusion.[27]

Therefore, when disagreements and rebellions are stirred up in a Commonwealth – as they often are – the result is never that the citizens dissolve the Commonwealth – though this often happens in other kinds of society. Instead, if they can't settle their disagreements while preserving the form of the Commonwealth, they change its form to another (*ut ejusdem formam in aliam mutent*).[28]

The first passage is immediately followed by the anecdote of the Spanish poet; the second refers to revolutions. If consequently the latter are problematic, or even chimerical, it is perhaps because the insurgent peoples are lacking that new state of a human being who is no longer anything other than an ex-poet: 'praeteritae suae vitae tam oblitus . . .', having forgotten their past life.

But for now, let's restrict ourselves to deepening the relationship between common memory and political form. The institution of the State involves a relation to time: it is not enough that human beings occasionally, while an Assembly is constituted, renounce threatening one another; it is necessary that this renunciation is durable, that its promise takes hold ('fidem summum Reipublicae praesidium').[29] At that point, the Assembly is no longer simply constituted – it becomes an institution, and loses its unique, occasional, originary character, in order to become cyclical or periodic. The promise taking hold thus presupposes a common memory that the State seeks to cultivate in individuals.

On the one hand, Spinoza never stops repeating that only the threat of the death penalty guarantees the promise and enables each to count on the others: if each can keep their civil promise, it is by virtue of a fear that is durably fixed in their memory. We see that it is less a matter of indefinitely remembering the oath taken on day one, than it is of associating, in an imaginary rather than a testimonial memory, the crime of treason with the ultimate punishment. In order for the State to be eternal, it would need to perpetuate, by some public 'monument' (*signum*), the *aeterna memoria* of

---

[27] *Ethics* IV, 39 Schol.; CWS I, 569.
[28] *TP* VI, 2; CWS II, 532.
[29] *TTP* XVI, 21; CWS II, 286.

the punishment inflicted on the perpetrator of the crime of treason.[30] And Spinoza pushes this provision to the point of paradox: whoever disobeys, even if they do so in the interest of their people, is nevertheless subject to punishment by death.[31]

On the other hand, and more generally, given that human beings are led by their affects rather than by reason, only a common affective disposition is capable of uniting them and rendering them constant (*communis affectus*).[32] This idea conforms with the passages from the *Ethics* concerning the function and role of memory: so long as we do not have knowledge of our affects, the best we can do is to give ourselves correct rules for living, to inscribe them in our memory (*memoriae mandare*).[33] Not that it suffices to retain their articulation or meaning in words: our imagination itself must be affected by the everyday application of these rules in concrete cases. In this way one will give rise in the mind to associations that conform with reason; for example, 'joining the image of slander with the imagination of that rule' according to which it is appropriate to repay hatred with generosity. And this is the very principle of memory, such as it is described in the scholium to *Ethics* II, 18. But in the scholium to V, 10, it is a matter of modifying memory, of substituting, for the associative chain formed in the mind by chance encounters (*communis naturae ordo*),[34] another chain, one that is correct, right, conforming with reason (*ordo ad intellectum*).[35] The strategy in both cases is identical, but they do not have the same ambition, for lack of being able to count on the same striving for ethical perfection by each: one would thus join, in the minds of all, the image of reprehensible or desirable acts with the affects that are the most powerful in the *vulgus* – fear and hope.[36]

The clearest example is still and once again that of the Hebrews: the unbreakable attachment that tied them to the form of their State was born of the very equilibrium of that form. It was a mixture of patriotism and

---

[30] *TP* VIII, 25; *CWS* II, 574–5.

[31] *TTP* XVI, 48–50; *CWS* II, 291–2.

[32] *TP* VI, 1; *CWS* II, 532. *TP* X, 9–10; *CWS* II, 600–1.

[33] *Ethics* V, 10 Schol.; *CWS* I, 601–3. We will see, however, that one must distinguish between two manners of intervening in memory that conform with reason: the one is political, referring to the formation of a common passional memory, and which enables the multitude to raise itself to the civil state; the other concerns the ethical progress of the individual, and consists in tying together the representations of memory according to an order that conforms with the understanding. But at this stage, we can treat them together.

[34] *Ethics* II, 29 Schol.; *CWS* I, 471.

[35] *Ethics* V, 10; *CWS* I, 601.

[36] *Ethics* IV, 37 Schol. 2; *CWS* I, 566–8.

xenophobia, both objects of daily worship, and which 'had to become a part of their nature' (*in naturam verti debuerunt*).[37] The *ingenium singulare* of a nation thus refers to an acquired and not an originary nature: a complex of laws and mores, and on top of that a language, which itself also, according to the *Ethics*, amounts to a common memory.[38]

If now we turn our attention to the evolutions that Spinoza describes, what we see above all are declines: do these fall under the concept of trans-formation? A single passage suggests this, one inspired by the cycles con-ceived by the philosophers and historians of antiquity:[39] democracy tends to be transformed into aristocracy, and then the latter into monarchy. As we will see, this is above all a matter of a long decline toward tyranny, which properly speaking no longer refers to a political form but resembles the state of war (or of permanent illness). Moreover, two symmetrical remarks show that Spinoza indeed has in mind a society on the path to dissolution: foreigners take on the customs of the people, and the people take on the customs of foreigners – the boundaries of collective individuality become indiscernible.[40]

Hence the interminable agony that befalls the Hebrew State: in Chapter XVII of the *Theologico-Political Treatise* Spinoza describes an escalating cycle of collective debauchery and ruinous institutional reforms. After the death of Moses, the Hebrews were seized by a zeal for changes, but changes that in no way had the effect of establishing a new form: they led only to the destruction of the old ('great changes', *magnae mutationes*, 'gradually chang-ing everything', *omnia paulatim mutare*, up to the 'complete ruin of the state', *imperii totius ruinae*).[41] This was an involution, rather than an evolution. The Hebrews did not invent new practices, they did not pass from one custom to another – they lost the very meaning of practice and custom, and this decline translated into the supremacy of the new, of the desire for novelties (*rerum novandarum cupiditas*).[42] The important thing is there, in that species

---

[37] *TTP* XVII, 80; CWS II, 314.
[38] *TTP* XVII, 93; CWS II, 317. *Ethics* II, 18 Schol.; CWS I, 465–6.
[39] *TP* VIII, 12; CWS II, 570.
[40] *TP* VIII, 12 and X, 4; CWS II, 570 and 598–9. In the first passage, the negative phe-nomenon is not the assimilation of foreigners; on the contrary, as Spinoza explains, it is the native citizens' refusal of a complete assimilation, or in short of naturalisation. This creates a distinction that transforms the initial democracy little by little into an aristocracy, and eventually, owing to the natural extinction of the privileged families, into monarchy.
[41] *TTP* XVII, 106–8; CWS II, 320.
[42] *TTP* XVII, 16; CWS II, 299. Here, by contrast, one can decipher a line of influence

of collective amnesia, in truth negative, which little by little carried out the transformation. The post-Mosaic Hebrews had lost their memory, they forgot the past, and no longer fixed their memories. Spinoza explicitly associates forgetting with the dissolution of the State.[43] Memory and amnesia, respect for customs and innovative hysteria: this alteration is above all present in Chapters XVII and XVIII of the *Theologico-Political Treatise* – the very same ones that raise the question of revolution.

Hence the two following symmetrical passages. The first invokes forgetting:

> [The] people's spirit, angered and niggardly, began to lose its resolve, so that finally they failed in their loyalty to form a worship which, though divine, had still been discredited among them and was suspect, and desired a new worship.[44]

The princes then set about in vain to establish new forms of worship, which each time were swept away by the new sensibility, incapable of becoming habituated to it. The second passage, by contrast, valorises tradition, in a eulogistic commentary on the form of the Hebrew State prior to the fatal error:

> [The priests] could have no wish to issue novel decrees, but only to administer and defend customary and received ones.[45]

Let us attempt a preliminary synthesis.

1. The persistence of the memory of the form (laws and mores) renders transformation impossible; in order for a transformation to be carried out, there must have been a loss of collective memory. Whence the temptation

---

from Bacon, whose political works appear as number 141 in the inventory of Spinoza's library: 'The causes and motives of seditions are, innovation in religion; taxes; *alteration of laws and customs*; breaking of privileges; general oppression; advancement of unworthy persons; strangers; dearths; disbanded soldiers; factions known desperate; and what soever, in offending people, joineth and knitteth them in a common cause' (Bacon 1985: 104. Our emphasis). This passage should also be read alongside those of the *Political Treatise* on the causes of *indignatio*, which leads to insurrection (notably *TP* IV, 4; *CWS* II, 526–7). However, as we will see, the motif of innovation as a factor of decline is ancient, going back at least to Cato. [Curley renders *rerum cupiditas novandarum* as 'a craving to make fundamental changes'. – GM.]

[43] See, notably, *TTP* V, 15; *CWS* II, 142.

[44] *TTP* XVII, 100; *CWS* II, 318–19.

[45] *TTP* XVIII, 7; *CWS* II, 324. Translation modified [see note 20, above].

to ask whether it is not for this reason that the man transformed in the scholium to IV, 39 is an amnesiac. In that case he would be much more than an example of a subject transformed: rather he would be a veritable type, the very figure of the transformed subject. We would then be led to the hypothesis that this scholium casts the shadow of revolution over the political demonstration of the *Ethics*.

2. History does in fact present a phenomenon that can be identified with collective amnesia, but which, in the manner of attempted revolutionaries, seems to push the collectivity into an endless spiral in which transformation is never carried out, and in which the state of things regresses even behind its present form.

For all that, must we conclude that collective amnesia is necessarily negative in Spinoza? If that were true, why is the scholium to IV, 39 not clearly pessimistic about the fate of the Spanish ex-poet? The reader is inclined to judge the latter mad or senile, and yet the case is supposed to illustrate a transformation. The image of the infant is ambiguous in this regard: a second birth or a return to infancy? We will ask whether Spinoza did not also develop the concept of a formative, and not ruinous, collective amnesia.

The judgment on amnesia has to remain open all the more insofar as the scholium to IV, 39 is interrupted, as we have seen: Spinoza says he does not want to encourage superstitious speculations, as if certain real transformations might appear almost more marvellous than those of marvellous tales. But the interruption happens at the moment when Spinoza enters into an interrogation into infancy. With the recent exception of Pierre Macherey, commentators have hardly remarked on the extent to which childhood hovers over the whole end of the *Ethics*:[46] three scholia – such a recurrence is quite rare in Spinoza.[47] The *Ethics* leaves the reader with two final images: the impotent infant, growing perpetually in the vicinity of death; the impotent adult, living in fear of eternal punishments after death (there is, in Spinoza, beyond the first kind of knowledge, a stunning economy of images, which comes down entirely to a 'philosophical style').

Amnesia and Formation: The Birth of a State

We are looking for a potential case of a 'good' collective amnesia: is this not the situation of a people throwing off the yoke that oppresses it? The case of establishing a new political form always comes down, in Spinoza, to recently

---

[46] See Macherey, *Introduction* IV, 252, n. 2; and V, 71, n. 2.
[47] *Ethics* IV, 39 Schol.; V, 6 Schol.; 39 schol; CWS I, 569–70; 599–600; 614–15.

liberated multitudes. In the absence of a prior sovereignty, we hesitate, however, to speak of a transformation: would this not be instead an originary formation, a genesis, a constituting act? Yet such a formation would indeed presuppose a certain mode of the community's pre-existence or prior individuation, since a collective effort of liberation is manifest . . .

At the end of the analysis of the monarchical 'kind' and of the form that is best suited for its self-perpetuation (as Spinoza will thereafter seek to do for all kinds of regimes, having ruled out the idea of establishing the best kind by a transformation), the following remark occurs:

> All that remains is to point out that here I'm conceiving a Monarchic state established by a free multitude. These things can be useful only to such a multitude. One which has become accustomed to another form of state won't be able to uproot the foundations they've received without a great danger of overthrowing the whole state and changing its structure (*Nam multitudo, quae alii imperii formae assuevit, non poterit sine magno eversionis periculo totius imperii recepta fundamenta evellere, & totius imperii fabricam mutare*).[48]

Spinoza indicates for whom he is writing: a multitude who has no habit other than freedom. And he explains why: in other cases, it would be necessary to attempt a revolution, at the risk of ruin pure and simple. There are two possibilities: either the monarchical State pre-exists, and it is a matter of reforming it; or else, conforming to the word *instituitur*, which we will also see used on the ethical plane, the free multitude founds its State, or in other words forms itself. We must ask to what extent the *Political Treatise* escapes the practical aporia that seems to suggest such an alternative.

What are the odds of this second hypothesis, which obviously refers to a freed multitude? The chapter, before concluding, includes a sort of long coda dedicated to another Spanish history, that of the Aragonese multitude which, liberated from the yoke of the Arabs, opted for the monarchical form. This is thus, manifestly, the situation most favourable for Spinozist politics – or at least that which, in his own eyes, best illustrates its principles. The self-portrait that the first biographer beheld, where the young Spinoza adopted the air and costume of Masaniello, leader of the revolt of the Neapolitan multitude against the Spanish yoke in 1647, here takes on a philosophical importance.[49] One will recall finally that the United Provinces were born

---

[48] *TP* VII, 26; CWS II, 558.
[49] Colerus 1954: 1518.

of a revolt, by which the Dutch multitude liberated itself from the same Spanish yoke (though it is true that this case is ambiguous, since Spinoza reckons that in this way the Dutch merely re-established the ancient rights of the general provincial States, over against the counts).[50]

The eruption of the theme of amnesia at the heart of the political sequence of the *Ethics* dramatically condenses an essential double proposition of the *Political Treatise*: on the one hand, any enterprise of transformation must, by the force of things, lack a collective amnesia. For this reason, revolutions must go wrong, and must provide the defending body with one of the worst figures in politics (worst limit case). But, on the other hand, the heroic and victorious uprising of a submissive population means a birth or a renewal – that is, an immaculate formation (best limit case).

Every example of political success, in Spinoza, is tied to a liberation: from the Hebrews and their exit from Egypt, to the Dutch liberated from the Spanish yoke, passing through the Aragonese liberated from the Arabic yoke. The only obvious counter-example is that of the Romans when they rid themselves of their tyrant and established the Republic; but this was precisely because their minds were not yet habituated to monarchy; and their Republic, in Spinoza's eyes, was nothing more than a long state of war that led ineluctably to the worst, the reign of a single person, absolute monarchy.[51] In sum, the English lacked what the Aragonese had been capable of; and the present-day Dutch, executioners of the brothers de Witt, lacked what their own ancestors knew how to conquer, though without truly giving it form: a freedom without memory. For a revolutionary multitude may well aspire to freedom; it so aspires like the ignorant person who believes themselves free while being totally unaware of the causes that determine them:[52] the revolutionary multitude is unaware of the causes of the tyranny that oppresses it, and its life remains subject to the corrupt practices that maintain tyranny. By contrast, a 'free multitude' is without memory, like a newborn (is not the struggle for liberation itself an act of freedom, is it not what procures a freedom without memory?).

Consider Chapter V of the *Theologico-Political Treatise*: Spinoza juxtaposes the situation of the Hebrews after the dissolution of their State (under the Babylonian yoke, they quickly forgot the law [*loi*] of Moses), and their situation before the State (under the Egyptian yoke, outside of the laws [*lois*] of the Pharaoh, they obeyed only natural law [*droit*]: they had no proper

---

[50] *TTP* XVIII, 36–7; CWS II, 331.
[51] *TTP* XVIII, 35; CWS I, 330.
[52] *Ethics* I, App.; CWS I, 440. *Ethics* III, 2 Schol.; CWS I, 495–7.

political memory). The flight from Egypt was in this way a return to the state of nature, a state all at once unformed and constituent, calling for form, whereas the revolution only brushes past the state of nature, sitting atop a chimera without knowing it, an old form in new garb:

> When they first left Egypt, they were no longer bound by the legislation of any other nation; so they were permitted, as they wished, to enact new laws *or* to establish new legislation, and to have a state wherever they wished, and to occupy what lands they wished.[53]

They had their choice of form and of territory: what then did they have in common? What constituted them in advance as *a* multitude, even informally? Only language, like the amnesiac poet; language as the sole collective memory and identity, since the latter were not yet ritualised. And this linguistic difference suffices to make possible both slavery and disobedience, as we will see: a complex knot of servitude and freedom, of memory and forgetting.

The Adult Child and Chimeras

Let us imagine that we are in the presence of multitudes without past, deprived of any prior form, and which do not run the risk of transformation tied to the memory of previous practices: are not these multitudes in the situation of the *infans adultus*, the adult newborn or child born adult, which Spinoza compares to that of the amnesiac Spanish poet?[54] For this is a new adult, without past or memory, that seems to come to the world fully formed. A whole series of difficulties spring up: first, the child is entirely the opposite of a free being, according to Spinoza; second, the amnesiac is not properly speaking a child, since he is called an adult child; third, once again, is he not merely mad or senile?; fourth, in any case, what could be meant by this union of contraries, *infans adultus*, for the philosopher who harshly criticised chimeras?

The fifth and final Part of the *Ethics* defines the freedom of the human being and lays out the supreme kind of knowledge. The latter implies in particular a devaluation of memory: not only does one understand nothing of the species of eternity under which things are intuitively grasped insofar as it is confused with memory, but intellectual activity must come to occupy

---

[53] *TTP* V, 26; *CWS* II, 145.
[54] [See the section on childhood in the Notes on Translation, above. – GM.]

a greater part of the mind than memory does.[55] What could be meant by the first sentence of the scholium to IV, 39: 'In Part V I shall explain how much these things can be harmful or beneficial to the mind' (implying: which conserve or alter the individuating form of the body)?

The other scholium, to Proposition 39 of Part V, at the end of the book, explains that our task, in this life, is to change the body of childhood into another infinitely more capable, in such a way that the mind of childhood, almost entirely occupied by memory and imagination, is also changed into another, in which the understanding has the greatest share. It is as if Childhood here stood for the first kind of knowledge, and the growth of the individual for the passage from unconsciousness to wisdom or virtue (and why does Spinoza say *corpus infantiae*, rather than *infantis*?):

> Because human Bodies are capable of a great many things, there is no doubt but what they can be of such a nature that they are related to Minds which have a great knowledge of themselves and of God, and of which the greatest, *or* chief, part is eternal. So they hardly fear death.
>
> But for a clearer understanding of these things, we must note here that we live in continuous change (*in continua vivimus variatione*), and that as we change for the better or worse (*in melius, sive in pejus mutamur*), we are called happy or unhappy. For he who has passed from being an infant or child to being a corpse (*in cadaver transiit*) is called unhappy. On the other hand, if we pass the whole length of our life with a sound Mind in a sound Body, that is considered happiness. And really, he who, like an infant or child, has a Body capable of very few things, and very heavily dependent on external causes, has a Mind which considered solely in itself is conscious of almost nothing of itself, or of God, or of things. On the other hand, he who has a Body capable of a great many things, has a Mind which considered only in itself is very much conscious of itself, and of God, and of things.
>
> In this life, then, we strive especially that the Body of childhood may change (as much as its nature allows and assists) into another (*In hac vita igitur apprime conamur, ut Corpus infantiae in aliud, quantum ejus natura patitur, eique conducit, mutetur . . .*), capable of a great many things and related to a Mind very much conscious of itself, of God, and of things. We strive, that is, that whatever is related to its memory or imagination is of

---

[55] *Ethics* V, 23 Schol.; CWS I, 607–8; and V, 38 schol. and 39 schol; CWS I, 613–14.

hardly any moment in relation to the intellect (as I have already said in V, 38 schol.).[56]

Here again, we will restrict ourselves to starting out with formal remarks, since we will often return to this passage. First, its ambiguity does not derive solely from the analogy implicitly established between the development of the infant and the ethical process. It also arises from the fact that the scholium combines two incompatible interpretations of *mutatio*:[57] first as perfection (change for the better or for the worse), then as transformation (change of the body of childhood into another). What's more, these two interpretations seem to overlap in the same sentence: the transformation of the body 'into another' seems immediately contradicted by the specified condition, 'as much as its nature suffers'. For it is certain that no nature 'allows' transformation; it can be a matter only of one and the same nature, which is nevertheless called on to suffer a radical change, a rupture comparable to a metamorphosis. Second, the insistence on the heterogeneity of the two ages, infantile and adult, is the great common link between the two scholia (to IV, 39 and V, 39), and is no doubt why they both have in common, on the one hand, referring to cadaveric decomposition as a necessary antithesis (death is not necessarily *mutatio in cadaver*; childhood is not necessarily *transitio in cadaver* . . .), and on the other hand, raising the problem of memory.

Perhaps then we must not confuse the child and the adult child; perhaps they even stand at opposite ends of the political field. The adult child is amnesiac, the child as such has a mind dominated by memory (the apparent contradiction arising from the fact that the child is born without a past and yet has no other mental activity than the memorial [*mnésique*]).[58] It is quite true that adults are large children, in Spinoza: Moses, for example, needed to 'bind [the Hebrews] more to the worship of God, in accordance with their childish power of understanding'.[59] And part of what is said of the child in the *Ethics* also goes for the 'mob' or the 'common people' (*vulgus*) in the

[56] *Ethics* V, 39 Schol.; CWS I, 614. Translation modified.

[57] 'But the main thing to note is that when I say that someone passes from a lesser to a greater perfection (*a minore ad majorem perfectionem transire*), and the opposite, I do not understand that he is changed from one essence, *or* form, to another (*ex una essentia, seu forma in aliam mutatur*). For example, a horse is destroyed as much if it is changed into a man as if it is changed into an insect. Rather, we conceive that his power of acting, insofar as it is understood through his nature, is increased or diminished' (*Ethics* IV, Praef.; CWS I, 545–6).

[58] Of course, all these aspects will ultimately be clarified.

[59] *TTP* III, 6; CWS II, 112. Spinoza's Latin: 'puerili captu'.

Theologico-Political Treatise: subject to anger, to imitation, to envy, to vengeance (beyond which the mob, of course, is similarly incapable of liberating itself from the imagination and memory). But if the majority of adults are large children, there are also, it will be said, great children, *collective children* that are born in the heroism of an uprising against foreign oppression: are they, too, born as adults? This is a difficult problem, which for now we can only represent confusedly.

Let us remark in addition that the brushing past the state of nature that characterises the insurgent mob in the quest for a new form without being in a position to desire it (since it has desire only through its present form) strongly resembles the situation of the child brushing past death in a process of growth that must lead it to change its body without it being able to desire it any longer. The scholium to V, 39 is, in this regard, as strange as that of IV, 39: on the one hand Spinoza says 'body of childhood' and not 'of the child'; on the other hand he does not say that the child strives, but that 'we strive' (*conamur*) to make this body, which is nevertheless our own, change. This sentence, which just now we took in a figurative sense, must also be understood literally, by seeing under the term *conamur* the adults who take care of children, as if the required change were disproportionate in relation to the forces proper to the child. If in fact we turn to the hierarchical principle that will serve to frame the process described in the scholium to V, 39, it becomes difficult not to give this word a collective connotation, beyond its immediate distributive signification:

> And in proportion as the actions of a body depend more on itself alone, and as other bodies concur with it less in acting, so its mind is more capable of understanding distinctly.[60]

---

[60] *Ethics* II, 13 Schol.; CWS I, 458. See also *Ethics* III, 7 Dem.; CWS I, 499. – Of course, the formula 'other bodies concur with it in acting' also applies in the case where the wind pushes me back, etc. It remains true that the schema is applied at the end of the book to the growth of the infant, and that the plural *conamur*: 1. conforms to the rule that 'if a number of Individuals so concur in one action that together they are all the cause of one effect, I consider them all, to that extent, as one singular thing' (*Ethics* II, Def. 7; CWS I, 447); 2. only applies to human beings. Meanwhile, demonstrating that he does not conceive of the growth of the child abstractly, Spinoza more than once mentions the educative role of parents (*Ethics* III, Def. aff. XXVII Exp.; IV, App. Cap. XIII and XX; we will comment on these texts below, in Chapter 5). Let us add that the majority of concurring actions with which our body passively participates are temporary and do not attain to the 'unity' that defines an individual form, outside of exceptional cases such as, precisely, the gestation of the child and obedience to the State.

Provisionally, then, the claim would be as follows: a body experiences a mutation in certain lethal cases, close to transformation but without yet being one, and experiences it in impotence and unconsciousness. And once again the same claim is applicable at two levels: that of the insurgent multitude and that of the growing infant.

We insist on the following point: one cannot, in the strict sense, desire one's own transformation, in Spinoza. Striving to be transformed would amount to dying, even when another individual would take one's place. Thus it is not sufficient to conclude that revolutions necessarily fail: the very desire for revolution is a logical monster in a philosophy that bases desire on essence or form, and which even defines it as actual essence. Transformation implies a change of essence, whereas desire is the self-affirmation of a given essence. So too the transformation of the ex-poet, however one interprets his new life, still remains a death, a destruction, *corruptio generationem subsequentem includens*, according to the formula of the *Metaphysical Thoughts*: no subject ensures the transition. It can be called an individual death as well: the death of the desiring instance, an essence being unable to involve its own negation to any degree.[61]

One will remark at this juncture that suicide is thought in the *Ethics* as a transformation, and even as the temporary coexistence of two forms, as some kind of real chimera (when a person takes their own life, they are forced to do so by a will that is other than their own, and yet it is still they who do it).[62] But Spinoza never stops drawing attention, in his political books, to the often suicidal behaviour of sovereigns – to such an extent that one must not be content with a pessimistic judgment about revolutions, one must in addition *understand* them, account for them as *necessary*. This is macabre, but it follows nearly geometrically from the behaviour of the sovereign.

Hobbes will sometimes compare the political body on the path to dissolution to the unhealthy body of an infant born of sick parents and itself destined either to a premature death or else to shed its bad disposition.[63] The relation between the child and illness, in politics, also appears in Spinoza, when he wants to show the chimera that constitutes the reign of one alone, since supposed absolute monarchies generally are so in name only, and dissimulate

---

[61] *Ethics* III, 4–5; CWS I, 498 (followed precisely by two propositions defining the *conatus* as the actual essence of the thing).

[62] *Ethics* IV, 20 Schol.; CWS I, 557.

[63] Hobbes, *Leviathan* XXIX (Hobbes 2012: II, 498–500). This happens when the sovereign has allowed its power to weaken, and cannot re-establish it other than by an unpopular forceful action.

the real form – aristocracy – of the state: a child or an already senile king is like a sick king, unfit to take charge of the affairs of the State.[64] Child, unhealthy person, senile person: we rediscover in a certain way the elements of the scholium to *Ethics* IV, 39, which are now brought together to form the emblematic figure of a chimerical regime. By chimera, one must understand a contradictory being, combining two natures:[65] to be precise, the impossible and consequently ruinous coexistence of two forms at the heart of the State, the one apparent and the other hidden – a little like in myths, when one form involves another thanks to a magical transformation. In the illusory world of fictions, according to Spinoza, 'any form whatever is changed to any other'.[66] But *nature* knows nothing of such magical ambiguities: the individual forms do not communicate, they do not encroach upon one another.

What then is the status of these strange margins of indecision or transition, widened by illness – that of the Spanish poet, of course, but above all that of the child? The body of the child oscillates, according to the scholium to V, 39, between the cadaver and health. In the political field, these margins are assignable: they are the spectre of the return to the state of nature, which is not the same thing as a dissolution pure and simple.[67] Not chaos, but already a beginning: a society grasped at its point of genesis, or dangerously regressing toward it; less chaos, consequently, than a larval state, which always threatens the existence of the civil state, and whose paradoxical concept emerges periodically in the two *Treatises*. There is no complete dissolution other than into a greater, foreign body; and inversely, no birth other than in liberation. In any case the idea of a regression to the state of a pure multitude without ties is only an abstraction, the state of nature being characterised by a powerful social desire that has not yet found its formula or solution.

There is thus an interval between the formed multitude and its pure and simple abolition: society, which must lead us to the consideration of a problematic social state, halfway between individuality (the habituation of juridical dispositions establishing a regularity in the movement and rest by which the different parts of the multitude communicate) and nothingness (splitting apart or dispersion of the parts). This state of tension, between form and formless, holds together a double dynamic, which is why it appears

---

[64] *TP* VI, 5; CWS II, 533–4.
[65] CM I, I, n. a.; CWS I, 299.
[66] *Ethics* I, 8 Schol. 2; CWS I, 413: *quascunque formas in alias quascunque mutari, imaginantur.*
[67] *TP* VI, 2; CWS II, 532.

in two opposed figures, the Assembly (above all in the *Theologico-Political Treatise*) and Solitude (in the *Political Treatise*). The Assembly is constituting: it tends toward union or form, but does not yet possess it, even though it is not separable from the formative act that gives it meaning; it is less a state than an event, the process of individuation of a human collectivity. Solitude, by contrast, tends toward dispersion, a tendency hindered by the powerful social desire of human beings; it thus designates a limited and literally explosive state, that of a regime – 'tyranny' – that tends to negate itself by running up against the very limits of the human ability to obey its commandments, and by this fact turns over into the state of war.[68]

These formal margins of indecision do not in principle have any status in Spinozism, where the principle of contradiction imposes on being a clear division into distinct natures. But to stop there would be overly simplistic, and would amount to neglecting the rule to treat every thing as forming a part of Nature, which includes aggression or malformation, and more generally the process of composition-decomposition-recomposition that is the very becoming of the universe. In Spinoza, it is at once the case that things only exist as formed, and that the whole problem is a problem of form. There is moreover no objection, as we will see, to considering the monster, in politics or elsewhere; to attempt a first pass, let us say that its unity is simply unviable, amounting to an illusion, and that consequently it is not it itself that lives, but rather a plurality of forms grappling with others and which can only be destroyed. Spinoza's political meditations bear principally on these unviable situations, on these confused intervals of History that can endure for centuries, as attested to by Roman history. Spinoza's political thought is quite preoccupied with sickness (degradation) and death (ruin), with regression toward another form, with imminent or failed transformations, such that the analysis of the monarchical regime properly speaking is preceded by a long preamble[69] which invokes not only political transformations, the human limits of the conservation of form (tyranny), but also the latent forms disguised under the appearance of another form. Spinoza, who intends to define the best, thus begins with the worst: 'So a state thought to be absolute Monarchy is really, in practice, an Aristocracy. Of course, it's not openly an aristocracy, only covertly one. But that makes it the worst kind.'[70]

---

[68] *TP* IV, 4; CWS II, 526–7.

[69] *TP* VI, 1–8; CWS II, 532–4 (the first four paragraphs constitute a transition from general political theory to the monarchical regime in particular, and set up the problematic coordinates of a healthy study of the latter).

[70] *TP* VI, 5; CWS II, 533.

This involvement of one form within another, or rather of the true form hidden in another that is apparent and false, cannot but call to mind the theme of the *imperium in imperio*: a dominion within a dominion, a State within a State. If the human being is not 'in nature as a dominion within a dominion',[71] this is because it cannot at once be a part of nature, subject to universal laws, and also endow itself with autonomous laws; or rather the laws of its own nature are relations necessarily subject to other, more general, relations, such that the pretentions to take them as the very laws of Nature can only be a dream (a teleological Nature, made for the human being). And if the human being cannot be a chimera, the latter triumphs at least in the representation that the human has of itself, which illusion produces true effects. Should we then say that the chimera or transformation is metaphorically imported from politics to psychology, so that thereafter it is really transported from psychology to politics? It is true that we do not immediately see the relation between the literal and figurative usages of the formula *imperium in imperio*: in politics, Spinoza utilises it to decry the confrontation between kings and prophets that results from the transformation of the Hebrew State into a monarchy (he does not make recourse to it in decrying the latent aristocracy that is absolute monarchy).[72] What is it that makes us think there is, in spite of everything, a link between the three kinds of texts – the Hebrew kings who 'had a state within a state, and ruled at someone else's pleasure'[73] (literal sense); the imaginary conception of the human being 'in nature as a dominion within a dominion' (figurative sense); and so-called absolute monarchy that disguises an aristocratic regime (a suspected implicit injection of the figurative sense into the literal)? It is that each time it is explicitly a matter of the belief in or vain aspiration for a *potestas absoluta*, which cannot in any case belong to a single human being. It is because the king, who is a human being, tends to think of himself 'in nature as a State within a State' that his effective reign is structurally threatened by the State within the State.

The historical context matters. On the one hand, we witness, throughout Europe and ultimately in Holland, the apparently irresistible rise of absolute monarchy. But on the other hand, the chimera being a chimera, Spinoza recalls that the Dutch State, prior to the triumph of William of Orange, was in any case marked from its origins by a hesitation concerning the place of

---

[71] *Ethics* III, Praef; CWS I, 491. *TP* II, 6; CWS II, 509.

[72] *TTP* XVII, 107; CWS II, 320 (transformation leading to the State within the State); *TTP* XVIII, 15–19; CWS II, 326 (transformation and the advent of royal war).

[73] *TTP* XVII, 108; CWS II, 321.

sovereignty (the people did not know where true power lay). It was like a balancing act: in times of war, sovereignty was on the side of the Stadtholder; in times of peace it fell back over to the side of the Grand Pensionary and the Regents Assembly. The Dutch Republic thus had an uncertain status, it was 'malformed' [*difforme*], and its form always remained undecided.[74]

Let us return finally to this question of childhood as the sickly transition toward the adult. We have seen how the figure of the *infans adultus* is strange: it works as the approximative image of a certainly negative but real situation (the transformation of an individual), and yet it can only be a chimera, if it is true that the body of the adult is a different body than that of the child. When Spinoza returns to this figure a bit later, he treats it this time clearly as a chimera, and associates it with the absurd conception of the naturalness of vice that he had ceaselessly combated since the beginning of Part III of the *Ethics*:

> But if most people were born grown up, and only one or two were born infants, then everyone would pity the infants, because they would regard infancy itself, not as a natural and necessary thing, but as a vice of nature, *or* a sin.[75]

It is true that the image seems inverted: this is no longer an adult once again become newborn, but a newborn already grown up. And Spinoza seems to mean that the negation of childhood amounts to conceiving the latter as a vice, unless it is the other way around. As for the other two scholia, we will for now content ourselves with formal remarks, since we will return to them at length. We have here three texts – the scholia to IV, 39; V, 6; and V, 39 – that take up the relation between adulthood and childhood. The first presents a curiously real chimera (but one without a future), the second takes turns chimera upside down and treats it as such, the third simply invokes the passage (truly full of risks) from one age to the other. Regression

---

[74] *TP* IX, 14 (*deformi*); CWS II, 595. [Curley translates *deformi* as 'defective'. – GM.] The study of the monarchical kind echoes the Dutch problem: the value of monarchy is better seen in times of war, but the value of democracy comes out in times of peace (*TP* VII, 5; CWS II, 547). Based on Spinoza's reasoning, it would not be difficult to complete the analysis of recent Dutch history: when the position of Stadtholder was abolished in 1654, after the overthrow of the Prince of Orange, it was thought that this had, not transformed, but finally formed a State; however, the social memory of the reign of the counts persisted, and the formal indecision remained up until the final drama of 1672 (the lynching of the grand pensioner De Witt).

[75] *Ethics* V, 6 Schol.; CWS I, 600.

toward childhood, negation of childhood, exit from childhood. These are at the same time three successive approaches in the relation of the adult to childhood: not believing that one could have been an infant, or rather only believing it because one has seen other infants grow up; denying it in practice by seeing childhood as a privation and so considering it as a vice; finally, perhaps, conceiving the whole of life as an exit from childhood. This proposed reading will of course need to be justified and confirmed by the analysis, and we will only be able to do this after conducting a long inquiry into the Spinozist conception of transformation. We will only say a word about the first of the three ideas, which is perhaps the simplest, but which is the most astonishing (to the point that it generally passes unnoticed).

Spinoza's claim about the relation to infancy can be summarily stated in the following terms, which will later need to be nuanced or made more precise: *an adult does not remember having been an infant, it needs others to teach it to them.* Reread now the end of the scholium to IV, 39: 'If this seems incredible, what shall we say of infants? A man of advanced years believes their nature to be so different from his own that he could not be persuaded that he was ever an infant, if he did not make this conjecture concerning himself from others.'[76] To grasp the full scope of this idea, perhaps it is necessary to put the translation of the word *infans* by 'infant' [*nourrisson*] into perspective: we have adopted it because Spinoza himself invokes the inability to speak, to walk, to reason, with regard to the *infans*; when he speaks of the *puer* [child], it is already a matter of something else, of complex affective mechanisms that make it possible to model in certain respects the behaviour of the adult (whence, reciprocally, the *pueritia* [childishness] of the latter . . .), namely the problems of adolescence; and certain passages explicitly distinguish *infans* and *puer*. Nevertheless, in the very same sentence where Spinoza mentions the incapacities of the infant [*tout-petit*], he speaks of a quasi-unconsciousness of oneself that lasts 'so many years'.[77] In fact, in Latin *infans* has a strict sense and a broad sense: sometimes it effectively means what we understand in French by 'infant' [*nourrisson*]; sometimes it encompasses the first seven years of life, which the Romans reckoned were necessary to learn to speak properly.[78] It would thus find its equivalent in the expression 'early childhood' [*petit enfant*]. Thus we should not be tempted too quickly to identify Spinoza's idea with the 'infantile amnesia' of modern

---

[76] *Ethics* IV, 39 Schol.; CWS I, 569–70.
[77] *Ethics* V, 6 Schol.; CWS I, 600.
[78] See Ernout and Meillet 2001. *Infans* even occasionally designates an infant that has not yet been born.

psychologists, and form the provisional hypothesis that this idea concerns early childhood. The knowledge that one had been a *petit enfant* in no way proceeds from a memory; it is not memory that ensures the link between the two ages, but the observation of others (or what Spinoza sometimes calls 'vague experience'), and perhaps equally from hearsay.

Recall that the two examples of perception by hearsay, in the *Treatise on the Emendation of the Intellect*, are related to infancy: being born on such-and-such day, having such-and-such parents. Spinoza does not mean that the *petit enfant* only knows by hearsay that such-and-such adults are its parents: that would be a commonplace, and the first example would suffice. What he literally says, however strange it seems, is: the conviction *of an adult* that they had such-and-such parents can only be explained by hearsay, not by memory: 'Ex auditu tantum scio . . . quod tales parentes habui' ('I know only from report . . . who my parents were').[79] This is the point of view of an adult who thinks of their infancy, as in the scholium to IV, 39. Spinoza thus indeed seems to allude to an amnesia forever separating the adult from the infant [*petit enfant*] that they had once been. The idea, applied to parents, and thus to a period that might theoretically cover all of childhood [*enfance*], appears 'incredible', and too contrary to common sense. What might Spinoza have meant? And can we draw out a general concept of amnesia that does accord with his conception of the mind and the body?

One final question. Does not the absurd hypothesis of the scholium to V, 6 ('if most people were born grown up, and only one or two were born infants . . .') call to mind an image that is the inverse of the real social situation such as Spinoza sees it, in which the majority of adults remain children, except for one or two sages? Is this not the ephemeral image of that golden age denounced as a pure fable at the beginning of the *Political Treatise*?[80] If everyone were in fact born an adult, if human beings could be freed of their customs in order to judge things *sub specie aeternitatis*, it is clear that political transformation would no longer be a problem: the multitude would have chosen one of the three or four optimal political forms that Spinoza proposes,[81] and it would form itself [*s'auto-formerait*] eternally. Was it not for this reason that the demystified Christ of the *Theologico-Political Treatise* appeared at once as the philosopher par excellence, the one who perceived God and things by the third kind of knowledge, and as the one who constituted an exception to the rule of the absolute illegitimacy of revolt?

---

[79] *TdIE* 20; CWS I, 13. The verb tenses are obviously decisive.
[80] *TP* I, 5; CWS II, 506.
[81] Four, in fact, since the *Political Treatise* examines two cases of aristocracy.

At the end of Ch. 16, I explicitly warned that everyone is bound to keep faith even with a Tyrant, except someone to whom God, by a certain rev-elation, had promised special aid against the Tyrant. So no one is allowed to take this as an example, unless he also has the power to perform mira-cles. This is also clear from the fact that Christ told his disciples that they shouldn't fear those who kill the body (see Matthew 10:28). If he'd said this to everyone, the state would be established in vain . . . So it must be confessed that the authority Christ gave his disciples he gave to them only, and that others cannot take them as an example.[82]

As we see, transformation for Spinoza is not only an object whose ref-erent is often problematic (whether it is a matter of rendering a judgment on revolution, on alchemical transformation, on amnesia, on the growth of the infant, etc.): it is an issue that animates his thought, to the extent that it wants to be practical, and so cannot avoid the question of the status and modalities of its intervention.

Spinoza's philosophy places at the heart of its practical preoccupations the theme of the *conservation* of form. And yet, no philosophy has been so preoccupied with *rupture*: it proposes to the individual a new life, and to the collectivity new institutions. It thus never ceases to encounter the problem of transformation, its reality, its fantasy, and the limit states that belong to it; whence the crucial themes of amnesia and the development of children, but also, both in ethics and in politics, of slavery and suicide. There are three ways of escaping what Spinoza's philosophy induces us here to think: 1. interpreting it as a conservatism (including politically); 2. interpreting it as a transformism (including politically); 3. interpreting this antithesis – which exists only between two errors – as a contradiction attributable to the thinker.

The gravest error is perhaps the first, which alone does not seem to be devoid of sense (since it is clear, by contrast, that Spinoza is absolutely pessi-mistic about revolutions). And yet, the conservatism of the *Political Treatise*, when properly understood, understood as the irresistible self-affirmation of form that proposes to each type of regime that it reinvent itself from top to bottom in order finally to *exist* (to truly have a form), has something about it that would terrify the mind of any 'conservative' or 'reformist' in the usual sense of the term. 'Conserve': is this not again one of those words – like 'God' – by which Spinoza, in a certain manner, misleads his world, radically subverting its standard interpretation *by affirming its very sense*? The question of the practical significance of the Spinozist approach cannot be made more urgent.

We propose here three studies, which concern different domains, but which constitute three successive investigations of the same problem. It seemed like a good idea to concentrate our attention first of all on the manner in which ethical rupture was thematised in the early texts, less studied than the three latter parts of the *Ethics*. This is the first study: how the traditional schema of conversion is rethought, first within a new problematic of the 'element', and then that of the 'institutum vitae'. The second study takes up the *Ethics* and shows that the emergence of the theme of childhood is connected to the reconsideration of the same schema, and to a redefinition of the ethical journey. The third, finally, analyses the articulation of the metaphysical and political dimensions of the problem of transformation: the critique and subversion of the theologico-political order. We will see that the meditation on political transformism quite significantly exceeds the framework of a mere commentary on revolutions, and leads Spinoza to the highest stage of his thinking on collective freedom – the concept of the 'free multitude', late on the scene, still only embryonic, a new thought that occupied his mind when phthisis finally got the better of him.

First Study: Involving Another Nature/Involving Nature

The appearance of the ambivalent theme of the *infans adultus* at the two extremes of the ethical progression, namely the first and third kinds of knowledge, carries the investigation into the status of such a change, in the very last pages of the *Ethics*, to its highest degree. Everything happens, as we will see, as if the question of the continuity of essence, in the process of growth, could not be resolved: the book concludes without seeming to elucidate either the relation of the wise to the ignorant, or the relation of the wise to other human beings, and not even that of the wise to the 'former self' that they had been. Thus we must first of all concern ourselves with the delicate status of ethical change. The Preface to Part IV of the *Ethics* having reiterated that perfection is a transition, not a transformation, Spinoza multiplies the indications in favour of its being a rupture: the image of growth, treated as a quasi-transformation; the gap between the wise and the ignorant, compared to that of a specific difference; finally and above all, the incompatibility of the *instituta vitae* formulated so dramatically at the beginning of the *Treatise on the Emendation of the Intellect*. We will say that the ethical progression has all the traits of a transformation but without being one.

1

Ethical Transition in the *Short Treatise*

Proper Element and Foreign Element (KV II, 26)

In the *Short Treatise*, Spinoza poses the problem of passage or transition through contraries.[1] Victory over the passions logically cannot precede the knowledge and love of God-Nature: a relation of succession, a simple temporal juxtaposition of contraries, would be an absurdity, for the ignorant would find themselves in the situation of needing to cease being ignorant before they gained knowledge. One will here recognise the old Socratic paradox of learning. Contraries cannot coexist, but only the presence of the second term can make the first pass away: 'only knowledge is the cause of the destruction [of ignorance]'.[2] This paradox is delicate, because it has the air of a sophism: the contraries here are not two things of a different nature, but the absence and presence of one and the same thing (knowledge); consequently, to say that knowledge chases off ignorance is just a turn of phrase, since it chases off nothing other than its own absence. Except that ignorance, far from being a nothingness or an empty space, corresponds to a 'mode of knowledge'[3] that falls under what we might call a subjective polarisation; this explains the necessity of a rupture, of a change of life, there where common sense instead sees a progression. This is to say that ignorance and knowledge are even more opposed than contraries. If there is an opposition, or incompatibility, it is because ignorance is a state of confused

---

[1] *KV* II, 26; CWS I, 146–50.

[2] *KV* II, 26; CWS I, 146–50. Translation modified. [As Curley notes, the original text is ambiguous about what it is that is being destroyed here. He follows Meijer in supposing that it is the passions; Zourabichvili follows Appuhn and the Pléiade editors in supposing that it is ignorance. – GM.]

[3] *KV* II, 1; CWS I, 96–8. Translation modified.

perception of things that gives rise to its own illusion concerning the true and the good, and sustains a particular kind of life based on this erroneous evaluation. Whence the dramatic dimension of the *Short Treatise* and the *Treatise on the Emendation of the Intellect*: the ascent toward knowledge contains an intimate struggle between two rival subjective principles.

Commentators have always privileged the version found in the *Treatise on the Emendation of the Intellect*, often emphasising that it has the character of a stylistic exercise inherited from Roman stoicism. The *Short Treatise*, however, makes use of a striking image: that of one's 'element'.

> [Without] virtue, or to put it better, without being governed by the intellect, everything leads to ruin, without our being able to enjoy any peace, and we live as if out of our *element*.[4]

It is a given that each by nature seeks their good or their comfort, or in other words what is useful to them. But, depending on the mode in which they invest their striving, they will be headed either for their salvation or their destruction. Salvation is the sovereignty of the understanding or, in other words, virtue. Destruction is 'pursuing sensual pleasures, lusts, and worldly things'.[5] These are false goods that, because they lead us to neglect our conservation, constitute a foreign element for us, one incompatible with our nature. By contrast, there is the love of God-Nature, a type of union that constitutes the true good. Spinoza does not explicitly speak of a 'proper' good, perhaps because at that very moment he foresaw a difficulty: it is a matter of finding comfort not within ourselves, but in something infinitely greater than us – even if this does not mean a pure and simple alterity, because we participate in it, and because it grants us sovereignty.

It is remarkable that the decision between true and false goods here amounts to an affective ordeal: 'it [divine love] is such that one who enjoys it would not want to exchange it for anything else in the world';[6] 'we find that [worldly things lead] not to our salvation but to our destruction'.[7] It is enjoyment that makes us know our proper element.

---

[4] *KV* II, 26; *CWS* I, 146. [N.B. Zourabichvili says that the emphasis here is Spinoza's, but I don't know that this is true. At least in Gebhardt's edition, there is no emphasis: 'en wy als buyten ons element leven'. – GM.]

[5] *KV* II, 26; *CWS* I, 147.

[6] *KV* II, 26; *CWS* I, 146.

[7] *KV* II, 26; *CWS* I, 147.

Spinoza goes further than the 'great theologians' with their argument from recompense, according to which the renunciation of a life of frivolity is only justified by the conviction that one will obtain eternity in exchange (one will here recognise an anticipation of the final proposition of the *Ethics*, which will identify beatitude and virtue). This argument leads to an absurd consequence: if eternity is not a sure thing, you may as well just follow your inclination. The critique is here carried out through a double declaration of immanence: the absence of eternal life in no way diminishes the danger of perdition, since it also applies to this life, which one means not to waste; and the decision in favour of divine love is a function not of the hope for a life after death, but of the concrete experience of a supreme enjoyment here on earth. Spinoza can thus conclude:

> This is as silly as if a fish (which cannot live outside the water) should say: if no eternal life is to come to me after this life in the water, I want to leave the water for the land. But what else can those who do not know God say to us?[8]

'I want to leave the water for the land': it is surely remarkable that Spinoza here makes fish speak, and feels the need to adopt their point of view in order to illustrate a human problem.[9] He even seems somewhat taken with this fantasy, since the exposition of the concept of natural right, in Chapter XVI of the *Theologico-Political Treatise*, will also depart from fish and the way in which they 'enjoy the water', their proper element.

But the truly surprising thing concerns the aspiration for another life. The sentence has above all a polemical function, if one recalls the myth from *Phaedo*, at the end of the discussion about the reasons to believe in the immortality of the soul: the human being who gains access to the true heaven and to the 'things beyond' is compared to fish who 'rising from the sea see things in our region'.[10] One can hardly imagine a more concise or definitive reversal of Platonism: in Spinoza, the image of salvation has

---

[8] *KV* II, 26; *CWS* I, 146.

[9] In the *Treatise on the Emendation of the Intellect* Spinoza allows for a legitimate usage of fictions of essence. He gladly makes recourse to them in his correspondence: not only can humans often be compared to beasts, but one can imagine a speaking triangle (*Ep*. LVI [to Boxel]; *CWS* II, 421), a thinking stone (*Ep*. LVIII [to Schuller]; *CWS* II, 428), or even a complaining circle (*Ep*. LXXVIII [to Oldenburg]; *CWS* II, 480).

[10] 109e (Plato 1997: 94). This source seems to us to have greater significance here than the amusing Talmudic parable of the fox who tries to convince some fish to escape

become the image of perdition, in a joyous satire of the concern for tran-scendence (to make salvation depend on the belief in a beyond, and to aban-don oneself to the passions due to the inability to believe in this beyond, are one and the same thing). However, the sense of the sentence is not exhausted by the polemic. That is only the obverse of a positive and truly curious idea, namely: the other life is not that which one believes in, it is not beyond the present condition, like an uncertain destiny; it is in everyday life that human beings, without their being aware of it, do their utmost to live another life – and here we mean a non-human life, as if they tried to fly or to live in the water. The other life is that which, though scarcely viable, is led by the *vulgus*, by ordinary mortals.

Whence the transposition of elements and its humorous potential: the water is to the earth as the earth, in Christian mythology, is to Heaven, because human beings invent a heaven on earth without knowing it, and because it is on the earth that one must search for a celestial life – the attempt to actualise a life in an element other than our own. If there is no Heaven, then Heaven must be on earth!

Here again, we find a declaration of immanence: utopias are not merely pious dreams, destined to remain as such; all of vulgar life, marked by the pri-macy of the imagination, participates in an effective utopia, which as such is ruinous (and which Spinoza will later call a 'waking dream').[11] For human beings have a certain nature, and utopia amounts above all to the projec-tion of another human nature. To the extent that this other life on earth is the common condition of human beings, the tendency to project another human nature is natural, inherent to the passivity that is the native state of every human being. By contrast, eternal life, such as Spinoza conceives of it, is our own proper life, in the element that suits us: Heaven is brought down to earth, and this return to the proper element, as we will see, has for its paradoxical condition the union with 'God'.

The problem of happiness is in this way inverted, so that the change of element – or transformation – signifies our destruction, and not our salva-tion. To search for Heaven is what each does in their everyday life, and above all those who, denying any eternal life, believe they devote them-selves to the Earth. In this sense, the everyday, religious representation of salvation is only the reflection of the tendentious state of perdition that sus-

---

their fishermen once and for all by reconnecting with the life of their distant ancestors on the earth (see Filippo Mignini in Spinoza 1986: 745 n. 33).

[11] We explored the concept of 'waking dream' or 'dreaming with open eyes' in Zourabichvili 2002, ch. 7.

tains it: the aspiration to Heaven, to say it again, is the very logic of everyday life or the state of passion.

The key to this passage from the *Short Treatise* is found at the very end of the *Ethics*, in the second-to-last scholium, framed by two passages that propose to the reader the same ultimate vision of the opposition between the two extreme states of the human condition: maximal unconsciousness, impotence, passivity (the fragile life of the infant, the agitated life of the ignorant); knowledge, power, impassivity (the free and joyous life of the wise).[12] This scholium prepares the way for the second statement of practical immanentism, 'Blessedness is not the reward of virtue, but virtue itself',[13] which builds on the first, given at the end of Part IV: 'A free man thinks of nothing less than of death, and his wisdom is a meditation on life, not on death.'[14] Spinoza had just developed his highly novel conception of eternity; now he specifies its practical role, clearing away the misinterpretations of a life that would search for its meaning beyond death, beyond itself. The inversion of values that characterises vulgar life (taking license for freedom) has the effect of making it impossible to master the passions; then this mastery remains possible only by playing on the motivations of hope and fear, which implies the belief in a divided beyond (heaven/hell). Spinoza here describes a veritable *structure*, that of vulgar life, or of the salvation of the ignorant: one cannot make the choice to be at once ignorant and incredulous, which would be equivalent to suicide or falling into madness. This is the fate of the incredulous fish of the *Short Treatise*, who is held back from leaving the water only by faith in the eternal. The reversal of values is exacerbated: in the ignorant, what there is of rationality is on the side of superstition, whereas a sober imagination leads to the absurd and to perdition. To cease to be ignorant, one must believe: fiction comes to the ultimate rescue. The *Ethics* does not have to concern itself with the potential salvation of the ignorant, since its social role is to encourage the life of the wise – but this does not prevent it from implying such salvation. In practice, only the fear of hell explains why the majority of human beings are not mad or suicidal: it provides a passional manner of resolving or at least attenuating the dilemma of Medea (*Video Meliora proboque, Deteriora sequor*). Nothing better illustrates the structural function of transcendental faith in vulgar life than the way in which Spinoza

---

[12] *Ethics* V, 39 Schol. and 42 Schol.; CWS I, 614 and 616–17. We will see however in the following study that the equivalence of these two states of impotence, that of the infant and that of the desperately ignorant adult, is only a mirage.

[13] *Ethics* V, 42; CWS I, 616.

[14] *Ethics* IV, 67; CWS I, 584.

describes the fate of the incredulous. Whether or not they believe it, the incredulous person is marked by the eternal, and feels nostalgia for it:

> If men did not have this Hope and Fear, but believed that minds die with the body, and that the wretched, exhausted with the burden of Morality, cannot look forward to a life to come, they would return to their natural disposition, and would prefer to govern all their actions according to lust, and to obey fortune rather than themselves. These opinions seem no less absurd to me than if someone, because he does not believe he can nourish his body with good food to eternity, should prefer to fill himself with poisons and other deadly things, or because he sees that the Mind is not eternal, *or* immortal, should prefer to be mindless, and to live without reason. These [common beliefs] are so absurd they are hardly worth mentioning.[15]

Here we clearly see the terrible dilemma of vulgar life: the individual can only choose between two alienations, of which the one, for all its lack of inspiration, at least conforms in its effects with the prescriptions of reason (to deliver oneself from the bondages of fortune, in other words from immediate desires, which are tied to the irrepressible power of the affections of the body). The fish resolves to remain in the water only from the perspective of eternal life; the human only finds the resources for a minimal adherence to its proper element – rationality, outside of which it is impotent and unhappy – by projecting this end outside itself. A rationality outside of itself: such is indeed the life of the *vulgus*, governed in its private life by the fear of eternal punishment, in its public life by the fear of the State.

This theme of a fictive human nature projected by the passive imagination appears in Spinoza's later texts. First of all, concerning pseudo-philosophers, for whom to think means to moralise: 'they've learned how to praise in many ways a human nature which doesn't exist anywhere, and how to bewail the way men really are'.[16] But to project a fictive human nature amounts to extracting the human being from nature: 'they seem to conceive man in nature as a dominion within a dominion'.[17] The link with the tendency of the *vulgus* to live in an element other than their own is obvious: to extract the human being from nature is to take the fish out of water. One attributes to it a power it does not have (to immediately master its passions, to live on land), one ignores its true power (to understand through causes,

---

15 *Ethics* V, 41 Schol.; CWS I, 616.
16 *TP* I, 1; CWS II, 503.
17 *Ethics* III, Praef.; CWS I, 491.

to live in the water). Not that Nature in general is an element; but in this way one abstracts away from the relation between a particular nature and the element that suits it. To treat a thing *extra naturam* is to abandon the question of the element, and consequently of the limits, both positive and negative, of a nature. On the one hand (the *vulgus*), the other nature is simply that by virtue of which the passive human being leads their life; on the other (the moralist philosopher), the other nature is what enables them to condemn passivity as a vicious choice against nature. Spinoza himself establishes this relation: these moralists 'conceive men not as they are, but as they want them to be'.[18] In other words, this attitude is dictated to them by the inadequacy of their ideas, and tells us more about them than about the object they claim to study.

It is one and the same thing to abandon oneself to an element other than one's own, and to pass over the question of one's element in silence. It is a given that those other fish (that is, we ourselves) put all of their efforts into this dangerous game that consists in trying to live on the earth, without their knowing it; but some of them also fail to see that by hating this game, they go even further in the affirmation of this earth, by developing the abstract conception of an *imperial* fish, one that does not imply the water. They believe they cease adoring the earth by no longer thinking of elements, but in this way they are prevented from affirming the water (they miss out on having joy, on knowing how to enjoy their own nature in a way). Spinoza even says that the politics of these moralists can only be a 'chimera',[19] that is, the implausible and impotent combination of two essences in a nature that involves a contradiction: they affirm a human being that is not one, and they propose remedies suited to a being that does not exist and which, if it did exist, would have no need for them.

It's not just moralism at stake: we will see that tyranny also tends to operate by virtue of a fictive human nature, and consequently constitutes less a political form than a 'chimera'.[20] It is characterised by acts or commands that 'human nature abhors',[21] or in other words that are contrary to it. We are no longer merely dealing with those ambiguous constitutions we spoke of in the Introduction, straddling the line between two distinct political forms: the political chimera here reaches its peak, designating a regime that

---

[18] *TP* I, 1; CWS II, 503.
[19] *TP* I, 1; CWS II, 503. Translation modified. [Curley renders Spinoza's 'chimaera' as 'Fantasy'. – GM.]
[20] *TP* IV, 4; CWS II, 526. Translation modified.
[21] *TP* III, 8; CWS II, 520. Translation modified.

tries to govern real human beings as if they were another species. This is the problem of the natural limit of the juridical transfer of political authority, to which we will return in the third study: the threshold beyond which a human can no longer obey another without ceasing to be a human being. Just as one will not manage to make a table eat grass, no matter how much one wants it, in the same way 'the State does not have the right to make men fly'[22] – to make them abandon the earth for the air, on the model of the fish that leaves the water.

Let us now return to the passage from the *Short Treatise*. The problem of ethical change is raised there in two ways: from the point of view of transition (the paradox of learning) and from the point of view of the element. At this point, we must think them together. 'Without virtue . . . we live as if out of our *element*':[23] such is our ordinary condition. But Spinoza warned us already in §1 that 'the causes (or to put it better, what we call sins) which prevent us from attaining our perfection are in ourselves'.[24] This exteriority that threatens us is intimate. The metaphor of the element, so forceful a bit further on, here turns out to be too weak, insofar as in it exteriority seems to be dissociated from us; the difference between ourselves and the element must thus be attenuated, mediated, as our life is compromised by the hostile element only by virtue of the striving that pushes us there. Destruction and salvation correspond to divergent orientations of desire. We find ourselves within a foreign element, as our entire being demands. Consequently, it is not a matter of raising a rampart between the exterior and ourselves: what is exterior is not in itself to blame, is not a threat; everything depends on our relation to it.

So the question of transition reappears: what is it that plays the role of the middle term that ever since Plato has been necessary in order to think progress or learning?

> So we see that to reach the truth of what we maintain as established regarding our salvation and peace, we need no principle other than that of seeking our own advantage, something which is very natural in all things. And since we find that pursuing sensual pleasures, lusts, and worldly things leads not to our salvation but to our destruction, we therefore prefer to be governed by our intellect. But because this can make no progress unless we have first arrived at the knowledge and love of God, it is

---

[22] *TP* IV, 4; CWS II, 526–7. Translation modified.
[23] *KV* II, 26; CWS I, 146.
[24] *KV* II, 26; CWS I, 146.

most necessary to seek him. And because, after the preceding reflections and considerations, we have found him to be the greatest good of all goods, we must stand firm here, and be at peace. For we have seen that outside him, there is nothing that can give us any salvation. True freedom is to be and to remain bound by the lovely chains of the love of God.[25]

What does this passage say? The search for what is useful is natural to us, is intimate, and yet it is the purveyor of salvation as well as destruction: for we deceive ourselves about the nature of the useful, and bring our striving to bear on false goods. The investment of our striving is confronted with an alternative: either sensual pleasures, or the sovereignty of the understanding (which is capable, the text said above, of providing us with a superior enjoyment). And we know by experience that the first path is ruinous.

Let us emphasise this point: up until now, Spinoza has insisted above all on the positive experience of a superior joy for turning us away from the impure and dangerous joys of passion:

when we who love something come to know something better than what we love, we always fall on it at once, and leave the first thing . . .[26]

when we know and enjoy the best, the worst has no power over us.[27]

a love is destroyed by the perception of something else that is better . . .[28]

However, Spinoza already invoked a duality of solutions:

It is possible to rid ourselves of Love in two ways, either by knowledge of a better thing, or by finding that the thing we have loved, and have regarded as something great and magnificent, brings much misery with it.[29]

It is only in a note in Chapter 19 that these two paths start to fall into place. There Spinoza presents the process of perfection according to a ternary schema, corresponding to the triad laid out in Chapter 2: opinion, which produces passions; right belief, which shows us what is good and bad in

---

[25] *KV* II, 26; *CWS* I, 146–7.
[26] *KV* II, 5; *CWS* I, 107.
[27] *KV* II, 19, n. c; *CWS* I, 130.
[28] *KV* II, 19; *CWS* I, 133. Translation modified.
[29] *KV* II, 5; *CWS* I, 104.

passions; and true knowledge, which carries out our deliverance.[30] And he
brings this schema into relation with a Christian triad: Sin, the Law that
identifies sin, and the Grace that delivers us from it.[31] The logic of transition thus seems to imply such a ternary schema, which introduces a middle
term between the state of passion and the accomplishment of deliverance,
the positive condition (experience of a joy of an intensity superior to that
produced by the passions) itself being subordinated to a negative condition
(acute awareness of the ruinous character of the passions).

Now, in Chapter 26, Spinoza argues from ruin and not from joy. If he does
so, it is in order to avoid falling into the circle of transition; for if we positively know, because we have enjoyed it, that our salvation resides in intellection, the knowledge would presuppose knowledge, and perfection would
amount to a happy accident. In fact, the rest of the text raises the problem
of transition, identifying 'seeking God' as the middle term. The penultimate
sentence confirms this argumentative approach: it is not because we have
already encountered God that we know that we must seek it, but simply by a
process of elimination ('outside him, there is nothing . . .').

Spinoza does not hesitate between the two paths, the positive and the
negative. Once again, the experience of a superior joy is a leitmotif that runs
throughout Part II of the *Short Treatise*. Except that this enjoyment does not
arise by chance; rather, it results from a patient effort, it is the crowning
achievement of the investigation. It presupposes knowledge, which is only
obtained by way of a rational meditation. But mere right belief, being wholly
external, as such has no power to produce a rupture: 'though Reason shows
us something that is better, it does not make us enjoy it'.[32] Right belief
makes us see, it 'indicates' (*aanwyst*):[33] we do not yet see the thing, but we
know what it would have to be, by demonstrative necessity. It is thus only
a sign of the thing, a 'message' that it addresses to us (*boodschaft*).[34] We
remain in an external though necessary relation with the thing, without
union or love, since the relation to the object passes through the mediation
of a sign.[35] Reason or right belief has no efficacy of its own: it only orients
the subject, 'it brings us to (*brengt tot*) a clear understanding, through which
we love God',[36] it is 'only like a stairway, by which we can climb up to

---

[30] [*KV* II, 2; *CWS* I, 98–9. *KV* II, 19, n. b; *CWS* I, 129.]
[31] [*KV* II, 19, unmarked footnote; *CWS* I, 130.]
[32] *KV* II, 21, n. a; *CWS* I, 138.
[33] *KV* II, 4; *CWS* I, 103.
[34] *KV* II, 26; *CWS* I, 147. Translation modified.
[35] See Boss 1982: 144: 'The thing is grasped at a distance.'
[36] *KV* II, 4; *CWS* I, 103.

the desired place'.[37] It is the moment of the dilemma or inner conflict par excellence, when knowledge is still impotent to modify our behaviour.[38] Since conversion is, if we can put it like this, undertaken by right belief but only carried out by true knowledge, one can no longer attribute the rupture to anything but the two complementary terms taken together. Right belief indeed corresponds to that transitory stage where the future encroaches on the present: we have not yet left behind passional life, and yet the movement of conversion is taking shape or being prepared. It arranges, from within passional life, the conditions for exiting it. It is between-two-loves – even though this state is not viable[39] and Spinoza is consequently forced to make correspond to it a specific 'desire' born of reasoning, which is nothing other than the necessity of seeking God articulated in the passage that we are commenting on.[40] Reason is in fact 'like a good spirit which without any falsity or deception brings tidings of the greatest good, to spur us thereby to seek it'.[41]

Let us now return to this passage and reread it. Its formulation seemed barely coherent at first glance, since the experience of the ruinous character of the passions led us to 'prefer to be governed by our intellect', but we could not progress toward this governance without *first* (*alvoren*) knowing or loving God; we must thus begin by seeking God. We have tended to think that the progress of the understanding is mixed up with the progress toward God, but the passage makes it a matter of two successive processes, ordered in relation to one another. The only clarifying path, at least if we take the syntax seriously, is to invoke on the one hand the way in which right belief

---

[37] *KV* II, 26; *CWS* I, 147.

[38] Chapter 21, on Reason, begins with a paraphrase of Ovid's celebrated formula, which will reappear in Part IV of the *Ethics*.

[39] 'given the weakness of our nature, we could not exist if we did not enjoy something to which we were united, and by which we were strengthened' (*KV* II, 5; *CWS* I, 105). The division of the concept of love, in Chapter 5, gives rise to a triad that does not overlap with the one we have just laid out. In this way the intermediate love dedicated to objects 'not corruptible through their cause', namely the 'modes that depend immediately on God' (*KV* II, 5; *CWS* I, 105, 107) (or Natured Nature, movement and rest being the only two immediate modes that we know, given *KV* I, 9), does not correspond to the stage of right belief or reason. Rather what is at stake is the first stage of clear knowledge. On progress in clear knowledge, see below, our remarks on *KV* II, 26 §5.

[40] *KV* II, 5; *CWS* I, 105. The necessity of seeking God is there the consequence of reasoning. The invocation of a 'desire which proceeds from reasoning' comes from the end of Chapter 21 (*KV* II, 21; *CWS* I, 138).

[41] *KV* II, 26; *CWS* I, 147.

or reason leads us toward the love of God (without producing it), and on the other hand the degrees in the love of God at stake in Chapter 5.

Let us return to the last part of the passage: not only does it confirm our proposed strategy, but above all it rigorously defines the inside-outside relation by underscoring the paradox – our proper element is God,[42] outside of which there is no salvation, and in which we coincide with ourselves, that is, we seek our own proper utility. While God is not we ourselves, this is no longer an external thing: we are with God in a relation of participation. That is why this union is not a matter of dependency and why it can be called freedom. The term 'union' is certainly ambivalent when it is a question of the relation between a part and its whole. We are not foreign to this whole with which we are united, but it exceeds us; better still, we only rejoin ourselves by participating in this whole that is greater than ourselves. Paragraph 9 draws out the consequences of this:

> From all that has been said, it can now be very easily conceived what human freedom is. [The bondage of a thing consists in being subjected to external causes; freedom, on the contrary, in being freed of them, not subjected to them.][43] I define it as follows: it is a firm existence, which our intellect acquires through immediate union with God, so that it can produce ideas in itself, and outside itself effects agreeing well with its nature, without its effects being subjected, however, to any external causes by which they can be changed (*veranderd*) or transformed (*verwisseld*).[44]

Here a real definition frames a nominal one: only the joint reading of the two enables us to understand Spinoza's logic. It is by being unified with God that one agrees with oneself, and is protected from transformation. No doubt Spinoza is here speaking of affects; the ambivalence of ethical change is revitalised here, as the passage at least authorises one to speak of a transformation of affectivity (or of what one could call 'subjectivity', to use an anachronistic term). However, just previously, Spinoza had explained that 'the more things, through their greater essence, are united with God, the more they also have of action, and the less of passion, and the more they are

---

[42] As Gilbert Boss writes, 'we live in God (or in nature) as the fish lives in the water' (Boss 1982: 167).

[43] [Gebhardt brackets this as probably a reader's summary; Curley, like Appuhn, places it in a footnote. Zourabichvili interpolates it here while indicating its status as a note. – GM.]

[44] KV II, 26; CWS I, 149.

also free of change (*verandering*) and corruption (*verderving*)'.[45] Here it is no longer a matter of affects, but of their subjects. Inalterability can be understood in two ways: 1. The union with God gives affectivity a constancy that rules out any regression to a previous stage (the adjective *vaste*, at the beginning of the passage, here rendered as 'firm', corroborates this idea). 2. This union frees us from an existence in which transformation threatens us. The more we are united with God, the more the danger of death or transformation recedes – which means, *a contrario*, that passive life is characterised by the perpetual risk of transformation. Insofar as we have not rejoined our own proper element, transformation weighs on us like a mortal threat. Is this the meaning of a somewhat enigmatic sentence from the *Ethics*: 'if one is among such as do not agree at all with his nature, he will hardly be able to accommodate himself to them without greatly changing himself (*magna ipsius mutatione*)'?[46] At the very least, it indicates another possible response to the question of the element suitable for a human life: society. To be united with God, or with other human beings? It is not by chance that Spinoza utilises the formula *Homo homini Deus*.[47] The *Treatise on the Emendation of the Intellect* always poignantly underscores this risk of transformation, which is inherent to the state of passivity.

A New Birth (KV II, 22)

However, before getting to the *Treatise on the Emendation of the Intellect*, let us note to what extent Part II, Chapter 26 of the *Short Treatise* clarifies *a contrario* Chapter 22, which defined the nature of ethical change.

The entire book is designed to kindle in the human being a new kind of love that, in being substituted for the old kind, will ensure their supreme happiness. Thus what is transformed is the love, not the subject that experiences it. But Spinoza, at the end of Chapter 22, uses the term 'rebirth' (*Wedergeboorte*), which means an 'other, or second, birth' (*andere of tweede geboorte*).[48]

This image, drawn from Christianity, corresponds to the rite of baptism.[49] But Christianity itself inherited it from ancient rites of initiation, which seem to have superimposed upon the passage from one age to another

---

45 *KV* II, 26; *CWS* I, 148.
46 *Ethics* IV, App. Cap. VII; *CWS* I, 589.
47 *Ethics* IV, 35 Schol.; *CWS* I, 563.
48 *KV* II, 22; *CWS* I, 140.
49 As Mignini points out; see Spinoza 1986: 719.

(from childhood to adulthood) the theme of a purification of the soul, and thus of a change of the mode of existence; and they identified the new mode of life with a new life, as if a new being rose up in place of the old – the same, and yet new, whence the idea of a rebirth.[50] This double dimension cannot but call to mind the scholia to the two propositions 39, on the growth of the infant (Part V) and on the transformation of the amnesiac (Part IV).

The question is clearly one of knowing whether the image is introduced here merely as a symbol, which would be wholly unremarkable, or if instead it takes on a philosophical status. Consider the following passages:

> Jesus answered him, 'Very truly, I tell you, no one can see the kingdom of God without being born anew.' Nicodemus said to him, 'How can anyone be born after having grown old? Can one enter a second time into the mother's womb and be born?' Jesus answered, 'Very truly, I tell you, no one can enter the kingdom of God without being born of water and Spirit. What is born of the flesh is flesh, and what is born of the Spirit is spirit. Do not be astonished that I said to you, "You must be born anew".'[51]

> So if you have been raised with Christ . . . you have died, and your life is hidden with Christ in God. When Christ who is your life is revealed, then you also will be revealed with him in glory. Put to death, therefore, whatever in you is earthly: fornication, impurity, passion, evil, desire, and greed (which is idolatry). On account of these the wrath of God is coming on those who are disobedient. These are the ways you also once followed, when you were living that life. But now you must get rid of all such things – anger, wrath, malice, slander, and abusive language from your mouth. Do not lie to one another, seeing that you have stripped off the old self with its practices and have clothed yourselves with the new self, which is being renewed in knowledge according to the image of its creator. In that renewal there is no longer Greek and Jew, circumcised and uncircumcised, barbarian, Scythian, slave and free; but Christ is all in all![52]

And now look at Spinoza's writing:

> When we become aware of these effects, we can truly say that we have been born again. For our first birth was when we were united with the body. From this union have arisen the effects and motions of the [animal]

---

[50] See volume 1 of the *Dictionnaire de théologie chrétienne* (Doré 1979).
[51] John 3:3–7 (*NRSV*, 1886). Translation modified.
[52] Colossians 3:1–11 (*NRSV*, 2071).

spirits. But our other, or second, birth will occur when we become aware in ourselves of the completely different effects of love produced by knowledge of this incorporeal object. This [love of God] is as different from [love of the body] as the incorporeal is from the corporeal, the spirit from the flesh. This, therefore, may the more rightly and truly be called Rebirth, because, as we shall show, an eternal and immutable constancy comes only from this Love and Union.[53]

Leaving aside the reference to an ethical conversion, two similarities jump out: the rebirth through the spirit, and the rebirth in God (via Christ, who himself, according to Paul, is a 'second Adam'[54]). Spiritual elevation by the knowledge of and participative union with God: all this coincides with the Christian myth. But that is not the interesting thing: we must ask ourselves to what extent Spinoza actually thought of ethical conversion as a second birth, to what extent a religious tradition could have inspired a set of philosophical concepts without contaminating it as such. In the *Metaphysical Thoughts*, Spinoza had warned about the possible slide from the literal to the figurative senses of the word 'life': 'this term is often taken in an extended sense, to signify the conduct of some person',[55] and he notes that a change in that kind of conduct, 'in which there is no transformation of the subject',[56] cannot be identified with a transformation. But this is just what the apostle seems to do when he identifies the change of the mode of life with a new life, even though the idea of transformation seems logically justified by the radical heterogeneity of the body and the spirit . . .

Must not this merely be a manner of speaking, one that has some power in the Christian imaginary of its audience? Surely yes, since the rupture inherent to ethical transition is an 'emendation' and not a transformation – though it does imply a rupture, which is precisely what we are trying to think here. But the question is of knowing to what extent – to recall a theme from Part V of the *Ethics* – the image conforms with the order of the understanding. Chapter 26 gives us a glimpse: the image of two elements leads us to think of passional life as a state of alienation, in which human beings look for joy in an element that is not their own, because they forge a fictive idea of their own nature. Passional life is their destruction, because they are in a situation of living or putting all their strivings toward living in a non-human

---

[53] *KV* II, 22; *CWS* I, 140.
[54] 1 Corinthians 15:45 (*NRSV*, 2021).
[55] *CM* App. II, 6; *CWS* I, 325.
[56] *CM* App. II, 4; *CWS* I, 321.

manner, as if they were a being of another nature. Consequently, ethical transition consists in effectuating the opposite movement, in coming back from that unviable other-life, in which the human being tends to become an other, to the life that is their own – and not simply to the mode of life that corresponds to them. We see that in fact it is no longer simply a matter of modes of life: on the contrary, if one mode of life can be devalued in relation to another, it is because it tends to express a life ontologically other than that of its subject, and which puts the latter in danger (we will see how the *Treatise on the Emendation of the Intellect* accentuates and dramatises this aspect). Ethical transition thus appears as *the obverse of a tendential transformation*: it crosses the line of heterogeneity in the other direction. Or rather, while the subject continually approaches it as an asymptotic limit, coming dangerously close to death, the movement of conversion enables it to escape from what we can legitimately call the attraction of death, insofar as heterogeneity had indeed been the object of a love. 'New birth', then, is not simply a striking image, a spectacular allegory: it fully corresponds to the logic at play here. Is this logic not discernible in the words of Christ, according to John? 'Do not lie to one another, seeing that you have stripped off the old self with its practices and have clothed yourselves with the new self, which is being renewed in knowledge according to the image of its creator.'[57] It is a matter of learning to perceive ourselves as an other, living in the manner of an other that we are not, and of making that other-us die out, to the extent that its alterity is revealed.

However, we would falsify the sense of the *Short Treatise* if we put too much stress on the same-other, proper-foreign opposition, forgetting that it continues to depend on that of the body and the mind; this would make us incapable of understanding why Spinoza never again explicitly took up the theme of the new birth. How can he speak of a 'rebirth' when it is merely a matter of the soul converting its love, and not itself being transformed? The *Short Treatise* lays out a logical configuration that is undisturbed by the paradox of 'rebirth', that is, of a transformation of the self: the curious theory of love, in all its ambivalence.

The Ambivalence of 'Union'

In the *Short Treatise*, Spinoza develops a conception that he would later abandon, although it brings together the lineaments of a logic of salvation

---

[57] [While Zourabichvili makes it sound like this quote comes from the Gospel of John, in fact it is drawn from Paul's letter to the Colossians, cited above. – GM.]

that would come to fruition in the last part of the *Ethics*. We know that the theme of salvation by active, intellectual conversion, of a love henceforth turned toward God, is not Spinoza's invention: rather, it belonged to a certain 'common sense' of the time. In the Renaissance, Giordano Bruno had distinguished between two forms of love, the one passive, the other active; Descartes also made this distinction, and the 'Grand siècle' drew to a close in full 'dispute over pure love' (Fénelon and Bossuet). What deserves our attention here is on the one hand the quasi-ontological status of love in the *Short Treatise*, which itself raises the problem of essence and of transformation; and on the other hand the participative logic – due, no doubt, to the identification of God and Nature – that enables Spinoza to escape the classical problem of 'theandry', the fusion of two beings of different natures that would, from his point of view, appear as a chimera.

The paradoxical effect of union is a whole composed of two different things: 'by [love] we understand a union such that the lover and the loved come to be one and the same thing, or to form a whole together'.[58] But we never exist outside of such a whole: 'it is necessary that we not be free of [love], because, given the weakness of our nature, we could not exist if we did not enjoy something to which we were united, and by which we were strengthened'.[59]

But as the whole is composed of different things, it must therefore be possible to distinguish union from the chimera. Spinoza does not deny the difference in essence between the united terms: the human being is usually united with things that have little or no essence.[60] At the same time, he affirms that 'the essence of a thing does not increase through its union with another thing, with which it makes a whole. On the contrary, the first thing remains unchanged.'[61] He indicates however that the being united to things lacking in essence tends to suffer their fate,[62] and that the effects of the union depend on the essence of the thing to which we are united.[63] It is true that the first claim comes from one of the two Dialogues, but nothing in the main body of the text decides for or against it. It is hard to reconcile the idea of a whole or of a single thing with the idea that the united beings

---

[58] *KV* II, 5; *CWS* I, 105–6.

[59] *KV* II, 5; *CWS* I, 105.

[60] *KV* II, 5; *CWS* I, 106. ['if they are so miserable who love corruptible things (which still have some essence), how miserable will they be who love honor, wealth, and sensual pleasure, which have no essence?']

[61] *KV* I, Second Dialogue, 4; *CWS* I, 77.

[62] *KV* II, 5; *CWS* I, 105–6.

[63] *KV* II, 22; *CWS* I, 140.

have different essences: the remark about effects seems to indicate that the loved object imposes its own destiny on the lover, coming to rule over the latter's nature – in short, that the existence of the lover conforms to an essence other than its own. Furthermore, salvation resides in the conversion of our love toward another object (God), whose essence is not any longer identical with our own, even if the logical relation is no longer of the same kind.

If despite all this the heterogeneity of essences does not constitute a problem, it is because Spinoza believed he had resolved the difficulty by means of the epistemological relation between idea and object. This solution is surprising, on the one hand because it identifies love with a strong epistemological relation (union), and on the other hand because it leads to the conclusion, via the conception of the mind as the 'idea of the body', that the mind *loves* the body. This latter trait will be absent in the *Ethics*: it testifies to a distant Platonic influence, according to which desire only bears on external bodies through the soul's attachment to the body. In the *Short Treatise*, the concept of the 'idea of the body' makes it possible to treat, on the same plane and analogically, the relation to one's own body and the relation to God (other bodies, invoked at first, are quickly forgotten). If the chimera is avoided, it is because Spinoza constructs his concept of union on the model of the epistemological relation, which combines two natures without mixing them up (unlike the fictive idea of an extended mind). But are the body and mind in fact of a different *nature*? To admit this would by the same stroke pluralise God, by contesting the attribution of the attributes of thought and extension to one and the same essence. Let us see what the text says. 'For assume that the body is united with the soul, according to the common doctrine of the Philosophers; nevertheless, the body never senses, nor is the soul extended. For then a Chimera, in which we conceive two substances, would be able to become one. And that is false.'[64] This remark, which appears only in one of the two manuscripts (manuscript B), requires caution. It occurs in the context of Spinoza's objection to the partisans of the faculties, who take the Understanding and the Will to be real beings. Spinoza simply means to show, by analogy with the body and the mind, the non-relation that irreducibly separates the supposed faculties, and which consequently makes it impossible to think their functional conjunction or the passage from one to the other. His procedure here is acrobatic, since

---

[64] *KV* II, 16; *CWS* I, 123. [This quotation comes from a part of the text that Gebhardt had printed as a note; Curley follows Meijer in introducing it into the main body of the text. – GM.]

the analogy is only possible if one temporarily adopts the adversary's point of view: Spinoza does not intend to reduce the duality of mind and body, but rather to show that it is formal and not numeric. On the other hand, the chimera generally designates the confusion of two essences under the same attribute. But ultimately is not this confusion, or at least the tendency toward this illusion, just what Spinoza condemns? The traditional conception, or non-conception, of the union of mind and body consists in searching for a transition from one to the other, on a homogeneous plane. This is the critique that he will levy against Descartes and his famous pineal gland in the Preface to Part IV of the *Ethics*: the supposed point of contact between the mind and the body still belongs to extension, it consists in linking them together under the same attribute, as if it were a matter of two different natures. Therefore, by conceiving the relation of the lover to the loved on the epistemological model of an objectal relation, union no longer runs the risk of conjuring a chimera.

Nevertheless, the problem reappears. Spinoza certainly does not say that the body and the mind differ essentially: the concept of the mind as 'the idea of the body' implies that it takes its essence from its object – 'our soul being an Idea of the body, it has its first being (*wezen*) from the body'.[65] But then, does not the mind change in nature – is it not transformed – by being united with another object? The body to which the mind is 'united' is not transformed without the latter also being transformed.[66] Finally, the union with that immutable and eternal thing that is the divine nature radically disrupts the life of a human being, and the scope and status of this disruption remains precisely to be defined. The theory of love and its conversion invokes a perceptive relation of the mind to the body proper to God, and in this way agrees with the concept of the 'idea of the body'; but it diverges from it significantly when it comes to the consequences of the change of the object. This is the ambivalent status of conversion: is it perfection, or transformation? Spinoza is looking for the philosophical formula of the 'second birth': a renewal of the same, a rupture that would not be a transformation. If salvation is on the side of the useful or of our own proper element, 'reintegration' has for its object our reclamation of ourselves; a transformation would annul any idea of salvation, or rather it would leave the problem intact, since the new being would strictly speaking have gained nothing from 'its' metamorphosis.

---

[65] *KV* II, 22, n. b; *CWS* I, 140. [Curley notes that this is bracketed by Gebhardt and may have been a reader's comment. – GM.]

[66] *KV* II, Praef. 10; *CWS* I, 95.

Thus the theory of love in the *Short Treatise* is torn in two logically opposed directions. Sometimes, in conformity with the concept of the mind as the 'idea of the body', essence is not independent of the object, love being an *essential* relation; at other times, the text gives us the impression that the mind alone constitutes the essence of a human being, the body being only one of its possible objects, which is indifferent to its essence. We will say that Spinoza tries to force the new conception of mind-body solidarity, which will prevail in the *Ethics*, to coexist with the old moral schema according to which only our soul pertains to us, where the body constitutes a foreign power. Spinoza is already in possession of a new theory of the body proper, but his theory of love contradicts it.

In truth, the text only attains a rather weak cohesion. If in fact the idea changes to the extent that its object changes, the union with another thing constitutes us otherwise; under these conditions, is not salvation a metamorphosis? Moreover, having spoken of the union of the mind with the body, Spinoza invokes the union with perishable things: if we follow this reasoning, must not the mind become the idea not only of the body but of a certain number of other objects? Must it not become the mind of another thing? The long note in the *Short Treatise* only mentions the birth and death, that is, the transformation, of the body proper: the mind is not transformed by abandoning the body for another thing, but by assuming the repercussions of the body's transformations. Once again, the text superimposes and at times conjugates heterogeneous theoretical strata.

Spinoza begins by saying that the idea and its object are necessarily united because 'the one cannot exist without the other';[67] this goes just as much for the relation of the mind and body. Then, concerning God, he says that our union with it is natural, for 'without him we can neither be nor be conceived'.[68] We see at once the similarity and dissymmetry of these two relations: the latter is without reciprocity. Or rather, the former is a relation of *reciprocal presupposition*, each of the terms having a meaning only in relation to the other; the latter is a relation of *implication*, thought on the model of participation. Our idea presupposes that of God, because we participate in it; no doubt the relation of the idea and the object acquires an ontological value with the concept of the idea of the body, but still this is different than the ontological relation of part and whole. In fact, it is only because the soul becomes the point of reference, tending to take on everything essential about the human being, that the relation to the body proper and the rela-

---

[67] *KV* II, 20, n. c; *CWS* I, 136.
[68] *KV* II, 22; *CWS* I, 139.

tion to God can appear on the same plane, as concurrent. For the question is indeed of their concurrence: is this merely a rhetorical effect tied to the dramatisation of the process of salvation?

If we are by nature united with God, then the union is not to be confused with love, which is only its conscious form. This is why Spinoza speaks of 'the union we have with him by Nature and by love'.[69] Inversely, once we have made the conversion, the union with God relegates the union with the body, which no longer persists, to an inferior rank. This actually leads to relativising the paradox of conversion: love, unlike union, plays no onto-logical role, and we do not need to think that Spinoza limits essence to the soul. Contrary to certain interpretations, we must consider love and union as concepts that are distinct in certain ways. Every human being is born united to a body on the one hand (as the 'first cause' of its soul, the 'first thing' it perceives[70]), and united to God-Nature on the other hand. But its love is exclusive, and bears either on the body and what effects it, or on God alone.

This reading is of course not entirely justified. We once again run into formulas that raise problems for the concept of the 'idea of the body' by identifying union and love: 'if the mind is united with the body only, and the body perishes, then it must also perish; for if it lacks the body, which is the foundation of its love, it must perish with it'.[71] By contrast, if the mind manages to be united with God, the body no longer takes the mind along with it in death: the mind is delinked from its union with the body, and the latter is no longer essential. Spinoza in this way develops a very abstract conception: the union with the body becomes one case among others, an unexceptional and fortuitous whole whose sole privilege is having been first in the life of the mind and which can be dissolved: 'the soul, being an Idea of this body, is so united with it, that it and this body, so constituted, together make a whole'.[72] And above all:

> And because the first thing the soul comes to know is the body, the result is that the soul loves the body and is united to it. But since [. . .] one love is destroyed by the perception of something else that is better, it follows from this clearly that *if we once come to know God (at least with as clear a knowledge as we have of our body), we must then come to be united with him even more closely than with our body, and be, as it were, released from the*

---

[69] *KV* II, 22; *CWS* I, 139.
[70] *KV* II, 22; *CWS* I, 139–40.
[71] *KV* II, 23; *CWS* I, 141.
[72] *KV* II, 19; *CWS* I, 132.

body. I say *more closely*, for we have already proven before that without him we can neither be nor be understood. This is because we know him, and must know him, not through anything else (as is the case with all other things), but only through himself (as we have already said before). Indeed, we know him better than we know ourselves, because without him we cannot know ourselves at all.[73]

This passage allows us to understand the contemporaneity of the two unions, the union with God simply being 'closer' than that with the body, and implying a 'detachment' from the latter. This superiority of the one over the other comes from the fact that we imply God, in an essential involvement, since we are a part of God. The life turned toward God is this relative detachment that leads to a survival of the mind in spite of the death of the body. But Spinoza often emphasises this even more strongly, as if union itself, and not merely love, were exclusive: 'we have noted that the Soul can be united either with the body of which it is the Idea or with God, without whom it can neither exist nor be understood (*of met het lichaam . . . of met God . . .*)'.[74]

Now, if the mind can in this way take leave of the body without renouncing its own essence, but on the contrary does so in order to *be* perfected and to ensure its salvation, it is because the whole essence of a human being is condensed there. Nothing says it better than this remark, which comes just at the moment where 'rebirth' is invoked: 'For our first birth was when we were united with the body.'[75]

To complicate things further, the concept of 'idea of the body' will contaminate the analogy of the two relations, to the body proper and to God, and seems consequently to presuppose a certain fusion or identification with God. Whence the resurgence of the spectre of transformation, now in such a way as to be compatible with salvation, since it implies an elevation – an apotheosis. If there is in fact an analogy on the one hand between the two relations, and on the other hand also between these two relations to the object called love and knowledge, then the mind, the idea of the body that it was initially, becomes the idea of God – though only 'to a certain extent' (*eenigzins*) and not 'as it is' (*zo hy is*), that is, not as it thinks itself.[76] This fusion is therefore partial, or rather unilateral, that is, without reciprocity. It

[73] *KV* II, 19; *CWS* I, 133. Our emphasis.
[74] *KV* II, 23; *CWS* I, 140–1.
[75] *KV* II, 22; *CWS* I, 140.
[76] *KV* II, 22; *CWS* I, 139.

is symptomatic that Spinoza here shrinks back from the question of essence, even though he had suggested that essence is not itself modified by love.[77] It is no less symptomatic that this idea would be contradicted at the end of the book, at least if, in Chapter 26, we dynamically interpret the first proposition of §8: 'the more things, through their greater essence, are united with God . . .'.[78] The letter of the text suggests a hierarchy of natural beings, but Mignini discerns here an increasing participation in the divine essence.[79] For the relation of participation is such that it enables a partial identification without essential alteration. When Spinoza says that the union with God is reinforced, he means our consciousness of that union; but it is true that this consciousness makes the human being's way of life accord with the ontological condition that is its own, if indeed it is possible to speak of a reinforcement or intensification of this union in the ontological sense of the term.

If we ask, in sum, why Spinoza rejected this first conception of the intellectual love of God, the principal reason is the contradiction between the concept of the mind as the 'idea of the body' and the analogy that leads to treating on the same plane, and in a very abstract manner, the union with God-Nature that constitutes ethical conversion and the existing union with the body. This is the total ambivalence of an immediate epistemological relation conceived as love. Beyond that, this conception tends to define essence by the mind alone. In the *Ethics*, this ambivalence will be cleared

---

[77] *KV* II, Second Dialogue, 4; *CWS* I, 77. All commentators reveal their discomfort on this point. Gilbert Boss, referring implicitly to Chapter 22's *eenigzis*, suggests that the soul 'can also become to a certain extent the Idea of God' (Boss 1982: 152), but does not bring up the difficulty such a claim implies: does the soul then cease to be defined as the idea of the body? And to what extent is it identified with God? He risks winding up with a formula that he knows is unacceptable, but which has the merit of indicating precisely, if furtively, the problem: 'The wise actually accedes, by a "second birth", to an immortality that is no longer that of the sensible body, but so to speak that of its new body, that is, that of the eternal being that has become the object of its love' (Boss 1982: 153). In short, Boss invokes a mystical body, that of God or the Son of God, recalling no longer the baptism but the Eucharist. We know the brilliant discovery on this point that will be found in the *Ethics*: namely, the mind insofar as it 'expresses the essence of the body under a species of eternity' (*Ethics* V, 23 Schol.; *CWS* I, 607). Here one should consult Filippo Mignini's commentary: 'But insofar as the object of love towards God is the pure understanding mind as the idea of the body, how could this love not only be sustained but conserved as an immortal part of that same mind, which has no object after death?' (Spinoza 1986: 723–4). Mignini underscores that, in the *Ethics*, the immortality of the mind will be based on the definition of the latter as the idea of the essence of the body, which as such is eternal.

[78] *KV* II, 26; *CWS* I, 148.

[79] Spinoza 1986: 749.

away both by abandoning the analogy (and the correlative idea, dependent on the tradition, of love of the body), and by the creation of a new concept: the essence of the body expressed *sub specie aeternitatis*.[80] Then it can no longer be a question of a double birth, by the flesh and by the spirit, and philosophy as a practice will need to find a new image of itself.

---

[80] *Ethics* V, 23 Schol.; CWS I, 607. [Zourabichvili refers to V, 29 Schol. – GM.]

2

Ethical Transition in the *Treatise on the Emendation of the Intellect*

Spinoza thus poses the question of transition a second time.[1] The interest of the *Treatise on the Emendation of the Intellect* for our inquiry is as follows: 1. The problem is that of the incompatibility of two *instituta vitae*. 2. Each of these is characterised by a particular type of 'love' (or a particular type of the determination of striving). 3. The primitive *institutum* that we must mourn betrays a state of tendential transformation.

The Logic of Ethical Transition: Conversion and Dilemma

The interest of the prologue of the *Treatise on the Emendation* is that it tells a story of transition. We know that the first sentence, which is of exceptional density, introduces the reader to a double temporality of caesura ('Postquam me experientia docuit . . .'[2]) and delay ('constitui tandem inquirere . . .', repeated insistently at the start of the second sentence: 'Dico, me tandem constituisse . . .'[3]). Pierre-François Moreau has recently shown[4] that the two statements that seem at first glance to constitute the content of the empirical lesson do not refer to the same moment: 'Postquam me experientia docuit, omnia, quae in communi vita frequenter occurrunt, vana, et futilia esse . . .'[5] and 'cum viderem omnia, a quibus, et quae timebam, nihil neque

---

[1] As the analysis that follows is particularly focused on certain literary details of the text, it has seemed to us worthwhile, if a bit pedantic, to quote the Latin directly and to refer to the translation in footnotes.

[2] 'After experience had taught me . . .' (*TdIE* 1; *CWS* I, 7).

[3] 'I resolved at last . . .' (*TdIE* 1; *CWS* I, 7); 'I say that I *resolved at last* . . .' (*TdIE* 2; *CWS* I, 7).

[4] Moreau 1994: 75.

[5] 'After experience had taught me that all the things which regularly occur in ordinary life are empty and futile . . .' (*TdIE* 1; *CWS* I, 7).

boni, neque mali in se habere, nisi quatenus ab iis animus movebatur . . .'[6] are separated, in subjective chronology, by a whole unstable period referred to by the adverb *tandem*. Léon Bruncshvicg already underscored that this introductory sentence summarises by itself the entire trajectory described in the prologue.[7] We are even more willing to subscribe to Moreau's conclusion insofar as the second statement reappears in §9, right at the same time as the discovery, and in the comedown after the paroxysm of §7. The initial caesura is thus a double trigger, and it includes a concrete duration that leads the subject of the initial empirical lesson, who kicks off the process, to the 'emendation' properly speaking and announced in the title. This lesson, in fact, which no doubt induces a tendency to be disaffected with regard to the preoccupations of everyday life, does not yet suffice to carry out what is announced as a necessary renunciation ('rejectis caeteris omnibus'[8]), which presupposes – just as in the *Short Treatise*, ignorance and the passions are not rejected prior to the advent of knowledge, for it is knowledge that pushes them back – a positive conversion of affectivity toward another type of object.[9] But – and this is the reason for the space opened up by the adverb

---

[6] 'I saw that all the things which were the cause or object of my fear had nothing of good or bad in themselves, except insofar as [my] mind was moved by them . . .' (*TdIE* 1; *CWS* I, 7).

[7] Brunschvicg 1971: 4. Brunschvicg had the originality to cite the first sentence only at the end of his paraphrase of the prologue. This however can lead one to think that the judgment of *vana & futilia*, which is not separated from the statement about good and bad, comes at the end of the process. He also presents things as if Spinoza, at the start, was moved only by a theoretical curiosity, or by a vague moral imperative ('Human beings have different ways of life, each must choose their own . . . Spinoza begins by looking at the human beings around him. How do they live?' [Brunschvicg 1971: 1].). He has the right idea when he makes Spinozism centre on the question of 'how to live?', but he does not go far enough; the question remains theoretical for him, whereas the prologue shows it arising in the very course of existence. His paraphrase, where the dynamic tension can only faintly be seen, presents a voluntaristic subject of the Cartesian type – 'through meditating on this contradiction, he is turned toward the remedy . . . he resolves to search for it using all his forces' (1971: 3–4) – that betrays the letter of the text. See below, our remarks on the use of the verb *cogo*, to push, to force, to constrain.

By contrast, Victor Delbos, who also begins his book with the invocation of the prologue, places the emphasis on what separates Spinozist doubt from Cartesian doubt: 'The doubt with which Spinoza begins is a practical doubt, engendered and fortified by anxieties, deceptions, and real sadnesses; whence the urgent necessity of surmounting them. One can dispense with science, but not with life' (Delbos 1893: 16).

[8] 'all others being rejected' (*TdIE* 1; *CWS* I, 7).

[9] Note the symmetry of the expressions 'ab iis animus movebatur . . .' and 'a quo solo . . . animus afficeretur . . .'.

tandem – the new object is not yet known, and its discovery will turn out to presuppose in reverse the rupture of which it initially appears to be the condition. The originality of the prologue is that it describes a complex dynamic that resolves the dilemma, and which, quite the opposite of a method arising from reasoning *a priori*, only gets underway via an irreducible experience; here we will see a desire held in suspense, caught between its deception and its uncertainty, and gradually discovering the conditions of its own recovery.

In what does the dilemma consist? Insofar as the true good is not known, insofar as its existence and the possibility of obtaining it are uncertain, the prospects are that of the void or nothingness: 'primo enim intuit inconsultum videbatur, propter rem tunc incertam certam amittere velle'.[10] But everyday goods, even when they are no longer considered as being of the highest rank, do not amount to nothingness: they offer certain 'advantages' (*commoda*). So they appear once again as favourable when one compares them with nothingness. The abstention described in §2 seems in this way to reopen the question of knowing whether the supreme good does not consist in everyday goods, in a hypothetical or sceptical mode that judges with the empirical certainty announced in the first sentence. We will speak of a movement of reflux: the uncertainty of the alternative engenders a tendency that counterbalances the movement of disaffection.

The first phase thus presents a radical mutation of affectivity. Certainly not a transformation, since the subject – here the *animus* – is implicitly supposed to remain identical to itself; but rather a conversion, a radical mutation affecting the choice of the object of desire, marked by wavering between *ab iis animus movebatur/a quo solo, rejectis caeteris omnibus, animus afficerentur*. Whence the idea of abandonment and renunciation (*amittere, abstinere*, paragraphs 2 and 6) that lingers over the entire prologue, and which constitutes the dilemma. Immediately, an alternative is posited, which seems to refuse in advance any third way. But practice immediately contradicts the theoretical simplicity of this choice: it includes some risk, because the alternative term is only an empty concept, the idea of a good of which we possess only the form, without yet knowing whether it exists or whether it can be attained. One possibility is thus that this choice can only be made between a devalued whole and nothing – which, by the same token, leads to an at least partial or tendential rehabilitation of the whole ('videbam nimirum

---

[10] 'for at first glance it seemed ill-advised to be willing to lose something certain for something then uncertain' (*TdIE* 2; CWS I, 7).

commoda . . . et si forte summa felicitas in iis esset sita . . .',[11] a hypothesis
that in itself contradicts the end of the first sentence). But the other possibility is that opting for this whole would compromise the chances of attaining
the supreme good. The dilemma thus consists in this: obtaining certainty
about the second choice itself depends on the choice.

Already, in the *Short Treatise*, the hypothesis of the absence of eternal life
led to the revalorisation of everyday goods, in the eyes of the 'great theologians'. Except that Spinoza denounced a sophism there, and he relied on the
force of our disaffection with regard to everyday goods to escape from this
illusion, buying enough time at least to discover the supreme good and to
enjoy it. Then what was at stake was more than a disaffection: a feeling of
maximal sadness – destruction – in the idea of continuing to pursue those
goods. Spinoza thus did not take seriously the risk of reflux: he saw only a
contradictory reasoning, not a necessary subjective tendency. And he went
straight to the question of utility, where the striving for self-conservation
was reanimated, the pursuit of everyday goods turning out not only to be
vain (procuring no salvation), but ruinous, a vector of destruction. In the
Treatise on the Emendation of the Intellect, by contrast, the demonstration
by way of utility, which has for its object the transformation of a growing
indifference into a repulsion, does not begin until §6: we must wait for the
question to become subjectively necessary.

We invoked a reflux, after an initial surge – but does not the very writing
of the prologue obey a logic of flux and reflux? The way in which Spinoza
presents his postponements, which wholly and clearly anticipate their ultimate conclusions, has often been characterised as a formalism. The regime
of writing required by the problem that he poses is not however that of suspense. Studying the prologue is taxing, and the reader is tempted to declare
that it is inelegantly structured: one discerns in it no clear succession, in
spite of the general progression, and any scholarly attempt at dividing it up
seems discouraged in advance. §1 presents two events: the empirical lesson
and the resolution that follows from it. §2 returns to the end of the preceding
in order to widen the gap between the lesson and the resolution, by way of
the dilemma of gains and losses, one of the alternatives being very uncertain.
§§3–5 reject a first solution, that of a compromise, on the grounds that the
competing modes of existence reciprocally exclude one another; they lay out
a first digression into the three goods ordinarily pursued: sensual pleasure,
honours, and wealth. §§6–9, armed with this reciprocal exclusion, raise the

[11] 'I saw, of course, the advantages . . . and if by chance the greatest happiness lay in them
. . .' (*TdIE* 2; CWS I, 7).

question of utility, and recall the dilemma in order to immediately attenuate its scope: there begins a new digression into the three goods, whose goal is to demonstrate their harmful character (this is the true solution); at this stage, the resolution is grasped. §10 and 11, by contrast, present the form of the true good, but return to a reservation formulated during the preceding development concerning the capacity to hold to the decision made (§7), in order to respond with the dynamic of exercise and the relative rehabilitation of the three goods, now as means (a supplement to the solution). Consequently, the dilemma is cleared away, and the writing can get back without any obstacle to its enunciative progression, in a linear mode.

We know that the solution of the dilemma is the furthest thing from a gamble; Spinoza is manifestly in search of a dynamic of choice that excludes any act of faith. Nevertheless, he refrains from simplifying the problem by annulling the paradox of a choice that presupposes itself. So the way out resides in a dynamic internal to the dilemma. And this is the second influence of experience on the pathway of 'emendation': the text multiplies the *videbam, viderem, vidi*, 'I saw' – in other words, I learned gradually, by doing and not by reasoning. In the *Short Treatise*, the dynamic of salvation resided first in the acute feeling of destruction, and then in the positive experience of an incredible enjoyment, the first being the pivot of a reversal, the second the point of no return. Similarly here, the last-ditch and hopeless effort of someone fatally ill (§7), a burst of life that is pure because it is unmotivated, provokes and finds along the way the experience that fulfils it – at once the promise of enjoyment and the fleeting but real anticipation of that enjoyment, which is all the more promising as it allows one to see and to get a taste for what it promises in advance. There is here something like an immanent providence, a joyous encounter that is due only to the striving proper to the subject, to its vital obstinacy, and not to any external support. Faith does not save, in Spinoza – what saves is the power, the voiceless declarations, of life.

It is nevertheless remarkable that, unlike in the *Short Treatise*, the last-ditch effort here is not something available in advance. Knowledge of what is useful does not enter into the equation until §6. In fact – the adverb *enim* in §7, which initially seemed odd, clarifies this – the remedy is uncertain, but the *search* for it, in the face of supreme danger, becomes itself a *bonum certum*. Then hope is reborn, a hope that is empty but of another nature than the hopes invoked earlier, in §5. What is certainly good, supremely good, is to seek to avoid death and to conserve ourselves in the form of existence that is our own (the concept of proper utility). Thus the supreme good anticipates itself, without contradiction, in the striving that is ultimately devoted to it. What follows will show that there is no difference between the search and the possession, insofar as the striving to be conserved of the being reconciled with itself only happens with the *summum bonum*. Between the search and the possession, the difference is one of degree, not of nature: if the process that will lead to the rejection of the everyday and the consolidation of the new is not yet completed, it is at least underway.

How then are we to define the practical phase that effectuates the transition? This is the object of §11, which closes out what is customarily called the prologue. Spinoza returns to that hopeless hope described in §7, the last gasp in the face of the supreme danger, in order to develop its implications. He recalls (at the end of §10) the reservation he had formulated concerning the search: *modo possem serio deliberare*, 'if only I could resolve wholeheartedly'.[12] The striving is there, it is available, but everything happens as though the conditions for its being carried out were still lacking. The conversion just begun must still be accomplished, and the game is not yet over: 'Nam quamvis haec mente adeo clare perciperem, non poteram tamen ideo omnem avaritiam, libidinem, atque gloriam deponere.'[13] The necessary condition for an immanent conversion – without appeal, without support – is required, but it is not yet sufficient for carrying it out. But at least from this point onward balance is restored: the mind has put an end to its 'distraction', or its exclusive occupation with what it wrongly took for the supreme good, even if it is not yet exclusively won over by the supreme good, according to the demands of the first paragraph. *Versabatur* responds to the *versari* of §7: the subject is no longer 'turned toward' or 'plunged into' the 'supreme danger', at the height of its 'distraction', but is turned toward the thoughts that precisely denounce this danger, and by contrast conceives the form of the true good. Additionally, this new nascent orientation is accompanied by an inverse movement, *aversabatur*, by which the subject 'turns away' from the three ordinary objects of desire, accomplishing what the initial empirical lesson could only begin negatively. The word is opposed to *distrahitur* (§§3–5), expressing a contrary or corrective movement – the very movement of *emendatio*. The movement of conversion has thus begun; but it is a slow movement whose outcome is not a sure thing, completely unlike an instantaneous about-face.

---

[12] *TdIE* 7; CWS I, 8. [Curley follows Koyré in understanding *deliberare* here to mean 'resolve' in the sense of deciding as a consequence of deliberation, rather than as 'reflect upon'. The French is *délibérer*. – GM.]

[13] 'For though I perceived these things so clearly in my mind, I still could not, on that account, put aside all greed, desire for sensual pleasure and love of esteem' (*TdIE* 10; CWS I, 10).

Now this constitutes the second empirical revelation, after the initial lesson: the beginning of the conversion is in fact the entire conversion, but in a fleeting mode. Spinoza effectively says, without any equivocation, that at this stage the supreme good is known, even if this knowledge can be perfected ('postquam tamen verum bonum magis ac magis mihi innotuit . . .'[14]) – which confirms the identity of the search and the possession. Or, more exactly, the search is a possession that is still too rare and brief. The mind thus discovers the true good in its striving to find it, and discovers secondarily that this experience of the true good includes its own dynamic, namely that it tends of itself to become more frequent (*frequentiora*, §11) and longer. A differential ear picks up here an echo of the *frequenter* of the first sentence of the prologue: the word now no longer means the cyclical or discontinuous reiteration that characterises everyday life, but the progressive suture of a segmented duration that tends toward the continuity of the eternal. Finally – this is the third element of this new empirical revelation – we witness the correction of the initial problem, which definitively opens the field for the movement of conversion. The problem is poorly posed insofar as one sees the three perishable goods as enemies; in truth, the enemy is simply the tendency to take them as supreme ends. The conversion now recuperates for itself the whole attractive force of these three goods (what §2 called their *commoda*, their 'advantages'), which up until then had been directed against it: invested in now as means, they become precious aids: 'sed contra ad finem, propter quem quaeruntur, multum conducent . . .'[15] All the initial resistance to the conversion, which made necessary the dramatic detour through the supreme danger in order to awaken the decisive energy, really consisted in these 'advantages', which everyone recognises. The poorly posed problem had as its corollary the naive and absurd attempt at a compromise; now we discover that perishable goods can be reconciled with the *institutum novum* – but precisely because we wrongly believed that they constituted the *institutum communi vitae*.

Spinoza is thus not content to demonstrate the impossibility of a compromise, for the latter leaves us before a practical aporia that must be resolved. So great is our deception regarding the proper place of everyday goods that, when faced with the alternative between the certain and the uncertain, we cannot simply renounce them. So there arises a new invocation

---

[14] 'nevertheless, after the true good became more and more known to me . . .' (*TdIE* 11; CWS I, 10).

[15] 'On the contrary, they will be of great use in attaining the end on account of which they are sought . . .' (*TdIE* 11, CWS I, 10).

of experience: 'perveni, ut viderem',[16] then 'Hoc unum videbam . . . Nam videbam . . . postquam vidi . . .'.[17] This experience is that of the medita-tion, which teaches us two things: the one is theoretical, although it will subsequently have a practical effect of persuasion, namely the superiority of the good sought over everyday goods. Doubtless, we cannot yet foresee its content, but we at least know its form, that of a stable good that procures a pure joy, which consequently is suitable for ensuring our salvation, whereas the pursuit of perishable goods takes us away even from caring about our salvation. The other empirical lesson is practical: the very exercise of the meditation contributes to detaching the subject from false goods, at least during the meditation. Now practice creates its own habituation, reinforced by the progressively increasing awareness of the true good, and above all by the discovery of something crucial: the problem is less one of purely and simply renouncing false goods in order to pursue the true one than it is of righting an inverted hierarchy, that of means and ends. In this way, false goods turn out to be goods all the same, though now as means, subject to the pursuit of the supreme good (but when their relativity is not recognised, they falsely appear as the only goods). This is not a return to the compromise that had earlier been abandoned: the incompatibility of the *instituta* remains intact, but its nature has been corrected. What cannot be reconciled is not perishable goods and the stable good, but a mode of life that sees the former as an end in itself, and another mode that sees them merely as means. Consequently, the *commoda* procured by perishable goods are no longer an obstacle to the search for the true good; nor are they a refutation of the feel-ing of disaffection that we experience in relation to them. They do not leave us indifferent, but we cannot find our salvation in them. Clearing away the ambivalence points toward abandoning the old mode of existence.

The Role of 'Striving'

The importance of the idea of force, of constraint, of striving throughout the prologue cannot be overstated. The dilemma, i.e. that aberrant but inevitable striving to hold open the absurd question of the compromise, opens onto what Spinoza presents as the only possible issue: the subject's reflection on 'utility'. Better still, the dilemma *forces* one to think utility ('cogebar inquirere, quid mihi esset utilius . . .'[18]). *Cogebar*, which in §2

---

[16] 'I came to the conclusion that . . .' (*TdIE* 7, *CWS* I, 8).
[17] 'I saw this . . . For I saw . . . after I saw . . .' (*TdIE* 11, *CWS* I, 10).
[18] 'I was forced to ask what would be more useful to me . . .' (*TdIE* 6; *CWS* I, 8).

had a purely logical sense tied to hypothetical reasoning, will now take on a dynamic or categorical sense, which is even clearer in the following paragraph ('Videbam . . . me cogi, remedium, quamvis incertum, summis viribus quaerere . . .'[19]). It is remarkable that the reappropriation of striving as such, which in the *Ethics* will be thought in terms of 'activity', has constraint as its point of departure. This is not a contradiction, but the passage from one regime of necessity to another – from a constrained necessity to a free necessity, as the letter to Schuller puts it.[20] The passive formulations simply illustrate how the decision here is foreign to a voluntary choice of a Cartesian type. The effect of constraint corresponds to a degree of the mind's maturation such that the decision, or conversion, cannot but result from it. 'Hoc unum videbam, quod, quamdiu mens circa has cogitationes versabatur, tamdiu illa aversabatur et serio de novo cogitabat instituto':[21] the subject bears witness to the mutation of the mind that is none other than its own. This is in no way to say that the subject as such was ever not thinking. An engaged witness – but not a voluntary one – of its own becoming-active, it is mixed up with a process of which it is not in charge.

If the introduction of the concept of 'utility' appears to be so decisive to us, it is because it is the criteria in relation to which the *instituta* are opposed and hierarchised in the final analysis. And the moment of its appearance is also the moment when the dynamic starts up again, now in favour of the search. Spinoza justifies the opposition or incompatibility (*opposita*, §6) two times: first, by the 'distraction' inherent to the pursuit of the three perishable goods; and then by the respective position of the two *instituta* with regard to utility or self-conservation. But these two instances are bound together, insofar as the 'distraction' does not pull the mind from the meditation without also pulling it from itself and its own power. Reconnecting with one's own power – we will return to this below – is the most general principle of the 'emendation'; for it is through one and the same process that the forces of the subject reconnect with their originary function of self-conservation, and the subject wins the force necessary for the completion of its own 'emendation'. In every way, §§6 and 7 constitute the prologue's point of inflection, the threshold where everything turns over.

---

[19] 'For I saw that . . . I was forced to seek a remedy with all my strength, however uncertain it might be . . .' (*TdIE* 7; *CWS* I, 9).

[20] *Ep*. LVIII [to Schuller]; *CWS* II, 429.

[21] 'I saw this, however: that so long as the mind was turned toward these thoughts, it was turned away from those things, and was thinking seriously about the new institution' (*TdIE* 11; *CWS* I, 10). Translation modified.

This is the only point on which we disagree with Pierre-François Moreau's analysis. He insists on the absence, in the prologue of the *Treatise on the Emendation of the Intellect*, of the concept of 'striving' (*conatus*) such as it is laid out in Part III of the *Ethics*,[22] and reproaches Victor Delbos, who made use of the idea of life in order to organise his commentary, for 'binding the experience of human life to relations between *conatus* and Reason'.[23] In fact, the complete concept of 'striving', thought in its relation to production and explication, is absent from the prologue. But Delbos does not presuppose it either, it seems to us; or rather he presupposes at most 'striving' as it is defined in the *Metaphysical Thoughts*, prior to the prologue: the striving of a thing to conserve its being;[24] and this is the precisely the definition that Spinoza goes on to provide for 'life'.[25] Doubtless the *Metaphysical Thoughts* emphasise that life only metaphorically extends to include customs, but reread the first three paragraphs of the prologue: 'ordinary life' (*communi vita*),[26] 'conduct and plan of life which I shared' (*ordo et commune vitae meae institutum*),[27] 'most things which present themselves in life' (*quae plerumque in vita occurunt*).[28] Not only is the term indeed present, but it is a matter of organising life otherwise, of asking after a 'new conduct' (*novum institutum*). Life, in the *Treatise on the Emendation of the Intellect*, is a differentiable notion: into kinds or modes, we say; into *instituta*, says Spinoza. Later we will see that the word *institutum* has the content of a true concept, but let us for now point out the obvious presupposition of the prologue, from the first sentence: everyday or not, life is characterised in general by acts oriented toward the search for the supreme good – since one can infer from these acts what kind of life is at stake: 'Nam quae plerumque in vita occurrunt, et apud homines, ut ex eorum operibus colligere licet, tanquam summum bonum aestimantur . . .'.[29] Life in general appears as a straining toward enjoyment.[30] The fact that such a tendency is always invested in a precise and variable object in no way prevents its logical presupposition as a determinable con-

---

[22] Moreau 1994: 219–22.
[23] Moreau 1994: 51–2.
[24] CM I, 6; CWS I, 314.
[25] CM II, 6; CWS I, 326. (Although there he uses the word *vis*, 'force', instead of *conatus*, the concept at stake is the same.)
[26] *TdIE* 1; CWS I, 7.
[27] *TdIE* 3; CWS I, 7.
[28] *TdIE* 3; CWS I, 7.
[29] 'For most things which present themselves in life, and which, to judge from their actions, men think to be the highest good . . .' (*TdIE* 3; CWS I, 7).
[30] See *fruerer* (*TdIE* 1; CWS I, 7); *fruitio* (*TdIE* 4; CWS I, 8).

cept, as one might say in a post-Kantian manner; correlatively, the object too is problematic, a pure *desiderandum* or *quaerendum*.[31] Without desire in general, the alternative between the certain and the uncertain would in no way constitute a dilemma, for it would not arise for a life indifferent to the good.[32]

In §7, all the claimants to the title of supreme good are submitted to the criteria of the 'conservation of our being': for – this is the second presupposition – the supreme good competing with ordinary goods is superior to them as much in terms of utility as in terms of enjoyment. These two criteria coincide in the expression *valde desiderandum*, in §10,[33] which refers explicitly to the idea of a 'remedy' (through the resonance of the expressions *summis viribus quaerere*, in §7, and *totisque viribus quaerendum*[34]) and to the idea of 'joy', which had just been expressed. The inference seems obvious: if life is the search for the supreme good, and if the supreme good is at once enjoyment and utility, the most general presupposition of the prologue is clearly the tendency to enjoy *and* to conserve oneself, the tendency to enjoy self-affirmatively. If we momentarily restrict ourselves to these remarks, without even accounting for the theme of the knowledge of our own power, which will appear further along in the *Treatise on the Emendation of the Intellect*, we see how what is at stake in the prologue is the reappropriation of our 'distracted' forces, the self-appropriating conversion of our everyday strivings, and finally – but this is already redundant – to tip the scales in favour of the emendation, or the *novum institutum*. Consequently, why not say, quite rigorously and with Victor Delbos: 'One must, therefore, when one desires the supreme good, make a return to oneself, and this act of reflection, far from stopping life in its tracks, marks the moment where it begins to take hold of itself and govern itself'?[35]

---

[31] *TdIE* 10; CWS I, 9–10.

[32] By way of comparison, consider this remark from the *Short Treatise*: 'So it is necessary that . . . given the weakness of our nature, we could not exist if we did not enjoy something to which we were united, and by which we were strengthened' (KV II, 5; CWS I, 105).

[33] 'greatly to be desired' (*TdIE* 10; CWS I, 9).

[34] 'to seek [a remedy] with all my strength' (*TdIE* 7; CWS I, 9); 'to be sought with all our strength' (*TdIE* 10; CWS I, 9).

[35] Delbos 1893: 17. See Moreau's critique, Moreau 1994: 52.

The Concept of *Institutum*: The Logic of Convergence

The question of the dilemma – does the reflex toward everyday goods compromise the search? can the search not allow for a compromise? – is answered twice. 1. Compromise is impossible, for the search for everyday goods 'distracts' the mind and carries it away from any meditation (the dilemma of *instituta*). 2. However, this articulation of the problem turns out to be posed in an imprecise way, and rectifying it allows us to foresee a reconciliation that, far from relativising the rupture between the old and the new, instead frees it to be carried out (the thematic of means and ends).

Let us now see how Spinoza moves from the empirical impossibility to the theoretical impossibility, how he thinks the heterogeneity of the two *instituta*. The second lesson that, after the initial sentence, presides over the caesura – a lesson that concerns the relation between evaluation and affectivity – gains all its sense here, at the same time that the thematic of the *instituta* and that of means and ends converge.

Let us thus return to the beginning of the prologue, when Spinoza asks whether 'emendation' implies a change in the mode of existence, or whether one might be able to embark on the quest for the supreme good all while continuing to live as before. The answer, to tell the truth, seems to be understood in advance, since the initial sentence indicates that the conquest of the true good has for its condition that one 'rejects everything else' (*rejectis caeteris omnibus*). However, the dilemma tied to uncertainty leads to the eventuality of a compromise, to the hope of not having to choose, and thus to the radical questioning of the alternative. Spinoza's negative answer is as clear and immediate as the seductiveness of this hypothesis is persistent. Look at the text: 'Volvebam igitur animo, an forte esset possibile ad novum institutum, aut saltem ad ipsius certitudinem pervenire, licet ordo, et commune vitae meae institutum non mutaretur; quod saepe frustra tentavi.'[36] Here again, Spinoza invokes a refutation by experience itself, and the parallel with the initial sentence is striking: *saepe* corresponds with *frequenter*, *frustra* with *vana & futilia*.

What is essential for us now is that the psychological attractiveness of the compromise provides Spinoza with the occasion to underscore, on the one hand, the link between the way in which one designates the supreme good and the mode of existence in which one finds oneself,

---

[36] 'So I wondered whether perhaps it would be possible to reach my new goal – or at least the certainty of attaining it – without changing the conduct and plan of life which I shared with other men' (*TdIE* 3; CWS I, 7).

and, on the other hand, the incompatibility between different modes of existence.

One rarely translates the two uses of the word *institutum* in the same way, which obscures the clarity of the text.[37] But the word designates, in all cases, a regular conduct, a regulated manner of acting, whether this is a matter of a learned habit or a programme for the future.[38] We need to understand what produces the homogeneity of such a tissue or what constitutes this order – in other words, what the logic of this 'institution' is.

To be precise, it is a matter of clearly knowing whether the conduct implied by the search for the supreme good is compatible with the ordinary conduct of life, in short whether it can be grounded in the present mode of existence, or whether it involves an other mode of existence that excludes it; the negative answer, at the end of the sentence, clearly emphasises the confrontation of two *instituta*, which henceforth applies for heterogeneous modes of existence. It is impossible to bring about one without changing (*non mutaretur*) the other. The text, which opposes the *ordo et commune vitae institutum* to the *novo institutum*, anticipates the answer in this regard.

If the *novum institutum* is incompatible with the *commune vitae institutum*, as is so clearly marked at the beginning of §6, it is because the latter is characterised by the search for objects that 'distract the mind': the expression *distrahitur mens* appears three times. These objects are wealth, sex,[39]

---

[37] Koyré, for example, translates the first use of the word as 'projet', 'recherche', 'dessein' (among other occurrences in §6 and 9), but the second use as 'conduite'.

[38] See Pfersmann: 'The constant order that ties [this existence] to that of others . . . A durable order of actions by which the social and private life of an individual are maintained' (Pfersmann 1988: 57 and 61, n. 15); and Moreau: 'What then does this term designate? It designates the structure, the tissue, the organisation of life; it is not by chance that it is associated with *ordo*. Common life does not form a mere juxtaposition of activities, it constitutes a homogeneous tissue' (Moreau 1994: 110).

[39] In the *Treatise* as later in the *Ethics*, the word *libido* most of the time and without any ambiguity designates sexual desire. Koyré translates it as 'volupté', a word that today has taken on a prudish connotation absent from the text. When Spinoza does use the word *voluptas*, it is in the most general sense of an 'ill will', turned toward the appearance of the good, as opposed to a 'good will' (Spinoza, referring back to the scholastic gloss of Aristotle, then plays with the proximity of the words *voluptas* and *voluntas*); see *KV* II, 17. It is remarkable that in §11, when *libido* is conditionally rehabilitated, Koyré translates it as 'passion charnelle', as if he wanted to make sure the reader would not get mistaken about what was at stake. Following Appuhn, Moreau translates it as 'plaisir'. But when Spinoza wants to speak of pleasure or enjoyment, that is to say not desire as such but its satisfaction, he says *gaudium*, or even *fruitio*, as moreover is the case in §4, where Moreau is therefore obligated to say 'jouissance du plaisir'. On the other hand, wealth and glory are also pleasures, and so too is thought become active.

and honours. That the mind is distracted means that its ability to conceive of another good is minimised ('ut minime possit de alio aliquo bono
cogitare').[40] Symmetrically, the next sentence says that the mind's being
blocked from thinking anything else is maximised ('quo maxime impedi-
tur, ne de alio cogitet . . .'[41]). However, the first formulation has a general
meaning, whereas the second concerns sex, where the mind is above all
'suspended' – Spinoza clearly plays on the two senses of attachment (to sex)
and interruption – during the time of desire, then 'troubled' (*perturbat*) and
'dulled' (*hebetat*) after the orgasm [*jouissance*]. In short, the mind is obsessed
and then dazed, and these are the two possible states of distraction: filled
up/emptied out. The mind, not available for any other thought, has the
illusion of being satisfied, which gives it a disposition that runs counter to
the search. Spinoza in fact tells us the reason for this abdication of the mind:
the illusion of being in the presence of a good, which determines it to a
posture of 'rest' ('ac si in aliquo bono quiesceret . . .'[42]). The mind is turned
away from all striving, thinking it possesses the key to all striving to think in
general, which is thinking the supreme good. The present objects of desire
'distract' – turn away and obsess – the mind because one 'seeks them only for
their own sake' ('non nisi propter se quaeruntur . . .');[43] in other words, they
are 'assumed to be the highest good' ('quia tum supponuntur summum esse
bonum . . .'),[44] or 'good through itself' ('supponitur enim semper bonum
esse per se . . .').[45] This indeed is the root of the mind's blockage, of the
exclusivity that the three objects of desire enjoy in it, of its unavailability
for anything else.

But Spinoza says, emphatically: '[as] the ultimate end toward which
everything is directed' ('tanquam finis ultimus, ad quem omnia dirigun-
tur').[46] This formulation, better than any other, tells us why the initially
sought-after compromise is nonsense, and how the two *instituta* are incom-

---

Rousset, with the word 'sensualité', finds a better solution, even though it is a bit out-
dated, as he explains; see his commentary (Spinoza 1992: 150). This discussion is of
little importance, as long as we all know what it is that we are talking about. For our
part, judging it simpler to call a spade a spade, we say: 'sex'.

[40] 'The mind is so distracted by these three that it cannot give the slightest thought to
any other good' (*TdIE* 3; *CWS* I, 8).

[41] '[the mind] is quite prevented from thinking anything else' (*TdIE* 4; *CWS* I, 8). See
too a bit further on, in §5, 'magno impedimento'.

[42] 'as if at peace in a good . . .' (*TdIE* 4; *CWS* I, 8).

[43] *TdIE* 4; *CWS* I, 8. Translation modified.

[44] *TdIE* 4; *CWS* I, 8.

[45] *TdIE* 5; *CWS* I, 8.

[46] *TdIE* 5; *CWS* I, 8.

patible: each of them is effectively defined by its relation to a centre of convergence that organises life. In this way, the present life is not only a sum of activities, a usage of time to which it would be possible to add a bit of philosophy. Its circumstances are not merely negative, not just deficiencies (*vana & futilia*): they involve an evaluation, they affirm a conception of the supreme good, however erroneous it may be. 'Distraction', in this sense, comes down to an illusory phenomenon: if the mind cannot think of anything else, it is because it adheres to the three objects as to goods and orients all its strivings toward them. Spinoza even seems to draw a distinction within the *institutum commune vitae*, such that, if we are obsessed with glory, 'we must direct (*dirigenda*) our lives according to other men's powers of understanding'.[47] By this he indicates a decentring of the strivings of the subject, which now converge upon another subject; we will return to this shortly.

By now we know that the mind searches all the less insofar as it thinks it has found the good and rejoices in its apparent discovery; it is thus not a matter merely of resolving an uncertainty, but of extirpating a false belief. We understand that ordinary life cannot accommodate philosophical inquiry, which, undertaking the search with a different centre of convergence, leads the whole set of its constituent parts into a movement of divergence and redistribution. We will see in this regard that the *novum institutum* does not eliminate the three principal constituents – money, sex, glory – but submits them to a different centre of convergence. An impatient reader might be tempted to object: Spinoza castigates, in the regime of everyday life, the fixed preoccupation of the mind, but is this not still true of what he proposes? Think again of the initial sentence: 'I resolved at last to try to find out whether there was anything which would be the true good, capable of communicating itself, and which alone would affect the mind, all others being rejected . . .'.[48] Without a doubt, it is a matter of substituting one centre of convergence for another, and it should come as no surprise that we find the same image in the remarks preceding the exposition of method: the convergence of all the sciences toward a single goal ('me omnes scientias ad unum finem et scopum velle dirigere . . .'[49]), the convergence of all our acts and thoughts toward that end ('omnes nostrae operationes, simul et cogitationes, ad hunc sunt dirigendae finem'[50]).

---

[47] *TdIE* 5; CWS I, 8.
[48] *TdIE* 1; CWS I, 7.
[49] 'I wish to direct all the sciences toward one end and goal . . .' (*TdIE* 16; CWS I, 11).
[50] 'all our activities and thoughts are to be directed to this end' (*TdIE* 16; CWS I, 11).

Except that one of these centres is exclusive, by virtue of the illusion that determines it (the *institutum commune vitae*, reserving for the three ordinary objects of desire the place that should by rights belong to the pure intellect, excluding the latter), whereas the other is hierarchising (the authentic supreme good, in the *novum institutum*, does not exclude its rivals but subordinates them).

Distraction, Possession: The Shadow of Transformation

Let us return to 'distraction'. *Distrahere* can mean 'pull in different directions' (it is a pulling, even a tearing: the cohesion of the subject is put in danger), but also 'pull away from' (an attraction that is at the same time a wandering, an obsession that turns one away). What is pulled in different directions is the subject; what it places at a distance is the true good. Are the two senses of the term conjoined in the prologue? They would be, if one could demonstrate that Spinoza establishes a link between the good and the self. This is precisely what happens after the three paragraphs on distraction: first with the notion of the 'useful' (§6), then, at the moment when the story reaches its highest dramatic point, with the implicit notion of health (§7). The question of the useful rises when the antagonism of the *instituta* is recognised as irreducible, and the radicality of the alternative definitively puts an end to any possibility of compromise: in this sense, the first sentence of §6 closes the parenthesis opened in §3 ('Nam . . .') with the goal of clarifying the failure of attempts to avoid the choice. Full awareness of the antagonism is even what forces one to think of the useful, or the 'more useful' ('cogebar inquirere, quid mihi esset utilius . . .'[51]), and at the same time procures the force of thinking, in a moment in which the striving born of the initial empirical lesson, counterbalanced by the persistent seduction of perishable goods, appears to get stuck in the dilemma of the uncertain. For to change one's life only has a meaning if it is 'useful'.

§§6 and 7 mark an intensification, an acceleration of the story. They abruptly cast new light on what preceded them concerning the respective weight of the givens between which the choice is made, concerning the ontological status of the two *instituta*.

1. We in fact witness a reversal of the tendency. Spinoza reminds us that the choice appeared up until now to be that between a 'certain good' (the 'advantages' procured by the three objects of ordinary desire: wealth, sex, and glory) and an 'uncertain good'. But the analysis of the three objects

[51] 'I was forced to ask what would be more useful to me' (*TdIE* 6; *CWS* I, 8).

revealed them to be quite uncertain, at least 'regarding their nature' (*sua natura* – what follows in the text will show that they are implicitly taken as certain 'regarding their attainment', *quoad ipsius consecutionem*);[52] whereas the new and still unknown object toward which the search tends is at least known in its form (this must be a 'fixed good', *fixum bonum*),[53] and turns out to be by contrast certain regarding its nature, and uncertain regarding its attainment. The advantage that seemed to belong to the *institutum communae vitae* is thus annulled in favour of an equilibrium between two goods that are partially certain and partially uncertain. But this equilibrium in turn topples over at the beginning of §7, in favour of the *novum institutum*: by a complete reversal, what was taken for a certain good – the three objects – now appear as a 'certain evil', whereas the uncertain good – the object sought – has acquired the status of a 'certain good'.

But 2. this spectacular about-face carried out in nine lines is followed by an explication ('Videbam enim . . .') which introduces the theme of death. The stakes of the initial empirical lesson are heightened: only valorising those things that are *vana & futilia* not only deprives us of the best, but exposes us to the worst; we have left behind the logic of risk and security for a logic of perdition and salvation, in which reasoning of the type 'a bird in the hand is worth two in the bush' has no place. Now, the objects of the choice will be re-evaluated in view of the threat of death, or according to the criteria of self-conservation. §7 carries this out as follows: 'illa autem omnia, quae vulgus sequitur, non tantum nullum conferunt remedium ad nostrum esse conservandum, sed etiam id impediunt, et frequenter sunt causa interitus eorum, qui ea possident, et semper causa interitus eorum, qui ab iis possidentur'.[54] The vocabulary testifies well to the radicalisation of the aim here: whereas the 'hindrance' up until now concerned the faculty of thinking of something else, or strictly speaking the very exercise of thought, it is henceforth a matter of the conservation of life; in the same way, *frequenter*, which referred in the initial sentence to the vanity and futility of our ordinary life, is now related to the mortal risk that weighs upon us. The slide from *possident*

---

[52] *TdIE* 6; CWS I, 8. Translation modified.

[53] *TdIE* 6; CWS I, 8. Translation modified. [Curley renders *fixum bonum* as 'permanent good'. – GM.]

[54] 'But all those things men ordinarily strive for, not only provide no remedy to conserve our being, but in fact hinder that conservation, often cause the destruction of those who possess them, and always cause the destruction of those who are possessed by them' (*TdIE* 7; CWS I, 9. Translation modified). [As you can see, here Spinoza's Latin here is *conservandum*. Curley renders this as 'preserve our being' and 'hinder that preservation'. – GM.]

to *possidentur*, playing on the classical ambivalence of 'possession', accentuates this reframing.

In order to understand this passage, it is tempting to relate it to the *Ethics*, and there does not seem to be any good reason not to do so. The *Ethics* will state that the essence of a thing cannot involve a contradiction, or in other words a thing does not contain in its nature what explains its own destruction; for that, one must have recourse to an external causality.[55] In fact, the three objects of ordinary desire – *omnia* [all of them, every one], according to the leitmotif that characterises them throughout the prologue – are henceforth designated as the 'cause' of our perdition, and if one adds to this the idea of 'possession' that appears at the end of the sentence, everything is in place for us to invoke such an external causality. Sex subjects us to a being other than ourselves, honour to the masses, wealth to money and material goods. Not that it is a matter of maleficent forces that manipulate us from without; one must rather pay attention to the precise constituent parts of these *omnia*. Under the general appellation of 'goods', one can first of all distinguish the passions (*avaritia, libido, gloria*, §10) and their objects (§§3–5: *divitia, honor*, and . . . and what? Spinoza does not have a name for sexual pleasure: he says *fruitio illius*, implying *libido*, and then – only in §17 – *deliciae*). But second of all, the object is separated: wealth refers to the concrete presence of money (*nummi*, in §§11 and 17) or of material 'goods' (*opes*, in §8), honour to the masses (*vulgus*, in §5) – we must now distinguish, in the object of passion, between the enjoyment and its concrete means. Here again, sex is the exception: whether or not this is by chance, the *Treatise on the Emendation* does not mention the partner(s) that its enjoyment requires according to the *Ethics*. Enjoyment and concrete means: it is true that in this text attainment and possession are used interchangeably; however, it seems important to us to remark that the first designates an external thing, and the second the effect this thing has on us. In the common mode of existence, we enjoy the effect produced on us by other bodies (sex), by praise or marks of public esteem (honour), by the material goods that we know to be ours (wealth). The two moments – the external body and its effect – form a triad with passion, which amounts to a choice of an object, a selection of a body and its effect.[56] For the masses are one thing, and it is another to wed one's body and soul to its smallest waverings, because one has taken glory as one's end; money is one thing, and it is another to make it one's sole obsession

[55] 'No thing can be destroyed except through an external cause' (*Ethics* III, 3; CWS I, 498). See too *Ethics* III, 4.
[56] See Appendix 1, below.

and to orient the whole of one's existence toward its unlimited acquisition; a partner, finally, is one thing, and sex, as the fixed idea impregnating the whole fabric of life, is another. The object as such does not possess us, or only possesses us insofar as we, making all our strivings converge upon it, potentially become other than ourselves.

Perhaps we can now understand the recurring presence of the statements about the evaluation of good and evil: a first time in the initial sentence, precisely as the condition of the ethical decision; a second time in §9, right after the passage that we have commented on, in which the story turns over in favour of the decision; a third time at the end of the prologue (§12). We are at the second stage. Spinoza had said: objects are not good or bad in themselves, but only insofar as they move the soul (§1). Now he seems to maintain the opposite: happiness and unhappiness depend on the quality of the object loved ('in qualitate objecti . . .',[57] implying: *sita est*). But from this point forward he has in view an evaluation of modes of existence themselves, no longer the evaluation in which each mode consists. There is a superiority of the 'eternal and infinite thing'[58] over things 'that can perish',[59] based on the criteria of affect: such a thing procures for us a pure and continuous joy. The quality of the object thus remains relative (the values attributed to them are only *respective*, §12), consisting in its manner of affecting us; it is nevertheless objective, because it is relative to what we are, to our supposed nature. So too the *Treatise on the Emendation of the Intellect*, after the prologue, does not turn toward the search for the supreme object without inquiring into our nature, namely into our power to understand (starting in §13). Relatively to a nature, one can hierarchise the possible objects of its desire: everything that is capable of affecting it. This hierarchy would change if the subject affected were of a different nature. In consequence, the objective evaluation of modes of existence in relation to a given nature can remain completely unknown; in which case – since Spinoza has here no criteria other than experience (affect) – human beings do not place certain pleasures into doubt, and remain ignorant of the superior mode of existence. It is thus at once true that the judgment of an object's value depends on the way in which we are affected by it, and that our happiness or unhappiness depends on the quality of the object. The reasoning of §9, its strange allure aside, testifies to this. In the explication ('Nam . . .'), Spinoza seems first to abandon the theme just laid out

---

[57] *TdIE* 9; CWS I, 9.
[58] *TdIE* 10; CWS I, 9.
[59] *TdIE* 9; CWS I, 9.

of a quality proper to the object: he invokes an indifference with regard to an object that is not loved, namely the possibility of not being affected by perishable things, which constitutes rather a development of what was said in §1. But this is a convoluted way of making us see the superiority of the love of an 'eternal and infinite thing', as the end of the sentence indicates: Spinoza begins by devaluating the love of things 'that can perish' in order to make us realise what we would gain from disposing of them. We must thus complicate the schema: the same objects do not always affect one and the same nature in the same way, for everything depends on the evaluation that is its own, on the hierarchy that it establishes, on the centre of convergence that carries out the synthesis of its life, or in other words on its mode of existence. We seem to contradict ourselves by ultimately subordinating affect to judgment; but the hierarchy, as we have seen, depends precisely on experience.

The schema thus involves three moments: (1) the manner in which we are affected by perishable things (2) depends on the way in which we evaluate them, that is, (3) on our general affective experience.[60] In clear terms, if we have not known pleasures other than those of sex, opulence, and glory, it is inevitable that we will place them at the forefront, and that all the strivings of our existence will converge toward them, or some of them. The evaluation would change if our affective experience were broadened, and this would be a mutation of affectivity itself – of the way in which we are affected by perishable things. Whence the importance of the power 'to think of something else' (*de alio cogitet*).[61]

Thus the moment of *amor*, which is variable by virtue of experience, is indeed related in the prologue to the question of *instituta*. What is it that we love? That is: what is it that we prefer, by which are we most vibrantly and positively affected (*valde desiderandum*, §10)? The hierarchy of our affects and the evaluation that it implies determines our mode of existence, our *institutum*. This is why, to repeat ourselves, 'possession' (*possidentur*) is not a relation between two terms, subject and object, with the second determining the desire of the first: the key moment is indeed that of desire, but what determines desire is the experience of objects, not the objective action of each of them on us, as in a physical system. The effect of an object on us depends on its nature as much as on ours, but it also depends on – it varies in virtue of – our broader experience, the effect potentially produced by other types of objects on us.

---

[60] See Appendix 2, below.
[61] *TdIE* 4; CWS I, 8. Translation modified.

'Possession' thus implies a conversion of subjectivity of the highest order: it is not a phenomenon of mere domination. And it is this that interests us: how, in this third term encircled by the notions of *amor*, of *institutum* and the image of the centre of the convergence, the subject becomes other, and does not merely suffer the law of another; how the incorporation – we would need to be able to say 'inspiration' – of the other into the subject results in a gap between the latter and the self, which the verb *distrahere*, as we can now better see, names so precisely. In French, in fact, we would have to say: 'distrait *de soi*',[62] because the word has taken on for us the sense of a slackening of the mind, like a 'diversion'; we no longer hear the double idea of ripping or pulling, and of turning away or attraction toward a point away from oneself.[63] *Distrahitur mens* – such is the way in which Spinoza designates the subject separated from itself, gathering its forces in the affirmation of a mode of life that contradicts its nature, in the conservation of a nature other than its own.

Sex, glory, and avarice: in each of these three cases, life has its centre outside of itself, as if the desires and the acts of the individual converged toward something other than itself. It is the case – if we may use the language of the *Ethics* – that the life of the wealthy must 'involve' something external to it, money and material possessions; that the life of the ambitious involves the masses; that the life of the debaucher by definition involves beings other than itself. But what does it mean to involve something other than oneself? Such a relation is much more profound than the dual relation that relates a subject to an object, as when one says that one picks up a stone or waves to a friend. The relation concerns an effect produced by a subject, but which does not have this subject as its sole cause. It is thus the effect, not the subject, that is involving: it involves the subject, plus something else.[64] This is why we say: the life of the wealthy, the life of the ambitious, etc. A life is a sum of effects, but also of the strivings that produce them, and which themselves come down to effects. When the wealthy person is engaged in increasing their fortune, their desire may well involve money (and also that which resembles it, via envy – see §9), but they nonetheless aim at their own satisfaction, not that of money, which, as a matter of fact, has no individuality of its own. Their concern in this, however, is to increase and conserve their money, rather than to increase their own power and

---

[62] Koyré in fact puts 'de soi' in quotation marks.

[63] For this reason, Koyré translates *distrahere* as 'attiré et distrait' ['attracted and distracted'].

[64] See *Ethics* II, 16; CWS I, 463.

to conserve themselves: they transfer their effort of conservation toward something else, and through this give money an existence of its own. The ambitious person comes to 'defend' the honours they possess rather than their life (*defenderent*, §8): their striving for conservation persists, but is displaced onto a thing other than themselves, and it is precisely in this sense that they are possessed, or that their possession becomes *passive*. Generally speaking, perishable things are 'harmful' (*obesse*, *oberunt*, §11) to the extent that they are 'sought for themselves' (*propter se quaeruntur*), pursued as ends and not as means. Far from merely forgetting ourselves, from losing sight of our own interest, we are positively engaged in making another thing prosper. It would consequently be insufficient to call these strivings useless, as if they were merely neutral with regard to our conservation: 'all those things men ordinarily strive for, not only provide no remedy to conserve our being, but in fact hinder that conservation'.[65] Whence the radical shift we invoked above, where the initial 'certain good' turned out to be a 'certain evil'. In sum, we harm ourselves *because* we concern ourselves with the prosperity and the conservation of something other than ourselves.

'Involving another thing' is thus said of the effects of a subject led into a becoming-other, into a becoming-other-than-human, whence it takes into consideration a third moment: outside the subject and the object, that which the subject becomes (and, correlatively, what the object becomes through the becoming of the subject). In this way the attraction exerted by this category of external things turns into the formation of a mode of existence out of sync with the self, whose centre of convergence implies a divergence with the self. Spinoza does not say that we are manipulated by something other than ourselves: he speaks less of the fatal attraction of these things on us than of our unrestrained strivings to acquire and conserve them. It seems consequently that our very striving is decentred, and that it pursues goals other than our own conservation: the conservation of honours, of money ... The *vulgus*, ordinary humanity as Spinoza sees it, resembles a mass of eccentrics [*excentriques*], of extravagant individuals who all diverge from human nature (he will also see them as 'sleepwalkers', in the *Ethics*).

One will thus speak of a transformation: they lead a life other than their own, a life contrary to their essence, whose centre of convergence is honour. What is aimed at or affirmed through us is not we ourselves, but wealth, honour, sex, as if these ends attained through our concern for them an autonomous existence; as if these foreign natures, corresponding to centres

---

[65] *TdIE* 7; CWS I, 9. Translation modified. [See note 54, above. – GM.]

of convergence that these ends constitute, were almost incarnated in us. Is this not to affirm one of the 'chimeras' or 'fictions' that will be subject to such scrutiny later in the *Treatise* (§53–64)? Is not the ordinary human being an objective mixture of human and money, or money beneath a human figure? Is it not a mixture of the human and the masses, a masses-human? Is it not finally a woman-man, more than a man for women (and vice versa)? The masses become honour in us, money becomes wealth, women become desire [*volupté*]. The duality of the object and the good indicates perfectly the decentring of individual strivings toward a foreign life: 'defend honours', that is to say the life of that other than ourselves that we fictively form with another; the 'excesses of sex' (*nimia libidine*), in other words the violent and obstinate affirmation of a life that is not our own, but that of an implausible hybrid in which our own nature is no longer clearly distinguished from the series of our possible partners. Once again, Spinoza names the sexual object at no moment of the prologue (we have here invoked women only by referring to the *Ethics*). As the objects of enjoyment such as glory and wealth explicitly presuppose means such as the masses and money, is this not a sign that the object in itself becomes secondary?

Consequently, there are not only two modes of existence at play, two *instituta* for one and the same subject, but – thanks to the radicalisation – the at least tendential transformation of a human being toward an other-than-human. The whole point of the prologue of the *Treatise* is to insist on the unviable character of this other-than-human life, which allows for no prospect other than death; such a life is not viable because it is a 'chimera', the confused idea of a nature that does not exist, because it involves different natures. §58 is very striking in this regard: Spinoza first of all says that the power of fiction is in inverse proportion to the understanding, for the result of the prologue is precisely the resolution to 'emend the intellect and render it capable of understanding things in the way the attainment of our end requires',[66] and in particular to 'know exactly our nature, which we desire to perfect' ('Nostram naturam, quam cupimus perficere, exacte nosse . . .').[67] It would thus appear that the period of the dilemma, whose twists and turns the prologue relates, is at the same time the most conducive to fiction. §58 concludes with an exemplary list of transformations that a non-emended mind might take pleasure in forging. Small wonder that the *vulgus* ties its fate to money, to sexual partners, and to the masses. Such is the chimera proper to the *commune vitae institutum*: not being able to think the human

---

[66] *TdIE* 18; CWS I, 12. Translation modified.
[67] *TdIE* 25; CWS I, 15.

being without money, women, the masses; to conceive its nature only in relation to another.

It is interesting that, in the *Treatise on the Emendation of the Intellect*, the theme of death arises at the precise moment when the individual, choosing without having a clear awareness to conserve something other than itself, becomes resolutely foreign to itself: in the *Ethics* as in the *Political Treatise*, this contradiction will be that of suicide. Spinoza here means that we do not perish under the blows struck by the external world, but because we have adopted a mode of existence that renders us foreign to ourselves. One will remember the warning of the political works: the State has more to fear from its internal dissensions than from external aggressions;[68] 'emendation', whether ethical or political, has for its object above all putting an end to a suicidal situation.

However, the scholium to Proposition 20 of *Ethics* IV is not the only text that the prologue calls to mind: does not the image of the 'fatal illness' (*lethali morbo*)[69] anticipate the scholium to IV, 39? The spelling is not insignificant, even if it was current for the time: *lethalis* proceeds by contagion from *Lethe*, the river of hell and of forgetting. But the exposition of mortal evil is also the moment, in the *Treatise*, when it becomes possible to dispose of the old ways: §11, as we have seen, implicitly describes the formation of a new habituation. Perhaps, then, one can identify the process of emendation with a transformation? Apparently not, because it consists in reconnecting with the concern for self-conservation; but it is a matter of putting an end to the centrifugal forces in the human, to a life that is from end to end chimerical, by a recentring on human nature properly understood, the centre of convergence of the *institutum novum*: 'to direct all the sciences toward one end and goal . . . in a word, all our activities and thoughts are to be directed to this end'.[70] 'Emendation' is the tendential transformation that we have just defined, but in reverse – or more precisely, the right way around.

'Homo concipiat naturam aliquam humanam sua multo firmiorem'

This recentring presents a difficulty that Spinoza, as much in the *Treatise* as in the *Ethics*, cannot avoid: the difficulty of the model. What justifies giving

---

[68] The beginning of *TTP* XVII; *TP* VI, 6.
[69] *TdIE* 7; *CWS* I, 9. Bernard Rousset identifies the Ciceronian origin of this expression (Spinoza 1992: 4).
[70] *TdIE* 16; *CWS* I, 11.

oneself a model, if it is true that this notion implies the idea of imperfection, absent from the nature of a thing as well as from Nature as a whole? Precisely the first decentring which places us at a remove from ourselves and produces this illusion of being foreign to oneself. Spinoza says: the human being, in all its ignorance and weakness (*humana imbecillitas*), 'conceives a human nature much stronger and more enduring than his own, and at the same time sees that nothing prevents his acquiring such a nature' (*talem naturam acquirat*).[71] What it conceives is a nature superior to its own, an ideal or a model to which it wants to conform and which falls to the Spinozist critique of moralism; but perhaps it is also – still too abstractly and formally – Human Nature itself, the nature proper to the human, in relation to a power that is its own and that belongs to it to recover: *natura & potentia hominis* (§25), *vis nativa intellectus* (§31). Spinoza takes care to add a note in which he defines this 'native force'[72] of the understanding: 'what is not caused in us by external causes'.[73] It is from this that the individual is 'distracted', adopting a mode of existence precisely related back to an external causality. The sense of 'a human nature much stronger than our own' is thus explained by the cleavage, in the subject, between its present *imbecillitas* and what in it is 'native' or 'innate' (*innata instrumenta*, §32). The *Ethics* will say that 'men are born ignorant of the causes of things':[74] this originary power is originally separated from itself – which refers us once again to infancy, the chimera-producing age par excellence.

How troubling this formulation is: 'a human nature much stronger than our own'. Koyré informs us of Wenzel's and Cassirer's decision to see an error here, and to read 'naturam aliquam humana sua multo firmiorem' in place of 'humanam':[75] it would then be a matter of a nature superior to human nature, which would no doubt accord with the excoriating texts of the moralists, but which would here constitute, instead, a veritable obscurity. The formulation is remarkable in two regards. First, Spinoza expresses himself here as if he had undergone a project of transformation: a nature being given, one conceives of another, superior, that one undertakes to acquire. Second, this other nature is nevertheless related to the same being as the first, the human being: here is the apparent absurdity, that of a plurality of human natures.

---

[71] *TdIE* 13; CWS I, 10.

[72] *TdIE* 31, n. k; CWS I, 17. Translation modified. [Curley renders *vis nativa* as 'inborn power'. – GM.]

[73] *TdIE* 31, n. k; CWS I, 17.

[74] *Ethics* I, App.; CWS I, 440.

[75] See Koyré's note on the translation (Spinoza 1994: 98).

The indecisive superposition of two logics, that of transformation and that of progression by degrees, recalls the ambiguity of the scholium to V, 39 about infancy. We find ourselves here, however, at the heart of the Spinozist problematic, and everything happens as if only a logically aberrant formula were able to express it with precision. No doubt it is a matter on a first level of a nature superior to human nature; but it is also by this operation of the imagination, which clears a zone of potentiality in the consciousness that the individual has of itself, that on a second level the individual accedes to Human Nature, in other words to its own nature properly understood (human power or native force). The rest of the passage shows this unambiguously: 'What that nature is we shall show in its proper place: that it is the knowledge of the union that the mind has with the whole of Nature.'[76]

Here there is, still in the vocabulary of the *Short Treatise*, a very clear allusion to the highest stage of knowledge that a human being can claim – that intuitive knowledge that will be at stake in Part V of the *Ethics*, which deals precisely with 'human power'. Better still, in the Preface to Part IV, which constitutes in many respects a development of §§13 and 14 of the *Treatise on the Emendation of the Intellect*, Spinoza takes up again exactly the same idea: having denounced the usage of 'models' (*exemplaria*), because they lead one to judge things arbitrarily from the perspective of imperfection, he rehabilitates this usage on condition of understanding that the values of perfection and imperfection involve 'nothing positive in things'.[77] Consequently, Spinoza proposes to 'form an idea of man, as a model of human nature which we may look to', calling 'good' what helps us move closer toward it, and 'evil' what prevents us from attaining it, and human beings perfect or imperfect depending on whether they approach it more closely or not.[78] Then, he forestalls the objection: no, this is not a transformation. 'But the main thing to note is that when I say that someone passes from a lesser to a greater perfection, and the opposite, I do not understand that he is changed from one essence, *or* form, to another.'[79] But to the extent that the ordinary mode of existence decentres us toward a chimerical nature that is not our own but which we believe to be human nature, the affective mutation that leads from the *institutum commune vitae* to the *institutum novum* necessarily takes on the appearance of a transformation, it is a quasi-transformation: from that other-than-us that we believed ourselves to be but were not, to ourselves; from the

---

[76] *TdIE* 13; CWS I, 10–11.
[77] *Ethics* IV, Praef.; CWS I, 545.
[78] *Ethics* IV, Praef.; CWS I, 545.
[79] *Ethics* IV, Praef.; CWS I, 545–6. See the Introduction, above.

chimera in which we confusedly mixed up our nature with that of external things, to human nature properly understood. 'Emendation' carries out the inverse trajectory of 'distraction', and absorbs the virtual transformation inherent in the previous state.

In sum: 1. 'Emendation' is inseparable from a mode of existence (*institutum*), and thus implies a true caesura; the incompatibility of the old and new modes of existence is tied to the 'distraction' that characterises the mind when it is given over to the search for perishable goods. 2. This change is not a transformation, because it consists precisely in reconnecting with the striving for self-conservation that constitutes us ('distraction' is above all distraction from oneself), but it reveals *a contrario* the illusions that haunt the *vita communis*.

One final remark: the prologue to the *Treatise on the Emendation of the Intellect* shows that the 'new', contrary to what we saw in the *Theologico-Political Treatise*, is not intrinsically bad for Spinoza.[80] We will only more clearly distinguish the *seriam rei alii novae operam dare velle*[81] (or *operam novo alicui instituto dare*[82]) from the *cupiditas novandarum*[83] of the Hebrews of the Old Testament: 'new', which was in the *Theologico-Political Treatise* the mark of the height of instability, is here opposed to *communis*, to what is ordinary in the life of human beings, characterised by precarity and inconsistency, and is related to salvation. In the same spirit, we will compare an early remark from the *Political Treatise*: 'So when I applied my mind to Politics, I didn't intend to advance anything new or unheard of, but only to demonstrate the things which agree best with practice . . .',[84] and that which closes the *Short Treatise*: 'To bring all this to an end, it remains only for me to say to the friends to whom I write this: do not be surprised at these novelties . . .'.[85]

At the end of these two analyses, what can we conclude? It is clear that ethical change does not consist in a transformation, in a change of essence: it is not a matter of becoming another human being. But the coincidence with oneself of the striving for perseverance consists in putting an end to what is quasi-other in us, which splits us apart (striving, by nature, can never be exclusively determined *ab alio*). This quasi-other is not directly

[80] [Referring back especially to section 2 of the Introduction. – GM.]
[81] ['to wish to devote myself seriously to something new and different' (*TdIE* 2; CWS I, 7).]
[82] ['my working toward this new goal' (*TdIE* 6; CWS I, 8).]
[83] ['desire for novelties' (*TTP* XVII, 16; CWS II, 299). Translation modified. Curley renders this as 'craving to make fundamental changes'. – GM.]
[84] *TP* I, 4; CWS II, 505.
[85] *KV* II, 26, 10; CWS I, 149–50.

assimilable to a thing or to an external cause that inhabits us, as if we could designate it clearly and distinguish it from us. This is why we introduced the apparently anachronistic moment – but how could we do otherwise? – of subjectivity: alterity does not lodge itself in the self of the first kind of knowledge in the mode of a relation to another thing, but in the mode of a relation between two halves of a split striving. There is indeed, in Spinoza, a moment of the subject in the modern sense of the term, to the extent that, for him, the concrete manifestation of the striving toward the useful depends on the manner in which human beings represent the useful to themselves: this is the whole paradoxical gap between desire and essence, even though our essence is manifest through a desire that is always invested, up to a certain *quantum*. Spinoza carries out the study of these existential decentrings, of these focal points of subjectivation that coincide with chimeras rather than with the metaphysical distribution of essences. The ethical task consists in the individual's returning from an imaginary position of the self (dreamed essence) to its natural position (real essence): in this way we understand that it can be experienced as a transformation, as the acquisition of a new nature or of a superior human nature (the point of view of the *imbecillitas humana*).

In appearance, it is a matter of a movement of expulsion of alterity: no longer unconsciously confusing self and other, no longer mixing up essences and living as chimeras, from the point of view of a subjectivity that is itself chimerical. The concept of the inadequate idea presents a regime of double involvement: of ourselves and of something else. It is not a matter of putting an end to this involvement of the other, rather one must simply cease to *confuse* it with us. In reality, ethics consists in changing the regime of involvement, of passing from a first to a second kind of relation to the other: knowledge of the third kind does not for all that make of us empires within an empire; it means that we henceforth understand ourselves adequately as participating in Nature. We pass from a suffered belonging to a conscious and active belonging. Consequently, we do not cease to imply Nature; on the contrary, what is now at stake is an active relation to the other. Testifying to this is the transmutation of the affect of love, in parallel with the emergence of a non-chimerical regime of involvement.[86]

---

[86] We analyse this transmutation in Zourabichvili 2002, chapter 6.

Appendices to the First Study

Appendix 1

Triad of Vulgar Goods
('illa ... omnia, quae vulgus sequitur', *Treatise on the Emendation of the Intellect*, §7)

1. External things (nature)
2. Respective effects of these things on us (range of enjoyments)
3. Selection and evaluation (supreme good, mode of existence)

Appendix 2

Triad of desire or of affectivity

1. The manner in which we are affected by perishable things *depends on*
2. the manner in which we evaluate them *which depends on*
3. our general affective experience.

Second Study: The Rectified Image of Childhood

The importance of childhood, in Spinoza's thought, is generally under-valued or poorly evaluated.[1] The study of a theme that is, at first glance, marginal in an author often appears as a frivolous pastime, but it can be justified not only if this theme is the object of an original treatment, but if it plays a role in the general economy of the thought. These two prerequisites seem to be satisfied here. Spinoza's relationship to childhood is all the more remarkable insofar as it never solidifies into a *position*. One could even call it contradictory – as if there were a link with the situation in which reason is forced to face its other in the guise of the age that is reputed to be without reason. So too Spinoza begins by admitting that he doesn't really know what to think about childhood.[2] His disparate remarks, by their problematic

---

[1] Pierre Macherey is the only commentator to fully insist on the importance of the theme of childhood in Spinoza: 'This obsessional theme traverses the whole of the *Ethics*: for Spinoza, childhood is a state that is characterised principally in a negative way, as lacking: it is like a sickness . . .' (Macherey, *Introduction* IV, 252, n. 2); 'The theme of childhood frequently recurs in the *Ethics*, with a generally negative connotation: for Spinoza childhood is an imperfect state, which can only be characterised as lacking, at best as a kind of necessary evil' (Macherey, *Introduction* V, 71, n.2). Like him we note the importance of the theme, and we also agree that the Spinozist ethical problem is that of leaving childhood behind or of becoming adult, but we believe it is necessary to show in this chapter that Spinoza diverges radically both from the scholastic position and that of Descartes, and that it is both incorrect and insufficient to summarise the matter as being one of a wholly banal negative vision (this moreover is why Macherey tends to explain the obsession as a personal matter). Later we will have occasion to detail our points of agreement and disagreement with Macherey on this score. For now we will limit ourselves to this minimal suggestion: from the structurally sick child, it appears illegitimate to conclude that childhood is a sickness (how would this not be a 'vice of Nature'?).

[2] *Ethics* II, 49 schol; CWS I, 490.

coherence, nevertheless open onto a horizon that is distinct from all other thinkers of the seventeenth century, Locke included. Upon reflection, it would have been surprising if that were not the case: how could one imagine that the state of inquiry in the Dutch golden age – what is childhood: a mutilated humanity or a world apart? the supreme humiliation or a happy madness? – how could this not have led this thinker who demystified the ideas of privation and metamorphosis to be philosophically overinvested in the first period of life? When at the end of the *Ethics* the whole of ethical progression or becoming-philosopher is identified with the becoming of the child that grows up, the entire Spinozist economy of images is at play, explicitly having in view an emancipated imagination, all the better freed of chimeras as it becomes 'more distinct and vivid' and the more it is ordered under the guidance of the mind.[3] In order to confront the problem, Spinoza needed to make a strange but necessary detour through a figure that curiously has the air of a chimera: the *infans adultus*, adult-child or child-adult. This whole programme – to naturalise childhood, to develop an imagination ordered 'for' the understanding and in this way to re-establish, in conformity with common sense, an inverted image; in sum not to regret or be sorry for childhood – is admirably condensed in the scholium to V, 6, which must be cited in its totality:

> The more this knowledge that things are necessary is concerned with singular things, which we imagine more distinctly and vividly, the greater is this power of the Mind over the affects, as experience itself also testifies. For we see that Sadness over some good which has perished is lessened as soon as the man who has lost it realizes that this good could not, in any way, have been kept. Similarly, we see that no one pities infants (*infans*), because they do not know how [*nescit*] to speak, to walk, or to reason, and because in sum (*denique*) they live so many years, as it were, unconscious

---

[3] The allusion to a free imagination at the end of the scholium to Proposition 17 of Part II of the *Ethics* does not amount to a fiction: it anticipates Part V (most notably 6 Schol., studied above; 7 Dem.; and 10 and its scholium). Gueroult's reservations concerning the analogous passage in Letter 17 to Balling appears to us even less decisive insofar as they partially refute themselves (Gueroult 1974, appendix 10). Gueroult was however right to say that the question of the free imagination is above all that of language (since words are 'images'). But to take the full measure of the thing, on the one hand we must be attentive to Spinoza's efforts to introduce new linguistic usages (which we studied in Zourabichvili 2002, chapter 5), and on the other hand we must pose the problem, perhaps even more delicate still, of the status of the image in philosophical discourse (which we will try, or at least begin, to do here).

of themselves. But if most people were born grown up, and only one or two were born infants, then everyone would pity the infants, because they would regard childhood (*infantiam*) itself, not as a natural and necessary thing, but as a vice of nature, *or* a sin. We could point out many other things along this line.[4]

In order to understand the stakes of the figure of the *infans adultus* – which, recall, was introduced in the scholium to IV, 39 in order to imagine the transformation of an individual ('he could surely have been taken for a grown-up infant if . . .') and to highlight the gap that separates the adult from the infant that it had been ('A man of advanced years believes their nature to be so different from his own that he could not be persuaded that ever he was an infant, if . . .') – some summary historical considerations will prove useful.[5]

Spinoza did not make his interventions in just any context: in that paradoxical century that so often combined archaism and modernity, childhood gave rise to a particularly rich and complex set of discourses and heterogeneous attitudes, particularly in Holland, where scholasticism, Cartesianism, Calvinist preaching, the legacy of humanism, Hippocratic and Galenic medicine, but also the unforeseen tendencies visible in collective practices, in certain empirical medical approaches, in juridical reflection, and finally in poetry and painting – where all this was superimposed and often mixed together. It is not too much to say that the Dutch golden age was buzzing about childhood; and Spinoza's work clearly shows that he was not foreign to this context, even if the power and originality of his problematic exceeded the framework of the contemporary trends.

---

[4] *Ethics* V, 6 Schol.; CWS I, 600. Translation modified. [1. See the section on *infans* in the translator's introduction; here Zourabichvili renders *infans* as *nourrisson* and *infantiam* as *enfance*, retaining the Latin in parentheses. 2. Spinoza writes that infants 'nescit loqui, ambulare, ratiocinari . . .'. Curley translates *nescit*, plausibly enough, as the 'inability' of the infant. Zourabichvili will later insist on the aspect of *ignorantia* when analysing this passage, which is also clearly echoed in the *quasi sui inscius* of the end of the sentence. 3. Curley drops the *denique*, 'in sum' or 'in the end', which Zourabichvili emphasises. – GM.]

[5] *Ethics* IV, 39 Schol.; CWS I, 569.

3

The Figure of the *Infans Adultus*

The Child of Scholasticism, and the Contradictions of the Renaissance

Thomas Aquinas sought to think the relation of childhood to the age of adulthood under the condition of numerical continuity. Such a project needs to reconcile the same and the other, differences of quantity and quality. The problem is that it cannot be a matter of a mere *growth*, or augmentation (obesity, for example, is a disorder and not a result of growth). Consequently, it was necessary to add a second schema that would correct or limit the first, which would fix its terminus, its end. The Aristotelian tradition had imposed the schema of perfection. Difference is thus at once gradual (augmentation) and negative (a lack calls for fulfilment, it is a privation that is not however a mere negation, since becoming implies power or potentiality); and to do this, it is necessary to differentiate the concept of privation, in order to be able to think a privation that does not exclude the presence of form or the soul, without which the body would not exist. Such is *imperfection*.

The latter is not at all of the same nature when it is a matter of the body as opposed to the mind. Everything happens as if the process were redoubled, quantitative change being attributed to the body and qualitative change to the mind. In the body, in fact, perfection is tied to the possession of the quantity that naturally corresponds to the form. But animated beings, unlike inanimate ones, spring from a seed, and do not immediately receive the quantity that is their due when they receive their form: they are born imperfect, and are led little by little to their optimal size through the labour of nutrition.[1] The gap between the present quantity and the

---

[1] Gilson 2002: 235–6.

optimal quantity is only a matter of degree, so that the child must simply *get bigger*:

> But in the body of man, so long as he is alive, it is not with respect to matter that he has the same parts, but with respect to his species. In respect to matter, of course, the parts are in flux, but this is not an obstacle to his being numerically one from the beginning of his life to the end of it . . . It is also like this in the human body, for the form and species of its single parts remain continuously through a whole life; the matter of the parts is not only resolved by the action of the natural heat, but is replenished anew by nourishment . . . the work of nature adds to what a boy has from some other source to bring him to his perfect quantity. And this addition does not make him numerically other, for the man is the same in number whether he is boy or adult.[2]

It is entirely otherwise with regard to the mind. In that case, perfection is presented as a quasi-generation, the operation this time passing through contraries, since the child is initially deprived of reason and must *become reasonable*. It is here that the difficulties arise, and where one feels Aquinas oscillating between two claims. If the human being is defined as an *animal rationale*, then the child must somehow acquire humanity; and yet the soul that informs the body of the latter is not of a species other than the human. If this paradox is possible, it is by virtue of the unity of the soul and its specification by its final degree of perfection (intellection). In this way it becomes possible to think the human without the human, the human being deprived of itself, *a privation that would not be a mere negation*. The child lacks its own essence, its own form, and is itself lacking. Thomas Aquinas forcefully rejects the idea of a difference of essence, which would imply a transformation: that would be to lack what characterises childhood, the impotence proper to what is only *in potentia*. At the end of the day, growth amounts to an accident.[3] Childhood is defined by its negativity: to see in it a positive

---

[2] *Summa Contra Gentiles* IV, 81, 12 (Aquinas 1957: 306–7).

[3] See the commentary on Saint Paul's 'but when the complete comes, the partial will come to an end' (1 Corinthians 13:10): 'The saying of the Apostle refers to those imperfect things from which imperfection is inseparable (*est de ratione imperfecti*), for then, when the perfect comes the imperfect must needs be done away. Thus with the advent of clear vision, faith is done away, because it is essentially "of the things that appear not." When, however, imperfection is not inseparable from the imperfect thing, the same identical thing which was imperfect becomes perfect. Thus childhood is not essential to man [*non est de ratione hominis*] and consequently the same identi-

age would be to compromise numerical continuity. And this negativity is the consequence of a teleology: the child only exists for the human that it is called on to become and which it is not yet; childhood has no sense in itself. And this is the first claim:

> Therefore, since the child is potentially understanding, even though he is not actually understanding, there must be in him a potentiality whereby he is able to understand.[4]

> And thus a disposition becomes a habit, just as a boy becomes a man.[5]

This status of potentiality is fragile: it implies a *dynamic* vision of the child. Fallen into its present actuality, the latter loses the tenuous thread that ties it to the human species. And this is the second claim:

> [for] so long as man has not the use of reason, he differs not from an irrational animal; so that even as an ox or a horse belongs to someone who, according to the civil law, can use them when he likes, as his own instrument, so, according to the natural law, a son, before coming to the use of reason, is under his father's care . . . As soon, however, as it begins to have the use of its free-will, it begins to belong to itself, and is able to look after itself . . .[6]

The child seems to belong to the genus but without a specific difference; one might call it an animal in general, and thus a beast (since one recognises that it at least possesses motor function). It is not of another species; rather in truth it has no species. However it is necessary that it already possesses the form to a certain degree, without which its perfection would be unthinkable: the child is a human being as yet indistinguishable from beasts. If theology decided to recognise the immortal soul of a baptised child, popular culture seemed to reject the idea that the infant already contained a human persona.[7] We can indeed call this age *formless*, since Thomas Aquinas himself uses the language of *informitas* to describe the state of imperfection or unrealised

---

cal subject who was a child, becomes a man. Now lifelessness [*informitas fidei*] is not essential to faith, but is accidental thereto as stated above. Therefore lifeless faith itself becomes living' (Aquinas, *Summa Theologiae*, II-II q.4 a.4).

[4] *Summa Contra Gentiles* II, 60, 6 (Aquinas 1957: 185).
[5] Aquinas, *Summa Theologiae*, I-II q.49 a.2.
[6] Aquinas, *Summa Theologiae*, II-II q.10 a.12.
[7] Ariès 1973: 61.

actuality; but also in the sense of the impossibility of granting a form to childhood, whether because its permanent changes makes this implausible, or because its body is not yet thought to have any marked traits.[8]

The numerical and formal identity that covers over the difference between the child and the adult, and so the logic of radical perfection that is imposed upon it, has a counterpart: having sense only through its relation to a norm from which it stands at a remove, the child upsets, disturbs, troubles, its incompletion, signalling an abnormality that brings it into proximity with the mad, the mute, the dwarven.[9] This kind of proximity is certainly not absent from Spinoza's texts: 'tell me what sort of things these spectres or spirits are. Are they infants (*infantes*), fools, or madmen?';[10] 'If they ask me whether such a man [one acting like Buridan's ass] should not be thought an ass, rather than a man, I say that I do not know – just as I also do not know how highly we should esteem one who hangs himself, or children (*pueri*), fools, and madmen, etc.'[11] The question is whether Spinoza stops there, if he actually rests content with the schema of negation or privation that follows from the logic of perfection but which tends to turn against it, amounting to an opposition in nature. In fact, the link with *potentia* does not prevent an abyssal divergence from actual states from opening up, so that one can only think that the reality of childhood, of the incomplete human, seems not only to correspond with those who remain children or become so again (the latter only being adult children or adults fallen back into childhood, if one takes the latter as the paradigm of incompletion), but that it even risks toppling over into the territory of *animalia irrationalia*.[12] Spinoza's entire relationship to *potentia* and the idea of perfection is at stake here.

In sum, the child is a being that is *small* when it comes to the body and *deprived* when it comes to the mind. A double or even triple nothingness, as we will see: insofar as it is small, its body is the same as that of the adult,

---

[8] See Michel de Montaigne: 'I cannot entertain that passion for caressing new-born infants, that have neither mental activities nor recognizable bodily shape by which to make themselves lovable' (*Essays* II, 8; Montaigne 1993: 139).

[9] See Lett 1988.

[10] *Ep.* LII [to Boxel]; CWS II, 409. Translation modified.

[11] *Ethics* II, 49 Schol.; CWS I, 490. This trio is also found together in Hobbes: see *Leviathan* XVI (Hobbes 2012: II, 248); and in Locke: '*children, idiots, savages*, and *illiterate* people . . .' (*Essay Concerning Human Understanding* I, 2, §27; Locke 1997: 72]).

[12] By its negative form, which only defines beasts by the negation of the specific difference of the human, this scholastic expression used by Spinoza in the scholium to *Ethics* III, 57 seems to encourage confusing them with children, the simpleminded, and the mad.

from which it only differs as more or less; insofar as it gets bigger, it is only a becoming, ungraspable and fleeting (these are its two ways of being invisible); finally, deprived of reason, it is defined by what it is not. From this point of view, must not childhood fall prey to the Spinozist critique of the hypostasis of a mere mode of thinking, like the cases of blindness or death?

The relationship to childhood is thus caught between an alternative, whose two opposing terms will turn out to be cumulative: the child, as preformed adult; the child, as the adult's opaque prehistory, dwelling with those similar to it and with some analogous beings – the simpleminded, idiots – in an impenetrable world.

The Renaissance, which caught the traditional attitude off-guard by bringing a fascinated attention to bear on infants, often with a mixture of tenderness and terror, of gravity and hilarity, affirmed the heterogeneity of the two worlds and their constant exchanges – so that often one no longer knew whether the child mimicked the adult, or if it was the other way around. Sometimes it was a mirror: the madness of human beings presented in the impish behaviour of children. Sometimes it was a permutation of contraries to the point of indiscernibility, recalling the famous words of Saint Paul:

> For God's foolishness is wiser than human wisdom . . . But God chose what is foolish in the world to shame the wise . . . If you think you are wise in this age, you should become fools so that you may become wise. For the wisdom of this world is foolishness with God.[13]

Erasmus wonderfully summarised this ambivalent Renaissance attitude, still dependent on the scholastic schema since it could only be inverted. His novel, decisive idea of an apprenticeship of freedom through freedom did not prevent him from taking up in his own account the Thomistic idea of the *informitas* of the infant that does not speak (*infans*), which is consequently indistinguishable from the beast: education is precisely the acquisition of the human form, *logos* understood as language rather than as reason.[14] On the other hand, in his double-edged fiction, he testifies to a culture that celebrates the madness of the child, and which sees in its progressive maturation a regrettable loss of vitality. The absolute separation of the two universes thus reveals its own chimera, and the theoretician of education reappeared in secret to draw his own figure of the *infans adultus*:

---

[13] 1 Corinthians 1:25 and 27; 3:18–19 (*NRSV*, 2002 and 2004).
[14] See Jacopin and Langres 1996: 23–31.

What is it in children, that we should kiss them the way we do, and cuddle them, and fondle them – so that even an enemy would give aid to one of that age – except this enchantment of folly, which prudent nature carefully bestows on the newly born . . . whence comes this grace of youth? Whence but from me, by whose favor the young know so little . . . For who does not dread and shun as a prodigy the boy who has a man's wisdom?[15]

The Child of Painting and Medicine

The reduction of the child's growth to the augmentation of the parts of the body leads directly to the chimera of the *infans adultus*: the child as an adult in miniature. This confusion of the child and the adult is very old: in the Western world it dates back to the beginning of the Middle Ages, which marks a rupture with late Hellenism.[16]

It is well known that painting had long represented the child without recognising its specific traits or particular expression, especially insofar as the fashion offered up no transition between the infant's singlet and the adult's dress. Childhood was signalled only by a difference in size, the proportions of the body being the same as those of the adult: one passed from one age to the other by a mere change in scale. Fundamentally the adult was immediately given, which could not fail to have a relationship with the Aristotelian thesis of the anteriority of actuality to potentiality, taken up again by Thomas Aquinas:

> Now the perfect is prior to the imperfect, absolutely speaking, both by nature and in point of time. But in one and the same thing, the perfect is prior by nature but the imperfect is prior in point of time – for example, a man in point of time is a boy prior to being a perfect man; yet the perfect man is prior by nature, because this is what nature intends. Absolutely speaking, even in point of time the perfect is prior to the imperfect, because a boy is generated by some man.[17]

Things began to change however starting in the thirteenth century, slowly, with the representation of angels, of the child Jesus, and *putti*. This tendency

---

[15] Erasmus 2015: 16–7.
[16] See Ariès 1973: 53–5.
[17] Aquinas 1923, Book II, Lecture 5, §347.

came to a head abruptly in the seventeenth century, which invented both the costume and the portrait of the child.[18]

Velázquez perhaps marked a turning point when he exhibited the chimera of the *infans adultus*; the child of *Las Meninas*, dressed like a lady, with her appearance of greatness among dwarves, is really a child, but an adult-child shown as such, refusing the troubling transition of growth; the little prince Balthasar Charles was no more than ten years old based on his face and body, but Velázquez painted his equestrian portrait in king's garb (some years earlier, he had painted the infant in the company of a dwarf, and already wrapped him in a cumbersome royal costume).[19] In parallel with this, Velázquez was drawn to court dwarves, which at first glance constitute the inverse phenomenon of the adult child: hence, again, *Las Meninas*, which has them shoulder to shoulder. But the dwarves, not being children, projected onto the latter the shadow of monstrosity: it is they who drive childhood off the right path toward the age of adulthood, and arouse the vague suspicion of an opaque, disgraced world apart, in which adults do not appear.[20] The dwarf makes an adult out of the child, but not in the sense of a prematuration or hastiness, not even in the sense of the invisibility of childhood, but rather by means of a visibility that is too much, blinding, fascinating.

Thus there are two ways of separating the child from its development, confusing it with the adult: either one makes it an adult straightaway, or else one pushes its difference to the margins, among the adults separated from adults. The gap, the asymmetry between the child treated like an adult and the adult with a child's proportions, is glaring; their rapprochement renders the border between the two ages uncertain, and gives rise to exchanges between them, the contagion of the one by the other, troubling both. These are the two facets of the chimera, its front and back sides, but also

---

[18] See Ariès, 1973, chapter 2.

[19] *Prince Balthasar Charles with a Dwarf*; *Equestrian Portrait of Prince Balthasar Charles*. Comparing the latter with the *Equestrian Portrait of Philip IV* is striking: the attitude and characteristics are identical. The child-king, whether heir apparent or reigning, is obviously the *infans adultus* par excellence, by the fact of his stature and the finery that accompanies him. In a third painting, Balthasar Charles appeared at the same age in a hunting outfit. Notably, Pierre-Maxime Schuhl has studied, outside of *Las Meninas*, the series of paintings of the Infanta Margarita: see Schuhl 1964: 471–4. Even in Holland, Gerard Ter Borch produced a portrait in 1648 of a young two-year-old girl, with silk robes and a handbag (*Portrait of Helena van der Schalcke*).

[20] Simon Schama comments on a painting of Molenauer where one sees infants with dwarves, and decodes a compendium of all the behavioural ambiguities of adults and children (see Schama 1988: 554–5).

perhaps the collusion of two lines of influence that coexisted late into the seventeenth century, as much in Holland as in Spain: the one humanist or renaissant (the dwarf as disquieting mediation), the other 'classical', that is, unprecedented (the emergence of the child from beneath the chimera that had covered it over). This look at the child proper, in Velázquez, through the conscious display of the chimera, would find its accomplishment in the Dutch painting of the golden age, notably in Rembrandt (the portraits of Titus)[21] and Metsu (*The Sick Child*).[22] A difference in kind is apparent. Now, recognising the singularity of the child, the new painting flatly denies the negative difference established by scholasticism: it *sees* the child, where scholasticism by contrast enumerated what it did not see (walking, speech, faith . . .); it is not that it now finds childhood touching, but it no longer shares the humanist anxiety about its links with inhumanity, which still relied on scholastic equivocations (the infant is at once same and other, an adult in negative, a temporary animal). The child is made to exist positively; it has ceased, to utilise a Spinozist category, to be an imaginary mode of thought, and this not in order to close it off in a world apart, still marked by its wholly negative determination, even if – to repeat ourselves – humanism and its representation of the opaque devilries of childhood coexisted with the new sensibility late into the seventeenth century: the child is the human in becoming, neither pre-adult nor confined in an impenetrable sphere (Rembrandt paints his son in the process of growing and chang-

---

[21] A certain legend has it that Rembrandt, composing *Titus Reading* in 1656–57, attributed Spinoza's traits to his son. It is well known that Rembrandt was a friend of the Jewish community of Amsterdam. In that period, the future philosopher had just been excommunicated and had begun to frequent the school of Dr Van den Enden. The series of portraits of Titus, from 1650 (if the portrait of the child was indeed of Titus, then nine years of age) to 1663, when the fatal illness could already be seen in the young adult's features, tragically illustrates the scholium to *Ethics* V, 39: 'he who has passed from being an infant or child to being a corpse . . .' (*Ethics* V, 39 Schol.; *CWS* I, 614).

[22] It is true, as Simon Schama wrote, that 'the Dutch invented the poignant image of the sick child' (Schama 1988: 522). Note that Velázquez's series of adult children already contained one: *Portrait of Prince Philip Prospero*, dated 1661 (one might object that the presence of rattles and a bell on the prince's robe makes the adult side disappear completely; but the essential thing nevertheless remains – the contrast between the feverish little boy attached to the games of his age, and his costume, which is that of a child, no doubt, but a royal child, which marks the overwhelming quality of his being heir to a kingdom). In Spinoza, the chimerical nature of absolute monarchy is eminently manifest in the figure of the king that is a child, sick, or senile. Metsu's painting, as we will see, relates to a completely different aspect of his thought.

ing).[23] It was no longer distinguished either from the mad or the beast; it is presented in just the opposite way, appearing as the being that never stops separating itself both from the mad and from the beast. Under this aegis, it perhaps became the adequate image of humanity.

Medicine, for its part, also conceived of the child and its health on the model of the adult organism; one could not, however, say that on this score it underwent an evolution analogous to that of pictorial representation.[24] As the physiology referred to was that of the adult, the child as an organism seemed to be structurally morbid: the child's uninterrupted growth and fragility were interpreted, in Galenic-Hippocratic terms, as a structural humoral disequilibrium (a predominance of heat and humidity, from which there followed the necessity of additional nourishment but also a certain tendency toward cadaveric decomposition – Spinoza's texts, although they are very different in spirit, bear the traces of these two aspects). The child does not have the proportions of the adult, but no more does it have proportions proper to itself, since they never cease changing, and it was thought that it would be futile to search for a norm of health in the child: from the absence of stable form there followed its incessant variation, which would remain unintelligible if it did not find its law in a final cause – the achieved organism of the adult. In sum, it was childhood itself that needed to be treated and overcome.[25] We see how the outline of a recognition (the difference in proportions) was compromised by an anguished feeling of vertigo (continuous growth).[26] We are very close to distinguishing between distinct

[23] Schama also cites a drawing from 1630, where an infant takes its first steps. (See Schama 1988: 493.)

[24] Descartes' *Treatise on Man* testifies to this: figure 44 [in the English edition] undeniably represents an adult-child. In the *Treatise on Man*, the sole peculiarity of the child is that it is made of more 'tender' matter, which explains its growth: as its pores are easier to enlarge, the continual replacement of parts means that each time larger or more numerous parts enter into the composition, up until the point when its matter has hardened (Descartes 2004: 118; *AT* XI, figure 13).

[25] See Jolibert 1981: 49–51.

[26] Hermetic treatises, whose diffusion was considerable at the end of the sixteenth century, pushed farthest this idea of successive transformations of the human being through the different ages of its life. Thus if an adolescent is absent for a long time even their family members would not recognise them. Infancy properly speaking is only a dream, to the extent that what is inconstant lacks reality. So one must not speak of the infant but of the 'imagination of the infant'. The infant is that being 'ready to change state in hardly any time, indeed in so little time that at all hours and instants it does nothing but change' (François Monsieur de Foix, commentary on chapter XV of the *Corpus Hermeticus* [Hermes Trismegistus 1579: 670]). [N.B. the passage in

physiologies here, and what dissuaded doctors from doing so was less the gap between forms (the need for a continuity of identity in development) than the impossibility of fixing a form in the child (inconsistency).

Mechanism, at pains to eliminate the occult categories of quality and end, paradoxically accentuated the conviction that the culture was in the process of unsettling, and could only reconfirm the medical invisibility of childhood: it treated it merely as a difference in size, whose development was reduced to an increase. Let us observe Descartes' difficulties in *The Description of the Human Body*: he accounts for 'the diverse temperaments of each body'[27] by way of the theory of the humours, as did Spinoza.[28] But he avoids making use of this theory in his attempt to explain growth. In this way he posits a principle of diminution and augmentation which at the same time is the principle of organisation based on temperament, though the latter principle seemed not to interest him and he left it undeveloped. The principle con-sists in the friction between solid parts (composed of 'little filaments') and fluid parts (humours and animal spirits), the first being moved more slowly than the second. There then follows a description of growth, which in fact includes two aspects: growth properly speaking, which concerns the solid parts and by which the body is 'stretched out', and its disturbance, due to a humoral excess, by which the body is 'fattened'. The text's structure, in four paragraphs, deserves attention: Descartes inserts the reversible process of the production of fat within the account of an irreversible process, which has the form of a diptych, that of youth and aging. Paradoxically, it is the invocation of disequilibrium that least betrays the mechanistic intention here. Growth is, for Descartes, clearly teleological: at the start, the small filaments 'are *not yet* joined to one another very firmly',[29] so that the body retains its plasticity – that is youth; but 'as we get older'[30] – note the *explicandum* becoming the *explicatio* – the small filaments '*finally* attain such a degree of hardness'[31] that growth and nutrition are interrupted, and this is aging, which comes to an end in death by virtue of the 'disproportion' between the movement of the fluid parts and the absolute rest acquired by the solid parts (the friction,

question does not appear as chapter XV in other editions. It appears not as a chapter but as Excerpt III in Mead 1906; in the more recent and comprehensive *Hermetica* (Copenhaver 1992), it does not appear at all. – GM.]

[27] Descartes 2004: 184; *AT* XI, 249. Translation modified.

[28] Spinoza, *TTP* II; *CWS* II, 97–8.

[29] Descartes 2004: 184; *AT* XI, 249. Our emphasis. Translation modified. [Descartes writes *pas encore*, but there is no 'yet' in Gaukroger's translation. – GM.]

[30] Descartes 2004: 185; *AT* XI, 250.

[31] Descartes 2004: 185; *AT* XI, 250. Our emphasis.

Descartes suggests, ceases to be). It is clear that one goes from a loose articulation [*jointure*] to a perfect articulation, and that ultimately aging is nothing other than the underside of youth. The Cartesian vision is strange: life does not decline, it is a continual increase affected by a progressive slowing-down. Aging and death are presupposed; he does not explain them at all. We get just the sketch of a reason for them: the fleeting invocation of a disproportion. But in order for that reason to be developed, and to become *relations of movement and rest between parts of the body*, Spinoza would have to take up the reins, and perhaps after him Baglivi, and the notion thus strengthened would have to be reunited with the object of that other ephemeral allusion, the *temperament of the body*, in order to form one and the same thought of biological individuality.

Such is the embarrassment of the first mechanism, which only escaped teleology by reintroducing it under the table, and which left the traditional notions of equilibrium and proportion in the dark, alternately utilising and not utilising them. As youth and aging are only the same reversible mask, the difference between the child and the adult is completely blurred. In truth, the preference of the classical philosophers (Leibniz, Malebranche) for preformation confirms and even intensifies the age-old confusion: now one places the adult in the seed itself.

Medicine did evolve in Holland, however, but on a completely different front: within the theoretical aporia, the doctor paid unprecedented attention to the child. Treatises on paediatrics and childcare multiplied.[32] No one called into question the judgment concerning childhood: impotence, fragility, morbidity. But the consequence that was drawn from this started to be inverted: this theoretical quasi-nothingness no longer led to practical indifference, but rather to the urgency of dealing with and struggling against it.

The figure of the sick child manifestly did not have the same meaning for the doctor and the painter in the Netherlands of the seventeenth century. For the former, sickness was above all childhood itself – the unsteady form – and childhood was not dissociated from a constitutive fragility, but for these very reasons it thereafter deserved full attention; for the latter, sickness was no doubt essential to childhood, but this precisely reinforced its specificity, and contributed to rendering it visible for itself. One might say that Spinoza

---

[32] Schama 1988: 521 and following. Not only texts for experts like *De morbis infantum* but popular treatises were published in the Netherlands. It would be another century before France, lagging behind the rest of Europe, began to have an interest in paediatrics (Lebrun 1995: 135).

established the link between these two attitudes: it was necessary that medicine too definitively recognised that the face and the body of the child could not be obtained by reduction, but that they differed, in their figure and proportions, from those of the adult: there was no longer any *method* available for passing from one age to the other.

The Child of the Jurists

The conception of childhood also evolved in the domain of the law. If the question up until then had been above all that of the bastard, that is, of a demarcation between legitimacy and illegitimacy from the perspective of succession, henceforth there would be an attempt to define the status of the child as such, notably in light of cases of infanticide and abandonment ('exposure'). Nevertheless, the main thing was the appearance of a contestation of parental authority.[33] On this score Holland seemed to outdo all its European neighbours: the indiscipline and indocility of children, the unprecedented tolerance of parents, and finally the frequency and intensity of their conflicts with adolescents, were shocking to every visitor.[34] Spinoza, as we will see, resonated with these dramatic episodes, which no doubt saddened him, but which pushed him to reflect on the failure of education rather than to condemn the children morally. On the other hand, the evolution of customs was not without repercussions in juridical thought: Hobbes in particular displayed a remarkable modernism here. He held that paternal domination is derived 'from the child's consent' (for the child, obedience is owed to the mother, assuming that she looks after its conservation; however, the Latin version of the *Leviathan* seems to grant to the mother a right of life and death over her child);[35] but children, insofar as they do not have the use of reason, that is, of speech, can neither be called just nor unjust, since the law has no meaning for them and since 'they had never power to make any covenant, or to understand the consequences thereof'.[36] Nevertheless, Hobbes virtually identifies the child and the servant, and the right of life and death that he grants to the mother over her infant, determining the duty to obey her if she chooses to protect its life, is, if not analogous, then at least comparable to the convention by which the vanquished alienates their liberty to the conqueror in exchange for their life (the juridical relation is

[33] On these diverse aspects, see Jolibert 1981.
[34] See Zumthor 1960: 119–21.
[35] *Leviathan* XX (Hobbes 2012: II, 308–11).
[36] *Leviathan* XXVI (Hobbes 2012: II, 422).

founded in both cases on the avoidance of death, even if the infant does not *consent* [convient]).[37] So too paternal authority is hardly distinguished from despotism, which will justify – we will return to this – a clear and concise point made in the *Political Treatise*.

The seventeenth century thus displayed a new attention paid to the child, in the margins of philosophy, theology, and medical theory. We will see whether Spinoza was not precisely in the process of accomplishing the renewal of the problematic needed in order to give this attention its first philosophical formulation; better, whether he did not draw on it in order to renew philosophy.

The Parable of the First Man

The *infans adultus* was not just any myth, one chimera among others, in the Christian Europe of the seventeenth century. We saw its first manifestation in Saint Paul, with the distinction between two births, that of the flesh and that of the spirit, and the theme of a regeneration, of a surging forth of a new adult, stripped of the 'former man': this myth is so important in Christianity that it gives rise to the first of its sacraments, baptism.[38] But there is a second manifestation, almost more decisive still because it is tied to the fundamental doctrine of original sin. 'But if most people were born grown up, and only one or two were born infants . . .'.[39] Spinoza knows quite well that Scripture tells the opposite story: first the appearance of a first man, fully formed, and that of his wife, also fully formed, and then, after the transgression of the prohibition, the birth of Cain and Abel and the expansion of humankind.[40]

Spinoza comments on the biblical story of the first man on numerous occasions. Today's reader would naturally expect him first of all to refuse the idea of the first man. After all, could there be a first man in this philosophy? Would this not be to fall back into the fiction of a creation *ex nihilo*, or at least of a supernatural transformation? Genesis says: 'God formed man from

---

[37] *Leviathan* XX (Hobbes 2012: II, 312–14).

[38] Recall that the baptism of children was a late, medieval, invention, tied to the problem of the salvation of children who died prematurely, during a time of severe infant mortality. And ever since the Renaissance, voices spoke up (Erasmus, in particular) to demand that the young adult confirm the vows of its baptism.

[39] *Ethics* V, 6 Schol.; CWS I, 600.

[40] Incidentally, the text of *Genesis* is ambiguous when it comes to the two first born; it passes without any transition from their birth to their adult activities: 'Now Abel was a keeper of sheep, and Cain a tiller of the ground' (Genesis 4:2 [NRSV, 17]).

the dust of the ground . . .'.[41] But is its author any better than those who 'imagine that men are formed both from stones and from seed, and that any form whatever is changed into any other'?[42] This passage, which probably alludes to the myth of Deucalion and Pyrrha, which Spinoza knew at least from Ovid, is related to a theme analogous to that of the biblical first man: the rebirth of humanity after Zeus decided to destroy it.[43] Finally, the link between the *infans adultus* and metamorphosis lacking a rule is confirmed in Lucretius, whose critique appears to have inspired that of Spinoza:

> Moreover, so far as growth is concerned, the lapse of time required for the confluence of seed would be unnecessary, if things could arise out of nothing. Children, too young to talk, in an instant would become young adults, and trees would suddenly bound up out of the ground.[44]

In fact, production from out of nothing entails that anything can be born of anything: whether a human being emerges from nothingness or from a stone amounts to the same thing, in the absence of a germ or a seed that would ensure the causal continuity of the process. It is a leap, a progressive substitution, not a production properly speaking: it could never be understood how one would pass from the stone to the human being, since nothing in the nature of the stone involves human nature. Certainly, in the myths, dust and stone seem to stand for matter awaiting form, pure potentiality, but this manner of thinking is not acceptable for either Lucretius or Spinoza, who both reject final causes. In fact, *ex nihilo* means 'without matter' less than it does 'without a rule': when Genesis begins, the earth is already there, deserted and empty, plunged in darkness; but the will of God was absolutely first, with no law, no motive predetermining it (the good is only observed after the fact). It is this negation of the principle of causality that Spinoza

---

[41] Genesis 2:7 (*NRSV*, 17).

[42] *Ethics* I, 8 Schol. 2; *CWS* I, 413.

[43] Ovid, *Metamorphoses*, I. The contrast with the biblical story is staggering: the pair of lovers reproduces humanity chastely, via an anodyne gesture that counts as an immaculate conception *avant la lettre*: men and women emerge from stone without the least allusion to a state of childhood (and on the other hand, the hardness they inherited from the stone immediately disposes them to labour, a bit like Cain and Abel). This too is how Michelangelo envisioned them, when he sculpted his intentionally incomplete figures, caught still in the matter, and baptised them *Prigioni*: the birth of an adult, a metaphor of sculpture in general. When it comes to nature, Spinoza obviously rejects this hylomorphic model, which ever since Aristotle found its privileged illustration in the completed activity of the sculptor.

[44] *On the Nature of Things* I, 184–6 (Lucretius 2001: 8).

contests: metamorphoses amount to brute emergences, although the new form seems to proceed from the old. They do not have a cause, they juxtapose natures that cannot proceed from one another. Like Lucretius, Spinoza denounces this relation between metamorphosis and emergence *ex nihilo*, as is evident from the end of the scholium on suicide: 'But that a man should, from the necessity of his own nature, strive not to exist, or to be changed into another form, is as impossible as that something should come from nothing. Anyone who gives this a little thought will see it.'[45]

The first man is thus a myth, consistent with that of Creation. Spinoza does not take the time to refute its absurdity: he merely observes that it is appropriate to see it as a parable rather than an account. He is concerned with the use that is made of it in the explication of the present impotence of human beings to overcome their passions, and proposes a counter-interpretation, of which he humorously admits he is not sure that it 'agrees with the writer's intention'.[46] It is a matter of refuting the idea of the Fall, of original sin, by showing that it is contradictory.[47] In fact this idea presupposes an Adam who was initially perfect, endowed with a *mens sana*, that is to say, wise and free, exempted from the long and precarious route that ideally leads every human being from their first state as an unconscious and impotent infant to that of the wise and happy human being, defined precisely by the formula of Juvenal, *mens sana in corpore sano*.[48] But, under these conditions, the Fall is unthinkable, since such a person, capable of the right use of their reason and striving naturally to persevere in that state, could neither be tricked nor experience the mad desire to rise to the rank of God. If the real Adam – the one whose story Genesis tells – had been tricked, it is because he was a human being like all other human beings, who 'are born ignorant of the causes of things'.[49] Adam was certainly not an *infans adultus*.[50]

---

[45] *Ethics* IV, 20 Schol.; CWS I, 557.
[46] *TTP* IV, 39; CWS II, 135.
[47] *TP* II, 6; CWS II, 509–10.
[48] *Ethics* V, 39 Schol.; CWS I, 614.
[49] *Ethics* I, App.; CWS I, 440.
[50] Deleuze, comparing the plight of infants to the condition of the real Adam, is very close to raising the question of the *infans adultus*: 'That is why it is scarcely possible to think that little children are happy, or that the first man was perfect: ignorant of causes and natures, reduced to the consciousness of events, condemned to undergo effects, they are slaves of everything, anxious and unhappy, in proportion to their imperfection. (No one has been more forceful than Spinoza in opposing the theological tradition of a perfect and happy Adam.)' (Deleuze 1988: 19–20). However, we will have to modify this verdict slightly.

This critique was already that of the *Ethics*, where Spinoza invokes the myth of the first man in the commentary on a hypothetical proposition – 'If men were born free . . .'[51] – which anticipates the analogous hypothesis of Part V, 'if most people were born grown up . . .'.[52] However, this commentary suggests a clarification concerning the absurdity of this hypothesis: it presupposes considering human nature in abstraction from the rest of Nature, and so, consequently, considering the production of the human being by God as a singular production, detached from the order and connection of other things.[53] At bottom, the moralists denounced in the Preface to Part III, or the philosophers at the beginning of the *Political Treatise*, merely repeat the biblical conception of the first man when, reasoning on the basis of a fictional state of perfection, they conclude that nature is now tainted. Is childhood anything else, for Christianity, than the result and heritage of original sin? Spinoza denounces this inversion of the natural order by which, sidestepping the *res naturalis & necessaria* that is childhood, according to the scholium to V, 6, one lays on the shoulders of human beings (and those of children especially – we will return to the matter of education) the burden of a presumed Fall of which their tainted nature bears the trace, instead of stating the natural conditions of a progression.

In this scholium, Spinoza returns to the interpretation that he had given of the divine warning in Chapter IV of the *Theologico-Political Treatise*. On the one hand, he explains that 'God only revealed to Adam the evil which would necessarily befall him if he ate of that tree, but not the necessity of that evil's following',[54] so that Adam, through a 'defect in his knowledge',[55] perceived God's warning as the statement of a law of consequences arbitrarily established by a king, not as the statement of a causal link between the nature of the act and the evil that would follow it. On the other hand, by a kind of interpretive tour de force, Spinoza bends this warning toward his own precept, namely that one should act freely in view of the good, rather than constrained by fear of evil. We will see that this precept, as far as we are able to judge, is precisely the basis of the theory of education that Spinoza would have advocated, and which perhaps he would have elaborated after the *Ethics*.

---

[51] 'they would form no concept of good and evil so long as they remained free' (*Ethics* IV, 68; CWS I, 594).

[52] *Ethics* V, 6 Schol.; CWS I, 600.

[53] On this point we refer to Pierre Macherey's illuminating analysis: see Macherey, *Introduction* IV, 391 and following.

[54] *TTP* IV, 26; CWS II, 131–2.

[55] *TTP* IV, 27; CWS II, 132.

Cartesian Voluntarism, Spinozist Voluntarism

The first journey of salvation proposed in Part V of the *Ethics*, which works through memory, almost exactly mimics a process of transformation.[56] It is a matter of reorganising one's memory, of habituating it to other linkages. No doubt, Spinoza seems at first glance to have resorted, provisionally, to ancient formulas of traditional morals: contract good habits via sustained attention aimed at the living and practical internalisation of precepts. But this is the whole gap between the proposition and its scholium, whose function is different: if Spinoza there still speaks of 'committing to memory' 'sure maxims of life',[57] it is rather in order to win over the reader by providing some familiar impressions while they are on the doorstep of a strange voyage – one that will not be without paradox, even if it is a matter of extracting them from this familiarity by inviting them to carry out on themselves the great work of rupture. The ancient formula is only the primer for a much more radical process, which is meant to progressively replace it. What distinguishes ethics from traditional morals is that memory is no longer for it an auxiliary, an instrument for working on oneself, but the very stakes or object of that work. Memory is not a faculty but an order; now it is a matter of *establishing* the order conforming to the understanding, and consequently to *reform*, to *transform* the order of memory. The whole associative mechanism that constitutes our subjectivity – our *institutum vitae*, to use the concept of the *Treatise on the Emendation of the Intellect*[58] – must be, if not erased, at least edged out for the sake of another, one conforming to reason, that is, to ourselves.

There is here – perhaps one could say *finally*, since the text encouraged us to suspend our reluctance, only to bring the problem back up – a work of *transformation*, and even of *voluntary* transformation, of a conscious destruction of our own affectivity, of our own evaluations, of our own desires. Is this not the 'foreignness' that Spinoza was said to have maintained with his disciples, according to the questionable testimony of Lucas?[59] A voluntarism without free will, naturally also without 'states of the soul', where Spinoza reveals himself to be more radical than Descartes, at least if we

---

[56] *Ethics* V, 10, its Dem. and Schol.; CWS I, 601–3.

[57] *Ethics* V, 10 Schol.; CWS I, 601. Translation modified.

[58] There is not – as we saw in the preceding study – a subject in general in Spinoza, but rather different regimes of investment or 'determination' of that striving to conserve our being that defines our 'actual essence' or the actualisation of our essence: in contemporary terms, we would speak of regimes of subjectivity.

[59] See below, note 67.

take him literally: a concerted effort to eradicate childhood (by which we mean: the second age in which memory is formed and in which education does its work), to dissolve the self such as it has been passively constructed, sedimented. Descartes thought it sufficient to reach 'a mature enough age'[60] in order by a single stroke to be *reborn* [rené], fully equipped for a conversion that, requiring only time and application, turned out to be given from the start. 'So today I have expressly rid my mind of all worries . . .'[61] – here we are at the furthest possible remove from the scholium to V, 39. Descartes could subsequently remain the same: the leap in place matters not at all, the problem is not even envisaged. So tranquil is Descartes' conviction of appearing in the clarity of a new dawn that he can even continue to accept most of the beliefs from childhood, which he merely reorganises, under the name of 'mysteries', in a special domain exempted from the jurisdiction of human reason. But, for Spinoza, the affair is presented much less sunnily. Instead of early morning heroism, there is the nauseating stench of age, the foggy weight of depression: the things of life have lost their flavour, *vana & futilia*.[62] Spinoza's philosophy begins in sickness, it lacks those athletic awakenings that, from the first stirrings, bring to heel all the reasons to sink into the night. 'I see the better, and approve it' – everything is presented under the best auspices, but right here at the very start, it is not that I forget, but – 'I follow the worse.' Is it not a mere exorcism, a mere magic trick, that opening gesture of the *Meditations*? It is a happy man at least, or a 'first man', who thinks he has the resources for that easy and sovereign life. The conclusion of the scholium to V, 10 calls on us not to 'enjoy a false appearance of freedom'.[63] Either Descartes is the perfect sage, or else he is only dreaming; no doubt he was the first man, walking on land that was new and wholly open to free meditation by the fiat of the mature man, of the *vir perfectus*. But when Spinoza closes his book with the words *difficilia & rara*, these latter certainly do not have the same sense called to mind by the 'infirmity and weakness of our nature'[64] with which the *Meditations* conclude.

When it comes to Descartes' warnings about the importance of the prejudices of childhood, and the probable lesson that Spinoza drew from it,[65] it

---

[60] Descartes, *Meditation* I (CSM II, 12; AT VII, 17).
[61] Descartes, *Meditation* I (CSM II, 12; AT VII, 17).
[62] See the first sentence of the *Treatise on the Emendation of the Intellect*, which we commented on in the previous study.
[63] *Ethics* V, 10 Schol.; CWS I, 603.
[64] Descartes, *Meditation* VI (CSM II, 62; AT VII, 90).
[65] See Macherey, *Introduction* IV, 252 n. 2.

is appropriate to underscore how the problematic of childhood, in the latter, exceeds this theme: as a general rule, it is not in order to recall the Cartesian story that he invokes childhood. There are only two instances where this is not the case: in the commentary on the *Principles*, of course, where more-over he contents himself with a subdued paraphrase,[66] and in a passage of the *Theologico-Political Treatise*, where he invokes his own personal case. One must here note that, in Spinoza, the rupture with the memory slowly sedimented during childhood is not only more difficult, but charged with obvious and much more dramatic biographical resonances: religious, famil-ial, social, professional, linguistic ruptures, a rupture even in the change of his name, from Baruch to Benedictus. And in the same way that he did not believe it possible to break with the prejudices of childhood by a voluntary decision steadfastly pursued, but by an active labour on his own memory, Spinoza did not break with his past as a pious but sharp young Jew without endeavouring to convert his regard for the very materials of his past educa-tion, Scripture (by contrast, Descartes' Christian faith remained that of his childhood, at least publicly). And no doubt this labour began very early, in his youth.

Spinoza thus reclaims the Cartesian formula for himself,[67] but he is far from done with childhood. What interests him is just as much the amnesia that irremediably separates us from infancy. His problematic is that of a double rupture: the one, carried out long ago, of every individual with the infant that they had been; the other, problematic, beginning in adolescence, with the later childhood, subject to education. The pri-mary trait of childhood is that it is over [*révolue*]: we are no longer the same as when we were infants, it is not just that we have gotten larger,

---

[66] Descartes writes in article 71 of the first part of the *Principles of Philosophy*: 'The chief cause of error arises from the preconceived opinions of childhood' (CSM I, 218; AT VIIIA, 35). Spinoza writes: 'But because we have absorbed at an early age many prej-udices from which we are not easily freed . . .' (*PP* I, Prol.; CWS I, 235).

[67] Lucas testifies to this, to the extent that one can believe him: 'This is why he said that it was only those who had been released from the maxims of their childhood who could know the truth . . .' (Lucas 1954: 1552). Considering the gravity that this process took on in Spinoza's personal case, the rest of the sentence might have a ring of authenticity, unless we have to chalk it up to the antisemitism that also leads Lucas to accentuate the heroism of the Spinozist conversion: 'so that one must make *strange* [*étranges*: also 'foreign'] efforts to overcome the impressions of tradition, to erase the false ideas that the mind is filled with before one is capable of judging things by oneself' (our emphasis). We pass over the 'miracle' then invoked by Lucas: that would bring us back into a Calvinist sphere, where grace conditions conversion.

developed our conceptions.[68] And no doubt we remain childish in certain respects. Thus Spinoza develops a new problematic, one quite foreign to Cartesianism.

---

[68] Macherey sees in this problematic of rupture a mere consequence of the Cartesian legacy: 'The fact of necessarily needing to have been a child before being a human being, to take up a formula of Descartes which Spinoza surely often reflected upon, is the form that takes up temporal existence par excellence, which involves constraints that reason finds enormously difficult to accept, since they are contrary to its own vocation. This is why the human being is so bad at representing to itself that it had been a child and seen the world with the eyes of a child, which one can only conjecture about by analogy' (Macherey, *Introduction* IV, 252 n. 2.). Macherey has here found the best formulation possible ('and seen the world with the eyes of a child . . .') to characterise rupture, but his reasoning presupposes that 'the man of advanced years' of the scholium to IV, 39 is an enlightened human being practising reason, and not just anyone, as Spinoza seems to have meant.

4

Childhood and Philosophy

Let us ask whether this *pathos* of the humble creature, in truth so *arrogant*, in the Spinozist sense of an ambition satisfied by dreams, does not find itself destituted for the sake of a new image of thought, foreign to all rhetoric of poverty and glory: childhood, finally placed back on its feet.

Mechanism, with its inability to propose a new norm of health, seemed to us to reinforce the chimera of the *infans adultus*. We might even, in this regard, invoke the figurative example of the elephant passing through the eye of a needle (judging that its impossibility is obvious to everyone, Spinoza uses it as a distinct image conforming to the understanding, conducive to *illustrating the illustration* that lists of chimeras or metamorphoses already constituted[1]). What is clear is the opposition of the small and the large, and their mutual opposition. But what is stopping the imagination from mentally shrinking the elephant, as in Lewis Carroll, until it could pass through the eye of a needle? The fiction would be even easier insofar as it would not need to pass through a transformation: the elephant would conserve its figure, its proportions, in just the same way that Alice, warped by the idea of growing up, became enormous and then miniscule. Whence the gnomes that belong to the Jewish tradition. Whence too the Lilliputians and the Brobdingnagians, in Swift, next to whom Gulliver is sometimes a giant, sometimes a dwarf – and a dwarf even next to the queen's court dwarf, who uses him as a punching bag, and a *nanunculus* next to the little girl who takes care of him. 'I reflected what a Mortification it must prove to me to appear as inconsiderable in this Nation, as one single *Lilliputian* would be among us.'[2] This sensitivity to the relativity of the small and the large, which is

---

[1] CM I, 3; CWS I, 307. *TdIE* 54; CWS I, 24.
[2] Swift 2005: 78. Swift was born during Spinoza's lifetime, in 1667. The work dates from 1726.

characteristic of the age – to the extent, of course, that one can consider
Spinoza and Swift as contemporaries – clearly has nothing to do with the
idea of growth, and one cannot think the becoming of the child in these
terms; and this indeed is why Swift could draw through these oscillations
a satire of his own society (Alice, in her naivety as a young girl, confuses
becoming-adult with the excessive growth of a child). The example of the
elephant and the eye of the needle is thus quite tenuous, and it is almost
embarrassing that proof of this is found in Descartes:

> You are confusing understanding and imagination, and are supposing that
> we imagine God to be like some enormous man, just as if someone who
> had never seen an elephant were to imagine that it was like some enor-
> mous tick, which, I agree, would be extremely foolish.[3]

In reality, Spinoza himself suggests the precariousness of his example:
not only does one not conceive very well, if not by experience, why the
reduction would be chimerical, nor why the elephant in miniature would no
longer be an elephant, nor even a young elephant (the mere change in size, if
it is proportionate, is not supposed to affect the identity of the form, according to Lemma 5 in Part II of the *Ethics*), but Spinoza himself warns against
the danger of chimerising, if we can use this expression, a mere difference
in size, just because it is unusual: 'the size of a giant is rare, but nevertheless
human'.[4] The statement (rather than the image) of the elephant passing
through the eye of the needle remains in spite of all this appropriate for what
Spinoza means to say: we have a clear perception of the *present* opposition
of the large and the small (the memories of the elephant and the eye are
supposed to be recalled as such, in a fiction that concerns only existence).

Let us return to mechanism: nothing as yet allows us to say that it would by
nature be incompatible with a complex conception of psychological development. But it falls precisely to Spinoza to bring their compatibility into the
light of day, by elaborating the new concept of form that makes possible a
mechanistic thinking of norms. Consequently, if mechanistic medicine (or
iatromechanics) initially excludes all paediatrics, understood as a theoretical
and practical specialisation, and if in this way it paradoxically lags behind

---

[3] Descartes, *Replies to the Fifth Set of Objections* (CSM II, 252; AT VII, 365).

[4] See *TTP* I, 40 adn. III (CWS II, 91 n. 44), concerning those who represent prophets
as superhumans, because their imagination is *more* vibrant than is ordinary. Prophets
would be another species if they had *other* mental faculties than our own. Would a
microscopic elephant have other faculties?

a new social consciousness attested to by painters and certain doctors and atypical midwives,[5] on the other hand there could only be a mechanistic paediatrics, because only mechanism is capable of turning us away from the teleological vision that negates childhood by inscribing lack within it.

Henceforth one will no longer cast over the infant this gaze of the 'complete' adult that only discovers its own negation in it, and which consequently sees nothing other than the abyss between two incompatible ages, between the being that presently is and the *nothingness from which it came*. One will adopt, on the contrary, the theoretical point of view of the child, not as a matter of childishness, but because this is the *right way* to consider human life: from the point of view of a being exposed to death and whose body as well as mind must become strong, and of the parents[6] that support it in this process. Spinoza disputes, as we will see, the chimerical position of the complete human being: it is they, the false adult, this incorrigible dreamer, that will deserve throughout the *Theologico-Political Treatise* the epithet *puerilis* – the final avatar of the figure of the *infans adultus*. The human being only becomes an adult by exiting the dream; and it is necessary that it be aware of this.

Infantile Impotence: Neither Privation nor Misery (scholia to *Ethics* V, 6 and 39)

The meaning of the scholium to V, 39 is now clear. The comparison of the adult and the infant, in the penultimate sentence, does not just have the aim of warning us about the necessary link between the capacities of the body and those of the weakened mind. It tends to make childhood and even *infancy* the common condition of human beings, and the point of view from which one must set out again in order finally to grasp a true ethical discourse: a discourse that is not set up for disappointed virtue, which neither ironises nor whines about the infantilism of adults, which no longer sees in childhood an unsurpassable ontological limit (being children of God). For to bring the human back to infancy is not to curse it, but to remind it of the elementary concerns that it owes to its body and its mind – through which the text, reciprocally, bears the traces of a new cultural attitude toward the infant. One will refrain from objecting that Spinoza rehabilitates in this

---

[5] See the analysis of the journal of Catharina (Vrouw) Schrader in Schama 1988, chapter 7.

[6] See our remarks in the Introduction on the use of the first person plural in *Ethics* V, 39 Schol.: *conamur*.

way the chimera of the *infans adultus*: on the contrary, as with the 'waking dream', *vigilando somniare*, he uses it to show that childhood properly understood extends much further than one thinks, and that it is appropriate to put an end to this state of affairs by exiting it.

And if we read carefully, we see that this comparison is prepared for in the preceding sentences:

> But for a clearer understanding of these things [the link between a healthy body, and thus a healthy mind, and serenity in the face of death], we must note here that *we* live in continuous change, and that as *we change* for the better or worse, *we* are called happy or unhappy (*felices aut infelices dicimur*). *For one who has passed from being an infant or child* to being a corpse is called unhappy. On the other hand, if *we* pass the whole length of our life (*totum vitae spatium*) with a sound Mind in a sound Body, that is considered happiness.[7]

The text appears quite confused, insofar as it inextricably mixes together three considerations: 1. The perpetual oscillation of the power to act. 2. The decisive orientation that the course of life takes, decrepitude or beatitude. 3. The undecided becoming of the child between death and survival. One must therefore read it as such, not seeking to dissociate what Spinoza clearly imagined together. However, nothing indicates that we are dealing with a confused representation: we see, instead, a distinct image in the process of being formed, a synthesis in progress that will be brought to its conclusion without ambiguity in the sentences that follow. The life of a human being oscillates, torn between happiness and unhappiness, *like* the child is perpetually caught between life and death. In this sense, childhood is already in advance an image of life as a whole.

One will note the passage's Aristotelian resonances. Aristotle still hesitated between two schemas: the conception of happiness as the decisive turning-point of life, the formation of a virtuous ἕξις or *habitus*, and the impossibility, for this reason, of calling a child happy or unhappy; the complementary criteria of a 'life come to an end', and consequently the uncertainty to the very end, allow for the possibility of a reversal of fortune.[8] The

---

[7] *Ethics* V, 39 Schol.; CWS I, 614. Our emphasis. Translation modified.

[8] *Nicomachean Ethics* I, 10 (Aristotle 2004: 16). See *Theologico-Political Treatise* III, 13: 'But the means which lead to living securely and preserving the body are chiefly placed in external things, and for that reason they are called gifts of fortune, because they depend for the most part on the governance of external causes of which we are igno-

expression *felices aut infelices dicimur*, in Spinoza's text, strongly recalls the Thomistic transposition of Aristotle's text: *puer non potest dici felix*, 'children cannot be called happy'.[9] The image of childhood is already virtually in place, beneath the description of the condition of the adult.

It would be false to maintain that childhood, in Spinoza, is the paradigm of impotence: that would be to confuse it with melancholy, anorexia, suicide. No doubt it is there to a certain indiscernible degree: like them, it is characterised by a near-total dependence with regard to external causes. But with this important difference: children are neither melancholics, nor anorexics, nor suicides – 'their bodies are continually, as it were, in a state of equilibrium'.[10] And Spinoza does not call them 'defeated' (*victus*)[11] or 'unhappy', but caught in an undecided becoming between health and death. Childhood is certainly a state of impotence, but to present things in this way would be to freeze them in place. On the contrary, Spinoza describes the *Passion* of the child ('quantum ejus natura patitur . . .', which refers back to the potentiality expressed at the beginning of the scholium, 'non dubium est, quin ejus naturae possint esse, ut . . .'[12]) as the advent [*avènement*] of its power to act. At bottom, childhood is not impotence itself – impotence is native – but the progressive, painful, dramatic blooming of the power to act. It would be a mistake to insist on the miserable condition of the child in Spinoza: this thread common to the seventeenth century goes for plenty of philosophers, but precisely not for Spinoza. It is Christian philosophers, from Saint Francis de Sales to Bossuet, by way of the Oratorians and Port-Royal, that make the *misery* of the child into a theme. It suffices to pass from Pascal or Malebranche to Spinoza to sense a monumental shift.[13]

---

rant. So in this matter, the wise man and the fool are almost equally happy or unhappy' (CWS II, 114).

[9] *Commentary on the Nicomachean Ethics* I, 14 (Aquinas 1964).

[10] *Ethics* III, 32 Schol.; CWS I, 513. For the sense of this formulation, see below.

[11] *Ethics* IV, 20 Schol.; CWS I, 557.

[12] *Ethics* V, 39 Schol.; CWS I, 614.

[13] See note 39, below. Let us pause for a moment on Ramond's commentary. He is one of the rare few (along with Macherey and Bove) to take up Spinoza's remarks on childhood. And above all, he notes Spinoza's hesitancy concerning the change of essence, or transformation (Ramond 1995: 215–16). But his eagerness not to see misery in the child – a word once again foreign to Spinoza's vocabulary and tone – leads him to pass over in silence the truly important problems of memory and *privatio*, by underscoring only the quantitative gap in power between the adult and the infant, which, it's true, is considerable, but which is not lesser than that between the sage and the drunk, and even – a problematic reversal! – between the *puer*, whose body is continually 'as if in a state of equilibrium', and the melancholic, etc. Whence this highly objectionable

'Nemo miseretur infantis':[14] no pity for children! This cry would nicely sum up the Calvinist attitude, but it does not resonate in the same way at all in Spinoza. Take the Spinozist definition of pity (*commiseratio*): 'a Sadness, accompanied by the idea of an evil that has happened to another whom we imagine to be like us'.[15] We immediately glimpse the ambivalence of pity, which lies in this case in the belief that *evil happens to children as such*, whose unawareness [*inconscience*] and physical debility are only its manifestations (and what is this evil, if not the *naturae vitium seu peccatum* to which the scholium to V, 6 alludes – the evil of childhood as such as punishment for the Fall?). For if we imagine that children are like us, on the one hand we see ourselves in them only as infirm, deprived of the faculties that we possess, and on the other hand they bring us back to the image of our own impotence. Whence the tendency of pity to turn over at once into contempt (*contemptus*), a special sensitivity to that of which an object is deprived which finds its expression in mockery (*irrisio*), and at the same time into *humilitas*, an affect that 'human nature, considered in itself, strains against as far as it can'.[16] We obtain more or less the picture of the moralistic preacher from the Preface to Part III of the *Ethics*. In the mouth of this sinister person-age, 'no pity!' is only a cry of hate.[17]

By contrast, there are two unequal ways of escaping this sadness, of refus-ing to enter into the game of pity. There is, first of all, that of the 'man of advanced years' whose analogical conjectures concerning children are

sentence on the scholium to V, 6: 'For childhood is for Spinoza a miserable state: only our habit of thinking it necessary makes it tolerable; and *this is the only reason why, contrary to what could be the case*, "no one pities infants"' (Ramond 1995: 215, our emphasis). But the contrary precisely could not be at all, or exists only in the heads of theologians and other embittered melancholics . . . Once again, the philosophical interest of the case of the infant seems clear to us: it represents the putting to the test of a philosophy that denies all validity to the concept of *privatio*. There must follow in Spinoza a general re-evaluation of the relationship of philosophy to childhood.

[14] *Ethics* V, 6 Schol.; CWS I, 600.

[15] *Ethics* III, DA XVIII; CWS I, 535.

[16] *Ethics* III, DA XXIX Exp.; CWS I, 538. Translation modified.

[17] Contempt and mockery are in the last analysis related to hate (*Ethics* IV, 45 cor. 1). – Dutch Calvinism condemned outpourings of sorrow upon the death of a child. Preaching a resignation drawing near to insensitivity, pastors explained to parents that their children would find themselves better off in paradise than in the 'valley of tears' of the mortal world. Schama underscores that the death of the infant was a nightmare for the Dutch family of the seventeenth century, which belies the claim of their indif-ference supposedly due to cultural conditioning by demographic reality (Schama 1988: 679). What transpires with Pierre Balling's feelings in Letter XVII to Spinoza goes in this direction.

less intense than his propensity to 'believe their nature to be so different from his own':[18] children tend to appear to him as foreigners, as beings of another species, to whom the category of privation no longer applies. One can surmise however that this illusory solution does not prevent the soul from hesitating, and that its proponent, as Pautrat translates it, does not himself 'seem to resemble a man'.[19] The philosopher – joined by a certain popular wisdom, given the *nemo* of the scholium to V, 6 – does not take for an unhappy accident what they know to be a matter of natural necessity (the state of childhood, to which weakness and the vicissitudes of illness are inherent). When Spinoza writes that it 'would be as absurd if a circle were to complain that God did not give it the properties of a sphere, or a child who is suffering from a stone, that he did not give it a healthy body',[20] he laconically highlights under what condition childhood in general appears pitiable to us: when we ascribe to the child a nature that it does not have, which amounts to subtracting it from the natural order in order to inscribe it in a magical order of chimeras and metamorphoses where the attributions of properties are wholly accidental and arbitrary, while the mixture of natures sustains the mirage of privation.[21] Let us add, to close the dossier on pity, that the latter is not just a sad passion, but a passion of an imitative nature and, on this score, is eminently childish.[22] In truth, childhood as such should neither make us rejoice nor be saddened: this is the price of contemplating it truly. But what adults, parents or not, do not oscillate between these two poles? Who other than Spinoza knew how to level such a gaze without pathos? Perhaps Chekhov?

If we return to the scholium to V, 39, it is clear that we now better understand the choice, in the final sentence, of the expressions *infantia* (instead

---

[18] *Ethics* IV, 39 Schol.; CWS I, 569.

[19] *Ethics* IV, 50 Schol.; CWS I, 574. [The Pautrat translation, which Zourabichvili here cites, reads: this person 'n'a pas l'air de ressembler à l'homme'. Curley: 'seems to be unlike a man.' – GM.]

[20] *Ep.* LXXVIII [to Oldenburg]; CWS II, 480.

[21] It is not by chance that Spinoza takes the example of a sick child in this letter: the child is exemplary of physical weakness (for moral weakness, he goes on to invoke an adult). Every child is more or less a sick person, though no longer in the sense of traditional medicine. Here therefore the natural condition of childhood is at stake, rather than the particular nature of a particularly 'unhappy' child (in the sense of misfortune – as in the scholium to V, 39 – and not misery; strictly speaking the distribution of happiness and unhappiness is still in suspense in the child). As for the link between misery and privation, one will note that Spinoza already availed himself of the argument of the circle and the properties of the sphere in Letter XIX to Blijenbergh.

[22] *Ethics* III, 32 Schol.; CWS I, 513.

of *infans*) and *in hac vita* (instead of *in infantia*), where the latter takes the reins from the *totum vitae spatium* invoked a few sentences earlier: 1. the striving to change the body and the mind of childhood into another body and another mind *incomparably* more powerful becomes coextensive with life as a whole (*totum vitae spatium mente sana in corpore sano percurrere = in hac vita conari, ut corpus in alium et mens in aliam mutentur, quae ad plurima apta sint*[23]); 2. childhood correlatively becomes the principal stake of philosophy. Let us now reread the final sentences (the scholium invoked at the end concerns access to knowledge of the third kind):

> And really, he who, like an infant or child, has a Body capable of very few things, and very heavily dependent on external causes, has a Mind which considered solely in itself is conscious of almost nothing of itself, or of God, or of things. On the other hand, he who has a Body capable of a great many things, has a mind which considered only in itself is very much conscious of itself, and of God, and of things. In this life, then, we strive especially that the Body of childhood may change (as much as its nature allows and assists) into another, capable of a great many things and related to a Mind very conscious of itself, of God, and of things. We strive, that is, that whatever is related to its memory or imagination is of hardly any moment in relation to the intellect (as I have already said in P38S).[24]

Finally, how can one not think that, throughout the whole scholium, the figure of the *delicate person*, one such as Spinoza, takes shape? The apparent confusion that we are invoking is nevertheless peculiar: the text passes from precarious health to the becoming of the child, with no transition other than that indecision between happiness and unhappiness. Everything happens as if these sickly states oscillate between two extreme destinies: the death of a child, and the perpetual health of the *dancing sage*.[25] Is it by chance

---

[23] In this second formulation, we have allowed ourselves to contract the following passage: 'in hac vita [igitur apprime] conamur, ut corpus infantiae in aliud . . . mutetur, quod ad plurima aptum sit, quodque ad mentem referatur, quae sui, et Dei, et rerum plurimum sit conscia'.

[24] *Ethics* V, 39 Schol.; CWS I, 614. Translation modified.

[25] Spinoza defines health as the body's capacity to do all that can follow from its nature (*Ethics* IV, 45 Schol.; CWS I, 572), that is, by its power to be affected and to affect in many ways (*Ethics* IV, 39 Dem.; CWS I, 568–9). Among the exercises and nutrients that he recommends are not just physical games, but music, theatre, perfumes, etc. This health therefore cannot be reduced to the performances of an athlete. It is instead

that Gilles Aillaud, in a play featuring Spinoza, attributes to him above all, and in an apparently arbitrary way, 'a gibbon's suddenness, quickness, and skill, as if he wanted to show that he was in our world like a fish in water, elusive [*insaisissable*]',[26] before curiously describing him as an *infans adultus*: 'this newborn that I rocked was an old ape . . . When he escaped me, it was as if the newborn who I wanted so much to hold in my arms had become a father.'[27] What does 'elusive' mean, in Aillaud's writing? Is it not the schema of activity, if we recall that the problem of the fish, in the *Short Treatise*, was that of putting an end to the dream of living outside the water?[28]

Spinoza clearly felt that he took part both in the sage and in the infant, insofar as his intellectual development had not come to an end and sickness threatened to interrupt it at each instant.[29] From this point of view, the scholium to V, 39 is as laden with lived life as the prologue to the *Treatise on the Emendation of the Intellect*. It is also hard not to be reminded of the sick child of Letter 78, whom fate has endowed with a weak body (*naturam infirmam*), but who does not complain, for that would be to dream of another essence, or to dream of oneself as a chimera, analogous to a circle that would have the properties of a sphere.

Finally, if the Aristotelian resonances are obvious, the scholium to V, 39 confirms Spinoza's more profound affinity with Lucretius. In addition to the chimerical figure of the *infans adultus*, there is also the idea, expressed at the beginning of the scholium, that leaving childhood behind would be putting an end to the fear of death:

> For, just as children tremble and fear everything in blinding darkness, so we even in daylight sometimes dread things that are no more terrible than

a matter of a body at once *agile* and *sensitive*. For lack of a better word, that is, of a word not only capable of bringing together these two meanings, but which remains close to Spinoza's experience, we propose *dancing*, which inevitably – but who would dare to say unpleasantly? – calls Nietzsche to mind. Recall that the latter had a passionate relationship with Spinoza. Certainly he came to consider him a 'sickly hermit' (*Beyond Good and Evil* §5 [Nietzsche 2002: 8]. Translation modified). But in the famous letter to Overbeck of 30 July 1881, he called Spinoza his 'precursor', speaking of a 'solitude for two', and concludes: 'Beyond that, my health is not as I had hoped' (Nietzsche 1996: 176).

[26] Aillaud 1987: 19.

[27] Aillaud 1987: 19–20.

[28] See the first study, above.

[29] 'But perhaps I will pursue these matters more clearly with you some other time, if life lasts' (*Ep.* LXXXIII [to Tschirnhaus]; CWS II, 487). See also Letter 28, to Bouwmeester, where Spinoza invokes his convalescence.

the imaginary dangers that cause children to quake in the dark. This terrifying darkness that enshrouds the mind must be dispelled not by the sun's rays and the dazzling darts of day, but by study of the superficial aspect and underlying principle of nature.[30]

So the great question reappears: why does the scholium to V, 39 appear so contradictory? Why does Spinoza invoke the exchange of one body for another, whereas he excludes in the same breath – 'quantum ejus natura patitur' – a change of essence? What is it that justifies a logical schema so close to that of emerging from a chrysalis?

Let us remark on the path followed since the *Short Treatise*: there, it was a question only: 1. of biological birth, as a transformation pure and simple, and of the movement analogous to that which makes another human being appear in place of a famous Spanish poet (which the reader can make sense of only by reference to the concept of 'element'); 2. of a 'new birth' or 'regeneration', purely spiritual, recalling the Christian symbolism of baptism and the Pauline theme of the Former Man. There was thus no place there for a philosophy of childhood, at once as comprehending it and as a point of view.

Henceforth philosophy is brought back to the perspective of childhood, in order to remind us, leaving all disparagement behind, that our problem is that of leaving it, and that it is this that makes the child what it is, and that it does not suffice to humiliate ourselves by seeing ourselves as large children, but that we must still so to speak *become* the children that we had been, with which we have broken without for all that ceasing to be them, even freezing within us that which is only development, gestation. The philosophy of the first man dreams of a fictive human nature, and by the same stroke it dreams of childhood as a sort of prehistory of the human being, an uncomfortable vestibule of life, populated by miasmas and phantoms. At once it denies the break (continuous growth) and never ceases blaming it (the yawning gulf between the non-human and the human). For there is no being of the child, no special essence that would differentiate it from the adult; no more is it a non-being, the absurd negation of its own future.

We must help the logic in order to pull it out of its dreamlike wandering astray. Why is childhood not a world? Why is growing a development and not a transformation? First of all, because the child, perfect in its being, would have no reason to leave it behind: it would be an *infans adultus*, a 'completed' child, as one says of a human being. Second of all, because it would be incomprehensible that each life would include the succession of

---

[30] *On the Nature of Things* II, 54–60 (Lucretius 2001: 37).

two essences (there must remain a difference between this and the case of the adult amnesiac, who is really transformed). Third of all, because from the perspective of the infinite understanding, the duality of the child and the adult does not make sense: God does not produce children but human beings – who are born at the lowest point of their power to act and think. This truism must be recalled: cut off from its becoming, the child no longer grows. Which means simply that the child *is* development.

One will object that we have fallen into an even worse sophism, which bears some relation to the mirage of the suicidal fish described in the *Short Treatise*: how could life be confused with childhood if it is the act of leaving it behind? How could the child be this being in perpetual negation of itself? But we are trapped in the paradox of becoming only if we allow ourselves to be: it falls to us not to hypostasise the child. The difference between the child and the adult becomes in Spinoza a pure *difference in perspectives*: the perspective of the threshold (the child in development), the perspective of dreaming with open eyes (pseudo-adult, *infans adultus*, the child petrified of thinking itself an adult and of contemplating childhood upside down, negatively, from the height of its illusion and its deception). The new frontier is between the *becoming-adult* of the child and the satisfied *childishness* of the apparent adult. And just as there is no child-being, but a native state of impotence from which the child extracts itself neither painlessly nor without help, there is no adult-being, since that would be the state of the perfect sage. The difference between becoming-adult and the fiction of adult-being explains Spinoza's famous declaration: 'I do not presume that I have discovered the best Philosophy; but I know that I understand the true one.'[31] Is this not, to the letter, the gap between *adolescens* and *adultus*? We will see further on what Spinoza has to say about adolescents.

Here and there the *Short Treatise* alludes to childhood, as to a certain regime of affectivity (the *Ethics* will not refute it on this point); but it never envisaged it as a development. On the contrary, it was a given that ethics was addressed to the adult, to the circle of young adults to whom Spinoza gave his lessons. But the two births, that of the flesh and that of the spirit, were symptomatic of a thought still imprisoned by the chimera of the *infans adultus*: a foetal life separated from its future since it could reach it only through death; a human being arising wholly new and pure. Yet the doctrine betrayed a blinding contradiction, which certainly referred to different levels of the text but which, left in its state, testified to the still unfinished character of the thought: the coexistence of the new thesis of the mind as

[31] *Ep.* LXXVI [to Burgh]; CWS II, 475.

the idea of the body, and the archaic thesis of the mind divorced from its body in order to be united with God. In revenge, when all the consequences of the concept of the *idea corporis* were drawn out, the relation to the body, far from being effaced, was transmuted, and the theme of childhood emerged as the schema of this transmutation. Conversion became immanent, something as 'natural and necessary' as childhood.[32]

We have still not answered the question. Why does perfection have the appearance of a transformation, as if Spinoza, for his part and in his own way, had needed to search, like Leibniz, for the formula of a 'transformation of an already formed animal'?[33] The conditions of the problem are as follows: perfection involves a rupture, but the latter must be thought properly, and not as if it arose from nothingness; for if it is accepted that the infant *could* accede to reason, the status of such a potentiality, in a philosophy that affirms the actuality of all power, must no longer be the same as it had been in scholasticism. It still appears however that Spinoza remained scholastic on this point: the child is deprived of reason, but as it is called upon *by nature* to conquer it, it was not possible for him to maintain in this case, as he had done in the case of blindness in the correspondence with Blijenbergh, that the privation that we imagine is ontologically only a mere negation;[34] reason was thus for him as well a positive negation, consisting of a being 'in potentia'. Obviously, Spinoza could not say so; but the hypothesis that appears unavoidable to us, given the importance of the scholium to V, 6 and the analysis we have provided of the scholium to V, 39, is that he could no longer think so, either.

One will note that the scholium to V, 6 refrains from using the word *privatio*. Instead it clearly opposes a conception that conforms with common sense, according to which the infant 'does not know' how to speak, walk, or reason, an ignorance which leads one to consider childhood (*infantia*) as

---

[32] *Ethics* V, 6 Schol.; *CWS* I, 599–600.

[33] Leibniz, Letter to Arnauld, 9 October 1687 (Leibniz 1967: 149).

[34] The idea of privation is that of a property that a thing lacks but yet which pertains to it by nature. It is a being of reason that is born of a comparison: see *Ethics* III, DA 3, Exp. (the case of sadness, which supposes the comparison of a present state with a past state); IV, Praef. (the case of imperfection and that of impotence). Spinoza thus says that 'privation is nothing positive, and that it is said only in relation to our intellect, not in relation to God's intellect' (*Ep.* XIX [to Blijenbergh]; *CWS* I, 359). Consequently, one must accept that even a blind person who has lost their sight is not for all that *deprived* of it; not seeing is a 'pure and simple negation', abstract in relation to their *new* nature (*Ep.* XXII [to Blijenbergh]; *CWS* I, 377). Individual transformation is implied by, and forms the physical correlate to, this affirmative ontology.

a 'natural and necessary thing', and a fictive conception, which is obtained by way of the shortcut of the dream of a human being born as an adult, and according to which childhood amounts to a 'vice' or a 'sin' of Nature.[35] This repeats the claim made in the Preface to Part III: 'nothing happens in nature which can be attributed to any defect in it'.[36] It is thus also a very clear allusion to the moralists, all the more so as childhood turns out to be the state of impotence par excellence. In fact, Spinoza wrote in that same Preface:

> they attribute the cause of human impotence, not to the common power of nature, but to I know not what vice of human nature, which they therefore bewail, or laugh at, or disdain, or (as usually happens) curse.[37]

According to Thomas Aquinas, Creation includes all degrees of perfection or goodness (from the noblest to the most vile being). But the difference does not merely concern the unequal attribution of perfections; it also stems from the capacity to degrade a perfection that one possessed, and this degradation is the very definition of evil. It is true that the latter is nothing, it has no reality, but this is not any longer a mere absence or negation; it is the 'lack of a quality that [the thing] should naturally have',[38] that is, a *privation*. If the human being is defined by reason, the privation of the latter is not explained simply by a merely potential possession; it is the mark of a loss. So too the child is culpable, even if the sin whose burden it bears is that of the first man. Childhood itself is the degradation of the human being, and the presence of children, and the necessity of being born a child, are the incessant and humiliating reminder of original sin. Posed in this way, the theme could clearly be exploited in a variety of ways depending on the theologian. Calvinism, dominant in Holland, went furthest in cursing the child: it was scandalous to pay them the least attention, to care for them when they were sick, to concern oneself with their education; scandalous even to kiss them before putting them to bed, and to grieve their passing.[39]

---

[35] *Ethics* V, 6 Schol.; CWS I, 600. Translation modified. [See above, Second Study, n. 4. – GM.]
[36] *Ethics* III, Praef.; CWS I, 492.
[37] *Ethics* III, Praef.; CWS I, 491.
[38] Gilson 2002: 185. We here follow the analysis from 183–8.
[39] Schama 1988, *passim*. Calvin: '[All] have been enveloped in original sin and defiled by its stains. For that reason, even infants themselves, while they carry their condemnation along with them from the mother's womb, are guilty not of another's fault but their own. For, even though the fruits of their iniquity have not yet come forth, they have the seed closed within them. Indeed, their whole nature is a seed of sin; hence

Spinoza is thus opposed to the idea that childhood lacks anything, and that it can be considered as in a state of privation. He disagrees with Christian thought except on one point: the child's state of extreme impotence and consequently of dependence. The impotence of the child is in no way the mark of the degradation of the first man, whose original perfection, presupposed by sin, is only a chimerical dream. This is why Spinoza uses the verb *nescire*: if the infant does not speak, or walk, or reason, it is obviously because it cannot; but this impotence, which incidentally is *stricto sensu* only a minimum of power, only a power that is insufficient when compared to that of external causes, is only the result of an *ignorance*. It doesn't know anything about what its body can do, nor what its mind can do; children are, 'as it were, unconscious of themselves'.[40] To say that childhood is 'a natural and necessary thing' is equivalent, at the end of the day, to saying: 'all men are born ignorant of the causes of things'.[41] Deprived of nothing, the infant must simply learn to affirm its nature.

And if 'the power of thought is dormant in infants', as Descartes wrote,[42] this is not, as he believed, breaking with Thomism in a Platonic fashion,[43] because their soul is too exclusively turned toward the body; rather, as V, 39 and its scholium say, it is because its body is not yet sufficiently cultivated.

---

it can be only hateful and abhorrent to God' (*Institutes of the Christian Religion* I, 2, 1 [Calvin 2006: 251]). This double argument, which is not unique to Calvinism, appears in the *Canons of the Synod of Dordrecht* (1619); see Fatio 1986: 327, articles 2 and 3. From the corruption of descendants, one passes to the corruption of children as such (childhood in the literal sense), and then to the corruption of human beings in general, reduced to the infantile condition (childhood in the figurative sense). – With the notable exception of Descartes, who was more circumspect even though he clung to a negative conception to which we will return, and Leibniz, who was indifferent to the question, Christian philosophers insisted on the image of *moral* misery that, to their minds, constituted childhood. Pascal, writing about the great men of this world: 'No, no, if they are greater than we, it is because their heads are higher, but their feet are as low as ours; they are all at the same level, and rest on the same earth, and by that extremity they are as lowly as we are, as the rest of us, as children, as beasts' (*Pensées* S635/L770 [Pascal 2004: 188]). For Malebranche, even the child born of a pious mother is entirely turned toward the body and is born a sinner: 'it is clear that it is disordered and deranged, and that there is nothing in it not deserving the anger of God' (*The Search after Truth* II, I, 7 [Malebranche 1997b: 123]).

[40] *Ethics* V, 6 Schol.; CWS I, 600.
[41] *Ethics* I, App.; CWS I, 440.
[42] Descartes, *Replies to the Fourth Set of Objections* (CSM II, 160; AT VII, 228). [N.B. Here Descartes is in fact quoting Arnauld back to him, though he does not dispute the claim; see CSM II, 143; AT VII, 204. – GM.]
[43] On this opposition to the Thomistic doctrine, see Moreau 1979: 38.

Spinoza clearly names the sole means of this cultivation, in a violently anti-Calvinist appeal: healthy and varied nutrition, as much for its moving parts as for its sensorial parts.[44] But this requires extreme care, because the body of the child can handle only a few things. In this regard, and in the context of the Netherlands of the second half of the seventeenth century, the *conamur* associated with the *quantum ejus natura patitur*, in the scholium to V, 39, resounds almost like a manifesto in favour of the development of paediatrics and childcare (the Preface to Part V of the *Ethics*, recall, underscores the decisive role of medicine).

Note on Gabriel Metsu's *The Sick Child*

A whole play of resonances links the scholium to *Ethics* V, 39 to Metsu's painting. Does the painting illustrate the scholium, or rather does the scholium comment on the painting? Metsu divides his canvas in two, across a diagonal that runs along the body of the child, and places in the lower half vibrant shades of red, blue, and yellow, the three primary colours, whereas the other half is almost veiled, drawing toward black-and-white, in spite of some dull yellows and browns: the child, grappling with sickness, is clearly caught between life and death ('Qui enim ex infante, vel puero in cadaver transiit, infelix dicitur, & contra id felicitati tribuitur, quod totum vitae spatium mente sana in corpore sano percurrere potuerimus'). The diagonal, which points upward toward the obscure representation of a Crucifixion, is transgressed near the bottom in the grey part by a cup that is colourful – no doubt because it contains a remedy. The painting would not be of interest if the positioning of the subjects repeated the chromatic division; but the chest and face of the healthy mother are in the dull half, whereas the child is completely within the vibrant triangle, colour and grey meeting one another on its pale face. It is said that the painting recalls the Virgin and Child, especially that of Van Dyck in the Wallace Collection in London. But what is the meaning of such a recollection, other than that *The Sick Child* is more precisely between the Virgin and Child and the Lamentation of Christ? In reality, the potbellied divine babies of the Dutchman have little to do with Metsu's child. The analogy is merely formal, which suggests that the Passion, as we said above, is henceforth that of the child, because it designates the painful and uncertain blooming of the power to act ('quantum ejus natura patitur . . .'), whereas the mother incarnates the *conamur* that surrounds the frail and unsteady little body. The gaze of the child has no pathos to it (V, 6

---

[44] *Ethics* IV, 45 Schol.

schol.: 'nemo miseretur infantis . . .'),[45] but the unlimited Patience that it expresses, taking leave at once of the mother, the painter, and the preacher, denies that its impotence is a pure privation. What the enlightened ones call 'religious connotations' (consolation, atonement, etc.) fall into the background, in a painting that no longer symbolises anything other than the fragile gap between *conamur* and *patitur*. If we were to see redemption here, that would have to be on the canvas itself, somewhere between the gaze of the child, leading out of frame, and the corner of intense red fabric that covers the mother's knee. But above all Metsu traces a counter-diagonal whose point of departure at the lower right is indicated by the gaze of the child, and whose direction is indicated – by the black *arrow* that occupies the centre of the canvas.[46] This second diagonal is favoured by the painter twice over: it points toward what context suggests to be a map, where he wrote his signature. We will say that the painting leads on the one hand to *The Allegory of Faith*, where Vermeer reproduced Jordaens' *Crucifixion*, which Metsu also imitates, and on the other hand to *The Allegory of Painting*, where the same Vermeer puts his signature on a map. It hardly matters that dating suggests otherwise: that only deprives us of anecdotal evidence; there remains the obvious shared set of problems. In sum, why does this painting, without being 'Spinozist', seem to us to resonate strangely with the scholium to V, 39 such as we have analysed it? As in Spinoza, the undecided proximity of life and death proper to the development of the child did not raise the latter to the rank of being the preeminent figure of the human condition (first axis and the chromatic division) without the image of childhood being rectified at the same time: read the map of nature, stop searching for a relation between misery and its atonement (second, methodological, axis).[47]

The Childishness of Men

Before pursuing the resolution of the problem of rupture, it would be useful to examine the remarks on the childishness of men in the *Theologico-Political Treatise*: taking into account this difference in perspectives (becoming-

---

[45] In order to be convinced of this, one need only compare it with *The Sick Girl*, by the very same Metsu two or three years earlier, where the mother in black wipes her tears.

[46] The arrow is a typical feature for Metsu: see *Woman Reading a Letter*. [This seems to be the painting to which Zourabichvili meant to refer, as it prominently features Cupid's arrows on a bucket in the centre of the frame. The painting he names is *Girl Receiving a Letter* (*La jeune femme recevant une lettre*), which does not contain any arrows. – GM.]

[47] On the importance of the cartographic model in the painting of the Dutch golden age, see Alpers 1983, chapter 4: 'The Mapping Impulse in Dutch Art'.

adult/being frozen in childhood) pushes us to re-evaluate them, to see in them something other than worn-out rhetoric. When it comes down to it, it is like the relationship to the corporeal and mental weakness of children, which cannot be an object of distress: how could Spinoza have given himself over for so many pages to something he despises – to satire and mockery (*irrisio*)?[48]

Perhaps we should first of all recall that the transformation invoked in the scholium to IV, 39 has no concrete sense that is acceptable without qualification, except on the political plane: the same parts take on a new relation of movement and rest among themselves, obeying a new fundamental law – that is revolution. Since the Introduction we have underscored the significant location of the scholium at the heart of the political sequence of the *Ethics*, as well as the analogous link established in the *Theologico-Political Treatise* between transformation and amnesia (the failure of all revolutions, tied to the memory of the old political form). But on the other hand, the Hebrews are described as a people that is without political memory, that is, childish, in search of a form: 'When they first left Egypt, they were no longer bound by the legislation of any other nation; so they were permitted, as they wished, to enact new laws . . . Nevertheless, they were quite incapable . . .'.[49] '[Moses] taught them in the same way parents usually do children who are lacking in all reason.'[50] In sum, the Hebrews alone did not know how to form a State, they owed their salvation to Moses, who conducted himself like their father. If the problem was how the newborn Hebrews would leave childhood behind (with the flight from Egypt being equivalent to a birth), the conditions of the process are quite similar to those that we saw in the scholium to V, 39: *conamur*, that is, an external striving that makes up for the striving of the newborn, which is still infirm because it is ignorant of all things. And the problem itself is posed in nearly identical terms: to acquire a true body, a true form, this time in the political sense (*societatem formare*).[51]

But if the history of the Hebrews is politically exemplary, it is just because of the contrast between their extreme childishness and the duration of their State, which attests to a successful *form*.[52] Could we speak of a paradox of *happy children*? This happiness is more collective than individual: *continua*

---

[48] On the opposition between laughter (*risum*) and mockery (*irrisio*), see *Ethics* IV, 45 Schol. On the critique of condescension, see *Ethics* III, Praef., and *TP* I, 1.

[49] *TTP* V, 26–7; *CWS* II, 145. We find the same idea at XVII, 26; *CWS* II, 301.

[50] *TTP* II, 47; *CWS* II, 107. Appuhn translates it as 'privés de raison', but the verb is *carere*, which designates a simple absence, without any idea of suppression.

[51] *TTP* III, 6–9; *CWS* II, 112–13; and IV, 28–9; *CWS* II, 132–3.

[52] *TTP* III, 6; *CWS* II, 112.

imperii foelicitas.[53] From the point of view of individual salvation, in fact, there is no reason why the Hebrews would be any happier than anyone else,[54] if by true happiness one understands, leaving fortune aside, virtue or love of God,[55] and consequently the tranquillity of the mind that has put an end to mental and affective fluctuation.[56] One formula aptly summarises the idea: 'only the temporal happiness of the body and the peace of the state';[57] in other words, the two aspects of *felicitas* – *mens sana in corpore sano* – were divided, distributed between the individuals and the community. And Spinoza remarks that the prophecy of Isaiah contained two promises: *mens sana in corpore sano* for the free and charitable (the wise), and the security of the state, material prosperity, and conservation of the body for those who at least observe the ceremonies (the ignorant).[58]

What then is this Mosaic teaching, analogous to that which parents have for the smallest infants? Spinoza says that the general problem was that of making the Hebrews obey: he never stops recalling their legendary disobedience.[59] But to see in this the proper character or nature of a nation would be, according to him, a 'childish' response, for Nature creates only individuals, and the character of a nation can only arise from the 'laws and mores' to which it is habituated. Spinoza thus invites us to distinguish between a native disobedience – the problem of political childcare, one might say – and a disobedient *habitus*, owing to certain failures of an institutional order (the mistake, in fact, lay in having changed the constitution).[60] Original disobedience is a universal given; persistent disobedience is only the sign of a failure of education.

The content of the teaching is a 'rule of true life', the famous Ten Commandments, which, given the 'childish comprehension' (*puerili captu*) of the Hebrews,[61] Moses could not teach via reasoning, but by a play of terrible threats and marvellous promises, even if he used persuasion rather

---

[53] *TTP* III, 19. [Curley translates *foelicitas* here as 'prosperity'. – GM.]

[54] *TTP* III, 13; *CWS* II, 114.

[55] *TTP* IV, 12–14; *CWS* II, 128.

[56] *TTP* IV, 42; *CWS* II, 136.

[57] *TTP* V, 2; *CWS* II, 138. ['solam corporis temporaneam foelicitatem, & imperii tranquillitatem'.]

[58] *TTP* V, 10; *CWS* II, 141.

[59] For example, *TTP* III, 19 and 41–2 (*CWS* II, 115 and 121); V, 28 (*CWS* II, 145); XIII, 8 (*CWS* II, 258); XVII, 93 (*CWS* II, 317), etc. [In these passages Spinoza refers to the Hebrews' *contumacia/contumax*, variously rendered by Curley as 'obstinacy', 'stubbornness', or being 'stiff-necked'; Zourabichvili writes of their 'insoumission'. – GM.]

[60] See the Introduction, above.

[61] *TTP* III, 6; *CWS* II, 112. Translation modified.

than dissuasion as much as possible. In this way he adapted his discourse to the level of comprehension of his public, soliciting its imagination and seeking above all to engrave strong associations in its memory (Spinoza underscores that even children can be reached by prophecy).[62] And, just the same as if it were a matter of infants who do not have the least idea of what is useful for them, he established what today we would call a regime that was totalitarian – extending the death penalty to the smallest details of private life (how to shave, dress, labour, celebrate, etc.)[63] – and, what's more, egalitarian.[64] Spinoza does not describe here an ideal city, as if the human community could arise of itself fully clothed, but a political infant, incapable of conserving itself: 'in order that the people, who were not capable of being their own masters, should hang on the words of its ruler, he did not permit these men, accustomed as they were to bondage, to act just as they pleased'.[65] The Hebrews had certainly not broken away from any political form: the Egyptian yoke had habituated them to slavery, and thus they were born slaves. And their first years could thus only be years of submission, under the enlightened guidance of a despotic but just father. From another point of view, however, they were born free, called to self-determination (return to the state of nature, primitive democracy).

One might be surprised that Spinoza would pass a positive judgment on such a regime, in a book in which he claims that democracy is 'the most natural state, and the one which approaches most nearly the freedom nature concedes to everyone'.[66] But that surprise would be abstract. Only the notion of *political childhood* enables us to understand this. It is not a matter of tyranny; on the contrary, it was the failure of Moses' system that led the Hebrews ineluctably to tyranny.[67] Moreover, Spinoza explains that behaving out of obedience (*ex mandato*), though it is not freedom, is nevertheless not by its nature slavery, for everything depends on the 'reason for the action', *actionis ratio*.[68] The slave is one whose mandated behaviour, which

---

[62] *TTP* II, 47 (*CWS* II, 107); V, 7 (*CWS* II, 140); and XI, 7 (*CWS* II, 242): 'the greatest of the Prophets, Moses, did not make any argument'.

[63] *TTP* XIII, 24–6 (*CWS* II, 262); XIV, 6–7 (*CWS* II, 264); XV, 42–5 (*CWS* II, 281–2).

[64] *TTP* XVII, 97 (*CWS* II, 318) and following: the hereditary privilege accorded to the Levites as a reward for their not worshipping the golden calf was the decisive political mistake during the time of Moses.

[65] *TTP* V, 30; *CWS* II, 146.

[66] *TTP* XVI, 36; *CWS* I, 289. Translation modified.

[67] *TTP* XVII, 103; *CWS* II, 319, and following.

[68] *TTP* XVI, 33; *CWS* II, 288.

in this way approaches suicidal behaviour, renders him 'useless to himself'.[69] But children are not slaves, insofar as they do what is useful for them *ex mandato parentis*.[70]

Finding themselves after the flight from Egypt in the state of nature, the Hebrews turned immediately to God, to whom they transferred their sovereignty. What then is the meaning of the *theocracy* thus proclaimed? Why does Spinoza not see in this a dreaming with open eyes, as in the case of those who believe that the Bible was really written by God and sent to human beings?[71] From a certain angle, the theocracy was in fact a chimera, and even doubly so, since it consisted in representing God as a king and in giving oneself over to God as a sovereign.[72] But perhaps there is a way in which the newborn people perceived as in a dream a real condition:

> By the very fact that they believed they could be preserved by the power of God alone, they transferred to God all their natural power to preserve themselves, which previously they perhaps had thought they had of themselves. As a result, they transferred all their right.[73]

The newborn certainly had a *conatus*, and on that score conserved itself through what the *Theologico-Political Treatise* calls the 'internal aid of God'. However, the power that it had at its disposal was wholly disproportionate to that of the external causes that acted upon it, and as it knew neither its own body nor its environment, its strivings were insufficient to conserve it, and its survival depended on 'external aid'.[74] In the same way, the Hebrews lived first in a brief period of primitive democracy that corresponded to their independence as a newborn people; but they quickly gave themselves over to God. This decision was moreover inspired by Moses, because it was the only form of non-oppressive, non-tyrannical dependency. The theocratic choice was thus the obscure recognition by the Hebrews themselves that they could not find in themselves their own law, that they were not aware of what would be useful and enable them to conserve themselves. So they needed to obey, and that is why they *learned to obey*. Everything happens as if the first education had obedience as its sole content, the infant not being

---

[69] *TTP* XVI, 33; CWS II, 288.
[70] *TTP* XVI, 35; CWS II, 289.
[71] *TTP*, beginning of XII (CWS II, 248).
[72] See below, third study.
[73] *TTP* XVII, 29; CWS II, 302.
[74] The definitions of these two kinds of 'divine aid' are found in *TTP* III, 9; CWS II, 113.

able to understand why they were being made to do one thing rather than another, or each thing in this way rather than that. It thus tacitly transfers its power to conserve itself to its parents, *conamur*, which is not so far from the Hobbesian idea of a well-founded obedience that the infant would no longer have once they reach the age of entering into agreements (as in Hobbes, the Spinozist educator – Moses – wields, or else possesses, a power of life and death over their pupils[75]). And this obedience is vital, since without it the infant would be abandoned to itself: external aid is, in this sense, the first setting into motion of internal aid. We will eventually return to this decisive mechanism.

But Spinoza also appears to count on a second mechanism: the internalisation of obedience, which is supposed to carry out the progressive transmutation of slavery into quasi-freedom. Here he is looking for the key to the passage from the first childhood to the second, from *infans* and *puer* to *adolescens*, an ambiguous and transitory age:

> Especially conducive was the extreme training in obedience they were brought up with. They were obliged to do everything according to a definite legal prescription. They weren't permitted to plow as they pleased, but only at certain times and in certain years, and only with one kind of animal at a time. Similarly, they could only sow and reap in a certain way and at a certain time. Without exception their life was a continual cultivation of obedience. (On this see Ch. 5, concerning the use of Ceremonies.) To those who had become completely accustomed to it, this regime must have seemed no longer bondage, but freedom. The inevitable result was that no one desired what was denied, but only what was commanded.[76]

Nevertheless this education failed, and the promising young State slowly made its way toward its downfall, frozen in a kind of *aging childhood*. The brilliant educator had committed an irreversible misstep: upon his death the people returned to their first disobedience, synonymous with the greatest submission. There then began the tyrannical drift, the slow death of the State.

Obey: such is thus the salvation of the ignorant. This is childhood become viable for itself and tolerable to others (liberated from without, via passion,

---

[75] See *TTP* IV, 7 (CWS II, 127) and following: 'fear of the gallows' is what sustains commands in the final instance (compare this to the end of Letter 23 to Blijenbergh).
[76] *TTP* XVII, 88–9; CWS II, 316.

from the slavery of its passions). The majority of individuals remain there: 'Everyone, without exception, can obey. But only a very few (compared with the whole human race) acquire a habit of virtue from the guidance of reason alone'[77] (liberation from within, by the transmutation of passions into actions). But the disobedient, the one who does not cultivate reason and does not even know how to obey, is 'inhuman, and almost a beast'.[78] This is the *infans adultus*, the great infant, an adult hardly different from a newborn, who, given the types that Spinoza scatters across his oeuvre, might be a suicide, a sceptic, a bloodthirsty beast, a madman. They alone can be said to be *deprived*,[79] and it is in this sense that they differ from the infant. The latter, neither fortunate nor misfortunate, has before it the prospect of two extreme fates, and an unlikely fate that nevertheless ensures its salvation: good fortune, or immanent reward (becoming adult); misfortune, or immanent punishment (infantilism); and finally to be, as the saying goes, wise beyond one's years [*enfant sage*], and to remain so up to the end of one's days. If Spinoza insists so strongly on the importance of the words of James, that 'man is justified by works and not by faith alone',[80] it is because the child precisely cannot be judged, for one cannot be known in advance.

The principal result of this analysis is the following: the first important stage of childhood is learning to obey. Far from imposing a servile fate upon the infant and then the child, it is a matter of: 1. rendering it capable of receiving 'external aid', without which it would not survive; 2. extracting it from disobedience, a condition that is slavish in the psychological and political sense of the term, since disobedience – or submission to one's passions alone – also means corruptibility; 3. carrying it, in a manner that is still slightly aporetic (utilising hope rather than fear, encouraging the internalisation of obedience), to the threshold of the second stage – becoming adult, that is to say free, wise, loving God in the sense of Part V of the *Ethics*.

We will soon see that the difference between children in becoming and adults remaining children must be deepened in light of certain points in the *Ethics*; in particular the body of the child is said to be, 'as it were, in a state of equilibrium',[81] whereas the childish adult is seen to be torn apart by its contradictions, in perpetual 'fluctuation'; and the child does not have the same

---

[77] *TTP* XV, 45; CWS II, 281–2.
[78] *TTP* V, 41; CWS II, 149. Translation modified. [Curley has: 'he is devoid of human feeling, and almost a beast'. But Spinoza seems to mean something stronger than this when he writes: 'inhumanum tamen esse, & paene brutum'. – GM.]
[79] *TTP* IV, 21 and 41; CWS II, 130 and 135–6.
[80] *TTP* XI, 21 and XIV, 14; CWS II, 247 and 266.
[81] *Ethics* III, 32 Schol.; CWS I, 513.

relation to memory as the adult. Before getting to that, let us simply under-line how the problem of the 'free multitude', in Spinoza's work, exceeds the framework of the Mosaic solution (namely, legislating down to the smallest details of existence). A reader at the end of the twentieth century cannot encounter this solution without shuddering, but Spinoza did not need to accept it either. On the one hand, the age of the prophets is over: 'God, however, has revealed through his Apostles that his covenant is no longer written with ink, or on stone tablets, but written on the heart, by the spirit of God.'[82] What does the Christian rupture mean, in political terms? That the problem is henceforth that of democracy.[83] On the other hand, Spinoza sees fit to specify that the Mosaic model is at antipodes with Dutch aspirations: 'such a form of state could be useful, perhaps, only for those who are willing to live by themselves, alone, without any foreign trade, shutting themselves up within their own boundaries, and segregating themselves from the rest of the world. It couldn't be at all useful for those to whom it's necessary to have dealings with others . . .'.[84] But why make this clarification, if not because the Dutch, like the Hebrews, were a new, child, people, for whom conse-quently there arose the problem of affirming its liberty, of learning to be free? Simon Schama remarks that no theme preoccupied Spinoza's compatriots more than the dialectical relation between play and instruction, between freedom and obedience:

> And because that theme was rooted in adult concerns, it meant that the trials of growing up Dutch were perhaps more acute than those of grow-ing up anywhere else. For it meant, in effect, that the adulthood (not to mention the Republic) into which one grew turned out to be exercised by the same quandaries as those alleged to be particular to childhood. To be Dutch at all, at least in the seventeenth century, was to be imprisoned

[82] *TTP* XVIII, 2; CWS II, 322.

[83] As Matheron writes: 'No more divinised sovereigns, no more legislating God, no more institutional taboos, no more privileged value accorded to a singular community: the State, laicised, demystified, given its true nature as an instrument conceived by human beings and for human beings, could be organised and reorganised freely. But what became sacred was the community in general: together you can make and remake the laws as you please, Christ essentially said, but each of you, personally, must then respect them with all your heart; and since they are only ever imperfect means, carry them out without contradicting them by going as far as you can in the direction they point: strive, in the sphere of your existence where their authority fails, to make reign in everyday life the greatest possible harmony among human beings' (Matheron 1971: 68–9).

[84] *TTP* XVIII, 2; CWS II, 322–3.

in a state of becoming: a sort of perpetual political adolescence. . . . If their children were more cherished than in any other previous European culture, the regard was born of a certain obsessive self-regard in which they saw themselves in the guise of children attempting to make their way.[85]

The Autonomisation of the Body

We initially made some progress in answering the question concerning the conditions of the problem: the rupture implied by development is not the inverse of a privation. There remains the problem as such: why must there have been a rupture? Spinoza no doubt encountered a difficulty in this, and the solutions that it was possible to envision were highly conjectural. We see two possibilities here: formation and autonomisation.

Given the preceding analysis, let us try to unpack an analogy suggested by Spinoza numerous times. He compares States to individuals, the Hebrews having left Egypt to a childish people, and it has even sometimes been said that he invites us to proceed in the opposite direction, deciphering politics in the history of an individual. That was the case, clearly, in the scholium to IV, 39; and we might ask ourselves whether the whole analysis of the becoming of the Hebrews after the flight from Egypt does not furnish us, inversely, with an at least plausible key to the *mutatio* of the infantile body in the scholium to V, 39. Here are the elements of the analogy.

A *spatium vitae* is created by a certain union of bodies destined for a common fate. The intrauterine life of the foetus is that of a body living under a law that is other than its own, in a state of total dependence, but which affirms itself more and more like a State within a State. The moment comes when its growth compromises the integrity of its relation of rest and movement within that of the whole, and in which the divergence becomes threatening for the part as well as for the whole: it leaves. And like the Jews freed of the Egyptian yoke, it is now *born*: certainly free, since it is no longer submitted to a foreign law, but still only knowing how to live in a state of dependence, and still incapable of affirming its own law. It is only in this sense that Spinoza could have once said, in the *Short Treatise*, at the risk of falling into the chimera of the *fœtus adultus*, that the child's coming into the world counts as a transformation.[86] Once again, Lucretius:

[85] Schama 1988: 495 and 515.
[86] KV II, Praef. n. 10; CWS I, 95.

Consider too how a baby, like a shipwrecked sailor tossed ashore by the savage waves, lies on the ground naked, speechless, and utterly helpless, as soon as nature has cast it forth with pangs of labor from its mother's womb into the shores of light; and how it fills the place with its woeful wailings – as is only reasonable for one destined to traverse so many evils in life.[87]

Let us continue: the parts are constantly being renewed, integrated within the whole according to a hierarchy of complex levels (for the political body: individuals, families, tribes, villages . . .), and can change their relation without for all that coming apart, as certain functions are maintained (the conservation of language, as in the scholium to IV, 39, being analogous to the circulation of the blood). The *generation* of the community, properly speaking, is nothing other than 'continual regeneration': this is the nutrition of the political body, an incessant succession of generations. Is not a generation the nutrition of a people? But the body must not just be maintained in life, it must grow, be fortified, and welcome in as many foreign bodies as possible, provided that it knows how to integrate them: 'ways of increasing the number of citizens more easily must be thought up, so that a large body of men is brought together'.[88] What's more, it comes to pass that in the wake of a crisis or a particularly grave illness, the body whether political or individual is submitted to a change in form.[89]

---

[87] *On the Nature of Things* V, 222–7 (Lucretius 2001: 143). We have modified the translation to emphasise the word *transire*, rendered as 'traverse', which Spinoza uses in the scholium to V, 39 on the subject of the becoming uncertain of the child. One will here also recall, anachronism aside, Kant's formidable commentary on this passage by Lucretius, which intersects with the complex problematic of childhood in the *Theologico-Political Treatise*, a servile condition but one that has the prospect of freedom: 'Even the child who has just wrenched itself from the mother's womb seems to enter the world with loud cries, unlike all other animals, simply because it regards the inability to make use of its limbs as *constraint*, and thus it immediately announces its claim to freedom . . .' (Kant 2006: 168). [Translation modified: as Zourabichvili says, he amends the French translation of *De Rerum Natura* that he cites to emphasise the *traverser* in the final sentence, and I modify the quoted English translation in the same way. – GM.]

[88] *TP* VI, 32; *CWS* II, 541. The cause of the decline of democracies into aristocracies comes from the refusal to naturalise foreigners. The increase of the parts is ensured at the level of individuals, but their renewal is hindered at the level of families: the latter are extinguished one by one, and the survivors constitute an oligarchy divided into factions that will make the aristocratic regime degenerate into a monarchy (*TP* VIII, 12).

[89] For a comparison of the relevant passages, see the Introduction, above.

But here is the important thing: the development, we said, is not only a growth but a rupture; it is necessary that the body of childhood must endure a *mutatio*, which however is not a transformation.

From there we get a first hypothesis, which has two aspects: 1. Perhaps the foetal and childish forms are partially chimerical, to the extent that the first involves the form of the mother, and the second because at first it still involves the mother from which the child can hardly be separated, and afterward it involves the parents or adults that care for it, although in these two latter cases the involvement is of a lesser degree, as they no longer seem to furnish the very *element* of its existence, in the sense of the *Short Treatise*. For the child like the infant does not know how to take care of itself: they are useless to themselves, like the slave dependent on its master, the obsessive hung up on pleasure, the suicide hung up on the gallows[90] – all of which are paradoxical Spinozist figures of those who 'do not belong to themselves'. This is the ultimate meaning of *conamur*: not to strive with others, as when a community is formed, but to be able to affirm oneself only by belonging to another. 2. Under these conditions the infant must find its viable form, like the child-people must find a political form that will not lead it back to the state of nature from which it rightly intends to extract itself. And who can fail to see that the assembly is an individual at rest, exactly as described in the first half of the definition of the *Ethics*? The parts of the people draw themselves together as *assembled* and as literally *convened* [convenantes],[91] but each immediately returns to their own activities, and all their movements must conserve among themselves a proportion that corresponds to the initial *convention*. Whence the necessity of passing from the form at rest to the form in movement, a transition that constitutes the veritable establishment of a political form.

The whole of childhood is here taken as a *formation*, a process during which the form is affirmed by being sought after, where the growing parts seek their best arrangement. The child, and still more the infant, is caught between life and death, like the assembly called constituent rests on the border of the state of nature insofar as the relations at the heart of the political body are not yet regulated – a fragile, poorly assured composition, which

---

[90] *Ep.* XXIII [to Blijenbergh]; CWS I, 390. – Twice Spinoza says that not to belong to oneself is to be dependent or hung up on the words of another (*TTP* V, *penderet*; XX, *pendeat*), notably concerning the infant Hebrew people entirely dependent on Moses. [In the above sentence and here in the footnote, 'dependent on' and 'hung up on' render the same phrase, 'suspendu à', which has both of these senses in French. – GM.]

[91] The Hebrews were supposedly capable of a *pacte* (*TTP* XVII), and the capacity to enter into a pact presupposes a reciprocal promise, or convention.

has not yet found its viable relation, which is different for each individual as for each people. Must we interpret the rupture in the body as the correlate of the advent of reason in the mind? That would be true for Thomas Aquinas, who makes the age of reason correspond with puberty. Spinoza's text instead allows us to glimpse two ruptures with uneven repercussions: 1. from *infans* to *puer* (learning to walk and talk), perhaps accompanied by amnesia; 2. the crisis of adolescence, where the body is developed enough that reason can now be cultivated, but where the individual also finds itself exposed to the passions properly speaking, money, sex, power – the problem now being that of an *active* forgetting. But all of this will need to be confirmed by a more careful study of the Spinozist doctrine of memory.

This hypothesis is however unacceptable, for an obvious reason, however well its elements seem to fit together: it leads us back to the Thomist schema of actualisation, and thus of childhood as privation. An alternative hypothesis must therefore be advanced: this will retain certain analogical features of the first (the whole-part relation), but while trying to explain the rupture without recourse to the idea of privation; it is based on the alternative of dependence and independence, of the part's belonging to the whole and its secession, and its self-determination as a whole. It would imply abandoning the strict recognition of one and the same concept of form in physiology and politics: the form – a certain relation of rest and movement between parts – is already present in the foetus, and the rupture consists in that the parts of the body, habituated to having no constant relations between them other than under the law of another constant relation, one of a superior order that integrates them, must learn to affirm their own relation for itself, and no longer solely under the 'ambient pressures' that account for the formation of the body and its conservation insofar as it is integrated within that ambience, pressures that now prove to be hostile: the ambience has become foreign; the element has become external. The body no longer forms an individual with its environment; nutrients must be found outside, drawn from a diversity that is sometimes suitable, sometimes not. For, as we mentioned in the Introduction, the scholium to V, 39 is clarified on this point by the scholium to II, 13 (itself united with definition 7 of that Part), which invokes the 'concurrence' from which the developing body frees itself, taking leave of a larger individuality of which it was only a part in order to affirm its own individuality.

This schema, which we will call *autonomisation*, and which alone appears to us capable of resolving the problem, throws into relief the passage from *conamur* to *conor*, as the key to the change suffered by the body: the development of motor, linguistic, and rational capacities consists not in the parts of the body entering into new dynamic relations (which might seem to be a defensible option, since the passage from crawling to walking, if we stick with superficial considerations, makes the hands available and completely reorganises the perceptive field), but in that the individual becomes capable of conserving itself. The development of capacities implies a rupture, because it happens through a reappropriation of *conatus*. It is this, no doubt, that is marked in the change of figure or apparent proportions of the body: the members are not just larger but blossoming and as it were revitalised; the corresponding attitudes, skilful and assured. It is this change that the painters discovered, and which is thus not a mere illusion. In no case, however, can we confuse it with a change in proportion and rest among the parts, which would affect the body in its individual identity.

The problem of memory will only become more complex.

5

Childhood and Memory

More forcefully than any other philosopher, Spinoza affirms the rupture, now understood to be mental, that separates us from childhood. Starting with the annotations to the *Short Treatise*, and then in the scholium to IV, 39 of the *Ethics*, it seems that, if the mind is the idea of the body, there can be no transformation of the body without a transformation of the mind, which manifests as amnesia. Consequently, if the doctrine is to be coherent, the psychology of memory, such as it is laid out in the *De natura corporum* of Part II of the *Ethics*, must allow for at least certain hypotheses concerning the nature of this amnesia, especially when it comes to the question of whether it is total (effacement of memorial traces) or subjective (the images remain, but it is as if they were not experienced).[1] But at the same time, Spinoza seems to indicate a different direction: namely, that amnesia must be also thought in the absence of transformation, if at least it is legitimate to apply it to childhood.

And everything invites us to go in this direction: it would take some bad faith to refuse the rapprochement of the two scholia to propositions 39. That of Part IV underscores the abyss that separates infancy from the age of adulthood; that of Part V invokes the change of the body of childhood into another, more capable body. It is remarkable, in the first, that from this abyss there follows for any 'human of advanced years' a sort of *fluctuatio imaginationis* between two beliefs: a belief in a difference in nature between the infant and oneself, which implies a transformation, and a belief in one's having been an infant at some point. Spinoza does not explicitly articulate the thesis of amnesia, but the latter is the link that justifies the passage from the anecdote of the metamorphosised human being to the question of the relation that we maintain with our own childhood. Furthermore, the

---

[1] We carried out this enquiry in Zourabichvili 2002, chapter 4.

relation in question falls under the 'vague experience' defined in the *Treatise on the Emendation of the Intellect*: an analogical inference drawn from the observation of those resembling me. I know that I was at one point an infant, like I know that I will one day die: the conviction is of the same order in both cases, foreign to memory. This is to say, at least, that memory, supposing that it remains, is incapable of vanquishing my tendency to believe in an insurmountable gap between the infant and myself. Was Spinoza aware that this idea of an external relation to one's own childhood is already found in Saint Augustine?

> I am loath to dwell on this part of my life of which, O Lord, I have no remembrance, about which I must trust the word of others and what I can surmise from observing other infants, even if such guesses are trustworthy. For it lies in the deep murk of my forgetfulness and is thus like the period which I passed in my mother's womb.[2]

How can we account for this forgetting and this foreignness? We will try to gather together all the elements available to us concerning the becoming of memory.

The Amnesiac Regime of the Fascinated *Infans*[3]

As memory is a 'connection of ideas' that 'is in the Mind according to the order and connection of the affections of the human Body',[4] it is not given at birth, but is constituted in the course of experience. Its formation is thus a process typical of childhood, and it is scarcely plausible that the context surrounding its logical description is down to chance:

> Let us suppose, then, a child, who saw Peter *for the first time* yesterday, in the morning, but saw Paul at noon, and Simon in the evening, and today again saw Peter in the morning. It is clear from P18 that as soon as he sees the morning light, he will immediately imagine the sun taking the same course through the sky as he saw on the preceding day, *or* he will imagine

---

[2] *Confessions* I, 7 (Augustine 2006: 38).

[3] [As you will see below, when Zourabichvili speaks of 'fascination' (*fascination*) or of the child's being 'fascinated' (*fasciné*) he does so as a translation of Spinoza's 'admiratio', which Curley renders as 'wonder' (*Ethics* III, DA IV and Exp.; CWS I, 532). – GM.]

[4] *Ethics* II, 18 Schol.; CWS I, 465.

the whole day, and Peter together with the morning, Paul with noon, and Simon with the evening . . .[5]

Spinoza takes the example of a child because he needs, in order to lay bare the mechanism, to posit a naive subject that *encounters* things, that is, who sees them 'for the first time'.[6] The child is required as the being par excellence for which there is something new. The passage describes a double associative circuit: the course of the sun during the day, in other words a succession, and the one-by-one association of each moment of the journey with one person in particular.

Now if it is inherent to memory that it is a connection [*enchaînement*] and not merely an inscription, if the recollection of the memory is associative, an object that would leave an isolated trace on the brain would have no chance of coming back up in the mind. The idea would be certainly given, but impossible to reactivate. One will object that this case is scarcely plausible, since no object in the world is ever given by itself. But it is precisely the case, with the exception of the passage that we have just cited, that Spinoza only gives examples of isolated childlike perceptions. Take the waking dream of the winged horse:[7] not only is there no perception of present things that could come to trouble the imagination of the monster whose intensity is consequently hallucinatory (we can suppose the child in the night, or entirely gripped by its vision and paying no attention to its environment), but the imagination is here presented as a curious product of memory. The *composition* of the two images is not the result of an association, but corresponds to a spontaneous movement of the body[8] or even to a desire.[9] The

---

[5] *Ethics* II, 44 Schol.; CWS I, 480–1. Our emphasis.

[6] Pierre Macherey is right to affirm that the child, in Spinoza, plays the role of an 'experimental model', which makes it possible to see an affective mechanism 'functioning in its bare state' and to draw from this 'the simplified sketch of the majority of our behaviours' (Macherey, *Introduction* III, 257–8). He says this concerning the scholium to III, 32, which we will comment on below, but the remark seems to us also to apply – if not even more clearly – to this scholium, where the reason for making recourse to the persona of the infant is crystal clear. Laurent Bove, in the same spirit, explains that 'it is the hidden child that continues to live in the passions of the adult', the child being the 'epistemological model' of the common behaviour of human beings (*vulgus*) (Bove 1996: 106). These remarks are tied to what we have thought it necessary to identify as the *pueritia* of the adult – the characteristic behaviour, not of the child properly speaking, in becoming, but of that forever frozen child that is the ordinary adult.

[7] *Ethics* II, 49 Schol.; CWS I, 485–6.

[8] *Ep.* XVII [to Balling]; CWS I, 352–4

[9] *Ep.* LII [to Boxel].; CWS II, 408–9.

images are aroused outside of any associative process, and if we do not know 'what the Body can do',[10] we suspect that among other things there is a power to reawaken isolated traces whose ideas, simultaneously, are presented in the mind in monstrous combinations, so that certain physical states like sleepiness or fever are favourable for the non-associative mobilisation of certain memories, and perhaps for the reactivation of unrelated memories that are normally inaccessible in waking life. It is certainly reasonable to believe that the child already capable of imagining a winged horse also ties in its memory the idea of the horse to the context of the street, or the carriage, etc., without which it could not have formed it; the same goes for the idea of the wing. However, these connections have no hold on the child: the unique and monstrous image has filled its mind. Spinoza names this phenomena *admiratio* (fascination). It is a matter of a 'singular imagination' that 'has no connection with the others', and to which for this reason 'the mind remains attached': fascination is thus produced each time a new sensation, *which does not recall anything*, is presented.[11]

Let us take up the case of the winged horse, and turn our attention to this astonishing passage:

> But to show that in our view this inclination [desire] is not free, and to make quite vivid what it is to pass over and be drawn from one thing to the other, we shall imagine a child who comes to perceive a certain thing *for the first time*. For example, I hold before him a little bell which makes a pleasant sound in his ears, by which he acquires an appetite for it. Let us see now whether he could omit having this appetite or Desire? . . . What, then, might it finally be that could lead him away from this appetite? Nothing else except that by the order and course of Nature he is affected by something that is more pleasant to him than the first thing.[12]

What is at stake is no doubt a fiction, a thought experiment: the child's first perception. The reader might for a moment think that what is at stake is the first perception of a bell, but Spinoza specifies a few lines later that 'this is all he knows'.[13] In one sense, this hardly matters: the fascination of the bell will be succeeded by another fascination, for an equally new object, and which in its turn will count as a first perception. The infant ignorant of all

---

[10] *Ethics* III, 2 schol; CWS I, 495.
[11] *Ethics* III, DA IV and Exp.; CWS I, 532.
[12] *KV* II, 17, 4; CWS I, 127. Our emphasis.
[13] *KV* II, 17, 4; CWS I, 127.

things will go from fascination to fascination, the mind each time gripped by isolated singularities. No doubt the affections leave traces in the brain,[14] but without any connection, so that the infant has no memory. It is doubtless necessary that the mind is habituated to objects in order to be capable of considering them together and, consequently, associating them: if the child of the scholium to II, 44 saw the sun for the first time, it would pay no attention to Peter, to Simon, etc. And if it saw a man for the first time, it would pay no attention to the sun.

Does the digression on memory in the *Treatise on the Emendation of the Intellect* confirm this analysis? Apparently not: 'the more singular a thing is, the more easily it may be retained'.[15] But what does Spinoza mean? He invokes a phenomenon of confusion: if you have only ever read one comedy telling a love story, you will retain a more distinct memory of it than if you have read a large number of them, which you will tend to mix up. But above all, he invokes the criteria of the 'intelligible', or of sense: 'If I give someone a large number of disconnected words, he will retain them with much more difficulty than if I give him the same words in the form of a story.'[16] In a certain way, memory here presupposes itself: not only because it is the condition for language, but because it consists in a link. The story is a connection: its memorisation is easier, because its different parts are presented in it as associated with one another, according to a dramatic progression. But the perceptive experience of the infant is very close to the situation of this person who is given 'a large number of disconnected words': they possess no means of memorising them.

Let us thus posit that the mental activity of the infant is without memory: it follows from this that infantile amnesia, the absence of memory of our early years, is explained less by some hypothetical transformation than by the fact that memory only begins to form at a later stage. The infant is incapable of tying down its ideas of affections, it retains them in isolation, and they can only re-emerge thanks to some spontaneous, even pathological, corporeal movement. Our earliest experiences were not forgotten; they were never fixed in the first place, or rather they were the object of a retention without memory.[17]

---

[14] Although Spinoza, in the *Ethics*, seems to hesitate between it needing to be the case that an affection is produced 'frequently' in order to leave a trace (*Ethics* II, Post. 5 after 13; CWS I, 462), and the mere condition that it is produced 'once' (*Ethics* II, 17 cor.; CWS I, 464).

[15] *TdIE* 83; CWS I, 36.

[16] *TdIE* 81; CWS I, 36.

[17] Descartes already developed a very interesting doctrine of unconscious fixation, but he

But that was only a first period. There then came the automatic formation of memory, which certainly did not put an end to the state of quasi-
unconsciousness of oneself that characterises infancy for Spinoza.[18] Let us
pause on this state of unconsciousness of oneself: it seems to us that it brings
us to three characteristics of childhood.

1. A discontinuous regime of perceptions, which the acquisition of
memory only complicates. The mind of the child is monopolised by present
perception, which the variable play of external solicitations and involuntary
associations ceaselessly replaces one for another. In this way it takes place
without any accounting for the change of subject, the new idea completely
effacing the old. As Fénelon observed: 'The child puts a question to you, and
before you answer, her eyes wander to the ceiling, she counts all the figures
on the paper, or the panes of glass in the windows; if you wish to recall her
to her first object, you constrain her as really as if you confined her in a
prison.'[19]

2. The child, up to a certain age, is incapable of vague experience, it draws
no lessons from experience: so too it is 'useless to itself', unaware of danger,
as is commonly said. No form of education seems to have any hold on it:
explanation is all in vain, and threats carry no weight. The fundamental
motive of dissuasive education is the principle of choosing the lesser of two
evils – a 'universal law of human nature'[20] and a direct expression of *conatus*
– by virtue of which an individual is capable of renouncing something. But
the child, at least up to a certain age, is not yet governed by this principle:[21]
its present impression demands everything of it; it suffers when punished,
but is unable to identify punishment as such (for that would imply a causal
link), and has no fear of it. Whence Spinoza's confusion, as he sometimes
compares children with madmen and suicides.[22]

explained it on the basis of the necessity, in order to form a memory, of attaching each
perception of a new object to a conception, and through the child's inability in this
regard. That is why, he said, we retain in ourselves the vestiges of confused sensations
from our intrauterine life, which affect us but which we do not identify as memories.
See Descartes' letters of 4 June 1648 to Arnauld (CSM III, 354–6; AT V, 192) and
29 June 1648, again to Arnauld (CSM III, 356–9; AT V, 219).
[18] *Ethics* V, 6 Schol. (CWS I, 600); V, 39, Schol. (CWS I, 614)
[19] Fénelon 1831: 38–9.
[20] *TTP* XVI, 15; CWS II, 285.
[21] The infants that the childish Hebrews resembled must be supposed to be older than
this.
[22] *Ethics* II, 49 Schol.; CWS I, 490.

3. Finally, the child is unconscious of its states of passion and incapable of mastering them, whether this is a matter of its compulsion to speak or an excitation that renders it intransigent.

Of these three points, the first only concerns the infant, the second concerns the young child and some adults (for example, criminals in whom the prospect of execution arouses no fear), and the third is the model of everyday human conduct, which is why *infans* and *puer* begin the list of the great somnambulists, as much in Letter 58 to Schuller as in the scholium to III, 2 of the *Ethics*.

In What Sense Is the Body of the Child, 'as it were, in a state of equilibrium'?

The third point warrants our slowing down, for it refers to an important passage that has never been given a very clear interpretation. Spinoza had just developed his doctrine of the 'imitation of the affects' when he writes:

> Finally, if we wish to consult experience, we shall find that it teaches us all these things, especially if we attend to the first years of our lives. For we find from experience that children, because their bodies are continually, as it were, in a state of equilibrium (*continuo veluti in aequilibrio*), laugh or cry simply because they see others laugh or cry. Moreover, whatever they see others do, they immediately desire to imitate it. And finally, they desire for themselves all those things by which they imagine others are pleased.[23]

Spinoza here invokes experience, not memory,[24] in order to describe a totally extroverted behaviour: children, at least very young ones, do not yet have

---

[23] *Ethics* III, 32 Schol.; CWS I, 513. [N.B. Spinoza's Latin: 'Nam pueros, quia eorum corpus continuo veluti in aequilibrio est . . .'. This should not be confused with the 'body of childhood' (*corpus infantiae*) of V, 39 Schol. – GM.]

[24] Contrary to what Macherey thinks: 'In this passage of the *Ethics*, Spinoza seems to fleetingly remember the child that he himself had been' (Macherey, *Introduction* III, 257 n. 2). Spinoza, as we have seen, conceives only an external relation to childhood, by means of the observation of others. He calls this 'vague experience', and indeed it is the word 'experience' that is used here. Let us note that in the last years of his life Spinoza was a tenant of the Van der Spycks, who had four children, and that Dutch children were very visible in general, allowed to play in public places and the forecourts of churches, to the great surprise of visiting foreigners (Zumthor 1960: 119; Schama 1988: 509). Colerus affirms that Spinoza talked with the Van der Spyck children, 'teaching them how they needed to be obedient and submissive to their parents' (Colerus 1954: 1520). We must receive this testimony with circumspection, on the

differentiated characters, they are not intrepid, or rather daring, or rather timid, according to the terms that human beings customarily use when they want to compare themselves with one another[25] (and which nothing stops them from regularly and unfairly applying to infants). If human beings are to a certain extent justified in doing so, it is because they actually differ from one another by their *ingenium*, their proper complexion, temperament, character, nature.[26] *Ingenium* is the product of a certain 'temperament of the body' and a sedimentation of experience in the body and the mind. In this sense, Spinoza can speak of the *ingenium* of an adolescent like Casearius,[27] which would have been imprudent in relation to the Van der Spyck children: no doubt very young children can let us glimpse the first hints of an *ingenium*, since, past the first age of pure fascination, they begin to experience; but we can also suppose that the whole of childhood is necessary to create this sort of fate, and that certain traumas are capable of abruptly inflecting it. Whatever the case, the 'equilibrium' invoked clearly signifies that childish affectivity is still deprived of *habitus*, so that the mind oscillates between sadness and joy without ever stably dwelling in or recognising one or the other. There is no childish melancholy, and this is the reason for a singular difference at the heart of impotence, between the child in becoming and the suicide who is always wallowing. In the same way, the child has no obsessional desire: its desire is variable, subject to the law of external determination or somnambulist automatism. The reverse is obvious enough, as Pierre Macherey underscores: namely, the extreme facility with which external influences mould their memory, which does not oppose this with any preestablished configuration.[28] Equilibrium in a way dooms itself, in almost no time at all.

The choice of the word 'equilibrium', with its positive connotations, might be surprising, and we must thus assure ourselves of its meaning. If childhood is a fundamentally morbid age, midway between the cadaver and the *mens sana in corpore sano* (together health and freedom), on the other hand since antiquity equilibrium has been the criteria of health par excellence. This legacy persists in Spinoza, in his demand that equal concern be

one hand by placing it back into its proper educational context (Colerus condemns the doctrine but insists on Spinoza's irreproachable virtue), on the other hand by relating it to the complex problematic of the parent-child relationships that we will analyse further along.

[25] *Ethics* III, 51 Schol.; CWS I, 522.
[26] On the notion of *ingenium*, see Moreau 1994: 395–404.
[27] *Ep.* IX [to de Vries]; CWS I, 193–4.
[28] Macherey, *Introduction* III, 258.

taken for all the parts of the body. This is what justifies Laurent Bove's original and stimulating interpretation, in a section entitled 'The Joyful Passion
of the Infant':[29] from the scarcely demanding desires of the child at a young
age, and the ease of satisfying them, he concludes that they are frequently
in a state of *hilaritas*, or 'cheerfulness', which is extremely rare or difficult to
obtain in adulthood. Recall that cheerfulness, in Spinoza, is the exact opposite of melancholy: a joy affecting all the parts of the body equally.[30] Bove
thus brings the quasi-equilibrium of the body of the child together with the
cheery equality of the satisfied infant. If this state is so difficult to attain in
adulthood, it is because it depends entirely on external causes, and as the
capacities of the body have by that point become very diverse, each having
its own needs, its conditions seem difficult to satisfy. By contrast, one can
imagine that the infant, in light of the state of dependence for what is useful
in which it finds itself (distinct – as we have said – from that of slavery),
and its unstable degree of power, to which there corresponds very simple
needs, does attain this form of passive joy. Once we recall how the figure
of the child plays the role of an epistemological model in the description of
the passional conduct of adults, we get the following overall judgment: 'In
Spinoza, however, there is also a positive perception of childhood included
in his ethical perspective.'[31]

We have no choice but to accept this claim, but for reasons other than
Bove's, about which we would express four reservations: 1. The problem of
the *hilaritas* of the adult refers, it seems to us, to that of *libido* and of sexual
pleasure described in terms of an illusory 'rest';[32] and if Spinoza condemns
the latter, it is because it completely separates the individual from what is
supposed to be its primary adult desire, intellectual *felicitas*; he substitutes for
this a list of successive concerns, in which sexuality stands out in its absence,
so that the implausible *hilaritas* can and must be replaced by a deft combination of local and varied *titillationes*, an alternating and periodic looking
after all the parts of the body.[33] 2. Bove writes that there is in the infant 'a
contentment or a fulfilment proper to its nature, that is, its singular relation
of movement and rest, the condition of its satisfaction';[34] we have stated
above the reasons for our opposition to an essentialisation of the body of the

[29] Bove 1996: 108–12.
[30] *Ethics* III, 11 Schol.; CWS I, 500–1.
[31] Bove 1996: 106.
[32] *TdIE*, 1; CWS I, 7. See the first study, above.
[33] *Ethics* IV, 45 Schol.; CWS I, 572.
[34] Bove 1996: 111.

child, which the author moreover ties to a perhaps slightly hasty essential-isation of *ingenia*, so that, on his account, such-and-such a relation of rest and movement prevents *hilaritas*, while such-and-such other one devotes the individual to a sort of joyous disequilibrium (*titillatio*).[35] 3. Consequently, he interprets the continual equilibrium of the body (leaving aside the *veluti* that nuances the expression) as already somehow participating in the 'joy of beat-itude'[36] laid out in Part V of the *Ethics*, which seems incompatible with the conditions Spinoza specifies on this subject: that the body of childhood is changed into another, more capable one, and that the understanding comes to occupy the greater part of the mind.[37] 4. Finally, if the hypothesis of a certain capacity of the infant for *hilaritas* seems plausible, it does not appear possible to infer it from the remark on the continual quasi-equilibrium of the body, which concerns the *puer*, supposedly capable of desires and affects that are already very diverse.

These objections lead to two remarks, the one concerning the sense of the word 'equilibrium', the other concerning the relationship between child-hood and beatitude. First of all, equilibrium can no doubt be understood in the medical sense of the term, in terms of the traditional doctrine of the humours, but only in relation to the relative states of disequilibrium that differentiate temperaments (bilious, choleric, phlegmatic, sanguine). This brings us back to the idea that the child does not yet have an *ingenium*.[38] On the other hand, it cannot here be opposed to morbid disequilibrium, since childhood is itself that morbid state in which the conservation of the rela-

---

[35] No doubt this will call to mind the opposition of the cheerful prophet and the sad one: see *TTP* II, 13; *CWS* II, 97.

[36] Bove 1996: 112.

[37] *Ethics* V, 39 Schol.; *CWS* I, 614.

[38] Pierre-François Moreau emphasises the slide from the traditional medical theory to the new conception of biological individuality when he brings together the Spinozist conception of *ingenium* with the *ingenio* in Huarte: 'In the latter, the notion of *ingenio* is used to explain why, although all souls are equal, individuals and nations have such different capacities, as much for knowledge as well as for practical activities. The diversity of *ingenios* was anchored, in turn, in that of the dispositions of the body – that is to say, the irreducible ways in which Nature had, for each singular individual, applied its laws. That which, in Huarte, referred to the mixture of the four humours supposes in Spinoza an equation in terms of rest and movement. But, in both cases, it is indeed a matter of developing a concept for figuring out the diversity of individuals, and for thinking the latter in relation to their corporeal determination' (Moreau 1994: 397–8). The expression *temperamentum corporis*, in chapter II of the *Theologico-Political Treatise*, marks the transition between the humoral conception and the mechanistic conception.

tion of rest and movement is never assured (for example, Dutch infants not only benefited from the protection and repletion provided for them by their mothers; they were also exposed, no matter the measures taken, to the miasmas of a particularly vicious atmosphere). Second of all, if it is clear that the quasi-equilibrium *of the body*, in a passage dedicated to mental oscillation, refers to a purely external determination of the mind, it seems important to insist here on the difference between the child and the adult: the former does not have a morbid passion that constitutes an overwhelming obstacle to the development of its intellectual faculties. From these two points of view, the child is not in danger of Medea's dilemma according to Ovid, that of seeing the better and approving it but doing the worse: on the one hand, the infant has not yet acquired the minimal rational structure of choosing the lesser evil, and it is moreover not yet capable of comparing two things; on the other hand, not yet being torn by violent passions lastingly inscribed within it, it does not resist diversion (we will return to this). The ideal would at bottom be to grow up like Christ, going straightaway to wisdom, from childish equilibrium to activity, without the detour through the passions: a successful education, which would make ethics a waste of time. Or rather ethics, the education to a life governed by reason,[39] would no longer be separable from education in the current sense of the term; for, as the scholium to V, 39 underscores, leaving behind the body of childhood and the mind that corresponds to it is the business of life in general.[40]

A first childhood without memory, a second childhood in which memory is formed: there remains a third state of memory, that of the adult in the true sense of the term, as it is described in Part V of the *Ethics*: only childish human beings cultivate memory and live in regret; to become free and active, in a word to become adult, is to change the body of childhood into another much more capable one that corresponds to a mind in which 'whatever is related to its memory or imagination is of hardly any moment in relation to the intellect'.[41] Here again, if it is true that he can serve as

---

[39] *Ethics* IV, App. Cap. IX; CWS I, 589.

[40] Perhaps Spinoza's reflection is itself in fact animated by the image of the childhood of Christ. The evangelist Luke speaks of the growth of Christ in terms very close to those of the scholium to V, 39, since they appear connected with intellectual development: 'The child grew and became strong, filled with wisdom' (Luke 2:40 [NRSV, 1833]); 'And Jesus increased in wisdom and in years' (Luke 2:52 [NRSV, 1834]). The story of Jesus' running away to talk with the theologians at the Temple cannot but invoke Spinoza's analogous precocity, at least if the beginning of Lucas's *Life of Spinoza* is to be believed (Lucas 1954: 1541–2).

[41] *Ethics* V, 39 Schol.; CWS I, 614.

a model, Christ is the memoryless, the splendid Amnesiac: he knew things by the third kind of knowledge, intuitively.[42] At least, he approached that state of complete a-mnesia (not forgetting, but absence of memory) – for to make of him a perfect man, a first man, an adult fully formed, would be to fall back into the chimera of the *infans adultus*, precisely, that is, to make of Christ the incarnation of God (all the Gospels, except for that of Luke, pass without transition from the newborn to the adult ready for baptism). And since the body brings with it a memory occupying at least a minimal part of mental activity, that would be at the same time to disincarnate him.

To make memory no longer occupy any more than a negligible part of the mind does not mean forgetting: a radical amnesia in fact supposes a transformation, a change of form or individual essence. And yet it is indeed a matter of a form of forgetting, but one that proceeds otherwise – by reorganisation. Becoming-adult means going to work on one's own memory in order to remodel its connections as much as possible, so that the conserved sensations are connected or reactivated, according to an order 'for' the understanding.[43] If it is true that memory consists not in the retention of simple ideal unities, but in the associative mechanism that makes them so many *stimuli* for one another, then there is indeed a dimension of forgetting in the ethical enterprise. Amnesiac, the human being who is free, reasonable, active, and adult tends to be so twice over: first in that it forges a new memory which is no longer that of its childhood, and then as a 'spiritual automaton', the mind that connects its ideas *sub specie aeternitatis*, gaining access to the synopsis that produces the demonstration as if beyond all memory.

And no doubt one must distinguish two, even three kinds of adult: 1. A very rare species, that of the sages who leave behind their child's memory and forge a rational memory and imagination, transmuting their passions into actions. 2. A common species, that of the pious or civil ignorant ones, who allow religion and the State to orient their memory in the direction of obedience, also conforming to reason to the extent that in this way they can, if not actively transmute, then at least passively surmount their passions. 3. A relatively rare species, that of the ignorant who resist all education, incapable even of obeying, who cling to their child's memory, and for whom there exists hardly anything other than torment.

Three stages, then, in the becoming-adult of the child, three ways too of being adult. If we stick to the path described by the scholium to V, 39: first, the infant has no memory and the individual, in its later years, consequently

---

[42] *TTP* IV, 32; CWS II, 133.
[43] *Ethics* V, 10; CWS I, 601.

retains no memory of this precocious period; then the child passively suffers the formation of a memory, according to encounters and education; finally, reaching the limit of its physical maturation, it can pursue its development by actively reforming its memory, which implies a second rupture with childhood.

We can foresee that two questions will arise here, which perhaps only amount to one and the same: one concerning adolescence, that is, of that age where the understanding emerges, in a perhaps inevitably conflictual relation with the memory forged during childhood; and one concerning education, or of the possibility of avoiding as much as possible the everyday passional drifts of the intermediary period, by going if possible continuously from the first memory to the second one.

Adolescence: Age of Reason, or Final Avatar of the *Infans Adultus*?

If one is to believe Lucas, Spinoza's critical reflection on Scripture (and thus on the very content of the education he received), which would lead to the *Theologico-Political Treatise*, began very early in his life: during the years of his adolescence; in other words – those of the scholium to V, 39 – during the critical years when the process of the mutation of the body of childhood is carried out, and during which there emerges a mind capable of knowledge. We can indeed call these years critical in advance, since the majority of minds that are ripened in this way, unlike that of the young Baruch, allow themselves to be absorbed forever in the waking dream of memory, as if the juvenile discovery of the power of reason had come to a sudden end. This makes it all the more important to study the remarks that Spinoza was able to make on the subject of adolescence:

> But skill and alertness are required for this [namely, to do things that serve to strengthen amicable relations among human beings]. For men vary – there being few who live according to the rule of reason – and yet generally they are envious, and more inclined to vengeance than to Compassion. So it requires a singular power of mind to bear with each one according to their character (*ingenio*), and to restrain oneself from imitating their affects. But those who know how to find fault with men, to castigate vices rather than teach virtues, and to break men's minds rather than strengthen them (*non firmare, sed frangere*) – they are burdensome (*molesti*) both to themselves and to others. That is why many, from too great an impatience of mind, and a false zeal for religion, have preferred

to live among the lower animals rather than among men. They are like children or adolescents (*pueri vel adolescentes*) who cannot bear with a level head (*aequo animo*) the scolding of their parents, and take refuge in the army. They choose the inconveniences of war and the discipline of an absolute commander in preference to the conveniences of home and the admonitions of a father; and while they take vengeance on their parents, they allow all sorts of burdens to be placed on them.[44]

This passage has some links to the scholium to III, 32: it is no longer the common provenance of pity and envy that is emphasised here, but the pronounced and almost unanimous penchant for the latter; the problem is no longer to illustrate by the example of children the universal process of affective imitation, but of knowing how to escape it; finally, where Spinoza had invoked a quasi-equilibrium of the body, he now speaks of a disequilibrium in the mind (inability to bear things *æquo animo*). The child has grown up, it is now a 'child or adolescent', who opts for the lesser evil (even if in an absurd and almost suicidal manner). Desire is no longer variable: it is focused on vengeance. We can say here, without needing to caricature at all, that one has passed in just a few years from mother's milk to vengeance, from the joyously primitive and healthy desire for regeneration to the sad and twilight desire to do evil to others and to oneself.[45] And paradoxically, indocility leads to a maximal docility, submission to the tyrannical discipline of the army, here compared with life among beasts.

This passage can lend itself to misunderstandings. 'Bear with each according to their character' is continued with 'children or adolescents who cannot bear with a level head the scolding of their parents'. Slipped in between these two expressions is a remark on how moral critique is burdensome for oneself and others, from which there follows, through impatience, the fate of the hermit (but one animated by a false religious zeal) or the soldier (but dictated by a concern for vengeance). Spinoza thus relates, back to back, parents and children, preachers and hermits. And here is the statement of the

---

[44] *Ethics* IV, App. Cap. XIII; CWS I, 589–90. Translation modified. [Curley's renderings of 'aequo animo' as 'calmly' and 'pueri vel adolescentes' as 'boys or young men' are perfectly viable; I have changed them only for the sake of a more intuitive fit with Zourabichvili's discussion. His decision to render 'ingenio' as 'understanding' is rather more problematic; see Moreau 1994. – GM.]

[45] Recall that the scholium to *Ethics* III, 2 (CWS I, 496) and Letter 58 to Schuller (CWS II, 428) both invoke, alongside the drunk's desire to drink and the chatterbox's desire to talk, the desire for milk of the *infans* and the desire for vengeance of the *puer*, as if it were a matter of two *types*.

problem: when adolescence comes, how is one to bear what is burdensome in others, how not to imitate them? One must admire the aphoristic force of the passage, the typically Spinozist capacity for dense, tight, seemingly clumsy writing, which does not immediately give up its meaning. Spinoza does not indicate the link between the two questions: it is left to the reader to decipher it with all the rigor required, while the positions of educator and educated, fleetingly indiscernible, float in their mind (which condemns the other? who teaches the lesson?).

The adolescent no longer wants to imitate, in other words it seeks to become adult: but is it in fact from obedience that they want to escape? Is it not rather an affective ambience by which the adolescent feels marked, and which they no longer want, because they perceive in it childishness, vulgarity? A passage from the *Short Treatise* recalls that children start out by spontaneously believing whatever their father says, having no knowledge other than by hearsay.[46] It is precisely at the moment when the individual comes into full possession of their corporeal and mental capabilities that they feel rise up within them, through ephemeral experiences, the possibility of an active usage of the mind: the influence of hearsay begins to wane. It is then that impatience tends to get the upper hand and to spoil the process: the adolescent separates itself from human beings rather than winning its independence among them, and in certain ways against them. The innocent equilibrium of the *puer* has given way to the disequilibrium of the *adolescens*, which has every chance of persisting until death. 'There being few who live according to the rule of reason': one will rediscover this theme in the very last lines of the *Ethics*, just after the invocation of the growth of the infant and its being aligned with the ethical enterprise, in a final scholium that recalls precisely the terms used to describe the infant ('as if he knew neither himself, nor God, nor things'[47]) in order to apply them, this time, to the ignorant in general, the childish adult. Confusing vengeance and freedom is certainly the tragedy of adolescence, which devotes human beings to a sad, 'childish' existence. It should come as no surprise that this is also the tragedy of revolution, insofar as the childhood-city relation sketches the contours of a common problem.

One will also find in this text the critique of educators, which echoes the programme of the *Treatise on the Emendation of the Intellect*: 'attention must

---

[46] 'We usually observe this [love that comes from hearsay] in children in relation to their father. Because he says that this or that is good, they are inclined to it, without knowing anything more about it' (*KV* II, 3, 7; CWS I, 101).
[47] *Ethics* V, 42 Schol.; CWS I, 616. Compare with V, 39 Schol.

be paid to Moral Philosophy and to Instruction concerning the Education of children'.[48] Spinoza's premature death invites us to dream (although this death, probably tied to a general state of exhaustion due to phthisis, was not entirely accidental, and the death of a phthistic has a certain air of *finality* [achèvement]): what would he have done after finishing the *Political Treatise*, if he had had a mind to? We know that he had started a retranslation of certain books of the Old Testament. But then? If by 'moral philosophy' we must understand the last three books of the *Ethics*, this in no way rules out that he would himself have wanted to elaborate this doctrine of education. It would be wrong to envision the latter as a special doctrine: based on the scholium to V, 39, where the development of reason is inscribed in the much broader process of a successful human life that leads from the condition of the infant to that of the sage, it would be nothing less than a rewriting of the *Ethics* for its unaware recipient or its rightful patient – the child. Besides, 'we can show best how much our skill and understanding are worth by educating men so that at last they live according to the command of their own reason'.[49]

What was Spinoza's reproach to the educators of his time? *Non firmare, sed frangere*: breaking young people's minds, rather than strengthening them. And consequently – for the *unde* of the passage cited refers as much to the unbearable character of their sermons as to the inability to bear that to which they contribute – making them impatient, throwing them into disequilibrium, ultimately casting them into an inauthentic existence in which what they absolutely require is compromised in advance by the vindictive mind that has caught hold of them. Not the hypocrisy of the falsely pious and pastors, but the unaware sincerity of a soul that would be pious, even though its energy feeds on hatred; or rather an ardour for combat that draws its force from vengeance, a capacity to obey that has nothing civil about it. In sum, the education of priests and rabbis, and of the families that revere them and are inspired by them, leaves room only for the choice between servile obedience and already embittered revolt. The *Theologico-Political Treatise* insists on this impasse:

> Still, we don't want to accuse the sectaries of impiety just because they accommodate the words of Scripture to their own opinions . . . We do censure them, though, for being unwilling to grant this same freedom to others, and for persecuting, as God's enemies, everyone who does not think as they do, even though they are very honest and obedient to true

---

[48] *TdIE* 15; CWS I, 11.
[49] *Ethics* IV, App. Cap. IX; CWS I, 589.

virtue. On the other hand, they still love, as God's elect, those who give lip service to these opinions, even if they are the most weak-minded. Nothing more wicked or harmful to the republic can be imagined.[50]

Thus we have two madnesses, two failures to live in society: 'living among beasts', and 'preferring the inconveniences of war and the authority of a tyrant'. So that it is true that the enigmatic individual quasi-transformation, that of the infant that needs us to make it become adult, hinges on the political problem (becoming citizen)[51] and its own crisis, the attempt at revolutionary transformation. And as for revolution, the seditious attitude of adolescents it at once disapproved of and excused: the fault lies with the tyrants, which here means the parents.

Two other passages from the *Ethics* confirm this crisis of traditional education. The one denounces repentance, the traditional means of all moral education of the Christian type, by showing that it is only founded on affective associations produced by education, which are variable according to custom and religion:

Parents – by blaming the former acts [which from custom are called *wrong*], and often scolding their children on account of them, and on the other hand, by recommending and praising the latter acts [which are called *right*] – have brought it about that emotions of Sadness were joined to the one kind of act, and those of Joy to the other . . . Hence, according as each one has been educated, so he either repents of a deed or exults at being esteemed for it.[52]

Repentance is not the revelation of a truth, but the servile exercise of a memory that overwhelms the mind and testifies to its docility; the repentant become aware of nothing, they merely obey the watchwords of their community. The other passage directly supports the reading that we are proposing. It accuses education of flattering the vindictive part of human nature: '[men are naturally inclined to Hate and Envy, and] Education itself adds to natural inclination. For parents generally spur their children on to virtue only by the incentive of Honor and Envy.'[53]

---

[50] *TTP* XIV, 3–4; CWS II, 264.
[51] 'Men aren't born civil; they become civil' (*TP* V, 2; CWS II, 529).
[52] *Ethics* III, DA XXVII Exp.; CWS I, 537.
[53] *Ethics* III, 55 Schol.; CWS I, 525–6.

What Is a Spinozist Pedagogy?[54]

Non firmare, sed frangere. The wish of rigorous Calvinism – to break the will of the child, who when all is said and done is judged a sinner – would not, it seems, ever have had much success in Holland, where unprecedented and particularly indulgent attention was paid to children.[55] Nevertheless, it must have had enough success to justify this digression (along with the scholium on the pleasures of life[56]). A passage from the doctor Van Beverwijck gives one an idea of the state of the question in the Holland of the seventeenth century:

> In all this upbringing and education, children should not be kept on too tight a rein, but allowed to exercise their childishness, so that we do not burden their fragile nature with heavy things and sow untimely seed in the unprepared field of understanding. Let them freely play and let school use play for their maturing . . . otherwise they will be against learning before they know what learning is.[57]

For his part, Christian Huygens, who was basically Spinoza's contemporary, militated for a ludic form of learning.[58] What would have been the great guiding principles of the Spinozist doctrine of education? We will try to discern them in the existing texts, without giving in to the temptation to

---

[54] The old article by Adolfo Ravà, 'La pedagogia di Spinoza', published in 1933, is terribly banal, even if it promises to begin with 'precise pedagogical ideas', insists on the 'great importance' of pedagogy for Spinoza, and conjectures that a longer life would have enabled its 'adequate development' (Ravà 1933: 195). He means above all to connect Spinozism to currents of thought, such as Stoicism but also Fichte and Comte, for which philosophy is not only a theoretical activity but an 'art of living', and which consequently 'imply a tendency for proselytism' (199). Parts III and IV of the *Ethics* appear to him as a 'grandiose social pedagogy, founded on psychology' (197), etc. Beyond that, it is a collection of biographical anecdotes that touch on teaching, which the reader can just as well find in Meinsma's *Spinoza et son cercle*, and the sketch of a scholarly programme that has nothing surprising about it: the importance of mathematics, of meditating on the Roman historians, etc. There is no question at any point of Spinoza's relationship to children. The only interesting remark concerns the *Hebrew Grammar*: 'Spinoza was, if we are not mistaken, the first to intuit the principle of modern linguistics of the fixity of phonetic laws' (204). And Ravà sees in this a linguistic approach of a Galilean spirit, desirous to eliminate exceptions and to extract the regularities of language.

[55] See Schama 1988: 557.

[56] *Ethics* IV, 45 Schol.

[57] Cited in Schama 1988: 557.

[58] Schama 1988: 558.

deduce from some dispersed remarks – which, when all is said and done, often have the character of mere *opinions* – all the details of a doctrine to which Spinoza, if he had started to elaborate it, would have needed to devote specific reflection based on unforeseeable results.

Let us recall, for example, the allusion of the *Theologico-Political Treatise*, when Spinoza invokes Moses' relation to the disobedience of the Hebrews: 'Next he terrified them with threats, if they transgressed those commands, and he promised them many goods if they respected them. So he taught them in the same way parents usually do children who are lacking in all reason.'[59] Can we see in this a conception of education? Pierre Macherey seems to think so, when he proposes to read Proposition 43 of Part IV of the *Ethics* as 'the sketch of a pedagogy' founded on useful corporal punishment: 'Pleasure can be excessive and evil, whereas Pain can be good insofar as the Pleasure, *or* Joy, is evil.'[60]

This proposition, in which one can see an accounting for a sort of immanent torture (disgust), of course remains interpretable to the letter as the unwelcome rehabilitation of a certain reasonable usage of corporal punishment, in reaction to the lenient drift of the Holland of the day, which was perhaps of service neither for adults nor children. And Macherey is right to recall Spinoza's insistence on the fear of punishment in political theory.

But the question is one of knowing more precisely how corporal punishment could serve as a pedagogical means. 'Pain', Macherey writes, 'can have value as a warning, by drawing attention to the excessive character presented by certain pleasures that exalt one part of the organism to the detriment of its overall equilibrium'.[61] And a bit further on: 'Why hesitate to make children suffer a little, if it will ultimately do them good, namely by preventing them from remaining children?'[62] Let us be clear: it is not a matter of delivering thought over to a sentimentality that would from the start rule out a possibility that philosophy must know how to consider and weigh serenely, in spite of ambient clamour. But look: pain is certainly *dissuasive*, at least for a child old enough to associate it with the reproached act and to choose the lesser of two evils (for the very young, these would be two singular perceptions without any relation, and the pain would simply remain pain). It is no less dissuasive than the fact of being burned: so-called vague experience leads one to avoid an act through the memory of its consequence. In order

---

[59] *TTP* II, 47; CWS II, 107.
[60] *Ethics* IV, 43; CWS I, 570.
[61] Macherey, *Introduction* IV, 264.
[62] Macherey, *Introduction* IV, 265 n. 1.

for pain to be in addition to this *persuasive*, and even to incline the child to pass a moral judgment on its act, it would be necessary that it had the effect of making it avoid the act by reason of its nature, and not of its consequence. In short, we see quite well how the child can be led to judge of good and evil on the basis of its *fear*. But we also see how the preceding runs counter to a fundamental Spinozist principle, which was destined for a brilliant posterity in the history of doctrines of education: 'He who is guided by Fear, and does good to avoid evil, is not guided by reason.'[63] Its scholium:

> The superstitious know how to reproach people for their vices better than they know how to teach them virtues, and they strive, not to guide men by reason, but to restrain them by Fear, so that they flee the evil rather than love virtues. Such people aim only to make others as wretched as they themselves are, so it is no wonder that they are generally burdensome (*molesti*) and hateful to men.[64]

Education can have no goal other than forming a free human being, or an adult in the non-trivial sense of the term. Certainly, as in politics, at first one can only seek to obtain obedience, but always while keeping in view the risk that it could all go to waste: *non firmare, sed frangere*. Politics, which takes human beings as they are, abandoned for the most part to a childishness without remedy, and whose goal above all is to lead them to live together, is

---

[63] *Ethics* IV, 63; CWS I, 582. Tschirnhaus was without a doubt the first Spinozist peda-gogue. See Tschirnhaus 1980: 222–3 (Spinoza's influence can be felt starting on page 214 – Tschirnhaus notably seems to have understood that Spinoza, far from condemn-ing the imagination, calls for developing its power). Closer to our time, William James closes his *Talks to Teachers* with the following words: 'Spinoza long ago wrote in his *Ethics* that anything that a man can avoid under the notion that it is bad he may also avoid under the notion that something else is good. He who habitually acts *sub specie mali*, under the negative notion, the notion of the bad, is called a slave by Spinoza. To him who acts habitually under the notion of good he gives the name of freeman. See to it now, I beg you, that you make freemen of your pupils by habituating them to act, whenever possible, under the notion of a good' (James 1992: 821). Lev Vygotsky cites these sentences by James in the part of his *Educational Psychology* devoted to the teaching of moral values, and he shows how Spinoza's proposition is opposed to that of Rousseau's *Emile*: 'Do not, in other words, turn morality into the internal policeman of the soul' (Vygotsky 1997: 227). More generally, Vygotsky's very important work on the development of the child was constantly inspired by Spinoza. Showing this would exceed the limits of this study, but the Russophone reader can be referred to Vygotsky 1996 (whose title would be translated as 'Play and its Role in the Psychic Development of the Child').

[64] *Ethics* IV, 63 Schol.; CWS I, 582.

already victorious when it manages at least to make them obey. But Spinoza also assigns to politics a second goal: to lead human beings to live a 'human life', to 'cultivate life' rather than to 'avoid death'.[65] Such is the problem of the 'free multitude', to which we will return in the final study. And so Moses tried as much as possible to use not only fear, but hope; and in his conclusions, Spinoza says that 'in each state the laws must be so instituted that men are checked not so much by fear as by the hope of some good they desire very much'.[66]

Learning to obey is the prerequisite of freedom, not only because the child only progresses under the guidance of an educator, but because the very content of obedience is the domination of immediate predilections. But it is a given that the means of obedience can compromise every step thereafter, by producing a murderous beast, sometime servile, sometimes vindictive. Such is thus the programme of all Spinozist pedagogy: to study the means of making one avoid evil as 'indirectly'[67] as possible from the perspective of the good, and in this way to encourage a mastery over oneself that would not be self-destructive but would coincide with the blossoming of capacities. It is up to the educator to make hope point little by little toward an immanent reward, toward virtue rather than a mere treat.[68]

To what extent do threats, if in fact necessary, remain a means of educa-tion? If they are not properly speaking a pedagogical instrument, is one at least entitled to prescribe them as a last resort? Spinoza's thought allows us unequivocally to distinguish between two cases: either the educator is led to use fear for lack of knowing how to make the student distinctly imagine the good that would follow from giving up what they are seeking, because they do not know how to show that it is *molestus*, troublesome, difficult, tedious, in which case punishment can only aggravate the situation (the only effect that education could have would be engraving in the student's memory a vindictive *habitus*, or developing a slavish submission which is contrary to its true goal); or else the educator finds themselves working in conditions close to those of the founder of the State, having to impose a minimal order on a disobedient multitude.[69] There remains between the two enough of

[65] *TP* V, 5–6; CWS II, 530.
[66] *TTP* V, 24; CWS II, 144.
[67] *Ethics* IV, 63 cor.; CWS I, 582.
[68] In very different epochs, Tschirnhaus (1980: 214–223) and Vygotsky (1997) both insisted on this point.
[69] See Jan Steen's painting *School for Boys and Girls*, reproduced in Schama's book, and the latter's commentary on it: a kind of animal chaos reigns in the classroom, where education and play are opposed instead of commingled (Schama 1998: 558–9).

a margin for an *auxiliary* recourse to fear, when the *habitus* of the student, spurred on by their own enjoyment, is still hesitant, and the student still knows those lethargic situations in which they are alienated from their own desire (but if threats and punishment become regular means, the risk is that the student will associate study with sad affects – a truism of the pedagogy of the age that the whole Spinozist theory of the passions confirms). We are in agreement with Macherey only from this point of view.

The difference between these two situations – the educator and their student, the educator before a classroom – corresponds in the *Theologico-Political Treatise* to the difference between the education of the turbulent mass of the Hebrews by Moses, already invoked, and the education of the first man by God, according to its rectified image (Adam born ignorant of all things):

> The first thing which strikes us is the story of the first man, where it is related that God told Adam not to eat the fruit of the tree of the knowledge of good and evil. This seems to mean that God told Adam to do and seek the good for the sake of the good (*sub ratione boni*), and not insofar as it is contrary to the evil, i.e., that he should seek the good from love of the good, and not from fear of evil. For as we've already shown, he who does good from a true knowledge and love of the good acts freely and with a constant heart, whereas he who acts from fear of evil is compelled by evil, acts like a slave, and lives under the command of another.[70]

We have at our disposal, on the question of discipline, a crucial passage where Spinoza invokes the tensions between parents and infants by comparing them with those that disturb a democratic State. This is a response to Hobbes, who does not mark an essential difference between paternal domination and despotic domination.[71] The comparison alone, in a context where it is a matter of refuting the pseudo-link between absolute monarchy and civil peace, nearly works as a pedagogical manifesto; but perhaps, at the moment when the Prince of Orange had just seized power, it also implicitly functions as a meditation on the Republic of the United Provinces.[72] 'No

---

[Zourabichvili refers to *The Schoolmaster* ('Le Maître d'École'), which is not discussed in Schama's book. – GM.]

[70] *TTP* IV, 38; CWS II, 135.

[71] See above, Chapter 3.

[72] Even if these latter were aristocratic in form, one can still think that this passage concerns them, not only thanks to the monarchical threat, but because the States here called popular or democratic were above all those where freedom of speech reigned.

doubt there are more, and more bitter, quarrels between parents and children than between masters and slaves. Nevertheless, it is not in the interest of a household to change paternal Right into mastery, and treat children like slaves.'[73] These lines echo the passage about adolescents on which we commented above: they are almost its solution. Once more, it is the conduct of the parents that is the cause: not, this time, the stupidity of their educational principles, but the possible drift of the exercise of their authority faced with the indocility of the children. Spinoza here invokes a tyrannical drift of the family, which compromises the very existence of familial links. What exactly is this 'interest of the household'? The child and the citizen, according to a formula already encountered above, do what is useful to them under the command of another, parents or sovereign, whereas the slave only does what is useful to the master.[74] And the establishment of the familial household is only justified by the desire for physical union animated by 'a Love of begetting children and educating them wisely', and a love inspired by 'freedom of mind'.[75] In other words, the role of the parents is to provide for the freedom of the child, this is the foundation of their authority, and consequently also its limit: the child becomes almost a citizen in their family.

A comedy by Terence, *Adelphoe*, might provide a clue to this conception of the role of parents, as the passage on the conflicts between adults and adolescents seems to echo it (such conflicts were, additionally, common in Dutch life).[76] The play presents two brothers, Aeschinus and Ctesipho: the first, a turbulent adolescent, debauched, on the verge of delinquency, is raised with indulgence and tolerance by his father's brother, whereas Ctesipho, remaining with the father, receives a rigid education (the father himself reproaches his brother for his leniency). But it is Ctesipho, not Aeschinus, who cannot bear paternal authority and threatens to expatriate by joining the service.[77] Better still, Micio, the tolerant uncle, makes a kind of profession of faith at the beginning of the play: 'This is the mark

---

[73] *TP* VI, 4; CWS II, 533. Translation modified. [Curley renders Spinoza's 'oeconomiae interest' as 'orderly management of a household'. – GM.]

[74] *TTP* XVI, 33; CWS II, 288. One will here note the usage of the word *liberi*, used correctly when it is a matter of relations with parents, that is to say of a juridical status that, for the father of the family, is opposed to the other category placed under their authority, the *servi*.

[75] *Ethics* IV, App. Cap. XX; CWS I, 591.

[76] *Ethics* IV, App. Cap. XIII; CWS II, 589–90.

[77] Terence 2006. [Zourabichvili refers to 'Act II, Scene 4 and Act III, Scene 3', but these divisions were not part of the original works and are not reproduced in this edition. See Brown's Introduction (Terence 2006: xiii). – GM.]

of a father, to get his son into the habit of acting rightly of his own accord (*sponte*) rather than through fear of another (*alieno metu*).'[78] Here now is Spinoza's praise of Moses: 'he took the greatest care that the people should do their duty, not so much from fear, as voluntarily (*non tam metu, quam sponte*)'.[79] But Micio continues: 'that's the difference between a father and a master (*dominus*). If he can't do that, he should admit that he doesn't know how to rule over his children.'[80] This time, we rediscover in advance the anti-Hobbesian distinction of the *Political Treatise*.

Truly, the reader would search in vain for the least moral depreciation of children in Spinoza. Childhood is only a state of impotence which one must leave and which the individual only leaves through education, and the collective connotation of the *conamur* of the scholium to V, 39 here takes on all its force based on the fact that education can turn into a tragic obstacle if it wagers on the internalisation of moral judgments through intimidation, rather than on the development of intellectual forces. Even Spinoza's precautionary measures before the instability of Casearius, his young student, were animated by a concern for education rather than by disapproval, and testify less to an annoyance than to a love and an explicit confidence.[81]

To conclude, let us draw the outlines of a Spinozist education: 1. Cultivate in equal parts all the capacities of the body and develop the power of the mind. 2. Appeal to hope rather than fear, by teaching love of immanent rewards (*acquiescentia in se ipso*, virtue). 3. Adapt oneself to the student's understanding, following the recurring themes of the Spinozist conception of prophecy (above all the kernel common to all religions: love of neighbour, justice, and charity;[82] then mathematics as soon as possible,[83] less for its own content than for its educative quality). 4. And from then on never forget the link between reason and affect. Pedagogues of a Spinozist inspiration, each in their own way, will know how to retrieve these four aspects.

---

[78] Terence 2006: 265.
[79] *TTP* V, 28; CWS II, 145.
[80] Terence 2006: 265.
[81] *Ep.* IX [to De Vries]; CWS I, 193–4.
[82] *TTP* XVIII, 20–22; CWS II, 261–2.
[83] Mathematics, 'whose truth no one doubts' (*TTP* XI, 20; CWS II, 246), is accessible to the most ignorant: 'Everyone grasps Euclid's propositions before they're demonstrated' (*TTP* VII, adn. VIII; CWS II, 185 n. 32). See also *Ethics* I, App.

Concluding Remarks on the Relationship to Childhood

And suddenly I saw a youth behind Gedali, a youth with the face of Spinoza, with the powerful forehead of Spinoza, with the sickly face of a nun. He was smoking and twitching like an escaped convict who has been tracked down and brought back to his jail. Ragged Reb Mordkhe sneaked up on him from behind, snatched the cigarette from his mouth, and came running over to me. 'That is Ilya, the rabbi's son,' Mordkhe wheezed, turning the bloody flesh of his inflamed eyelids to me, 'the damned son, the worst son, the disobedient son!' And Mordkhe threatened the youth with his little fist and spat in his face.

Isaac Babel, *Red Cavalry*[1]

1. At first Spinoza is astonished and perplexed. How could we have begun by being so weak, so unaware of ourselves, so far from the image we have of what a human being needs to be? Can it be that we no longer have anything but an external link with that numb and wholly somnambulistic being that we had formerly been?

2. In order to be able to think childhood correctly, one must first of all avoid the risk of the chimera of the *infans adultus* in all its avatars: miniaturised adult, first man, hypostasised child as an essence apart. To which we can add the quite real figure of the adult who has not grown up (childishness of the *vulgus*), the rare and problematic figure of the convalescent amnesiac, over which doubt still lingers (is this a new life or a vestibule of death?),[2] and finally the figure of the adolescent.

---

[1] Babel 2002: 235–6.

[2] It is also not out of bounds to see a certain irony here in regard to the Christian theme of the second birth, which the young Spinoza, in the *Short Treatise*, already reclaimed for himself. Once again, is not the ex-poet quite simply senile or, as one says, regressed

3. Now there is, for the first time in philosophy, an *active* gaze upon children. Not that it is a matter of loving them, of pitying them their fate, or of being moved by them. Between the humanist fascination with the opaque and snickering world of childhood in the sixteenth century, and the 'coddling' of a Madame de Sévigné of the eighteenth, and beyond the contradictions of a century of transition in which modernism and archaism coexisted, and were often interlaced with one another, Spinoza treated childhood without scorn or compassion, the child as a being in becoming. The relationship to childhood became the veridical ordeal of a philosophy that meant to grant no validity to the idea of privation, and which triumphed in this ordeal by rectifying the image of childhood, by appropriating it as the best illustration of itself. The child grasped in its becoming, at the end of the *Ethics*, is the very image, the unique, definitive image, conforming to the understanding, of becoming-philosopher.

Becoming-philosopher grasped in the image of the child: one must not confuse this claim with that of Gilles Deleuze and Félix Guattari, 'Spinozism is the becoming-child of the philosopher.'[3] Certainly we have not ruled out that the two claims might converge, but they have neither the same sense nor the same object. Deleuze and Guattari see in the Spinozist conception of the body (kinematic relations between elements and the composition of these relations) an essential affinity with the childish mode of interrogation. For our purposes, investigating the explicit and insistent presence of the theme of childhood in Spinoza, we were led to insist on the general critique of the scholastic category of privation. And no doubt we could for our part have invoked a 'becoming-child of the philosopher', that is, a properly *childish* inspiration in the philosopher. We would do so concerning the scholium to *Ethics* IV, 59: 'The act of beating, insofar as it is considered physically, and insofar as we attend only to the fact that the man raises his arm, closes his fist, and moves his whole arm forcefully up and down, is a virtue, conceived

---

to childhood? See Erasmus: 'and just as the gods of the poets customarily save, by some metamorphosis or other, those who are dying, in like manner I bring those who have one foot in the grave back to their infancy again, for as long as possible; so that the folk are not far off in speaking of them as "in their second childhood." If anyone would like to know the method of bringing about this alteration, I shall not conceal it. I lead them to my spring of Lethe – for that stream rises in the Fortunate Isles, and only a little rivulet of it flows in the underworld – so that then and there they may drink draughts of forgetfulness. With their cares of mind purged away, by gentle stages they become young again' (Erasmus 2015: 17).
3 Deleuze and Guattari 1987: 256.

from the structure of the human Body.'[4] That the whole gesture would first of all be a virtue in itself, graspable as such independently of its possible ends or motivations – who would make this discovery, if not the infant who obstinately gives itself over even to the action of beating, with no other apparent reason than the *acquiescentia in se ipso* that the action procures for it?[5] Is it not a infant's point of view that Spinoza asks us to adopt here? Becoming infant, that is, setting loose the share of innocence and power inherent to every gesture: no, definitely not, *nemo miseretur infantis*, childish impotence is not misery.

Childhood thus becomes coextensive with life as a whole, as is confirmed in another mode in the *Theologico-Political Treatise*: 'everyone is born ignorant of everything. Before men can know the true principle of living and acquire a virtuous disposition, much of their life has passed, even if they have been well-educated.'[6] One must thus reconnect with childhood, in a particular way that is situated, beyond all memory, at the furthest remove from 'regret'. It is not sad to need to begin by being a child: what is sad is to remain one. Childhood only appears pitiable *a posteriori*, when we cast a retrospective gaze at the sliver of power that we had, compared to the degree of capacity to which we have elevated ourselves, while we continue to rise: so, in fact, there is strictly speaking nothing to regret, and only the impotent adult, a monstrous infant beneath the exterior of a mature adult, can give itself over to hallucinatory nostalgia for its earliest years (one impotence traded for another, but at least then it had been pampered); unless, of course, the memory was that of *leaps* taken, and of the *acquiescentia in se ipso* that each time accompanied the discovery of a new capacity. In any case, childhood is not melancholic, it oscillates between joy and sadness, without ever being fixated on one or the other; with its back against misfortune, it is the very ambition for freedom and good fortune.[7]

---

[4] *Ethics* IV, 39 Schol.; CWS I, 580.

[5] 'Self-satisfaction (*acquiescentia in se ipso*) is a Joy born of the fact that a man considers himself and his own power of acting' (*Ethics* III, DA XXV; CWS I, 536. Translation modified.).

[6] *TTP* XVI, 7; CWS II, 283. Translation modified.

[7] The time has come to comment on Pierre Macherey's position. While we can only salute the way in which he has underscored the role of childhood in the *Ethics* better than anyone, we feel that he has somewhat underestimated the originality of Spinoza's aims. Let us cite this remarkable note, concerning the scholium to III, 2: 'Childhood, instead of being treated as an autonomous state, in which humanity would have no part at all, is invoked, completely without nostalgia, from the perspective of a genetic development, where it appears as constituting our own past as human beings . . .'. Up to this point, we couldn't have said it better ourselves. But what follows seems more

4. The memory of the child, a mélange of encounters, of filial piety and education, is modified in adolescence, *the age of reason*, either passing into the background by being transformed in the extremely rare case of the sage, or else being inflected as an effect of the unresolved tension between education and the forces of liberation, and the back-and-forth between these two. Childhood is the conflictual link between two processes that it should be possible to conjugate: education and development. We see how education properly conceived, itself reformed, might cultivate a memory favourable for the full blossoming of the capacities. But most of the time the child is frustrated, insofar as education is not focused on the problem of the development of its power to understand, according to the terms of the *Treatise on the Emendation of the Intellect*. Initially amnesiac, the child suffers within itself the formation, throughout its development, of a more or less bothersome memory, up until the point that its successful growth puts it into crisis and leads the individual to submit itself, whether by docility or pseudo-revolt, or else to reform itself.

objectionable to us: 'One thinks here of Descartes, when he invites us never to forget that we had been children before being human beings. In this passage of the *Ethics*, Spinoza seems to fleetingly remember the child that he himself had been, and he does so in a purely experimental, apparently objective state of mind, but from which a bitter feeling of derision is not wholly absent. *How sad to think that one could have been an child!*, this approach seems to imply. We see that the theoretical activity of the philosopher, who in principle casts over the reality analysed a completely disinterested gaze, remains traversed by imaginary phantasms; but the essential thing is that the weight of these phantasms, reduced to a minimum, does not outweigh that of demonstrative rigor' (Macherey, *Introduction* III, 257, n. 2). Here then are our remarks. 1. Spinoza minimises the Cartesian theme of the prejudices of childhood; he sees in it only one aspect of the relationship to childhood (in order to be convinced of this, it is sufficient to compare him with Malebranche). 2. Spinoza characterises the relationship to childhood as external, indirectly established via the detour of the observation of others, and not through the channel of personal memory. 3. To ascribe to Spinoza a distressed attitude with regard to childhood is to put him in contradiction with his typical norm of behaviour – or with what we might call his intellectual deontology (*non ridere, non lugere, neque detestari, sed intelligere*) – which, of course, remains humanly possible; but more importantly it would contradict Spinoza's own words in the scholium to V, 6. 4. We certainly cannot rule out that imaginary phantasms played a role, but the recurrence of remarks on childhood in the *Ethics*, if our analyses have not been erroneous, makes perfect sense without needing to suppose this. We do not rule out *a priori* the existence of such phantasms (we couldn't say anything of the sort); we say that, phantasms or no, Spinoza discovered the terms of a *philosophical* relationship to childhood, which was undeniably unprecedented.

In order to summarise the complexity of this relationship to memory and forgetting, we might gather together the elements of a fictional autobiography:

' – me, Bento, now Benedictus, merchant by inheritance turned philosopher and optician, notable son of the Jewish community of Amsterdam become a poor citizen without religion, wandering serenely in cosmopolitan Holland;

' – I see myself first in the relatively recent past, in adolescence, a critical period in which, before I was twenty years of age, as my hagiography underscores, I began to reason and posed questions to the rabbis that left them mute, consummating my rupture little by little until they decided to chase me out;[8] and for all that, I did not yet leave behind this troubled period in which I hesitated about what kind of life to lead, in which the world appeared to me absurd, chaotic, confusing,[9] and in which a mortified disgust arose in me;[10]

' – if I look farther back, which I do without pleasure,[11] I review the past of my childhood, during which I received that traditional Judaic education from which I separated myself, and of which I recall only the basis of my reformed memory, casting over it a gaze that can no longer belong to that time (mutation of my *institutum vitae*);[12]

' – finally, opaque and silent, there is that very remote past to which I am only attached by the external link of hearsay and vague experience: I was an infant, and those parents watched over me.'[13]

---

[8] See the beginning of Lucas 1954.
[9] *Ep.* XXX [to Oldenburg]; CWS II, 14.
[10] *TdIE*, prologue; CWS I, 7–10.
[11] *KV* I, 14 ('Of Regret'); CWS I, 118–19. Translation modified. [Curley translates *Beklagh* as 'Longing'. – GM.] *Ethics* III, DA XXXII and Exp. (CWS I, 539).
[12] *TTP* IX, 31; CWS II, 216–17.
[13] *Ethics* IV, 39 Schol.; CWS I, 569–70. *TdIE* 15; CWS I, 11.

Third Study: The Power of God and the Power of Kings

At the beginning of Part II of the *Ethics*, Spinoza remarks that the *vulgus* has a tendency to 'compare' or 'confuse' two powers of different natures, that of God and that of kings. This scholium marks a halting point, a pause, for both a recapitulation and a foreword, where Spinoza's impatience shows through. The progression is remarkable:

> But we have refuted this . . . we have shown . . . then we have shown . . . I could also show here . . . But I do not wish to speak so often about the same topic. I only beg the reader, over and over again (*iterum atque iterum*), to reflect carefully once more (*atque iterum*) on what is said concerning this matter in Part I, from 16 to the end. For no one will be able to perceive rightly the things I maintain unless he takes great care not to confuse God's power with the human power or right of Kings.[1]

Spinoza draws the reader's attention to three points: 1. The object of the whole second half of Part I of the *Ethics*, which the reader would have just read, was to distinguish between the two powers. 2. This distinction is not simple. 3. It is a waste of time to bother reading the rest if one has not incorporated its lesson. Sometimes Spinoza tells us to continue to read even if we feel like we have not followed the argument, or that we are not in agreement.[2] But here the alternative is clear: either you have understood, or else there is nothing to do but close the book. There is no ethics, in short, if you have not understood that God is not a king. Consequently, you must soak up this second half: read it *iterum atque iterum . . . atque iterum*, again and

---

[1] *Ethics* II, 3 schol; CWS I, 449. Translation modified. [Curley drops the emphatic repetitions: *iterum atque iterum . . . atque iterum* becomes a single 'repeatedly'. – GM.]

[2] For example, when he starts to 'speak Spinozan' (*Ethics* II, 11 Schol.; CWS I, 456).

again or more! The distinction between the two powers is key to accessing the ethics.

We must recognise that Spinoza has some reason for being impatient: even leaving aside the appendix, this is the fourth time since the start of the *Ethics* that he affirms this distinction between divine power and human power.[3]

The matter of the two powers is thus of central importance. We recognise it already in the first letter to Blijenbergh, from 1664, concerning the anthropomorphic language of the prophets: 'First, because God had revealed the means to salvation and destruction, and was the cause of them, they represented him as a king and lawgiver'[4] (for example, 'When Micaiah said to King Ahab that he had seen God sitting on his throne . . .'[5]).

Next we find it again in the *Theologico-Political Treatise*, on the subject of miracles: the vulgar 'imagine God's power as the rule of a certain Royal majesty',[6] they 'imagine God as corporeal and as maintaining a kingly rule, whose throne they deem to be in the dome of heaven';[7] finally, that miracles 'require causes and circumstances – as we have already shown – and that they do not follow from I know not what kingly rule [*imperio*] which the common people [*vulgus*] ascribe to God, but from his command and divine decree [*decreto*], i.e. . . . from the laws of nature and its order'.[8]

What are we to understand by the 'power of kings'? This biblical comparison is found almost everywhere in the Christian theological tradition (up through Saint Thomas Aquinas, in spite of his critique of metaphor). But it is significant that its Spinozist demystification coincides with a decisive stage in the history of monarchy: the rise of royal absolutism in Europe. Spinoza could in no way have had the same idea of a king that the prophets did in their time. Across this metaphysical polemic against confusing the power of God with that of kings, a topical wind was blowing.

---

[3] *Ethics* I, 8 Schol. 2 (*CWS* I, 413); 15 Schol. (*CWS* I, 421–4); 17 Schol. (*CWS* I, 425–8); 33 Schol. 2 (*CWS* I, 436–9).
[4] *Ep.* XIX [to Blijenbergh]; *CWS* I, 360.
[5] *Ep.* XXI [to Blijenbergh]; *CWS* I, 381.
[6] *TTP* VI, 3; *CWS* II, 153.
[7] *TTP* VI, 58; *CWS* II, 165.
[8] *TTP* VI, 69; *CWS* II, 168.

6

The Confusion of the Two Powers and the Baroque Drift of Cartesianism

Let us first of all ask what concept of royal power is at work in the scholium:

> By God's power ordinary people understand God's free will and his right over all things which are, things which on that account are commonly considered to be contingent. For they say that God has the power of destroying all things and reducing them to nothing. Further, they often compare God's power with the power of Kings. But we have refuted this in I, 32 cor. 1 and cor. 2, and we have shown in I, 16 that God acts with the same necessity by which he understands himself, i.e., just as it follows from the necessity of the divine nature (as everyone maintains unanimously) that God understands himself, with the same necessity it also follows that God does infinitely many things in infinitely many modes. And then we have shown in I, 34 that God's power is nothing except God's active essence. And so it is as impossible for us to conceive that God does not act as it is to conceive that he does not exist.[1]

The distinction between the two powers intersects with two others: that of divine and human natures,[2] and the distinction between conceptions of freedom.[3] The common person (*vulgus*) is inclined to attribute a body and a mind to God, and consequently to subject it to the passions; when it comes to philosophers, judging God's sovereign perfection by human perfections, they ascribe to God an understanding and a will. Spinoza has in mind the prophetic visions of the Old Testament studied in the *Theologico-Political*

---

[1] *Ethics* II, 3 Schol.; CWS I, 449.
[2] *Ethics* I, 8 Schol. (CWS I, 413); 15, Schol. (CWS I, 421–4); 17, Schol. (CWS I, 425–8).
[3] *Ethics* I, 17 Schol.; 33, Schol. (CWS I, 425–8; 436–9).

Treatise. The passage also repeats the expression *instar hominis*, which is utilised in the scholium to I, 15. However, the anthropomorphism here is of another nature: it consists in attributing to God a *potentia humana*; and then there is the polemic on freedom (the philosophers, whether we are talking about Thomas Aquinas or Descartes, have tended to confuse constraint and necessity, and to define God's freedom as 'free will', 'absolute will', 'arbitrariness' [*bon plaisir*], 'indifference').

A difficulty arises here: this 'human power', supposedly defined by 'free will' and the 'right to all things', in other words by a double power of deliberation and execution, seems to contradict the Appendix to Part I, which denounced in such free will an illusion, a prejudice, a human vanity (in the same way, in Part II, Spinoza would develop a critique of the notions of understanding and will as such). Kings are no exception. Free or absolute, the will of the king is only what it is insofar as it decides alone, supposing such a thing were possible, not in the sense of a power to choose between alternatives. Spinoza will show in the *Political Treatise* that this autonomy of decision is impossible. It is thus necessary to accept that the two attributes of royal power – arbitrariness and authority concentrated in a single person – amount to a politico-metaphysical fiction. The comparison of the two powers turns out to be doubly mystifying: it bases a superstition on another superstition. For it is their very impotence that leads human beings to engage in self-deception and to imagine God on the basis of the image they have of themselves.

Let us now note how free will is defined: a power of annihilation (implicitly: annihilation of what has been created, or in other words God can go back on its decision, its will can change), or of abstention (and Spinoza forcefully states the consequence: this amounts to denying God). In short, a fickle God and a God that does not exist – such are the conclusions brought about by the ordinary definition of free will, which however is formulated by the most ferocious partisans of the existence and immutability of God.

Refutation of the Power of Abstention

We must therefore do as Spinoza instructs us: we must return to and reread Part I of the *Ethics* starting with Proposition 16, namely everything concerning the mode of production of the world by God. Reread in particular the scholium to Proposition 17, which refutes the false, Cartesian-scholastic conception of the free cause:

> Others think that God is a free cause because he can (so they think) bring it about that the things which we have said follow from his nature (i.e.,

which are in his power) do not happen or are not produced by him. But this is the same as if they were to say that God can bring it about that it would not follow from the nature of a triangle that its three angles are equal to two right angles; *or* that from a given cause the effect would not follow – which is absurd.[4]

One thus understands by divine freedom a negative power of abstention, a power-to-not. God would manifest its omnipotence by not doing everything it could, by retaining its power (a power of retention or omission). Spinoza will strive to show how this conception goes astray: it actually posits the contrary of what it means to affirm, it compromises the power of God.

The principal argument is founded on the identity of cause and effect, or of essence and its properties. 'This is the same as if they were to say' – Spinoza cannot be unaware that Descartes says just that:

I turn to the difficulty of conceiving how God would have been acting freely and indifferently if he had made it false that the three angles of a triangle were equal to two right angles, or in general that contradictories could not be true together. It is easy to dispel this difficulty by considering that the power of God cannot have any limits . . .[5]

What Descartes considers to be 'incomprehensible', in view of the finitude of our understanding, is exactly what Spinoza rejects as 'absurd'. For Descartes, the necessity of the causal link would be imposed like a constraint on God from without, whereas for Spinoza it is the expression of the divine nature. The relation of an essence and its property is analytic: one cannot pull them apart without destroying the terms. A figure the sum of whose angles is not equal to two right angles would no longer be a triangle; otherwise, one would only construct the impossible mixture of two natures – a chimera. By impossible mixture, we mean that the two natures, being contradictory, can only destroy one another.[6] It is thus only through error that one can separate an essence from its properties. Still this error, stripped of its positive content, is at bottom only a misunderstanding, a misnaming of things:

---

[4] *Ethics* I, 17 Schol.; CWS I, 425–6.

[5] Descartes, Letter to Mesland, 2 May 1644 (CSM III, 235; AT IV, 118). See also the *Replies to the Sixth Set of Objections*: 'nor did [God] will that the three angles of a triangle should be equal to two right angles because he recognized that it could not be otherwise' (CSM II, 291; AT VII, 432).

[6] See *Ethics* III, 4–5 and their demonstrations; CWS I, 498.

And indeed, most errors consist only in our not rightly applying names to things. For when someone says that the lines which are drawn from the center of a circle to its circumference are unequal, he surely understands (then at least) by a circle something different from what Mathematicians understand. Similarly, when men err in calculating, they have certain numbers in their mind and different ones on the paper.[7]

Failures of language produce ephemeral chimeras, purely verbal beings – a courtyard flying into a neighbour's hen, for example.[8]

Before writing the *Ethics*, Spinoza had already reflected on this strange Cartesian claim. It is noteworthy that at that time he tied it to the question of divine immutability.[9] First, Spinoza carefully isolates *transformatio* from other kinds of change, for the absurdity of a change in God concerning essence would be immediately apparent: transformation implies 'the corruption of things . . . one which at the same time includes the generation following corruption',[10] so that a transformation of God would at once imply its death, contrary to its necessary existence, and the emergence of another God, or in other words polytheism, contrary to the unicity involved in its concept.[11] Then, having disqualified other species of change one by one, Spinoza introduces another argument, added in a note in the Dutch translation: if it is true that in God understanding and volition are identical, then the will by which God decreed that the sum of the angles of a triangle is equal to two right angles would be identical with its comprehension of this equality. 'For this reason, it will be as impossible for us to conceive that God can change his decrees as it is for us to think that the three angles of a triangle are not equal to two right angles.'[12]

The interest in this argument is that it ties the notion of an alternative to a change of decrees, but also and above all, although implicitly, to an unthinkable change of conception. Mutability, which is conceivable on the human plane, would for God amount to its not thinking what it thinks, to not conceiving how it conceives: it would introduce contradiction into it and threaten its identity. Alternatives, choice, would imply non-self-identity: a God other than itself, tending toward metamorphosis or

---

[7] *Ethics* II, 47 Schol.; CWS I, 483.
[8] *Ethics* II, 47 Schol.; CWS I, 483.
[9] CM II, 4; CWS I, 321–3.
[10] CM II 4; CWS I, 321. See also above, Introduction, n. 12.
[11] Spinoza had refuted polytheism earlier, in Chapter 2 (CM II, 2; CWS I, 318–9).
[12] CM II, 4; CWS I, 323.

pluralisation. Doubtless this is still only a first step, marked by the identification of God's understanding and will (which, as we know, is not a thesis unique to Spinoza). The next step, in the *Ethics*, will be the suppression of these two faculties, which will be brought down to the rank of modes or effects. But the formula of the *Metaphysical Thoughts* already suggests a direct link between God's essence and the nature of its production, of the same kind as that which unites a geometric figure and its properties: the decrees of God are analytically related to its essence, just as the equality of its three angles to two right ones are related to the essence of the triangle.[13]

We find confirmation of this in the commentary on Descartes' *Principles*, where Spinoza proposes a proof of the immutability of God that does not appear in the original text. This proof draws its support from the simplicity that had just been shown to pertain to God, and whose corollary is precisely the impossibility of separating God's decrees from its essence: 'From this it follows that God's intellect and his will, *or* his Decree, and his power, are only distinguished by reason from his essence.'[14]

This claim, at the heart of what is presented as a simple exposition of the *Principles*, has striking anti-Cartesian implications: to establish a link by nature between God and its decree, is by the same stroke to ruin its liberty of indifference and the contingency of the world it produces. Let us see now what follows from this:

> P18: *God is immutable*. Dem.: If God were mutable (*mutabilis*), he would not be changed only in part, but would have to be changed in respect to his whole essence (by P17). However, the essence of God exists necessarily (by P5, 6, and 7). Therefore, God is immutable, q.e.d.[15]

It could not be clearer, first, that alternatives and change come down to the same thing; second, that any change, in God, would amount to its transformation; and finally that such a transformation being contradictory, the supposed indifference of God is a pure fiction. It is clear too that just above, in the so-called exposition of the *Principles*, Spinoza was quite seriously working to refute polytheism, which was hardly a concern for Descartes.[16]

---

[13] See also *TTP* IV, 24–5; CWS II, 131.

[14] *PP* I, 17 cor.; CWS I, 260.

[15] *PP* I, 18 and Dem.; CWS I, 260.

[16] Polytheism is nevertheless invoked in the fifth Meditation, in the same problematic context: 'There are many ways in which I understand that this idea is not something fictitious which is dependent on my thought, but is an image of a true and immutable nature. First of all, there is the fact that, apart from God, there is nothing else of which

It has been said that the object of this refutation, which by contrast appears so often in Spinoza, is the denial of the substantiality of the world and consequently of its exteriority in relation to God.[17] In this regard it has been noted that the reasoning departs from the hypothesis of two Gods, as if it were a matter of refuting a possible dualism. This, however, is strictly speaking true only in the *Principles*:[18] the *Ethics* speaks of 'two or more Gods',[19] using the Cartesian turn of phrase, referring to the choice that God is supposed to have made, in the Thomist tradition but also in Descartes, at the moment of production. The choice is first between producing and not producing, since such is the mark par excellence of a free will – whence the Two; next it is between many possible worlds, as in Thomism – whence the Many. One will note that the *Metaphysical Thoughts*, which follow the *Principles*, still refer to the hypothesis of 'many gods'.[20] Finally, the Appendix to Part I of the *Ethics*, as well as the *Theologico-Political Treatise*, regularly refer to pagan polytheism.[21]

In Spinoza, the problem of polytheism is tied to the question of knowing whether the attribution of a free will to God is compatible with its unity and immutability; it is only indirectly, and through its consequences, that it touches on the exteriority of the world, as a corollary of its contingency. His reasonings might be borrowed in part from the tradition, but they nevertheless have a new and vital sense, by virtue of an original context which, as we will see, is that of baroque Europe.

Let us now return to the scholium to I, 17. The argument from causal identity might have sufficed; Spinoza will however produce a second, which is of another nature and which fulfils another function. The new argument is polemical. No doubt this is true of any argument when it intervenes in an adverse context, but we must distinguish between reasonings that support a thesis, and participate in a positive movement of enunciation, and reasonings whose sole interest is to invalidate those of the adversary, by

---

I am capable of thinking such that existence belongs to its essence. Second, I cannot understand how there could be two or more Gods of this kind . . .' (CSM II, 47; AT VII, 68). The link between pluralism and transformation is clearly established, even if Descartes hardly dwells on it. Spinoza will turn this link against its author, seeing in it the means to refute the doctrine of the creation of eternal truths.

17 This is Wolfson's position: see Wolfson 1934, chapter 4.
18 *PP* I, 11 and Dem.; *CWS* I, 254–5.
19 *Ethics* I, 33 Dem.; *CWS* I, 436.
20 *CM* II, 2 and 4; *CWS* I, 318–19 and 321–3.
21 *TTP* VI, 4 (*CWS* II, 153) and 31–2 (*CWS* II, 159); XIV, 25 (*CWS* II, 268), insisting on the unicity of God; XV, 6 (*CWS* II, 274); XVII, 109 (*CWS* II, 321).

revealing their internal contradictions. The difference, in this scholium, is very marked: Spinoza will now venture into a logical space that he takes to be fictive. On this point he explains himself in the scholium to I, 33, whose structure is similar in this regard: the geometric order does not on its own have the power to force entry into a mind that does not consent to the proof of the demonstration, protected as it is by a rampart of beliefs that discredit the conclusions in advance.

It is thus a matter of evaluating the adversary's argument: an exhaustive creation would amount to an exhaustion of God's power, 'so they preferred to maintain that God is indifferent to all things, not creating anything except what he has decreed to create by some absolute will'.[22] Spinoza responds in two steps. First of all, this argument presupposes that a part of the divine power remains potential, a claim to which he is opposed. Here he only recalls the conclusions of the geometric reasoning,[23] and so seems to beg the question; this leads him to formulate a second response, which has the appearance of a counterargument: a non-exhaustive creation would mean that God conceives an infinity of possibles 'which nevertheless he will never be able to create'.[24] God, in being prevented from doing all that it can, would impose a constraint upon itself, which would limit its power.[25] And what is this part of the divine power left never to be actualised, in order to prevent it from being exhausted? The supposed potential power is really only a nothingness, an impotence. In this way the contradiction becomes obvious: 'he cannot bring about everything to which his power extends'.[26]

Let us note that the refutation of the idea of finite substance, in the *Short Treatise*, showed precisely the aberration of such a conception: 'It [substance] cannot limit itself, for being unlimited, it would have had to change its whole nature',[27] that is, to be transformed. Everything thus happens as if the self-limitation of God, which as we have seen is the logical consequence of the retention of a part of its power, must lead to its transformation. Constraint presupposes a relation of exteriority that is in the case of God as impossible as suicide, since such a relation would no less be a relation to itself. It is striking that this problem of a power of omission occupies the next part of the *Short Treatise*. For if 'it is impossible that a substance should have

---

[22] *Ethics* I, 17 Schol.; CWS I, 426.

[23] *Ethics* I, 16; CWS I, 424.

[24] *Ethics* I, 17 Schol.; CWS I, 426.

[25] Macherey speaks of those 'negative or suspensive characteristics that place this power in a position to turn against itself, outside of all reason' (Macherey, *Introduction* I, 153).

[26] *Ethics* I, 17 Schol.; CWS I, 426.

[27] *KV* I, 2, n. 1; CWS I, 66. Translation modified.

willed to limit itself',[28] could it not turn out to be limited by its cause? It is therefore necessary to ask after God's conduct when it produces. The answer will hardly satisfy us, for it is still obediently Cartesian: 'That he could not have given more would be contrary to his omnipotence . . .'. (Had Spinoza already become himself, he would have stopped there.) 'That he could have, but would not, smacks of envy, which is not in any way in God, who is all goodness and fullness.'[29] We will soon see the answer given in the *Ethics*; what matters for now is that the *Short Treatise* really establishes, even if only implicitly, a relation between the power of abstention, wrongly thought to characterise divine freedom, and the idea of a transformation of God.

Refutation of the Power of the Alternative

But Spinoza is not yet finished with 'free will': he returns to it in a long scholium to which we have already referred, the second to I, 33. In the meantime – that is, from the second part of the scholium to I, 17, to the second corollary of I, 32 – he reduces the understanding and the will to the rank of mere effects of divine production, undoing still a bit further the fallacious link between God's freedom and its supposed will.[30] In the attribution of a 'free will' [*volonté libre*] to God, in fact, two things need to be critiqued, two anthropomorphic traits that both share in common an illusion concerning human nature: volition [*la volonté*], and arbitrariness [*le libre arbitre*]. From this point on, what counts is the identity in God of its power and its essence, only formulated in I, 34 (to which, incidentally, the scholium on the power of kings refers), though it was already presupposed in the second scholium to I, 33.

Let us again underscore how the attack targets Descartes in particular. The idea of a 'kingdom of God' is biblical in origin, and Spinoza cites the prophets on this score. But he immediately specifies that in their case the metaphor was perfectly justified, for they had no theoretical pretensions and spoke in a language suited to the vulgar, having only the goal of making them know the divine law, that is, of making them obey. This conception is already that of Thomas Aquinas.[31] For his part, Hobbes devoted half of

---

[28] *KV* I, 2; *CWS* I, 67.
[29] *KV* I, 2; *CWS* I, 67.
[30] *Ethics* I, 32 cor. 1; *CWS* I, 435.
[31] Aquinas excluded from theology, the highest doctrine, the recourse to metaphor, which on his account belonged to the lowest doctrine, poetics. However, it was still necessary that metaphor was suitable to holy Scripture, since it makes significant use of it. A first reason for this is that human knowledge departs from the sensible. But

the *Leviathan* to the 'king of kings',[32] but he specified that God's reign is exercised properly speaking only over creatures endowed with reason: the expression applies to the order of nature only metaphorically.[33] Leibniz, dis-regarding Spinoza's warning, will also fall in with this Christian lineage.[34] In this context, only one philosopher was happy to fully identify the power of God and royal power: Descartes.

'It is God who has established these laws in nature, just as a king estab-lishes laws in his kingdom.'[35] Descartes is in the process of laying out his doctrine of the creation of eternal truths, and he raises an objection to himself:[36] 'If God established these truths, he can change them, like a king changes his laws', but 'I understand them to be eternal and immutable'.[37]

he adds another: it is befitting 'that spiritual truths be expounded by means of figures taken from corporeal things, in order that thereby even the simple who are unable by themselves to grasp intellectual things may be able to understand it' (*Summa Theologiae* I q.1 a.9). However, there is an important qualification: if you must make recourse to comparisons, it seems more suitable to avoid 'nobler bodies', for 'simili-tudes drawn from things farthest away from God form within us a truer estimate that God is above whatsoever we may say or think of Him' (*Summa Theologiae* I q.1 a.9). Nevertheless, Aquinas seems to have been less vigilant about the reverse, since royalty seemed to him to approach divinity. (This is how he explained the ancient kings' rites of apotheosis, on which see Gilson.) ['The ruler of the people is the servant of God, and it is from God that this faithful servant will receive his reward. Those truly royal recompenses – honor and glory – will be his in fuller measure in the degree that his kingly office is higher and more divine. The pagans were confused in thinking that their kings became gods after their death. This is not the king's motive for governing justly. He has been God's deputy among his people, and he can therefore justly expect that, after leading his people to him, he will be closer to God in the next world and more intimately united with him' (Gilson 2002: 376).]

[32] As he explains in the last lines of Chapter XXX (Hobbes 2012: II, 552).

[33] *Leviathan* XXXI (Hobbes 2012: II, 554–6). (The question of God's royalty, understood in the literal, historical sense of the term, dealt with in XXXV, does not concern us here.)

[34] In Leibniz, God can be considered sometimes as the 'architect of the machine of the universe', and sometimes as the 'monarch of the divine city of minds', by virtue of the harmony of the two kingdoms of nature and grace. See *Discourse on Metaphysics* §§36–7 (Leibniz 1989: 326–8), and the correspondence with Arnauld (Leibniz 1989: 331–54); *On the Radical Origination of Things* (Leibniz 1989: 486–50); *Principles of Nature and Grace* §5 (Leibniz 1989: 638); and *Monadology* §§85–7 (Leibniz 1989: 651–2).

[35] Descartes, Letter to Mersenne, 15 April 1630 (*AT* I, 145).

[36] Geneviève Rodis-Lewis notes that this objection must have made an impression on Mersenne: in 1634, he wrote that 'God could change everything in physics.' See Rodis-Lewis 2000: 139 and 491 n. 57.

[37] Descartes, Letter to Mersenne, 15 April 1630 (*AT* I, 145–6).

And his response is as follows: 'Yes' – that is, the objection is admissible – 'if his will can change'.[38] Now, of course, it cannot change, since this would be a mark of inconstancy, and thus of imperfection. Descartes, as often happens to him, finds himself in quite a precarious position: 1. His intention, which will also be Spinoza's, is to affirm the omnipotence of God without limits. 2. God must thus not, unlike the ancient divinities, be subject to truths independent of it, so that the truth itself must bear the mark of its free will, or be the object of a creation (creation bears not only on existence but on essence). 3. But it is still hard to see how contingency could not lead to mutability, how the power of the alternative would not fade away simply by virtue of the fact that the will was exercised at some point. Does not the arbitrariness of the decision involve its variability? How would free will not be caprice?

A capricious God, which nevertheless could only violate dogma: this no doubt is too much for Descartes, but it is not yet enough for Spinoza. The question quickly bears on the logic of choice. Can one simply conceive of a capricious God? One will note Spinoza's reticence to think choice, which hardly plays a role for him in either case: one, implying an external constraint, namely having to 'choose the lesser of two evils' (Seneca's problem);[39] the other, implying an internalisation of constraint, and consequently an internal tension, 'I see the better, and approve it, but do the worse' (Medea's problem).[40] Only dependency directly opposes the subject to itself, makes it *fluctuating*. Choice is always between a bad and a good, that is, between two evils or two goods: it comes down to an affective mechanism that leaves no place for indifference. In fact, choice translates resistance into the spontaneous affirmation of a nature, and always presupposes at least one other nature. In order for God to have had a choice, it would have been necessary that a thread from the outside passes into it and compromises its identity.

One will not be surprised to rediscover at the level of God the same consequence as on the ethical level: the alternative is not external to the subject, it is its division, or at least its tendency toward division. And so Spinoza's conclusion is radical: to affirm that God has a choice is to dissolve its identity, it is to posit only a verbal unity. And it is to take away from God everything that one hoped to grant it: the gesture by which Descartes

[38] Descartes, Letter to Mersenne, 15 April 1630 (*AT* I, 145–6).
[39] *Ethics* IV, 20 Schol.; *CWS* I, 557.
[40] *Ethics* III, 2 Schol. (*CWS* I, 496–7); IV, Praef. (*CWS* I, 543); IV, 17 Schol. (*CWS* I, 554–5).

believed he would elevate monotheism to its highest and greatest form leads us to polytheism.

Not only do alternatives and change come down to the same logic, but this logic is operative at the level of essence: plurality of Gods = transformation of God. Such are the two polemical moments of necessitarianism: having a choice is to be able to change; and thus, to be other than oneself or to be transformed. And such is the object of *Ethics* I, 33, its demonstration and its second scholium.

Ethics I, 33, Its Demonstration and Second Scholium

Spinoza's strategy is as follows: the ruin of alternatives is the indispensable polemical complement to the positive demonstration of the necessary character of the production of things. *Ethics* I, 33: 'Things could have been produced by God in no other way, and in no other order than they have been produced.'[41]

The demonstration proceeds by way of absurdity, showing that the affirmation of an alternative leads to polytheism. If it is true that the production of the world follows from the necessity of the divine nature, then another world would mean another God:

> Therefore, if things could have been of another nature, or could have been determined to produce an effect in another way, so that the order of Nature was different, then God's nature could also have been other than it is now, and therefore (by 11) that [other nature] would also have had to exist, and consequently, there could have been two or more Gods, which is absurd (by 14 cor. 1).[42]

The reasoning seems to beg the question, since it is supported by what it is apparently supposed to demonstrate, the necessity of the link between God and the natural order. If there is this link, then alternatives lead to polytheism; but the latter is absurd given the definition of God; thus the link exists . . . The reasoning only seems to work on the basis of a separate hypothetical syllogism: if the order of the world necessarily follows from the nature of God, then the idea of an alternative must shatter the notion of God. Strictly speaking, the hypothesis remains to be demonstrated: what we took for question-begging was in reality a tautology. Ultimately, Proposition

41 *Ethics* I, 33; CWS I, 436.
42 *Ethics* I, 33 Dem.; CWS I, 436.

33 is only the polemical obverse of Propositions 16 and 29, which are cited as premises: the aspect that calls out the adversary. It adds nothing to them, it merely confirms them negatively. The appearance of question-begging thus comes from the fact that there was nothing to demonstrate: it simply relies on a claim already established in order to make the adversary's position appear absurd. Reasoning by reduction to absurdity, for whose insufficiency Tschirnhaus thought to reproach Spinoza,[43] here takes on, so to speak, a natural function: the polemical function. It is no longer an indirect proof of what is true, which has already been produced, but the refutation of the false, which follows from it.

And yet this approach is insufficient, since the polemic also implies that the adversary, shocked by this claim being put forth, would no longer have an ear for hearing reasons. The 'demonstration' was only a barely concealed provocation: Descartes, the polytheist! Descartes, who began his letter on the God-king precisely by denouncing the residual paganism of the scholastic conception . . .![44] Now we must bring the attack to the adversary's camp; if he is deaf to our reasoning, let his own be destroyed.

Here marks the passage to the second step of the polemic, which explains the tone of impatience with which the second scholium began, paving the way for the scholium to II, 3: 'From the preceding it clearly follows that . . . Nor does this in any way mean that . . . Indeed, from the opposite, it would clearly follow (as I have just shown), that . . . Of course, I have no doubt that many will reject this opinion as absurd, without even being willing to examine it' (*perpendere*, the same verb as in the scholium to II, 3), 'for no other reason than because they have been accustomed . . . But I also have no doubt that, if they are willing to reflect on the matter, and consider properly' (again, *perpendere*) 'the chain of our demonstrations, in the end they will . . . Nor is it necessary for me to repeat here what I said in 17, schol. Nevertheless, to please them, I shall show that . . .'.[45] The scholium finishes with these words: 'So I shall waste no time in refuting this absurdity.'[46]

Spinoza must agree to interrupt the productive course of the theses demonstrated *ordine geometrico*, in order to move temporarily into the logical space of absurdity, which he unfolds all the better to destroy it. In this space

[43] See *Ep.* LXIV [to Schuller]; CWS II, 438–9.
[44] Descartes, Letter to Mersenne, 15 April 1630: 'In fact, to say that these truths are independent of God, is to speak of it like Jupiter or Saturn, and to subject it to the Styx and the Fates' (AT I, 145). Note that God, for Aquinas, knows essences by contemplating itself; its creation bears only on existences (see *Summa Theologiae* I q.14 a.5).
[45] *Ethics* I, 33 Schol. 2; CWS I, 436–7. Translation modified.
[46] *Ethics* I, 33 Schol. 2; CWS I, 439.

there shimmer curious 'verbal beings': 'two or more Gods', as we have seen, but also the figure of a metamorphosing God, not identical to itself. Perhaps they coincide.

The second scholium to Proposition 33 introduces the idea of perfection: not only is the alternative a false notion, but it contradicts the supremely perfect nature of God. By contrast, the perfection of the production of things follows necessarily from the divine perfection. Why would imperfection follow from the notion of alternatives? Because if the production could have happened otherwise, God would have had another nature. Moreover, that nature, different from the one that follows from the consideration of the supremely perfect, would no longer be divine.[47]

One will note that the notion of choice does not play a role here: the alternative envisioned is objective, and Spinoza means 'if things had been *necessarily* produced in another way . . .'. The reasoning always operates within the register of necessity; the interrogation simply bears on the existence of an alternative within necessity, on the possibility of another necessity.

But, Spinoza adds, those who are 'accustomed' to conceive of freedom as the exercise of an 'absolute volition' (contrary to I, def. 7) run the risk of judging the thesis to be absurd even before having examined it, whereas this examination, if they submitted to it, would lead them to reject this false concept of freedom.[48] He overcomes his weariness (reflecting the impatience of I, 17) and initiates a new demonstration, whose goal is to show that even an important concession to the adversary (attributing to God a will pertaining to its essence) changes nothing with regard to the conclusion: the incompatibility of perfection and alternatives. Spinoza thus posits two premises: 1. Decrees also bear on essences (or else God would be impotent). 2. Decrees are eternal (or else God would be inconstant).

Let us analyse the reasoning here.

1. Spinoza begins by underlining that when properly understood, eternity, which is a divine perfection, excludes alternatives. In fact, eternity excludes *ante* and *post*, whence the double impossibility of change ('cannot') and the initial alternative ('could not have'). God is indissociable from its decrees ('it cannot be without them').

2. Will one object that God could have, without imperfection and from all eternity, decreed otherwise? But the alternative, this time attributed to God, never leaves any room for choice. And above all, Spinoza underscores that this objection leads straight to inconstancy (the possibility of changing

---

[47] *Ethics* I, 33 Schol. 2; CWS I, 436–7.
[48] *Ethics* I, 33 Schol. 2; CWS I, 437.

decrees). *For if* God had decreed otherwise, it would have had another understanding and another will. Supposing that this were possible, that is, without implying any transformation or imperfection (it being understood that transformation would mean degradation), it remains equally possible that it could decree otherwise today. Let us be more precise: if God had decreed otherwise *than it decreed* (henceforth, the subject that remains accepts the alternative), it would have had another understanding and another will *than those that it had*. Now if the present and an unreal past are compatible, the same would go for the present and the [real] past and the present that it led to. And if one considers the consensus of philosophers on the actuality of the divine understanding and on the impossibility of distinguishing the understanding and will of God from its essence, one comes back to the initial conclusion: worse than inconstancy, having had another actual understanding and another will would absurdly mean that God had another essence.[49]

At this point Spinoza can return to the hypothesis of a retention of power, whose refutation in the *Short Treatise* seemed insufficient to us, but which prefigured the judgment rendered in the scholium to *Ethics* I, 17: such a hypothesis amounts to attributing a certain impotence to God. This latter part of the scholium is difficult. Spinoza begins by stating the proposition again, just to add that if the necessity of the relation between the divine nature and the natural order followed from perfection, then the argument for such retention can no longer be maintained in any way. It is important to understand: 1. That retention becomes impossible since, in the absence of any alternative, what God can do, God does. 2. That perfection being in any case incompatible with alternatives, retention loses its meaning (not only does the concept of omnipotence do without it; it rules it out). Spinoza then makes room for an objection inspired by the *Replies to the Sixth Set of Objections*: if God is also the author of moral truths, then perfection or imperfection are not in things, and 'if God had willed it, he could have brought it about that what is now perfection would have been the greatest imperfection, and conversely'.[50] We find here once again the same type of reasoning as that concerning the triangle inseparable from its properties: the absurdity of the objection consists in positing the arbitrariness of the link between the essence of things and their content in perfection.

The *Short Treatise*, which contained a first version of this argument, proposed a helpful example: it is as if justice could refrain from being just. For

[49] *Ethics* I, 33 Schol. 2; CWS I, 437–8.
[50] *Ethics* I, 33 Schol. 2; CWS I, 438.

such is indeed the consequence of a conception according to which God has the power to indifferently attribute good or bad to anything whatever, and in this way to make it so 'that evil becomes good': one separates value from itself, one pretends that its meaning would be indifferent to the nature of things or the acts to which it is related. To such an aberration Spinoza has a cutting reply:

> This reasoning is as sound as if I said that God is God because he wills that he is God, therefore it is in his power not to be God. This is absurdity itself.[51]

Spinoza naturally means that one does not posit a subject by abstracting from its essence. This, moreover, is what comes through if one compares, in the *Metaphysical Thoughts*, the two formulas defining the changes that are not transformations: 'whatever variation there can be in a subject while the very essence of the subject remains intact'; 'change in which there is no transformation of the subject'.[52] In this way, to think that God could indifferently establish values, and then change them, amounts to saying that 'it is in his power not to be God', that is, to be this chimera that is and at the same time is not what it is, or rather is destroyed in order to become what it is not (we have already had occasion to underscore how striving to be transformed is a contradiction in terms, since 'no thing can be destroyed except through an external cause'[53]).

In the scholium we are concerned with here, to say that perfection does not reside in things but in a decree of God is in truth a sophism, for the two are not mutually exclusive: God creates the essences of things, which involve a certain degree of perfection.[54] To untie the link between the nature of a thing and its perfection presupposes that there was some play there, which comes down to introducing a gap in God between what it conceives and what it decrees, whereas it decrees precisely as it conceives: God, as Spinoza already underscored with regard to the triangle, 'understands necessarily what it wills', an ambiguous statement that might be interpreted in a Cartesian sense as a liberty of indifference, but which means simply that God's will and understanding, decree and conception are one and the same

---

[51] *KV* I, 4; *CWS* I, 83.
[52] *CM* I, 4; *CWS* I, 321.
[53] *Ethics* III, 4; *CWS* I, 498.
[54] On the scale of degrees of perfection or reality, see *Ethics* I, 11 Schol., and II, 13 Schol. (*CWS* I, 418–19; 457–8).

thing (it does not understand what it wills without reciprocally willing what it understands).

Spinoza here clearly denounces, in the Cartesian doctrine of the creation of eternal truths, the persistence of a primacy of volition in spite of the theoretical indistinction of the will and the understanding. Everything actually happens as if Descartes' God conceived all possibles on the one hand, abstracting from any consideration of truth or perfection, and on the other decreed concerning them an arbitrary distribution of the true and good.[55] The hypothesis of a power of omission leads at the end of the day to the absurdity of a schizophrenic God, who 'can bring it about by his will that he understands things in another way than he does understand them'.[56]

Finally, the relation between these two absurdities that constitute the inversion of values and the transformation of God is already stated in the second corollary to I, 20, on the basis of the identity of the essence and existence of God (a variant of the argument from simplicity, discussed above):

> It follows, secondly, that God, *or* all of God's attributes, are immutable. For if they changed as to their existence, they would also (by P20) change as to their essence, i.e. (as is known through itself), from being true become false, which is absurd.[57]

The Baroque – or its Banishment?

Let us recapitulate these multiple geometric incursions into the logical space of absurdity (a false space, of course, which shimmers only in words – but Spinoza likes to take his adversary at his word, and to lead him into his own verbal trap). To confuse the power of God with the power of kings, to create this half-divine, half-human chimera of a celestial monarch, is to dissolve the identity of the supremely perfect Being in polytheism and metamorphosis.

---

[55] Let us cite, for memory's sake, the incriminating passage from the *Replies to the Sixth Set of Objections*: 'As for the freedom of the will, the way in which it exists in God is quite different from the way in which it exists in us. It is self-contradictory to suppose that the will of God was not indifferent from eternity with respect to everything which has happened or will ever happen; for it is impossible to imagine that anything is thought of in the divine intellect as good or true, or worthy of belief or action or omission, prior to the decision of the divine will to make it so' (CSM II, 291; AT VII, 431–2). There follows, among other things, the example of the properties of the triangle.

[56] *Ethics* I, 33 Schol. 2; CWS I, 438.

[57] *Ethics* I, 20 cor. 2; CWS I, 428–9.

One could say that this Spinozist way of imagining Cartesianism, or rather of revealing its underlying imaginary, its fictional tendencies, is quite 'baroque'. However, one might also consider, or object, that the 'Baroque' is the drift that Spinoza condemns in the Cartesian doctrine of the creation of eternal truths, and which consequently he keeps at a distance. This point deserves our attention.

We have invoked the confession of Letter 30, where Spinoza admits that certain things, 'which do not agree at all with our philosophic mind, previously seemed to me in vain, disorderly and absurd'.[58] If one were to realise, beyond this, that the theory of death as transformation, as stated in the scholium to *Ethics* IV, 39, was an idea dear to the late Renaissance (or, if you prefer, to the precocious Baroque), one would be tempted to reconstruct a juvenile Spinozist melancholy whose conjunctural formula would be found in Ronsard:

One never dies, one simply changes
From one form into another, and this change is called
Death, when one takes on a new form.
(Discours à maître Julien Chauveau)

O death, your power is great and admirable!
[. . .]
All that has been remade flows like water,
And nothing under Heaven does not see itself anew:
But the form is changed into a new other,
And the world calls LIVING this change,
And DYING when the form turns into another.
(Hymne à la mort)[59]

In Ronsard, death and birth tend to become indiscernible, so that the mournful vision of a world where everything is corrupted is accompanied by a strange vitalism. The young Spinoza, animated solely by the desire to understand, and haunted by the discordance between reason and things, experienced and carried within himself this contradiction up to a 'fatal' point, as he indicated in the prologue to the *Treatise on the Emendation of the Intellect*. It is in the framework of this crisis, where the desire for rationality constantly runs into the apparent confusion of things, that we must locate

---

[58] *Ep.* XXX [to Oldenburg]; CWS II, 14.
[59] Cited in Jeanneret 1998: 43–4.

this old feeling. The latter certainly never surpassed the stage of a tendency or belief *at certain times*, since the same prologue, which described the reaction to the crises, relayed an active hesitation that ultimately opened onto the conquest of a thinking that was sure of itself. Spinoza's philosophy, produced by the ultimately surmounted crisis, bears within itself the refutation of generalised chaos: the confusion is in the mind, not in things; the universal and perpetual process of transformation, which is the very becoming of Nature, is governed by constant laws.[60]

It is not our aim here to discuss the criteria of the Baroque. We will adopt a minimal definition that will hopefully be acceptable, and call Baroque this acute relation to the unstable, to the confused, and to disproportion, of a mind affected by the infinite, which unevenly marks, in space and time, European culture from the final decades of the sixteenth century up through the second half of the seventeenth.[61] If we are concerned with the conditions of a debate rather than the statement of a *doxa* or doctrine, we can broadly identify three moments of the baroque spirit: 1. The resigned sentiment of the vanishing of all fixity, and the melancholy vitalism that follows from it (a position that Spinoza never subscribed to, and which is that of a scepticism that virtually renounces philosophy). 2. The unresolved crisis of reason (which Spinoza experienced while believing himself capable of overcoming it, whereas Pascal accepted it as an ultimate and irreducible given). 3. The crisis overcome, which accepts all the apparent chaos but believes it possible to decipher an order therein (Spinoza become Spinozist, along with Malebranche and Leibniz).

---

[60] See *Ethics* III, Praef.; CWS I, 491–2.

[61] It is customary to say that the United Provinces 'resisted' the Baroque – for example, see Lebrun 1967: 45. Only the Low Countries that remained Spanish, and thus Catholic, were open to it (the Rubens in Anvers, etc.), whereas Calvinism, needing severe places of worship, along with the commercial bourgeoisie, sought above all in painting a peaceful reflection of its everyday life, preventing its diffusion. This judgment must be relativised. We remarked in the previous study that Calvinism was incapable of preventing the evolution of Dutch customs in matters of childcare; in the same way, it quickly found itself needing to allow for the reintroduction of organs into churches. More generally, one need not imagine Holland, the most open and cosmopolitan place in Europe, as protected from a tendency that was sweeping across the whole continent. Spanish theatre (Lope de Vega, Calderón) found great success there, as well as *L'Astrée*, whose Dutch imitators were numerous, and the same goes for Racine, whose work echoes the baroque problematic of political power, etc. Finally, it is hard to deny that Rembrandt had a baroque sensibility (the interpenetration of contraries, continuous passages from one form to another, etc.).

Spinoza's philosophy belongs to this third moment: consider, for example, the decision not to become outraged by the disorder of human passions – as do those whose imagination is captured by the satisfying representation of a perfect human being – but rather to confront the apparent confusion in order to unlock its mechanism (the theory of the passions); or the Spinozist search for a law of variation, instead of opposing or superimposing the one and the many, the immutable and the changing, as irreconcilable domains (the theory of the individual); or again this typical manner of naturalising the extraordinary, by subtracting the supernatural from it (the theory of the miracle, of hallucination, and of omens). If the Baroque in art abolishes clear oppositions, the absolute delimitation of contraries, it finds its philosophical equivalent in the different ways of deciding on the scholastic refusal of fig-ures of madness, in the conviction of no longer being able to hold to reason shielded from the confused and the obscure by annulling them under the category of *privatio*: that is, recognising that thought is never clear (Pascal), or that on the contrary reason is legible beneath apparent disorder (Spinoza). These are also the two ways of introducing dreams into philosophy: the intu-ition of the indiscernible, or the need for a superior striving for distinction.

And it is because Spinoza wants to allow in his thought for maximal variety and variation that the need for the immutable is stronger and more radical in him than in anyone else, and more dramatically so given the con-dition of immanence, which has repercussions for God – as we have seen in his veiled critique of Descartes – and makes every concession to the immu-tability of the world. Spinozism demands the minimum of permanence or identity, provided that there is an immovable rock, ultimately so as to save knowledge but also the relative continuity of existences:

> created things, *or* all things except God, always exist only by the power, *or* essence, of God, and not by their own power. From this it follows that the present existence of things is not the cause of their future existence, but only God's immutability is. So we are compelled to say that when God has first created a thing, he will preserve it afterwards continuously, *or* will continue that same action of creating it.[62]

The significance of this precocious text, faithful to the Cartesian doctrine of continual creation, is that it guarantees future *conatus* through the immu-tability of God. It is clear that an inconstant, 'fluctuating' God, as Filippo

[62] CM II, 1; CWS I, 317.

Mignini put it,[63] in short a God that ceaselessly changes its decrees all the while itself passing through corresponding metamorphoses, would render essences unstable and would compromise any scientific or ethical method, not only because the object would mutate, but because the subject itself would proceed from one amnesia to another. There is here something like a properly Spinozist experience of the Kantian cinnabar, a hell that reveals Cartesianism pushed to its ultimate consequences and which leads us back to the first moment of the baroque, that of universal confusion, a dreamlike world of pure effects where everything metamorphoses instead of *being reproduced*, before an impotent and fascinated imagination.[64] It is precisely this that Spinoza saw, and was determined to banish – this was indeed how he participated in the Baroque.[65]

The Paradoxical Fate of Spinozism: Chimera against Chimera, and How the Relation to Polytheism Is Really Established in Spinoza's Thought

It turns out that the first refuters of Spinozism imputed to it what the system itself was designed to destroy: an unstable, polymorphous, corporeal God – that is, a chimera. They believed that they recognised the spectre that Spinoza demystified in the God of Descartes and the scholastics in Spinozism itself. It is true that his thought left itself open to this, when it proposed the most paradoxical, most acrobatic solution possible: *to truly distinguish the infinite from the finite presupposes making the finite immanent to the infinite*. 'Those who judge things confusedly and have not been accustomed to know things through their first causes – because they do not distinguish between the modifications of substances and the substances themselves, nor do they know how things are produced.'[66] Spinoza adds: from this there

---

[63] 'But if the divine will were free, that is, devoid of a necessitating internal rule, the very existence of God – which consists in a perfect essence – would not be necessary, but abandoned to the fluctuation of its will to be or not to be' (Spinoza 1986: 538).

[64] See the *Critique of Pure Reason*, 'On the synthesis of reproduction in the imagination', A100–A102 (Kant 1998: 229–30).

[65] Our aim here is not to produce an exhaustive analysis of baroque traits in Spinoza's work. Leaving aside the themes of dreams and amnesia, one would need to add the relativisation of values (not that value is intrinsically relative, but it only has sense when referred to a point of view: the feeling of the beautiful and the ugly is tied to the structure of our eye), the point of view of the worm in the blood, the fiction of a speaking triangle that takes God to be triangular, maybe also the thesis of an infinity of attributes, and finally the sprawling use of the adverb *quatenus*.

[66] *Ethics* I, 8 Schol. 2; CWS I, 413. Translation modified.

arises the belief in metamorphoses, the confusion of the divine and human natures.

The violence of the refuters was proportionate to the unheard-of insolence of this philosopher who essentially told Christians that their religion of 'mediation' (the mystery of the Incarnation) rested on a chimera worthy of ancient mythology. For Spinoza, the God-human who came to save human beings was no less fabulous than Zeus taking on a human form in order to seduce a young woman (and by contrast, it was in a totally different sense that Christ, according to Spinoza, was 'divine'). But it was apparently an analogous concern that animated the Christian philosophers. Take Malebranche: his concern for a radical distinction between the infinite and the finite led him to posit an infinite distance, a non-relation between the Most High and the unfathomable nothing to which sin reduces us, so that a relation is only possible in spite of it through a 'mediator', God-Human, at least for those who 'truly count their own being, and this vast universe we admire, as nothing', for the rest live in illusion and pride: 'They dare to approach God as if they no longer knew that the distance from Him to us is infinite.'[67] In short, each accuses the other of confusing what must be distinguished.

The effort of refutation thus bears principally on this notion of mode, which on the one hand ruins the doctrine of the Mediator, and on the other hand proposes a sort of substitute for it; this is why, following Malebranche, so many authors detected in Spinozism a divinisation of the creature, and at the same time a vivisection of the unique, simple, and nonextended God. In order to throw the accusation of producing chimeras back at Spinoza, to carry out this reversal vital for a Christianity threatened at its foundations, it would be important to remain deaf to the relationship between substance and its modifications. Less than a misinterpretation [*contresens*], there was here, by all evidence, in minds as sharp as those of Malebranche, Bayle, Fénelon, and Leibniz, an indispensable *misunderstanding* [*malentendu*]. Malebranche, as is well known, led the charge, even using that argumentative move so dear to Spinoza, which consists in denouncing in the adversary a confusion analogous to that of a bad geometer who gives to one figure the properties of another:

> What disorder, what discord between the divinity and its parts! What a monster, Aristes, what an appalling and ridiculous chimera! A God necessarily hated, blasphemed, scorned, or at least unknown by the better

---

[67] *Dialogues on Metaphysics and on Religion* XIV, 8 (Malebranche 1997a: 273).

part of what He is. For how few people would think of recognizing such a divinity? A God who is necessarily either unhappy or unfeeling in most of His parts or modifications, a God who punishes or exacts vengeance on Himself. In a word, an infinitely perfect being nonetheless comprising all the disorders of the universe. What notion is more full of visible contradictions! Surely if there are people capable of constructing a God on the basis of so monstrous an idea, it is either because they do not want to have one or they are minds born to seek all the properties of a triangle in the idea of a circle.[68]

Bayle, Lamy, and Leibniz would take up this argument in which modification is reduced to part, leading to a God that is composed and not simple, variable and not immutable, corporeal and not pure thought.

Fénelon had a slightly different approach. Certainly, he thundered against the idea that God could modify itself. But, clearly believing that Spinoza's God comes down to the *facies totius universi*, he intended to show that the universe would not satisfy his idea of the infinitely perfect. He compares the infinite universe with the internal movement of a quantity of boiling water confined to a pot:

> It is true to say that all this water boils, that it is agitated, that it changes its relations, and that in a word nothing is more changing internally, although it appears immobile from the outside. Exactly the same would go for this universe that is supposed to be infinite: it could not as a whole change its place; but all the different movements within that form all the relations, which constitute the generation and corruption of substances, would be perpetual and infinite. The whole mass would move ceaselessly in all its parts. But, it is clear that a whole that perpetually changes would not satisfy the idea that I have of infinite perfection . . .[69]

No matter the angle of attack (theory of the mode, of the plurality of attributes, or of the universe permanent in its variation), what is denounced is polytheism, or better a changing, contradictory, suicidal God.[70] It is a

---

[68] *Dialogues on Metaphysics and on Religion* IX, 2 (Malebranche 1997a: 150).

[69] Fénelon 1983–97: II, 626.

[70] The slander that consisted in denouncing in Spinozism a chimera in the strict sense of the term would have a long afterlife. It often devolved into an *ad hominem* slander: thus in the nineteenth century Foucher de Careil denounced 'the coupling of Descartes and the Kabbalah in a vigorous but deformed brain' (cited in Friedmann 1975: 20–1).

thorny affair, when one knows the ease with which a Malebranche or a Leibniz themselves made use of polytheistic rhetoric: 'God regards us in Jesus Christ as Gods';[71] 'so many little gods under this supreme God'.[72]

Only one path for refutation, much less often taken than that by way of the mode, remained plausible: how do we pass from the substantial unity of the attribute to the unicity of a substance comprising all attributes? Only Wittich, it seems, took hold of this problem in order to claim that Spinozism in fact hid beneath the chimera of the single substance an irreducibly plural God.[73]

Spinoza himself had been able to write: 'Regarding the attributes of which God consists, they are nothing but infinite substances, each of which must, of itself, be infinitely perfect.'[74] One will note that when Oldenburg asked him if this did not lead to a polytheism, he based his question on the thesis of the necessary existence of substance, without understanding that the concept no longer had its traditional application or extension.[75] In his defence, one must however take into account the intellectual conversion that Spinoza demanded of him, even if Spinoza was very careful in laying out his definition of God, which incidentally did not contain the word 'substance'. Similarly, at the beginning of the *Ethics*, there is an air of polytheism about Propositions 6–8, which is reinforced by the second scholium to I, 8 (although it unambiguously invokes God in its singularity) in its treatment of the substantial-modal relation as if it concerned 'substances' in the plural – which is somewhat paradoxical, in a scholium that also denounces mythological phantasmagoria. Spinoza is walking a tightrope here: the geometric progression – which must reform the traditional concept of substance step-by-step in order to culminate in the statement of the single substance (God, in Proposition 11), and in this way make apparent the chimera that would constitute the pluralism of substances – necessarily functions in a transitory and variable logical space, where the philosopher, without being able too strongly to anticipate his final claim (as in Letter 2, he gives to the reader,

---

[71] *Dialogues on Metaphysics and on Religion* IX, 6 (Malebranche 1997a: 156).

[72] G. W. Leibniz, Letter to Arnauld, 9 October 1687 (Leibniz 1989: 346). The 'small gods' are minds or rational souls. See also *New System* §5 (Leibniz 1989: 454–5). By contrast, consider his reluctance to allow such language in the Letter to Thomasius, 20/30 April 1669 (Leibniz 1989: 101), and *Monadology* §60 (Leibniz 1989: 649).

[73] Hubert 1995: 75.

[74] *KV* I, 6, n. a.; CWS I, 88.

[75] *Ep.* III [from Oldenburg]; CWS I, 169. Spinoza's response, in Letter 4: 'the second Proposition does not make many Gods, but only one, consisting of infinite attributes, etc.' (*Ep.* IV [to Oldenburg]; CWS I, 172).

like a sphinx, only the first hint of the definition of God), continues to speak the vulgar language of substance in the plural, which in his view is fictive, but real for the reader.[76]

Much later, Tschirnhaus would ask whether the infinity of attributes does not lead to an infinity of worlds.[77] Spinoza felt it was sufficient to point to *Ethics* II, 7, which states the identity of the order and connection between attributes. An infinity of worlds would lead to an infinity of orders, or in other words of simultaneous productions, as the improper term 'parallelism', which since Leibniz has distorted this doctrine, has often led people to believe. If this were the case – and we do not see how the logic of parallelism could fail to lead to this ultimate consequence – he would need to posit not a dozen divinities as in the Greek pantheon, but an infinity of Gods performing miraculously synchronous acts, implying who knows what preestablished harmony.

Of all the demonstrations of the unicity of God, the only interesting one is that which is not given as such, which does not begin from the pregiven concept of God or the single substance, but on the contrary gives rise to it. Ordinarily, Spinoza deduces the unicity of God from its nominal definition (supremely perfect being). Take two Gods A and B; they must know one another; thus, the necessity of the idea that A forms of B is in B, since the latter exists necessarily, and vice versa; and so each lacks the perfection that is found in the other; A and B are therefore only false Gods.[78] In the *Ethics*, this reasoning is obsolete, it being given from I, 5 onward that there cannot be two or more substances of the same nature (since considered in themselves, abstracting from their affections, they would differ in nothing). But I, 2 and 3 add another premise: if there were many substances, they would thus be of different attributes, having nothing in common between them and no causal connection. The originality here[79] lies in not making

---

[76] As Pierre Lachièze-Rey wrote: 'The hypothetical plurality of primary substance is, it is true, seemingly presented to us as a fact that, if it existed, would require a cause, which seems to imply the intervention of the principle of causality; but instead it is a matter of making us try to carry out, from within this plurality, a mental operation whose impossibility we will grasp in a manner as immediate as that of "making a square circle" or "representing an elephant passing through the eye of a needle"' (Lachièze-Rey 1950: 250).

[77] *Ep.* LXIII [from Schuller, speaking on Tschirnhaus' behalf]; CWS II, 436.

[78] *PP* I, 11 Dem.; CWS I, 254–5. There is an analogous line of reasoning in the *Metaphysical Thoughts*, with the added nuance that it pertains to multiple Gods, as we noted above. On the medieval origin of this reasoning, see Wolfson 1934: 79–11; and Gueroult 1968: 224 n. 8.

[79] As was already the case in the *Short Treatise* I, 2 (CWS I, 65–73), where the demonstration was less elegant.

the hypothesis of polytheism immediately absurd, which gives the reasoning a truly creative character: faced with this impious perspective, the reader is intellectually constrained to orient themselves toward the synthesis of the attributes.[80] The latter, as we know, is only accomplished from the point of view of the idea of God: there is thus a leap from one logical moment to another, from substance raised to infinity or the attribute raised to substantiality, to God, the absolutely infinite being that absorbs all being and to which there necessarily pertains, by its essence, every attribute. The second scholium to I, 8 precisely marks a pause between the two moments of the process.

Of all Spinoza's correspondents, only Hudde appears to be particularly interested in obtaining a *Spinozist* demonstration of divine unity. He got a first response: 1. The definition of a thing, involving only its essence, never indicates a number, and consequently the existence of a thing of which there are multiple examples is not explained by its essence but by an external cause. 2. The existence of God follows from its very essence. 3. Therefore 'the necessary existence of many Gods cannot be inferred'.[81] Spinoza's reasoning is valid, but it has the air of a sophism, since it posits as a premise that a mere definition cannot decide on number; whence this conclusion that, instead of positing the unicity of God, only rejects *the necessity of polytheism*.[82] One understands why Hudde felt he had not gotten a true answer to his question.

[80] Lachièze-Rey goes even further by suggesting that this intermediary moment of the demonstration was a moment of Spinoza's own thought: 'Under the influence of the radical distinction established by Descartes between extension and thought, was not Spinoza led to introduce into his own system an analogous distinction by transposing it into one between the attributes; was he not led to admit, if not as real, at least as possible, a plurality of self-positings [*autopositions*], each infinite essence forming with the corresponding *causa sui* a kind of world complete and closed upon itself?' (Lachièze-Rey 1950: 98). This question, as we have suggested above, must not be separated from the questionable 'parallelist' interpretation of the attributes.

[81] *Ep.* XXXIV [to Hudde]; CWS II, 26.

[82] In fact, this manner of demonstration leads to the claim that 'God is only very improperly called one and unique' (CM I, 6; CWS I, 312). (See also the analogous formula in the letter to Jelles: *Ep.* L; CWS II, 406.) This claim has the following implications. On the one hand, numbering a thing presupposes having antecedently related it to a common kind, so that the question – and the claim itself – of the unicity of God has as a theoretical framework the virtual position of a community of its *similars*, and consequently constitutes nonsense. On the other hand, one could simply say that the existence of God, insofar as it immediately follows from its essence, excludes all number, and thus plurality in particular. (On this question, see Macherey 2000). The question nevertheless has a sense when it is a matter of thinking the identity of heterogeneous

Spinoza thus gave him a second response, which resembles the formal arguments of the *Principles* and the *Metaphysical Thoughts*, but which is presented in a less awkward, more disturbing form, which is, one might say, baroque: it is as if a double momentarily detached itself from its original, by the mere play of the words God and Being, in order immediately to be reincorporated. 1. Take the following definition: God is understood as the Being whose essence involves existence, and which consequently (a previously established inference) is supremely perfect. 2. Suppose now a Being that necessarily existed, and which was thus supremely perfect. 3. The essence of this being can only be that of God. 4. If it existed outside of God, we would be dealing with a second exemplar, which according to the first response is 'absurd', for it would suppose that the existence of God followed from something other than its essence, which is indifferent to number.

But Hudde remained perplexed: 'and nevertheless you say that your difficulty – namely, where there could not be many beings, existing through themselves, but differing in nature, just as thought and extension are different, and can perhaps subsist by their own sufficiency – remains untouched'.[83] Having only Spinoza's responses at our disposal, we cannot know whether the question was initially put to him in this form. If that were the case, that would mean that he had initially been evasive, substituting the enumeration of God's properties for the synthesis of its attributes. Be that as it may, Hudde laid out the foundation of the problem before Spinoza: not at all imagining the reproducibility of God in many examples, he asks how to synthesise thought and extension, and why the latter are not Gods without communication. The response clearly hinges on the difference between 'infinite in its kind' and 'absolutely infinite'. Curiously, in his previous letter, Spinoza had granted to his correspondent that if a being, because it possesses a certain perfection, consequently exists necessarily, *for all the more reason* the perfectly infinite being must also exist; 'curiously', for this proposition was contiguous with the demonstration of unicity, but had no reason to play a role there since it secretly prepared the way for *another* demonstration. Now Spinoza lays out this latter: certainly extension and thought each exist by themselves; but then, by the argument 'for all the more reason', we can only attribute them to God which, if it possesses all perfection, must possess

---

attributes, because the problem of divine *unity* (and not unicity) is then tied directly to the hypothesis of a numerical plurality, thinkable under the kind common to the attribute.

[83] *Ep.* XXXVI [to Hudde]; CWS II, 30.

extension and thought among other things. The reasoning is audacious since it goes as far as possible in accepting a plurality of substances: this plurality is posited, *but thereby absorbed*.

Let us confess our trouble here: two truths are posited,[84] of which the one annuls the other. *As much as Spinoza refuted Cartesian polytheism, because it was a matter of denouncing the schizophrenic dissolution of the poorly conceived unique God, still he did not refute the polytheism of minor Gods, but rather clears it away simply by positing the properly understood unique God*: the necessary subsumption of all the infinities of a determinate kind under the absolutely infinite. The attribute is not a mode, it exists through itself. The concept of extension is formed, for example, without that of God, and thus it is sub-stance; its essence involves existence, and thus it is cause of itself. Extension is derived from nothing, it is absolutely a first cause; but *also* God must be posited, whose concept absorbs that of extension. God, one might say, becomes the subject of a multiplicity of substances; but this would be to say nothing, since the positing of God annuls the nevertheless irrefutable mul-tiplicity of substances.[85] If we must admit a logical gap here, we must also

---

[84] As Macherey underscores: 'It is necessary, then, to grant both aspects of the argument equal weight: considered from the point of view of the diversity (or infinity) of its attributes, substance is neither a fiction nor the representation of a pure possibility, which could not be constructed except by an enumeration toward the infinite, because such an enumeration has no sense except from the point of view of the imagination. But it is the same content, an identical reality that presents itself as diversity and then as unity' (Macherey 2011: 98).

[85] As Gueroult wrote, 'the unicity necessarily involved in the concept of God, not being possible without this union, is consequently *imposed* on substances that, consid-ered in themselves in their concept, are perfectly foreign to it' (Gueroult 1968: 226; Gueroult's emphasis). Gueroult concludes on this score that 'the *unicity* proper to the infinitely infinite nature of God is the principle of the *unity* in it of all the substances that constitute it' (1968: 226, Gueroult's emphasis), so that the mistake would be to search conversely for the unicity of God in the impotence of substances to exist without the others. And this makes plausible the hypothesis that Hudde, having seen Spinoza's last response in Letter 36, would await a demonstration of this kind ('I trust I see in what sense you understand it', Spinoza writes [CWS II, 30]). In a general way, Gueroult excellently summarises the problem: 'In fact, it would be vain to look in them [substances] for something that calls for their inseparability or their unity. Their irreconcilable diversity involves, on the contrary, with regard to each, their recipro-cal independence. After having rehabilitated them as possible ingredients of God by establishing their self-sufficiency and their self-causality, Spinoza could not then go on to relate them to God by arguing for their insufficiency and impotence. Unless he was lacking in the most basic logic, it would have been necessary for him to let down his correspondents and demonstrate the unity of substances, not by starting from them, but by conceiving that it is imposed on them from without – if not in spite of them,

concede that there is no real problem of pluralism, unless one asks after the very possibility of the concept of God, as Leibniz would later do.[86]

Let us return to the false problem raised by the first refuters. The sound contestation of Spinozist monotheism can only bear on the irreducible duality of approaches that characterise it in its foundation, and on the potential insufficiency of their articulation: the classical problem of the reconciliation of the real distinction and substantial identity of the attributes.[87] It does not fall to us to decide on this question; we sought only to make apparent the gap between the manner in which the first refuters thought themselves able to turn the Spinozist weaponry against him (the critique of a pluralist and transformist conception of God by way of anthropomorphism, initially raised by Spinoza against his predecessors and Descartes in particular) and the manner in which Spinoza himself could meet the problem of pluralism or polytheism on his own terms.

---

at least independently of them, by the infinitely infinite being whose nature demands that they would be united in it' (Gueroult 1968: 227).

[86] The question, as Friedmann notes, is that of proving 'the compatibility of perfections, infinite in number, that God involves' (Friedmann 1975: 131).

[87] Lachièze-Rey concluded that there is in this sense a definitive discord, in Spinozism, between a 'regressive analytic method' inherited from Descartes, based on the substantial-modal implication and the universe as a system of essences, and a 'progressive method', synthetic, based on the properly Spinozist intuition of immanent causality (Lachièze-Rey 1950, conclusion). For an overview of the debate at the heart of the German school, see Huan 1914, chapter 3. In sum: 1. Hegel and Erdmann lean toward a subjectivist interpretation of the attributes, holding that if each attribute is in itself and conceived through itself, one obtains a diversity irreducible to any synthesis, but they run aground on the objection that the infinite understanding alone cannot produce this heterogeneity. 2. Herder and then Fischer forward the hypothesis of a plurality of forces, in this way attempting to surpass the alternative of formalism (renouncing the reality of the attributes) and pluralism (renouncing the unity of substance), but inevitably exposing themselves to the charge of arbitrariness. 3. Camerer considers the question undecidable, and concludes that there is an insoluble contradiction at the heart of Spinozism. 4. Based on suggestions by Zulawski and Windelband, and without for all that claiming to completely resolve the question, Huan estimates that the diversity of the attributes is contemporaneous with God's action (modification).

7

The Transformist Dream of Absolute Monarchy

If the fictive attribution to God of a royal power has such consequences, must not kings, for their part, have something to do with polytheism and metamorphoses? Must not the call not to confuse the power of God and the power of kings be read in these two senses?

When we read the call in this other sense, we leave behind metaphysics for current affairs. Spinoza wrote the *Ethics* at a time when Louis XIV had progressively extended his hegemony across Europe, quickly attaining prominence over the sovereigns of Spain, England, and the Emperor, encountering immediate resistance only from the United Provinces and particularly from Holland. Outside of its dominant Calvinism and its upstart economic success, Holland represented political alterity in Europe, the refuge for all dissidents and all religious sects; it was there too that lampoons and gazettes were published that would be clandestinely introduced into the kingdom of France.[1] At the same time, the republican regime was itself threatened from within by the ascendence of monarchical absolutism, represented by the Prince of Orange. Louis XIV, though hardly in favour of an Orangist restoration for diplomatic reasons, led the punitive expedition[2] of 1672 that delivered the *coup de grâce* to the republican experiment.[3] This is

---

[1] '[T]heir insolence spurs me to turn all my forces against that haughty and ingrate nation', wrote Louis XIV in his *Mémoires* (cited in Mugnier-Pollet 1976: 176).

[2] The United Provinces, feeling threatened, had inspired the recent anti-French Triple Alliance, in which England and Sweden participated. But at the last minute, Louis XIV was successful in subordinating England by promising Charles II a territorial reward and help in re-establishing absolutism and Catholicism in his kingdom.

[3] All the safeguards of the *Political Treatise* against the catastrophic transfer of all sovereignty to a military chief in a situation of national distress are obviously related to this recent event, and have as their backdrop or grid of intelligibility the final decades of the Roman republic (the prestige of a Scipio, the dictatorship of a Sulla, and then

when Spinoza, solicited by the diplomat Stouppe, declined the offer of a royal grant.[4]

Everything thus happens as if the claim about the power of God and the power of kings had as its background these current affairs themselves: the relationship is too strong for it to be a matter of a mere coincidence.[5] It seems moreover that the comparison could only have a sense if kings, in the imagination of the vulgar, were already distinguished as exceptional beings, at the limit of the human. But this observation would remain only half convincing if Spinoza had not himself inverted the formula.

The Divinisation of Kings

If we turn to the study of monarchy in the *Political Treatise* (VI–VII), we see that it is carried out in two stages: first the exposition of a viable constitution (*fundamenta*), then its reconstruction in a demonstrative mode. Now at the point at which he announces, at the beginning of chapter VII, that he will 'demonstrate . . . in proper order' what he had previously only 'explained', Spinoza begins with the following remark: 'Kings are not Gods . . .' (and he had said *a contrario*: 'Persians were accustomed to worship their Kings as Gods, yet . . .').[6]

This theme was already present in the *Theologico-Political Treatise*. Is not the confusion of the royal and the divine implicitly there between the lines of the title itself? We know that the aim of that work was to combat any admixture of the theological in the political, any intrusion of the clergy into the affairs of the State, against the theocratic pretensions of the Calvinist consistory. Now, of the fearful and superstitious mass of human beings, the

---

Caesar . . .). See *TP* VII, 5 and 7 (*CWS* II, 547–8); VIII, 9 (*CWS* II, 568–9); X, 9 (*CWS* II, 600).

[4] Colerus reports the testimony of the spouses Van der Spyck, with whom Spinoza was lodging: he told them, after the famous visit with the French occupant, that 'in the interviews that he had had with M. Stoupe (sic), the officer had assured him that he would be employed of his own free will, and that he would not need to doubt that he would obtain, on his recommendation, a pension from the generosity of the king; but that for him, Spinoza, as he had no intention of dedicating himself to the king of France, had refused the offer made to him, with all the civility of which he was capable' (Colerus 1954: 1522).

[5] Pierre Macherey already suggested this relation to current affairs, in a remark that even allows one to glimpse the exchange between the Divine and the Royal by which, in the seventeenth century, God tended to be made into a king and the king into a God (Macherey, *Introduction* II, 61 and n. 2).

[6] *TP* VII, 1; *CWS* II, 544.

Preface says that they 'are easily led, under the pretext of religion, now to worship their Kings as Gods, now to curse and loathe them as the common plague of the human race'.[7]

There then follow the famous lines on royal absolutism:

> The greatest secret of monarchic rule, and its main interest, is to keep men deceived, and to cloak in the specious name of Religion the fear by which they must be checked, so that they will fight for slavery as they would for their survival, and will think it not shameful, but a most honorable achievement, to give their life and blood that one man may have a ground for boasting. Nevertheless, in a free republic nothing more unfortunate can be thought of or attempted. For it is completely contrary to the general freedom to fill the free judgment of each man with prejudices, or to restrain it in any way.[8]

The Dutch reader of 1670 could not but think of the young king of France, who Racine had years prior already compared to Alexander; the *Treatise* was written during a period of military preparations, offensive on the French side, defensive on the Dutch side (Louis XIV had already conquered Flanders). In the years following the invasion, the insistent remarks of the *Political Treatise* concerning the exclusively defensive legitimacy of wars[9] were referring not only to the anti-Hispanic bellicosity of the House of Orange but also to the aggressivity of the French, of which Holland would henceforth be the privileged victim (Spinoza would invoke Louis XIV by name in his critique of the marriages of warmongers[10]): absolute monarchy is pious and bellicose by nature – these are the two faces of its mystification.

The early remark of the Preface is taken further in Chapter XVII, which now provides examples: the apotheosis of Augustus, the divinisation of the Persian kings (as again later in the *Political Treatise*), and finally Alexander. If the comparison of Louis XIV and Alexander was at the time becoming

---

[7] *TTP* Praef., 8; CWS II, 68.

[8] *TTP* Praef., 10; CWS II, 68–9.

[9] 'War ought to be waged only for the sake of peace' (*TP* VI, 35; CWS II, 542); 'No doubt the majority of this Council will never have a disposition in favor of war' (*TP* VII, 7; CWS II, 548); etc.

[10] *TP* VII, 24; CWS II, 556. The reference is to the War of Devolution (1667–68), in which France, upon the death of the father of Maria Theresa of Spain, asserted its rights over the Spanish Low Countries. The peace of Aix-la-Chappelle, which followed in 1668, rang out like an alarm bell across all of Europe, at the very moment when Spinoza was writing the *Theologico-Political Treatise*.

a commonplace,[11] the *Theologico-Political Treatise* paints an image of the Greek conqueror that is, to say the least, complex: superstitious as hell,[12] although a shrewd man.[13] The idea is the following: 'when Kings assumed the rule in earlier times, to make themselves secure they tried to persuade people that they were descended from the immortal Gods. They thought that if only their subjects (and everyone else) didn't look on them as equals, but believed them to be Gods, they would easily surrender to them, and willingly submit to their rule.'[14]

But then finally comes the following remark:

> Others have had better success . . . in persuading men that Majesty is sacred, God's representative on earth, that it has been established, not by men's vote and consent, but by God, and that it is preserved and defended by God's particular providence and aid. And in this way Monarchs have devised other means to secure their rule, which I'll omit . . .[15]

Spinoza is alluding to the Gallic inversion of the traditional theological doctrine of the divine origin of all authority (according to the Pauline formula: *non est potestas nisi a Deo*). This traditional doctrine of divine right[16] is moreover also refused in the name of popular sovereignty: Spinoza maintains that the divine right properly speaking only exists by virtue of a transfer of sovereignty from the people to God, establishing a theocracy,[17] and grants the formula *Non est potestas nisi a Deo* validity only within the framework

---

[11] After Racine, Mignard would paint a portrait of the king as Alexander, etc.

[12] *TTP* Praef., 5; *CWS* II, 67.

[13] *TTP* XVII, 22; *CWS* II, 300. But shrewdness, as it appears from the start of the *Political Treatise*, is not a sufficient virtue in politics.

[14] *TTP* XVII, 20; *CWS* II, 300.

[15] *TTP* XVII, 24–5; *CWS* II, 301.

[16] [Throughout this paragraph Zourabichvili uses the word 'droit'. In this part of *TTP* XVII Spinoza uses the language of 'jus', as in: 'Quare absolute concedendum jus divinum ab eo tempore incepisse, a quo homines expresso pacto Deo promiserunt in omnibus obedire, quo sua libertate naturali quasi cesserunt, jusque suum in Deum transtulerunt, sicuti in statu civili fieri diximus'. Both Curley (*CWS* II, 293) and Silverthorne and Israel (Spinoza 2007: 205) translate this as 'divine law'. However, given that Spinoza's semantic field also includes 'lex divina', most notably of course in *TTP* IV: 'Lex distinguenda videtur in humanam, & divinam . . . per divinam autem, quae solum summum bonum, hoc est, Dei veram cognitionem, & amorem spectat', I prefer to render this *jus* as 'right'. – GM.]

[17] *TTP* XVI, 55–6; *CWS* II, 293.

of his immanentist reinterpretation[18] – two ideas clearly monstrous for a theologian. But in the passage cited, Spinoza targets more precisely the monarchist version of divine right, or in other words the absolutist conception of the king as vicar of God.

The current state of affairs is thus signalled anew, since this conception, already adopted by the English kings, was definitively imposed with its announcement in France under the reign of Louis XIV: it means that power is transmitted directly to God, contrary to the original theological conception that affirms only the divine nature of sovereignty but leaves to human beings the issue of determining the form of its exercise, which consequently implies, in the case of monarchy, an initial popular consent (an original contract). This disappearance of elective mediation leads to a sacralisation of the very personage of the king, and tends to lead back to the ancient practice of apotheosis.[19]

The figure of the Great King thus might play a certain role between the lines of Spinoza's text.[20] Belonging to the same generation, beginning their careers in the same year 1661, the one by a seizure of power, the other by a commentary on the great innovative thinker of the age, we see two brilliant points in a perfect relation of opposition: the Sun King and the expert lens grinder. It is likely that the king, in spite of the naive efforts of Colbert and the curiosity of the Great Condé, remained unaware of Spinoza, even if Schuller assured him that the *Theologico-Political Treatise* was 'thought very highly of by many people in Paris'.[21] It is sufficient that the *Ethics* and the two political works involve Louis XIV as a living incarnation of the figure to be demystified. It is sufficient, furthermore, that his long reign came to

---

[18] '[The] power by which natural things exist, and so by which they have effects, can't be anything but the eternal power of God itself' (*TP* II, 2; *CWS* II, 507). From this point of view the divine origin of *potestas* and popular sovereignty coincide.

[19] At his first *lit de justice* in Parliament (at the age of four and a half years old!) Louis XIV was told: 'The seat of Your Majesty represents for us the throne of the living God', the royal orders render you honour and respect 'as to a visible divinity' (Lacour-Gayet 1923: 263). A bit later, in *Le catéchisme royal* by Antoine Godeau, in 1650: 'You are the visible image of God in all his extension . . . May your Majesty remember at every moment that he is a vice-God' (cited by Néraudau 1986: 14).

[20] This suggestion is even adorned by a symbolic anecdote: Van den Enden, Spinoza's former teacher, in his old age moved to the Picpus neighborhood of Paris, perhaps in order to foment an attack on the king; he paid for it with his life in 1674. See Vernière 1951: 91 and following. This is the origin of the legend of Spinoza's voyage to France, and of the threat of his imprisonment. Vernière wonders whether Van den Enden, under torture, mentioned Spinoza's name.

[21] *Ep.* LXX [from Schuller]; *CWS* II, 461. Translation modified.

an end in conformity with the prognosis of the *Political Treatise* concerning autocratic regimes: war, misery, surveillance, intolerance – a society transformed into 'desolation' [*solitudo*].[22]

Monarchical Absolutism and Metamorphosis

Is it possible, then, that there is a relation between monarchical absolutism and metamorphosis? Evidently so, in the case of Louis XIV.

1. Among all the books of classical poetry, the most highly regarded in the seventeenth century was Ovid's *Metamorphosis*. One can especially get a taste for this at Versailles, all of whose décor it inspired, under the authoritarian rule of Le Brun. But even more, going beyond all plans, Versailles testifies to the submission of architecture itself, stone, marble, even down to the metal of the furniture, to the principle of metamorphosis: 'there is not an inch of Versailles that has not been modified ten times', said the princess Palatine.[23] It is often forgotten that the palace already existed, and that Louis XIV's intervention consisted not in constructing it, but in setting it into motion, at the same time affirming the new conception of the power of one alone: the transformations of Versailles began with absolutism, in 1661, and would never again cease until the Revolution. Under the reign of Louis XIV, they are the marks of fortune and of the royal will, which reflected in the monarch, at the exact point where he wanted to be absolute, the image of an irreducible multiplicity.[24] This official aesthetic, nourished on Ovid, had only one goal: to serve the glory of the king, to find the symbolic adequate to the absolute monarchy.

---

[22] *TP* V, 4 (CWS II, 530) and VI, 4 (CWS II, 533). Translation modified. [In the former, Curley renders *solitudo* as 'wasteland'; in the latter, as 'being without protection'. – GM.]

[23] Cited in Cornette 1998: 9. See also Beaussant 1981: 69–70: 'Before Louis XIV, there had already been three Versailles. With him, there would be a permanent metamorphosis, an incessant transformation – the Versailles of Le Vau, the Versailles of Mansart, of Robert de Cotte – a perpetual construction site about which the mistreated courtiers bitterly complained.'

[24] 'The palace was, in fact, in perpetual metamorphosis, and the stages, the transformations, the regrets of this royal construction site translate the transformations, the aesthetic confrontations, and some of the political stakes that marked the Grand Siècle. *The* Versailles [plural] say much more than the too-still image of the "king of glory" reflected by the glitter and sparkle of the great mirrors and crystal chandeliers of the Galerie des Glaces, which each night captured the radiance of the setting sun' (Cornette 1998).

2. The absolutist ideology consisted in the fabulous transmutation of the real. Louis XIV was not simply compared to a God, but to all the gods. Here is an example of praise:

> Your empire, Sire, will remain eternally, like your august name; even if all the Gods found themselves today in your enchanted palace, and by their presence rendered it with Your Majesty more considerable than Rome ever was, each of them would hasten to aid me in embellishing this Temple, of which you will always be the most beautiful ornament. Versailles is now a Pantheon; the ancient one was built by Agrippa who dedicated it to Jupiter the Vengeful; for me, Sire, I have no fear of passing into flattery, nor into profanity, in dedicating the new one to you, as to the Augustus Apollo of France . . . It is hardly wrong, Sire, that I call Your Majesty the New Pantheon, since His sacred person contains the perfections of the divinities of paganism: the intelligence of Saturn, the power of Jupiter, the valour of Mars and the radiance of Apollo.[25]

The king is all the gods at once, a Pantheon unto himself. But on another level, incarnating Jupiter, he constructs around himself, at Versailles, a Pantheon. Many historians have underscored his propensity to surround himself with little secondary gods: one absolute kinglet for painting (Le Brun), another for the belles-lettres (Boileau), a third for music (Lully). This pantheonic dream was also projected, diplomatically, across all of Europe, everywhere aiding the rise of absolute monarchy, provided that the sovereigns swore allegiance, beginning of course with Spain, England, and the Emperor.

3. The very life of this king was punctuated by spectacular reversals that belong to metamorphosis:[26] that of the end of the 1650s, when to everyone's surprise the sovereign, a politically irresponsible guitar player and chess enthusiast, evolved into an inventive and methodical politician; that of the 1680s, when the master of Europe, baroque and libertine, turned to devotion.

---

[25] Vertron 1686; cited in Néraudau 1986: 65. The author speaks of a 'pagan monotheism'; we would be inclined, instead, to speak of a Christian polytheism . . . Already Augustus was happy to multiply his divine links: descended from Venus, he willingly had himself represented as Mercury, as Apollo, as (triumphant) Jupiter. See Martin 1994: 426–34. The author advances an interesting idea: 'Above all, it was necessary to perfect the reconciliation of human beings through that of the gods' (426–7). In this way, Augustus worked to reconstruct the divided Pantheon: Juno, Minerva, Neptune, and finally Bacchus, with whom Marc Antony had been identified, were rehabilitated.

[26] On this subject see Beaussant 1981: 54 and following.

4. Until 1670, ballet was Louis XIV's preferred diversion. He himself played any role: Apollo, of course, but also Hercules, Alexander, some Roman emperor, and again a shepherd, a madman, a Moor, and even feminine roles. These are so many successive transfigurations of the body of the king: what in literature and painting are only metaphors here become living metamorphoses.[27] This of course affected the very content of the ballets, which drew much from mythology. Finally, the ballet had a notorious political role: the king assigned each their place, meaning notably for the nobles their transformation into courtiers.

In every regard, Louis XIV was the great concrete incarnation of transformation, in which all the elements of the problem raised by Spinoza were condensed. During the latter's lifetime, the mythological image of the king saw great success. It would later come into crisis, for many reasons: it became a cliché; some were repulsed by this political usage of mythology, or quite simply by the divinisation of royal authority; finally, it seemed to others still too weak to express the miracle that was realised in the royal body. For metamorphosis is inherent to the absolute monarch not only because it is supposed to hold together all talents, but also and above all through this double body that makes of it another Incarnation, that of the nation. But this mystery, this permanent miracle seems, to many, to be beyond all figuration.[28]

---

[27] Néraudau 1986: 119; and Beaussant 1981: 65: 'in this way, *Les Plaisirs de l'Isle enchantée* were a theatre, but this was not a representation. This was a transmutation, a translation on an epic and mythic scale of the royal personage and his entourage.'

[28] The monarchical taste for Ovid finally invites us to ask, in Ovid himself, after a potential relationship between the *Metamorphosis* and politics. This falls outside the scope of our investigation, but it is notable that Spinoza left behind two hints, though they are admittedly inconclusive: the strange definition of Ovid as an author of 'political matters', which is often taken to be a slip-up (*TTP* VII, 62; *CWS* II, 184), and the reference to the divinisation of Augustus (*TTP* XVII, 21; *CWS* II, 300). Recall the fury of Augustus and his sentencing the poet to exile in the year 8, just as he finished the *Metamorphoses*. Without revisiting the reasons for this sanction, which doubtless have never been made fully clear, one may take Ovid to be a particularly perspicacious witness of the great political mystification of his time: the progressive establishment of a monarchical regime under the cover of a republican restoration (the Principate). The final verses of the *Metamorphoses* invoke precisely the advent of Augustus (Spinoza, for his part, alludes to this at the end of *TTP* XVII). As Néraudau writes, 'Ovid places the metamorphosis of Augustus in line with other incredible metamorphoses and he makes the power of the Prince enter into the agitated world that created his poetry. He pushed to the extreme limit the mythological ambitions of power' (Néraudau 1997: 19–21). [Zourabichvili follows Appuhn in reading Spinoza as saying that Ovid is concerned with political matters; other readers take him to be discussing the author of the Book of Judges. See Curley's footnote on the matter (*CWS* II, 184, n. 29). – GM.]

The relationship between monarchy and transformation must now be verified in the analyses that Spinoza devotes to this regime. These analyses, as we will see, ceaselessly denounce a *political chimera*, a regime that exists only in the dream of a sovereign and a populace.

Royal Absolutism according to Spinoza: A Quintuple Chimera

The reminder that 'kings are not gods' is not incidental, and it is not in vain that Spinoza places it at the head of his demonstration of the optimal foundations of the monarchical regime in the *Political Treatise*. The originality of the approach is by now well known: on the one hand, the entire demonstration is based on the in fact and in principle impossibility of royal absolutism,[29] and reveals its falsehood: the reality of such a regime would in fact imply that kings were gods. On the other hand, it is precisely in the name of an absolutist conception of sovereignty that Spinoza carries out the demystification, and this is what directs the effort of optimisation toward a constitution at the furthest possible remove from royal absolutism.[30] We will see in the end that the entire analysis of monarchy is traversed by another argumentative theme that is its counterpoint: no longer the impossibility of the reign of a single person and its failure to be absolute, but its tyrannical and barbarous drift, the political avatar of 'dreaming with open eyes' that is the most common condition of human beings, nothing less indeed than the triumphant tendency in Europe – including Holland – at the moment when Spinoza wrote. Who could believe that a human being could stay above human passions, and in all circumstances have eyes only for the common good? 'No one is so alert that he doesn't sometimes lose focus',[31] that is, confuse the private and the public.

The study of monarchy includes two components, chapter VI and chapter VII. The three first paragraphs of chapter VI have an unclear status: they contain general remarks that seem to extend the previous chapters, and yet Spinoza slides imperceptibly toward the case of monarchy, as it appears in the middle of §3. We believe that the first four paragraphs constitute an introduction specific to the problem of monarchy, a set of premises that outline a problematic frame that the reader will need to keep in mind throughout the study: is it true that monarchy is the solution par excellence to the political problem? These premises can be reduced to two principal ones.

---

[29] See Préposiet 1967: 232–3; Matheron 1969: 404.
[30] See Giancotti 1985: 231–55.
[31] *TP* VI, 3; CWS II, 532.

1. The multitude, moved by its fear of desolation, desires the civil state, and obtains it only on condition of consenting to let itself be led 'as if by one mind' (*una veluti mente*).[32] To conclude that the solution lies in the reign of a single person would be poorly relying on experience, which shows that the durability of absolute monarchies is paid for by a pseudo-concord obtained through intimidation, by a peace that is only the 'absence of war' (*belli privatio*), and which deserves in reality the names of 'barbarism' and 'desolation' [*solitudo*].[33] Monarchy thus implicitly appears as a contradictory political solution: fleeing desolation for another form of desolation.

2. Since human beings are subject to the passions, on the one hand the condition in which they can 'agree' is the formation of a 'common affect';[34] on the other hand it is not realistic to entrust the care of the 'common well-being' to a single human being (absolute monarchy), hoping they will perform an abnegation of which no one is judged capable.[35] Moreover, this state of passion explains that the propensity to discord is as strong as the desire for concord, whence a perpetual, maybe inevitable tension,[36] which if need be is resolved by a reversal of authority that is less the pure and simple dissolution of the State than the death of one political form to the benefit of another form (just as an individual death, in the *Ethics*, is not necessarily a cadaveric decomposition but can be a transformation).[37] Why does the theme of transformation arise here? To understand this, it suffices to consider the examples of common affects likely to unite human beings: hope and fear, which the entire *Theologico-Political Treatise* demonstrated constitute the motive to obedience, but also the 'desire to avenge some common loss', in direct relation with the feeling of 'indignation' that animates insurrections against the tyrant.[38]

---

[32] *TP* VI, 1; CWS II, 532.

[33] *TP* VI, 4; CWS II, 533 (and also already *TP* V, 4; CWS II, 530). Translation modified.

[34] *TP* VI, 1; CWS II, 532.

[35] *TP* VI, 3; CWS II, 532–3. At the end of the previous chapter, Spinoza explained that Machiavelli's aim in *The Prince* was perhaps to 'show how much a free multitude should beware of entrusting its well-being absolutely to one person' (*TP* V, 7; CWS II, 531).

[36] *TP* VI, 2 and 4; CWS II, 532–3.

[37] *TP* VI, 2; CWS II, 532.

[38] *TP* III, 9; CWS II, 521: 'The third and final consideration is that things that cause indignation among most people are less within a Commonwealth's Right. For certainly men are guided by nature to unite in one aim (*in unum conspirare*), either because of a common hope or a common fear, or because they long to avenge some common loss.' [Translation modified.] The common fear here refers to the solitude of the state of nature, and one will note that Spinoza, in the *Theologico Political Treatise*, defined the

One will note that revolt, as in the case of adolescents, is for Spinoza a vindictive, sad, impotent behaviour, which nevertheless there is no sense in condemning, since it emanates from individuals pushed to the limit of what their nature can bear by 'troublesome' individuals who are false educators – parents, preachers, tyrants ('If there is no moderation in the mob, if they are terrifying unless they are frightened, it is because freedom and slavery are not easily combined'[39]). Faced with the alternative of self-negation or revolt, this negative outburst is the last indication of the health of the *conatus*.

The monarchical regime, though it seeks the absolute reign of a single person, is thus immediately placed under the twin signs of contradiction and transformation. We will now see in what aspects this double tendency manifests itself.

First Chimera: Behind the King, the Favourites and the Court

Spinoza insists first of all on the impossibility of ruling alone, whence the intrinsic paradox of monarchy. The question is not only that of the rationality of government, but of its practical possibility. 'Anyone who believes that one man alone can control the supreme Right of a Commonwealth is greatly mistaken.'[40] The burden of the State exceeds in every way the power of a single person: to consider everything at each moment, to be competent in all things, to make everyone obey. Consequently, after the common well-being has been 'committed absolutely' (*absolute committatur*) to someone,[41] this person must surround themselves with generals, counsellors, friends, 'to whom he commits (*committit*) his own well-being and that of everyone else'.[42] Thus there is a second transfer of sovereignty, by which the king, at a remove from the multitude of human beings, betrays their faith or sworn oath (*fidei*), by handing it over in turn to the loyalty (*fide*) of

---

contractual act in the same terms: *in unum conspirare* (*TTP* XVI). On indignation, see also *TP* IV, 4 (*CWS* II, 527) and *Ethics* III, 22 Schol. (*CWS* I, 507) and DA XX (*CWS* I, 535). [In *TP* III, 9 and elsewhere Curley tends to drop the language of indignation: here he renders 'quae plurimi indignantur' as 'things most people resent' (*CWS* II, 521). – GM.]

[39] *TP* VII, 27; *CWS* II, 559. Translation modified. ['Nihil praeterea in vulgo modicum, terrere nisi paveant: nam libertas et servitium haud facile miscentur.']

[40] *TP* VI, 5; *CWS* I, 533.

[41] *TP* VI, 3; *CWS* II, 532. On the impossibility of a single human being to consider all the affairs simultaneously and to be competent in all things, see respectively VII, 3 (*CWS* II, 546) and 5 (*CWS* II, 547–8).

[42] *TP* VI, 5; *CWS* II, 533.

a small number of people, capable of handling affairs and making the masses obey.[43] 'So a state thought to be an absolute Monarchy is really, in prac- tice, an Aristocracy. Of course, it's not openly an aristocracy, only covertly one. But that makes it the worst kind.'[44] Only just formed, the regime is immediately and by the force of things transformed, according to the logic of mythological metamorphoses: beneath the form, another form. And by a rather baroque play of successive iterations, the king might even fear a third transfer, this time carried out by his entourage: 'So the fewer the Counselors are, and the more powerful they consequently are, the greater the danger they'll transfer the rule to someone else . . . Moreover, if all power has been transferred unconditionally to one man, it can far more easily be transferred from that one to another.'[45]

In fact, the logic of the passions means that the reign of a single person incites envy, and that the king, at the same time that he must fatally rely on others, has to distrust everyone. This contradiction places the so-called sovereign in a relation of reciprocal fear with his subjects, and necessarily distracts him from the consideration of the common good by leading him to 'lay traps' and to make State secrets into the principle of his politics.[46] In

---

[43] TP VI, 3; CWS II, 532. On the necessity by which the king finds himself counting on the loyalty of his soldiers, see VII, 12 (CWS II, 549–50). *Fide* is also invoked concern- ing the absolute transfer to a military chief: see VII, 17 (CWS II, 552–3).

[44] TP VI, 5; CWS II, 533. See Balibar 1998: 71–2.

[45] TP VII, 14; CWS II, 551. Spinoza adds, citing Tacitus, that 'two common soldiers undertook to transfer the rule of the Roman people, and they succeeded' (alluding to the advent of Otho). This sentence is also cited in *TTP* XVII, n. XXXV (CWS II, 296).

[46] TP VI, 6 (CWS II, 534); VII, 27 and 29 (CWS II, 558–60). Here of course there is a whole critique of the baroque conception of politics, announced at the beginning of the *Political Treatise* (I, 2; CWS II, 504). See Naudé 1998: 23 and following; and Senellart 1989: 55 (on Naudé and his research into a 'legitimate Machiavellianism') and 99 (on Spinoza's relation to Machiavelli and his 'anti-tyrannical' analysis). Spinoza considers the problem of the legitimacy of a coup d'état in *TP* X, in a polemic against Machiavelli on the subject of the establishment of the dictatorship in the Roman Republic. Spinoza analyses it as a periodic transformation of the republic into a monarchy, with the risk that the latter will become lasting: 'Truly, since this Dictatorial power is absolutely Royal, the state can't be changed for a time into a Monarchy' (*in Monarchicum* – implying *imperium* – *mutari*) 'without great danger to the Republic, however short the time is' (*TP* X, 1; CWS II, 597). A bit later he cites the case of Scipio; and when, in his critique of Machiavelli's positive evaluation of the dictatorship as a remedy that periodically returns the State to its foundations, he invokes the danger that 'in their effort to escape Charybdis, they fall into Scylla' (*TP* X, 1; CWS II, 597), one is almost tempted to hear *Sulla*. Finally the danger materialised

this way the State is set into the spiral of tyranny, as the monarchy is easily destroyed, in favour or in the name of a popular uprising against oppression, to the benefit of another who will be more distrustful still. This is the framework, described in the *Theologico-Political Treatise*, in which Spinoza renders his pessimistic judgment on revolutions, which we mentioned in the Introduction.[47] Such a cycle not only reduces human beings to slavery, but robs the leader of the State of all freedom.

The contradiction inherent to royal absolutism leads Spinoza to this paradoxical conclusion:

> From all these considerations it follows that a King is less his own Master, and that the condition of his subjects is more wretched, the more absolutely the Right of the Commonwealth is transferred to him. So, to establish a Monarchic government properly, it's necessary to lay firm foundations for it. If this is done, the Monarch will be secure, and the multitude will have peace. Accordingly, a Monarch will be most his own master, when he's most attentive to the well-being of the multitude.[48]

Thus it is by way of realism, and not utopia, that Spinoza invites the monarch, not to relinquish the absolute authority of which he dreams but does not possess, but just to awaken from his dream, which turns into a nightmare as much for his subjects as for himself.

in Augustus, as he indicated in the *Theologico-Political Treatise*: 'in the end the state gave way again to a monarchy, changed only in name, as in England' (*TTP* XVIII, 35; *CWS* II, 331). Under the guise of a return to republican virtue, the establishment of the Principate in fact amounted to a monarchical transformation, the name serving to mystify the Roman people whose *odium regni* was legendary, but who, after so many years of civil war, tended to hate only the name of the king. Cromwell, somewhat differently than Augustus since he restored instead of established the monarchy (Spinoza explains that the Roman people were never accustomed to monarchy, killing three of its six kings), took the name of Lord Protector. Curiously, on the topic of Rome, the true transformation is not the one invoked (the Revolution of 509, putting an end to the tyranny of the Etruscan kings), but the Augustinian transformation, which not without ambiguity is compared to the pseudo-transformation of the English Revolution. Things become clearer in the *Political Treatise*, where the central problem is now the suicidal monarchical drift of every State (*TP* VII, 12; *CWS* II, 549–50), while Roman history becomes the principal point of reference (see above all VIII, 9 and X, 10 [*CWS* II, 568–9 and 600–1]). – On the reciprocal fear that engenders the pretension of reigning alone and the tyrannical spiral, see Matheron 1969: 405–20; and 'Spinoza, the Anti-Orwell: The Fear of the Masses', in Balibar 1994.
[47] See *TTP* XVII, 13–9 (*CWS* II, 298–9) and XVIII, 30–6 (*CWS* II, 329–31).
[48] *TP* VI, 8; *CWS* II, 534.

One gets the sense however that Spinoza hesitates between two visions, between two prognoses: the furious spiral of the ambition for power and reciprocal fear, which makes royal absolutism into an unstable and suicidal regime ('no one has sustained a violent rule for long; moderate ones last', according to Seneca[49]), and the heavy weight of oriental despotism ('No state has stood so long without notable change as that of the Turks. On the other hand, none have been less lasting than popular, *or* Democratic states. Nowhere else have there been so many rebellions'[50]). It is symptomatic that, in the second case, Spinoza abandons the pragmatic argument for a normative one: order, sure, but at what cost? He no longer invokes the likely ruin of the regime, but the breakdown into barbarism; no longer the grue-some fate of the tyrant, but the becoming-inhuman of its subjects.[51]

Second Chimera: The Tyrannical Dream of Transforming Nature

When Spinoza first deals with barbarism, that is, that regime of apparent peace where the subjects do not rise up because they are terrorised, 'deterred by fear' (*metu territi*),[52] he invokes the idea of a life reduced to 'the circula-tion of blood, and other things common to all animals', in contrast to a life deserving of being called human, which is defined above all by reason, that is 'the true virtue and life of the Mind'.[53] (In the *Theologico-Political Treatise*, Spinoza remarked that there are always people who dream of nothing but enriching themselves and filling their stomachs, willing for that to make any compromises: they easily accommodate themselves to such a regime which, in return, is supported by them.[54]) This calls to mind this passage from the scholium to *Ethics* IV, 39: 'I dare not deny that – even though the circula-tion of the blood is maintained, as well as the other [signs] on account of which the Body is thought to be alive – the human Body can nevertheless

---

[49] This phrase, cited twice in the *Theologico-Political Treatise* (*TTP* V, 22 and XVI, 29; *CWS* II, 144 and 288), is not repeated in the *Political Treatise*, although the theme of the political suicide of the tyrant is prominent there, along with the underlying figure of Nero.

[50] *TP* VI, 4; *CWS* II, 533.

[51] It seems to us arbitrary that Matheron ties together the two outcomes as two moments of one and the same logic (Matheron 1969: 418).

[52] *TP* V, 4; *CWS* II, 530. Translation modified.

[53] *TP* V, 5; *CWS* II, 530.

[54] *TTP* XX, 28; *CWS* II, 349.

be changed into another nature entirely different from its own.'[55] Of course, here the context is that of a difference in species, not of the individual: human beings reduced to the state of beasts. Spinoza allows himself this turn of phrase as a rhetorical and polemical fiction, but at the same time – a bit like Ovid speaking of love – the image of transformation does correspond to the reality of a nature taken to its limits, to the point of forgetting itself, dreamt otherwise by the tyrant, and dreaming itself otherwise.

In fact, when Spinoza asks whether the sovereign is bound by the laws [lois], he immediately answers no, in agreement with Roman law [droit] (according to a traditional maxim, *princeps legibus solutus*, 'the Prince is not bound by the laws'). But this is so that later he can distinguish between civil laws and natural laws: the sovereign can indeed change the legislation, and moreover only he is accustomed to doing so, but within limits such that he cannot commit suicide insofar as he is sovereign, and in so doing drag the whole body politic down with him. The *Civitas* is really comparable to a natural body, and the old medieval metaphor, taken up again by Machiavelli and Hobbes and constantly presented in the *Political Treatise*, hardly even counts as one there: like every body, the State (*Civitas*), or in other words a united, formed multitude, has no essence or identity other than the fundamental law or the set of laws forming the legislation that constitutes it. So that at the level of the sovereign, by one of those logical turns whose secret Spinoza possesses, civil laws and natural laws are mixed together, and the sovereign turns out to be completely bound by the laws (unless the State finds itself in a situation where its survival depends on a constitutional reform, analogous to a body's *magna ipsius mutatio* when it is necessary for its adaptation to new conditions:[56] if the sovereign alone is authorised to make the decision, the judgment, which in a way is immanent to the latter, is rendered by the reaction of the multitude, according to whether or not it consents[57]):

For if a State weren't bound by any laws, *or* rules, without which the State would not be a State, then we'd have to think of it, not as a natural thing, but as a chimera. The State sins, then, when it does, or allows to happen, what can be a cause of its ruin. We say then that it sins in the same sense in which Philosophers or Doctors say that nature sins. In this sense we can say that the State sins when it does something contrary to the dictate of

---

[55] *Ethics* IV, 39 Schol.; CWS I, 569.
[56] *Ethics* IV, App. Cap. VII; CWS I, 589.
[57] TP IV, 6; CWS II, 528.

reason. For a State is most its own master when it acts according to the dictate of reason (by III, 7). Insofar as it acts contrary to reason, it fails itself *or* sins. We'll understand these things more clearly if we consider that when we say each person can decide whatever he wishes concerning a thing of which he is the master, this power must be defined not only by the power of the agent, but also by the capacity of what he's acting on. If I say, for example, that I can rightly do whatever I wish concerning this table, I surely don't mean that I have the right to make this table eat grass. Similarly, even though we say that men are not their own masters, but are subject to the State, we don't mean that they lose their human nature and take on a different nature (*quod homines naturam humanam amittant, et aliam induant*). Nor do we mean that the State has the right to make men fly, or (what is equally impossible) to make men honor those things which move them to laughter or disgust. What we mean is that when certain circumstances are present, the subjects respect and fear the State, and that when those circumstances are absent, this fear and respect are destroyed. When they're destroyed, so is the State itself.[58]

This passage begins by warning us of a 'chimera': thinking that the State could be subtracted from the conditions of a certain nature in general, in other words that it could avoid depending either as regards its essence or existence on a certain number of laws that are the laws of its nature; thinking, in sum, that the State could be something supernatural. It concludes by throwing into relief a *transformist temptation inherent to tyranny*: prescribing for human beings a conduct contrary to their nature and which is addressed to beings constituted otherwise than they are – in other words, dreaming with open eyes that human beings could change their nature.[59] And when Spinoza attempts to bring together political tyranny and domestic tyranny, in a passage that seems to target Hobbes directly and of which we spoke in the previous study, he invokes precisely a transformation of paternal right into pure domination (*Jus paternum in dominimum mutare*), the parents becoming masters and children slaves.[60]

In the previous chapter, Spinoza gave examples of this conduct contrary to human nature toward which the king become tyrant tries to push human beings:

---

[58] *TP* IV, 4; *CWS* II, 526–7. Translation modified.
[59] Frederick II, the thirteenth-century precursor to modern royal absolutism, was known as *immutator mundi*, the one who could change the world.
[60] *TP* VI, 4; *CWS* II, 533.

by what rewards or threats can a man be induced to love what he hates or to hate what he loves? In this category we may put those things which human nature so abhors that it considers them worse than any other evil, as that a man should act as a witness against himself, that he should torture himself, that he should kill his parents, that he should not strive to avoid death, and the like, which no one can be induced to do by rewards or threats.[61]

In sum, Spinoza insists on the natural limits of authority, which he says are at the same time the *natural limits of obedience*. The tyrannical transgression bears on nature in general or reason, which is why, on the same page, Spinoza characterises it as 'insane' and 'mad'.[62] Whence the subtle conclusion according to which the State is not bound by its laws, since the natural laws by which it is restrained do not come down to civil right but to natural right, in other words the *right of war*, which is at work in two senses: the absolute right of the sovereign in regard to its subjects (obedience to the laws without which the community would be dissolved), and the right without contradiction of subjects in regard to the sovereign – as soon as the latter transgresses the limits of obedience and violates the community as such. And he explicitly invokes suicide in order to show that the respect for these natural laws in no way constrains the sovereign, *at least insofar as it is sovereign* (for insofar as what it commands is a chimera, the sovereign can dream of being constrained by Nature):

The only way the State is bound by [the right of war] is the way a man in the state of nature is bound to take care not to kill himself: to be able to be his own master, *or* not to be an enemy to himself, he must take care not to kill himself. This care, of course, is not obedience, but freedom of human nature.[63]

The tyrant is thus suicidal, not insofar as it is an individual, but insofar as it is the sovereign incarnating the State as a whole (though, from Nero to Hitler, it is possible to be both at once).

There is no point in insisting on how foreign this belief in the power of contradiction has come to appear after the twentieth century. It would be better to ask whether this belief had not already been demolished twice over:

[61] *TP* III, 8; CWS II, 520. See also *TTP* XX, 24–9; CWS II, 348–9.
[62] *TP* III, 8; CWS II, 520.
[63] *TP* IV, 5; CWS II, 527.

by the theory of individuality, whose aim is to determine what a body and consequently a mind can endure 'without any change of form',[64] once it is said that 'we do not know what a body can do', according to the formula that Gilles Deleuze threw into such relief;[65] and by the concept of 'vacillation of mind' (*fluctuatio animi*), which substitutes for the question 'is there a contradiction?' the question 'how far does the ambivalence go?'[66] What can a body do? How far does an ambivalence go? The responses to these questions can only be empirical, historical, shattering the conviction that experience has already revealed everything.[67]

We must go further still. Spinoza says that 'if men could be so deprived of their natural right that subsequently they could do nothing, except by the will of those who held the supreme Right, then the latter would be permitted to reign over their subjects most violently and with absolute impunity. *But I believe it could never occur to anyone to think that*.'[68] And he informs us that '*without any intellectual incoherence, we can conceive* men who believe, love, hate, disdain, or are overcome by any kind of affect whatever, solely in accordance with the right of the state'.[69] We see a reticence and at the same time a courage before a possibility that the mind is loathe to admit, but which it has no real reason to rule out. However, that is not the most profound point, which is in the following passage:

> I confess that someone can get prior control of another person's judgment in many ways, *some of them almost incredible*. So though that person does not directly command the other person's judgment, it can still depend so much on what he says that we can rightly say that to that extent it is subject to his control. But whatever ingenuity has been able to achieve in this matter, it has never reached the point where men do not learn from experience that each person is plentifully supplied with his own faculty of judgment and that men's minds differ as much as their palates do.[70]

Nobody can seriously claim that this judgment has been rendered obsolete by History. What it maintains is not a utopian glimmer from within the disaster, but confidence in an infinite and infinitely subtle capacity of life

---

[64] *Ethics* II, L4–7 and Schol. after 13; CWS I, 461. See above, Chapter 2.
[65] *Ethics* III, 2 Schol.; CWS I, 495. See Deleuze 2005, chapter 14.
[66] *Ethics* III, starting with 17; CWS I, 504.
[67] TP I, 3; CWS II, 504.
[68] TTP XVII, 4; CWS II, 297. Our emphasis.
[69] TTP XVII, 10; CWS II, 298. Our emphasis.
[70] TTP XX, 4; CWS II, 344–5. Our emphasis.

to evade its own negation, an almost anonymous, impersonal, involun-tary capacity of the terrorised being to deviate within consent, to be liter-ally incorrigible. It is certainly a paradox, but not a contradiction, for this thinker who reflected so much on the dramatic disobedience of peoples (the Hebrews and above all the Romans), on their inability to discipline them-selves and thereby take the first step toward freedom, to then at the end of the account wager on an irreducible disobedience as the final vitality and freedom under terror.[71] The human being is this complex nature at once desperately fragile and of unheard-of resistance, whose political behaviour ranges from the panicked and suicidal compulsion to place its fate in the hands of a providential person,[72] to being attached to a liberty of which it nevertheless has only an illusory representation (a glimmer of awakening while 'dreaming with open eyes', a glimpse as though through the clouds, which is due to the mere fact that it exists, and that consequently it exists with a certain nature).

Third Chimera: Changing Decrees (and the Theory of the King's Double Mind)

The reminder of the humanity of kings reveals another contradiction inher-ent to the monarchical idea: it claims to make the individual will, governed by the passions and thus variable, coincide with the law, which involves the idea of constancy. Thus there is no need to invoke a discourse that will come after the fact to justify monarchy by mystifying the mass of people: the seed of mystification is inscribed within its very logic. Before Locke, Spinoza said that absolute monarchy does not number among political forms, because it is in contradiction with the very idea of the state.[73]

---

[71] We agree entirely with Balibar's conclusion in 'Spinoza, the Anti-Orwell' (the 'incom-pressible minimum', the capacity to resist logically tied to individuality as such), in Balibar 1994: 33–7.

[72] 'Those who flee an enemy, overawed by fear, can't be restrained by fear of anything else, but rush headlong into rivers or into a fire, to escape their enemies' steel. So, how-ever properly a commonwealth may be organized, and however well its laws may be set up, still, in the greatest crises of the state, when everyone is seized by panic, as often happens, then everyone approves only what the present fear urges, without giving any consideration to the future or to the laws. All heads turn toward a Man who is famous for his victories. They release him from the laws and (a very bad precedent) continue his command, entrusting the whole Republic to his good faith. That's why the Roman state perished' (TP X, 10; CWS II, 600–1). William of Orange can surely be seen here beneath the traits of Augustus.

[73] 'Hence it is evident, that *Absolute Monarchy*, which by some Men is counted the only

The contradiction would be resolved if the will of the sovereign could be constant, if the royal capacity for decision could be separated from its inherent risk, capriciousness. We know that the rise of absolute monarchy historically took place under this condition, which however in no way limited the right of the sovereign: power was supposed to be absolute but not, for all that, arbitrary, since the law remained subject to Christian duties; the royal will was all at once guaranteed by custom or the 'fundamental law', and juridically unlimited; and notably the struggle of kings for personal power was concentrated on the question of swearing oaths, contested in the name of personal responsibility solely before God.[74]

For Spinoza, this can only be a matter of a mystification. He invokes the testimony of History: the Persians, for example, having indeed honoured their kings as Gods, for all that still did not grant them the right to change the laws.[75] The demonstrative rearticulation of the analysis of monarchy, in chapter VII of the *Political Treatise*, unambiguously clarifies the initial claims about the relation between the sovereign and the laws:

> For the fundamental principles of the state must be regarded as the eternal decrees of the King. Indeed, his ministers obey him completely if they refuse to carry out any commands he gives which are inconsistent with the fundamental principles of the state. We can explain this clearly with the example of Ulysses . . .[76]

The reminder that 'kings are not Gods' is redoubled in a reasoning that opposes the inevitably inconstant will of a human being to the actually divine type of will that the legislator must evince: *aeterna decreta*. And it is because the royal will must become divine that any absolute authority is denied to the person of the king. Ulysses, a figure of the wise king, himself demanded to be *bound* to the ship's mast so as not to yield to the song of the sirens. Whence the crucial distinction between absolute monarchy ('And nowhere that I know is a Monarch elected absolutely', *nullibi monarcha abso-*

Government in the World, is indeed *inconsistent with Civil Society*, and so can be no Form of Civil Government at all' (*Second Treatise of Government* VII, §90 [Locke 2003: 326]).

[74] See Bodin's argument on the subject of perjury (*On Sovereignty*, I, 8 [Bodin 2010: 27]). Bodin concludes that taking an oath is absurd, as it can only lead to a dyarchy, and to the purely religious character of the obligation to keep promises.

[75] *TP* VII, 1; CWS II, 544.

[76] *TP* VII, 1; CWS II, 544.

lute eligitur[77]) and the absolute obedience that is still owed to the sovereign. How would the will of the king become divine if not by tying the king to its own will, as to the rectitude of a mast? For 'if everything depended on the inconstant will of one man, nothing would be firmly established'.[78] In this way we can say that everything is done *ex solo Regis decreto*, and yet that the decree is eternal. This is summarised in the final formula: 'all right follows from the will of the king, but not everything the king wills is right'.[79]

Paragraph 1 of chapter VII of the *Political Treatise* can be taken as the direct counterpart of the scholium to *Ethics* II, 3: the warning not to confuse the power of God with the power of kings, viewed now from the side of politics. It is in fact at one and the same time that the tyrant-king passes for a God and that the vulgar image of a royal power of God is formed. It is imagined in God in the same way that the common people think they see God: as the power to destroy everything, that is to say the power to *change its decrees*, according to the formula of the second scholium to I, 33. And the problematic of the miracle, in the *Theologico-Political Treatise*, can also be considered from this point of view, that of tyranny, with the slight difference that the order of Nature is explained by the divine nature, whereas royal authority derives from the multitude by transfer: the monarch and the multitude are taken as two distinct powers, the transcendence of the divine right of kings resembling the transcendence of a God sitting on a royal throne. The demystification of the so-called absolute monarchs thus goes hand in hand with the rectification of the concept of God: not the power to change decrees, but on the contrary the power to hold to them. And for that, the king must be tightly bound . . .

It will be useful here to recall the account of the institutions of constitutional monarchy that Spinoza proposes to substitute for the chimera of royal absolutism. It is a matter of re-establishing a relation of immanence between the sovereign and the multitude, replacing the dismal confrontation of reciprocal fear. Spinoza thus returns to the problem such as it had been posed in the four introductory paragraphs: the multitude must somehow be led 'as if by a single mind'. This would happen if the king, instead of imposing its inconstant will on the multitude from without, which tends to keep it formless, really became the mind *of* the State: for each problem, the Assembly, which is as large as possible, submits to the king the major opinions that

---

[77] *TP* VII, 1; CWS II, 544.
[78] *TP* VII, 1; CWS II, 545.
[79] *TP* VII, 1; CWS II, 545. Translation modified. ['omne jus sit regis explicata voluntas; at non ut omnis regis voluntas jus sit'.]

have arisen from the debate, and it falls to the king to decide among them.[80] Instead of an unconditional transfer, carried out in a moment of panic, to a military chief, which will no doubt eventually lead to war but in which there is not even any clear difference between the civil state and the state of war, 'a multitude freely transfers to a King only what it cannot have absolutely in its power, i.e., an end to controversies and speed in making decisions'.[81]

It is at this stage that the old metaphor of the 'political body' takes on its importance and its interest. Treated for the most part as a commonplace,[82] it only truly plays a role with regard to monarchy, where it concerns either the place left empty by the monarch or assassinated quasi-monarch ('the Hollanders thought that to maintain their freedom it was enough to renounce their Count and cut the head off the body of the state', *imperii corpus capite obtruncare*[83]) or else the establishment of a well-formed monarchy:

> The King is absolutely to be considered as the mind of the Commonwealth; but the Council should be considered the mind's external senses, as it were, the body of the Commonwealth, through which the mind conceives the condition of the State, and does what it decides is best for itself.[84]

One will note the stunning and almost ironic contiguity of the words *absolute rex*.[85] But the essential thing is this: 1. Applied to monarchy, the image

---

[80] As Balibar has written, 'we might say that the king is the only individual in the body politic who has no "opinion" of his own, *no interiority*. In himself, he does not "think" any differently from the multitude. But without him the multitude would be incapable of thinking clearly and distinctly and so would be unable to save itself' (Balibar 1998: 72).

[81] *TP* VII, 5; *CWS* II, 547.

[82] See *TP* III, 1 (*CWS* II, 517), where Spinoza defines the State (*civitas*) as the *imperii integrum corpus*. An analogous expression is used in paragraph 2 (*totius imperii corpus et mens*) and paragraph 5 (*imperii corpus*).

[83] *TP* IX, 14; *CWS* II, 594–5. Like at the end of chapter XVIII of the *Theologico-Political Treatise*, Spinoza here alludes to the so-called First Stadtholderless Period, established by the general states of the United Provinces under the influence of the States of Holland, in the wake of the revolt of William II in 1650, whose aim was the establishment of an absolute monarchy.

[84] *TP* VI, 19; *CWS* II, 537–8.

[85] [Spinoza writes: 'et absolute rex censendus est veluti civitatis mens . . .'. The play is that 'absolute' does not directly modify 'rex' but 'censendus est': not that this is an absolute king, but that the king must absolutely be considered 'veluti civitatis mens'. On the problematic status of 'veluti', see Matheron 2020. – GM.]

includes a third term, the Council, surpassing the traditional duality of the sovereign (head-mind) giving form to the mass (body) by leading it. 2. This third term contributes to bringing an image initially understood in an Aristotelian sense (the soul as form of the body) slightly closer to the Spinozist conception (the mind as the idea of the body).

But if the king is the mind of the State, where do we locate the Council in this analogy? Its role of selecting and transmitting information invokes the sensory organs ('the mind's external senses'). But Spinoza immediately corrects the image by identifying the Council with the very body of the State. This identification is decisive, for the metaphoric relation of the mind and body is henceforth internal to the institutional system. The two images, in fact, do not amount to the same thing: in the first case, the relation is external, as if the king were related from without to a situation distinct from it. In the second, the *Civitas* becomes the subject and internalises the relation between the king and the population: the mind attains knowledge of *its* body ('Civitatis corpus, per quod mens Civitatis statum concipit . . .'). It no longer seems incongruous to paraphrase axiom 4 of Part II of the *Ethics*: the king feels that a certain body is affected in many ways. On this condition, it is indeed the mind *of* the State, in the sense that Spinoza elsewhere says that the mind is the idea of a body. Without the mediation of the Council, by contrast, the king would have only a blind relation to the situation, the mind would be related to its own body as to something foreign.

The king thus has a second body that distinguishes it from its body of flesh; but this is not a mystical body, in the sense of a permanent transfiguration of the body of flesh; and for this reason the king cannot be said to *incarnate* the State. Its second body is nothing other than the politically united population, which it perceives in an internal way, kinaesthetically, so to speak, through the intermediary of the Council. In sum, Spinoza proposes a theory of the *two minds of the king* – the idea of its body, the idea of the political body.

Consequently, the chimera of royal absolutism, or the vertiginous confrontation to which absolute transfer gives rise, implicitly corresponds to the image of a mind that no longer feels its body, or which only perceives it as an external aggression.[86] The mind seeks madly for a body that it could claim

---

[86] This is contrary to Hobbes, for whom the multitude becomes a people through its unconditional transfer to the king, and consequently is totally identified with it, to the point that it is absurd to say that the kingdom revolts against the king: only the multitude ['crowd'] does that (*De Cive* XII, 8 [Hobbes 1998: 137]). But for Spinoza, precisely, identification can never be the means of an unconditional transfer, which

for itself, and it tends to forge an imaginary one, precariously making use of a head that is poorly attached and which can fall off. Then there will remain a body without a head, a body that will reclaim, and can now only reclaim, that which really corresponds to it: a new tyrant.

In truth, this gap or opacity between the body and mind means nothing in Spinozist terms other than the onset of death for both: a political individual on the path toward dissolution. It is a double fiction: that of a civil state which is only a 'desolation' [*solitude*]; that of a sovereign which is only a tyrant. On the one hand, the relapse to the old dualistic sense of the image means that the political individual is not truly formed, that its parts tend to be united but under an always changeable law that is imposed from without. On the other hand, the idea of a body surviving without its head is only opposed to the Spinozist concept of *idea corporis* if one confuses head and mind: the body is stripped of its head, but the mind – or its memory, in the form of customs – remains. The body thus retains its form, and this is why it tends immediately to secrete a new head, identical to the preceding one, after each decapitation. However, the spiral radicalises the tyrant: the mind is progressively transformed, becomes amnesiac, at the same time that the body tends to decompose (such is the lamentable history of the decline of the Hebrew people, up to the complete dissolution of its State[87]).

Fourth Chimera: The Death of the King and Succession (TP VII, 25)

The king is a human being: by nature, it cannot reign alone, and its will is mutable. And it is also mortal. Now the viability of the monarchical political form requires corresponding divine perfections: omniscience and omnipotence, immutability, eternity. Whence the importance of the Council (or Assembly), on the one hand consultative and executive power, on the other hand responsibility for legislation.[88] But it is also necessary to resolve the problem of the continuity of the regime, which is the object of the stunning VII, 25.

The opening of this text – 'The form of the state (*Imperii facies*) should be kept one and the same (*una, eademque servari*)'[89] – strongly resembles the

---

can only give rise to a persistent and ever more dramatic confrontation between a head (the tyrant) and the body (the multitude) to which it is poorly attached.

[87] See above, Introduction.
[88] *TP* VI, 17; CWS II, 537.
[89] *TP* VII, 25; CWS II, 556.

sentence from Letter 64 to Schuller on 'the face of the whole Universe (*facies totius universi*), which, however much it may vary in infinite ways, nevertheless always remains the same'.[90] Here, the infinite change is on the one hand the succession of kings, each reign bringing its variation, and on the other hand the *summa mutatio et consequentur periculosissima* ['the greatest possible change, and consequently the most dangerous'] that would constitute – that constitutes? – the succession. Why this hesitation? Because this paragraph leaves the reader's head spinning. One cannot, at first glance, avoid the feeling that there is a blatant contradiction between the beginning and the end:

> Moreover, what I said – that the King's eldest son should succeed to his father by right, or, if there are no male children, the closest male relative – is evident both from vi, 13, and because the choice a multitude makes of a King ought to be eternal, if possible. Otherwise it must happen that the supreme power of the state often passes to the multitude, which is the greatest possible change, and consequently the most dangerous.[91]

> So the King's death is, in a way, the death of the Commonwealth. The Civil order returns to the natural order. As a result, the supreme power naturally returns to the multitude, who can therefore rightly make new laws and repeal old ones. So it's evident that no one succeeds to the King by right except the one the multitude wants to be his successor . . .[92]

The problem is parallel to that of the will: just as the decrees must be eternal, 'the choice a multitude makes of a King ought to be eternal, if possible'.[93] How to overcome the contradiction of a regime in which the mortality of the king must equal the necessary permanence of institutions?

At first glance, Spinoza seems to be on the same page as Hobbes when it comes to elective monarchy: power returns to the multitude upon the death of each king.[94] Elective monarchy is, if not a real democracy, at least a regime of *intermittent democracy*, just as the Roman Republic was an

---

[90] *Ep.* LXIV [to Schuller]; CWS II, 439.
[91] *TP* VII, 25; CWS II, 556.
[92] *TP* VII, 25; CWS II, 557.
[93] *TP* VII, 25; CWS II, 556.
[94] See *Leviathan* XIX (Hobbes 2012: II, 300). Hobbes is categorical: if the right to succession does not belong to the king, sovereignty is really popular, and monarchy is thus only apparent.

intermittent monarchy (the establishment of dictatorship).[95] Monarchy thus seems to concentrate all the risks of subversion: an occult aristocracy, a wild tyranny, and now dyarchy. We can even correct this approximation: the 'return to the multitude' is equivocal, and democracy is a specific form that does not spontaneously arise, even if it could have existed ephemerally in the hypothesis of an original contract. What is threatening is simply the return to the state of nature, as Spinoza comes to say: the State does not dissolve, but rather passes through a kind of perpetual reformation, which could indeed turn toward a transformation of the regime (whence the expression *mutatio summa et consequenter periculosissima*). Elective monarchy is less a malformed regime than a regime that must ceaselessly reform itself, which never finally establishes its form and truly leaves behind the time of constitution. This specific fragility, tied to the mortality of the sovereign, is a problem that does not arise either in aristocracy, provided it knows how to maintain its open ranks, or in democracy, unless – as Hobbes says – the people itself disappears.

Spinoza's position is nevertheless precarious: he can only speak in favour of the hereditary solution, and yet it possesses one of the principal attributes of royal absolutism. So he needs immediately to distance himself from the monarchist camp, and in particular from Hobbes ('those who maintain that the King . . .'): heredity, in fact, cannot mean arbitrariness [*bon plaisir*], unless one is to untie Ulysses at the most enchanting moment of the siren's song.

How can the hereditary solution be protected from the ideologues of autocracy? Once again Spinoza reasons on a tightrope, and his reasoning, as so often, contains misdirections. The first is its apparent overall linguistic incoherence. But there is a second: the invocation of the problem of inheritance. 'To understand this more clearly, note that children are their parents' heirs by civil right, not by natural right.' With this established at the start of the paragraph, one expects that Spinoza will say that the same goes for royal succession. But no: 'Concerning the King the reasoning is completely different'. But yes: 'the King's sword, *or* right, is really the will of the multitude itself . . .'.[96]

What is the meaning of this passage, without a doubt the most baroque that Spinoza ever wrote? Its clarity does not prevent it from being traversed by a rift that shakes the whole edifice of optimised monarchy. Spinoza does

---

[95] Indeed, Hobbes brings together the elective king and the Roman dictator: see *Leviathan* XIX (Hobbes 2012: II, 296).

[96] *TP* VII, 25; *CWS* II, 557.

not simply return to the hereditary solution: he had already forwarded that throughout Chapter VI.[97] He just thinks that the right of succession must be limited, that it cannot be left to the king to make just any choice. We implicitly come back to the problem of treason, or the risk of a second transfer of transferred sovereignty. This is why the spectre of tyranny reappears: 'men endowed with reason never give up their right so much that they cease to be men and may be considered as no more than cattle'.[98] Now we start to understand better. It is for the same reason that the right of royal succession both does not amount to the right of ordinary inheritance and nevertheless at the same time belongs eminently to the multitude: the State – as Louis the Great said – is the king, his will is law [droit]; it is thus suspended with the death of the king. If in the case of private inheritance the will survives the deceased through the power of the State that itself is 'eternal', but in spite of everything this power dies 'in a way', quodammodo, with the death of the king, this – if we are to avoid contradiction – must lead us to conclude that the truly eternal power, in the monarchical State, remains that of the multitude. The king has decisional power, but there is one decision and one alone that does not fall to the king to make: that which concerns his succession, whose rule is established in advance, and which is included in the clauses of the eternal election. Monarchy must be hereditary, but the right of succession belongs to the multitude, for a completely logical reason: just as the permanence of a human will relies on an incorruptible power which is that of the State, the royal will, which is in no way divinised by its confusion with the will of the State but which instead transfers its humanity to it, must in turn rely on a power capable of being made permanent – that of the multitude. So too the stability of the monarchical regime passes paradoxically through the greatest peril: the periodic brush with the state of nature. We will say that monarchy, Spinoza's speculative efforts notwithstanding, remains in spite of everything a contradictory political essence, a chimera.

One will ask what becomes of the Assembly. Spinoza doesn't say a word about it, probably for a precise reason: to invoke it here would be to admit dyarchy, the division of sovereignty. Now the beginning of the paragraph warned that sovereignty, in conformity with the concept inherited from Bodin and Hobbes, must be indivisible. Thus there is no escape from the alternative: either the Hobbesian solution of absolute transfer, which is absolute in name only and promises slavery, an inhuman life reduced to animal functions; or else the precarity of a discontinuous regime, which the

---

[97] TP VI, 13, 20, 37–8; CWS II, 536, 538, 542–3.
[98] TTP VII, 25; CWS II, 557.

multitude only renews because it wants to. This is because, without being divided, the sovereignty of the king only becomes absolute (the principal Bodinian criterion) – or only approaches the real absolutism that, according to Spinoza, can only be democratic[99] – through the union that the king forms with its enlarged and practically democratic Council, which constitutes its senses.

The greatest peril? It is still true that the Assembly survives the king:

The responsibility for educating the King's sons will also fall to this Council, as well as their guardianship, if the King dies and leaves an infant or child as his successor. But *so that the Council will not in the meantime be left without a King*, a Senior Nobleman of the Commonwealth ought to be chosen to take the King's place, until his legitimate successor reaches the age at which he can bear the burden of rule.[100]

This confirms: 1. That power indeed returns to the multitude, organised however in the most stable manner possible (an assembly of suitably old representatives elected by the people, according to a principle of equality of families). 2. That the Assembly only functions at the heart of a dual structure whose other space, left empty, must be refilled (the election by the Assembly of a regent from among the suitably old members of the family of the king). 3. That the essential thing is to avoid the political version of the chimera of the *infans adultus*, that of the 'child king'.[101] It is likely that the

---

[99] *TP* XI, 1; *CWS* II, 601 (democracy as *omino absolutum imperium*).

[100] *TP* VI, 20; *CWS* II, 538. Our emphasis. Recall that the nobility, in the constitution laid out by Spinoza, are born of the family of the king (in order to avoid the risks of The Fronde or of aristocratic drift): see on this subject VI, 13 (*CWS* II, 536). This presupposes – as Spinoza will moreover say at the end of chapter VII – a 'free multitude', still politically informed: it is not a question of depriving the old families, but of ennobling only one of them (how can one avoid thinking despite everything of the way in which Louis XIV brought the nobility to heel, after having resolved to exercise power?).

[101] *TP* VI, 5; *CWS* II, 533: 'Moreover, a King who is a boy or sick, or burdened with old age, is king at the pleasure of others.' See above, Introduction and Second Study (our remarks on Velázquez), and the footnote on the child Louis XIV. One will note that by making the Assembly responsible for the education – and, if need be, making it into the tutor – of the heir, Spinoza completely inverts Hobbes' remark in Chapter XIX of the *Leviathan*: 'there is no great Common-wealth, the Soveraignty whereof is in a great Assembly, which is not, as to consultations of Peace, and Warre, and making of Lawes, in the same condition, as if the Government were in a Child. For as a Child wants the judgement to dissent from counsell given him, and is thereby

Assembly will maintain the institutions; but as it is sovereign only in the interval of the sovereign's vacancy, nothing, absolutely nothing, prevents it from attempting a transformation of the regime. It thus seems that we can well and truly speak of a flickering democracy, even if we hesitate to say more than that, since the Assembly remains an organisation; still, this hesitation is justified, since only the Assembly has any institutional legitimacy in the exercise of sovereignty, the latter reappearing only once the regent is named. In theory, and if need be in practice, it is indeed a matter of a return to the multitude or to the state of nature. Monarchy is this regime condemned to regularly traverse the Acheron, and we cannot be surprised to rediscover in politics, though in a slightly different form, the link the *Ethics* established between death and transformation. Spinoza goes beyond the alternative of absolute monarchy and elective monarchy, which for him are both chimeras, but he stumbles into an irreducible contradiction, that of a regime that he tries to rationalise, and which gives his reasoning a contradictory appearance: however much the double problem of the single and variable human being might be resolved by the institution of the Assembly, Spinoza then runs into a discontinuity that the chimera of royal absolutism or still other fictions know how to overcome only in their dreams.[102]

Whence the final word on monarchy, which completely inverts the ordinary vision of the king as shepherd, father or protector of his people:

> necessitated to take the advise of them, or him, to whom he is committed: So an Assembly wanteth the liberty, to dissent from the counsell of the major part, be it good, or bad. And as a Child has need of a Tutor, or Protector to preserve his Person, and Authority: So also (in great Common-wealths,) the Sovereign Assembly, in all great dangers and troubles, have need of *Custodes libertatis*; that is, of Dictators, or Protectors of their Authoritie; which are as much as Temporary Monarchs; to whom for a time, they may commit the entire exercise of their Power; and have (at the end of that time) been oftner deprived thereof, than Infant Kings, by their Protectors, Regents, or any other Tutors' (*Leviathan* XIX [Hobbes 2012: II, 294). We will see, however, that Spinoza does not entirely reject this Hobbesian analysis, although his democratic sensibility leads him to approach the problem from a totally different angle.

[102] Still other fictions: for example, those of the immortality of the king, or the migration of the political body from one natural body to another, or even those of the Crown (in regard to which the dead king and the new king are one), of the Dynasty (royalty is transmitted by lineage and not coronation, which covers over the interregnum) and Dignity (in relation to which there notably developed the mythological image of the Phoenix, quite vividly for the kings of the seventeenth century). It is by virtue of a *persona ficta* that the famous formulas 'The king never dies' (invoked by Bodin, Bossuet, etc.) or even 'The king is dead! Long live the king!' have their sense (see Kantorowicz 2016, chapters 1 and 7).

We conclude, then, that a multitude can preserve a full enough freedom under a King, so long as it brings it about that the King's power is determined only by the power of the multitude, and is preserved by the multitude's protection (*praesidio*). And this was the only rule I followed in laying the foundations of a Monarchic state.[103]

Fifth Chimera: Return to Apotheosis, and Theocratic Truth

As Alexandre Matheron remarks, since the problem of monarchy is the very human person of the king, the logical solution, however fictive, would be to restore sovereignty to a divinity.[104] Either the king lets himself be seen as a god, or is himself God (theocracy). The two options were alive in Spinoza's time: 'You are gods, it matters not that still you die, your authority does not',[105] exclaimed Bossuet; and the claims of Gomarism, that Calvinist tendency that advocated a strict interpretation of the doctrine of predestination, and which triumphed with the 1619 Synod of Dordrecht, belonged to a theocratic project.

In both cases, the prize to be won was ideological in nature: finding the means of obedience. In both cases, too, the power of God was mixed up with that of an absolute monarch. But theocracy presents an originality: not only is power never exercised except by regents (beginning with its founder, Moses), so that the God-human mystification is not necessary, but above all the means is discovered by which to eternalise an initial will without running into the essential discontinuity of monarchy or courting the danger of a tyrannical drift (the sole premise being that the initiator is an enlightened absolute monarch).

Of course, this regime rests entirely on the teleological belief in a dialogue between God and human beings. It is at least in a way the truth of monarchy – that form of sovereignty that can only be possessed by God – and at the same time a question posed to democracy. For Spinoza does not insist in vain on the childishness of the Hebrews, *libres esclaves* based on the native condition of human beings, and through the supersensible supplement of the idea of their singular election.[106] But the only clear reason that human beings could have for transferring their sovereignty to a king is that they do not

---

[103] *TP* VII, 31; CWS II, 563. Translation modified.
[104] Matheron 1969: 447.
[105] Bossuet, 'Sermon sur le devoir des rois', 1662 (Bossuet 1997: 162).
[106] See above, Chapter 4.

know how to resolve their own controversies.[107] As it so happens, we have already diagnosed, in the transfer to God, a clear recognition of the same order: leaving matters to an adult, namely Moses in his relation to God, and more generally to the external aid of God (which, given its Spinozist definition, can also be applied to the care that adults provide for an infant). And we remain within this aporia: is not Mosaic education, apparently the only kind possible, an impasse? Does it not prevent any process of real liberation? What is this Hebraic confusion of *habitus* and liberty – the illusion of a slave, or the turn toward emancipation spoiled by Moses' fatal error?

Thus, to close the book on monarchy, we must do as Spinoza does at the end of chapter VII of the *Political Treatise*, and return to the question of the 'free multitude'.[108] But first we must recapitulate. We have seen royal absolutism, the political chimera par excellence, haunted five times by transformation: the tendency toward dissimulated aristocracy, the tendency toward the transformist dream, the tendency toward the variability of the will, the tendency toward periodic death, and the tendency toward apotheosis. The prognostic on this political form that is not one, and which nevertheless triumphed in Europe, is complicated: at once Spinoza announces its twilight, and sees in it the twilight of every State.

[107] TP VII, 5; CWS II, 547–8. It is here that Spinoza rejoins Hobbes in a certain manner (see above, n. 101), though with two differences: he does not speak of infantilism here; and where for the English thinker it is a matter of rendering a definitive judgment on democracy, for Spinoza by contrast this is the spur that forces his thought.
[108] TP VII, 26 and 30–1; CWS II, 557–8 and 560–3.

8

What is a Free Multitude? War and Civilisation

The *Political Treatise*, like every book of philosophy with political aims, ultimately has no sense other than as an intervention. Let us quickly move past the obvious: even less than in the *Theologico-Political Treatise*, if this is possible, does Spinoza here address himself to the masses. The latter, fighting for their own oppression by giving their favour to the partisans of the most rigorous interpretation of the doctrine of predestination, had already encouraged the execution of the Grand Pensionary Oldenbarnevelt in 1619; now they had lynched the Grand Pensionary De Witt, placing all their forces at the service of intolerance.

We know on the other hand that the Republic was an aristocracy in fact (dominated by the commercial class of the Regents, responsible for the staggering economic rise of Holland), but that this form was poorly ensured by equivocal institutions (the monarchic militaro-clerical pole of the Stadtholder, claimed by the House of Orange; the parliamentarian pole represented by the office of the Grand Pensionary, and dominated by the Regents).[1]

Finally, we know that Spinoza tended to privilege a fundamental alternative between the popular or democratic tendency, essentially peaceful, tolerant, and civilised, and the tyrannical tendency, by its nature bellicose, devout, and barbarous, incarnated by monarchy become absolute (incidentally, it was not the least of his merits to have somehow described in advance, in his analysis of the monarchical regime, the entire evolution of the reign of Louis XIV, from the real authority of Mazarin and the power of sedition of the Grands under the apparent reign of an infant king, up to the final devout and warlike act, plunging the country into misery).

---

[1] See the Introduction, above.

In this way, the people is at once *vulgus* and *multitudo*: a mass of anxious and credulous ignorants, and nevertheless the immanent source of all sovereignty, and thereby the source of its meaning. One cannot count on it; no more can one renounce it. There is an apparent ambivalence here only if one forgets once again the rectified image of child: the question is that of civilisation, and by all accounts Spinoza ties this question to the becoming of the multitude. Throughout the *Political Treatise*, in fact, the concept of the multitude is shaped by the free-slave distinction, which receives its full consistency in the opposition *barbari-culti*, *barbari-civiles*.[2] But civilisation has only one name: democracy. Aristocracies are only an effect of History, and the physics of human passions explains their genesis (the reticence of human beings to grant citizenship to others who have not, as they themselves have, contributed to the formation of their State, at the risk of their own lives) and their degeneration into absolute monarchies (the reduction of the nobility, in the course of time, to a small number of clans that tear each other apart).[3]

Prudence is never Spinoza's final word with regard to the people, but is only a realistic assessment which a consistent Spinozist has no reason to shamefully flaunt: 'The mob is terrifying, if unafraid (*terret vulgus, nisi metuat*).'[4] For one always forgets the end of the passage, after Spinoza has reminded us that repentance, humility, and respect, which are in themselves sadnesses and make human beings unhappy, were nevertheless preached by the prophets: 'Really, those who are subject to these affects can be guided far more easily than others, so that in the end they may live from the guidance of reason, i.e., may be free and enjoy the life of the blessed.'[5] One forgets the point of view of education, which was that of Moses. It is true that Spinoza was at the same time careful not to fall into 'dreaming with open eyes':

> Moreover, though we've shown that reason can do much to restrain and moderate the affects, we've also seen that the path reason teaches us to follow is very difficult. So people who persuade themselves that a multitude, which may be divided over public affairs, can be induced to live only according to the prescription of reason, those people are dreaming of the golden age of the Poets. They're captive to a myth.[6]

---

[2] *TP* I, 7 (*CWS* II, 506); and X, 4 (*CWS* II, 603–4).
[3] *TP* VIII, 12; *CWS* II, 570.
[4] *Ethics* IV, 54 Schol.; *CWS* I, 576.
[5] *Ethics* IV, 54 Schol.; *CWS* I, 576.
[6] *TP* I, 5; *CWS* I, 506.

Civilisation is thus not the multitude become community of sages. Rather it is the multitude elevated to concord, also called true peace, whose members, all while continuing to be subject to their passions, are at least dominated by joyous passions. And this is the difference between the two types of multitude. In order to treat this problem, let us begin by rereading in its entirety this decisive passage, which we have already spoken of numerous times:

4. A Commonwealth whose subjects, terrified by fear, don't take up arms should be said to be without war, but not at peace. Peace isn't the privation (*privatio*) of war, but a virtue which arises from strength of mind (*animi fortitudo*). For (by ii, 19) it's obedience, a constant will to do what must be done in accordance with the common decree of the Commonwealth. When the peace of a Commonwealth depends on its subjects' lack of spirit – so that they're led like sheep, and know only how to be slaves – it would be more properly called a wasteland [*solitudo*] than a Commonwealth.

5. When we say, then, that the best state is one where men pass their lives harmoniously, I mean that they pass a *human* life, one defined not merely by the circulation of the blood, and other things common to all animals, but mostly by reason, the true virtue and life of the Mind.

6. But note: when I say a rule has been set up for this end, I mean that a free multitude has set it up, not that the rule over a multitude has been acquired by the right of war. For a free multitude is guided by hope more than by fear, whereas a multitude which has been subjugated is guided more by fear than by hope. The first want to cultivate life (*vitam colere*); the second care only to avoid death. The first are eager to live for themselves; the second are forced to belong to the victor. So we say that the second are slaves, and the first free.

The end of a state someone acquires by the Right of war, then, is to be master; it has slaves rather than subjects. When we attend to the general right of each state, there is no essential difference between one created by a free multitude, and one acquired by the right of war. Still, we've shown that each has a very different end. Furthermore, the means by which each state must be preserved are very different.[7]

The general problem is to understand what it means, for Spinoza, to intervene in politics: what is the point, in practice, of this whole attempt to

---

[7] *TP* V, 4–6; CWS II, 530–1.

optimise each political form, the monarchical, aristocratic, and democratic?
Let us try to enumerate the conditions of the problem.

1. Spinoza maintains his preference for democracy: the human regime
par excellence (the only one that has no end other than concord), and
according to him the most rational one, not simply because the solution to
a problem has fewer chances of escaping a large assembly than a small group
of people, let alone one, but because there sovereignty is 'the most absolute'.

2. However, he places no hope in revolution, whose goal is certainly to
rise up against the tyrant, but which remains ineluctably caught in the spiral
of tyranny, unintentionally contributing to its barbaric drift.

3. In conformity with his general approach, which consists in treating
each thing as natural, and thus as individuated according to a form and a
conatus, Spinoza endeavours to construct, not an ideal in the Platonic sense,
but an optimal constitution for each type of regime, or in other words a veritable form, capable of conserving itself, and which can only be destroyed by
external causes.

4. Yet the reformism of the *Political Treatise* is aporetic: just as the addressee
of the *Theologico-Political Treatise* was the minority of enlightened minds (the
Preface) and ultimately any sovereign facing the alternative of a tolerant and
thus stable State and an intolerant State undermined by perpetual civil war
(the last chapter), the *Political Treatise*, judging by the rare passages invoking
the conditions for putting it into practice, is no longer addressed either to
sovereigns or to people in general – but only to 'free multitudes', as we underscored in the Introduction. The analysis of monarchy ends on this clarification, which amounts to once again dissuading any aspiring revolutionary, and
gives the example of the Aragonese, emancipated from the Arabs and having
no political memory liable to hinder the free formation of a State.[8] The
Dutch did not have a mind to *reform* the State, they put an end to the County
while maintaining its traces in the *malformed* system of the Republic.[9]

5. 'Free multitudes' correspond to cases of political birth or, strictly speaking, rebirth: their characteristic is that they do not yet have political customs. These are child peoples (whose degree of collective ignorance or
credulity is obviously variable).

6. Finally, Spinoza lays out a general schema for the decline of the State,
from primitive democracy up to the final monarchical barbarism.

What is the point of the *Political Treatise*? It would seem that the only
response is to allow time to run its course, which, by the play of circum-

[8] *TP* VII, 26 and 30; *CWS* II, 557–8 and 560–3.
[9] *TP* IX, 14; *CWS* II, 594–5: *reformando, deformi*.

stances or external causes, dissolves States bit by bit until they are weak enough to be annexed by other States. Is there a third option, other than reformist optimism and fatalistic pessimism? On the one hand, in fact, the reformist gesture is caught in a circle ('I'm conceiving a Monarchic state established by a free multitude. These things can be useful only to such a multitude'[10]). On the other hand, general pessimism tends toward a phys- ical description of a political universe analogous to that of bodies: all death is transformation, whether the same people change its regime (Spinoza invokes this possibility at the beginning of chapter VI but constantly rules it out elsewhere), or else allows itself to be absorbed by a greater whole, by invasion and annexation.[11]

There is however a difference between the political universe and that of individual bodies. In politics, the integration of a community as such is always problematic: if its individuating relation is the legislation of the State, the alternative is between dissolution pure and simple into the greater whole (assimilation of individuals) and the threat of a State within a State. In cases of oppression, put simply of annexation or colonisation, the second possibility will prevail. We have seen that Spinoza gives the example of the Jews and Christians, and of the conservation of their respective rites. Let us also keep in mind the familial Marrano experience of a religion cloaked beneath an apparent religion, and the possibility of a new Hebrew state invoked in the *Theologico-Political Treatise*.[12] From the point of view of the stability of the State as much as from that of concord and freedom, the solution lies in the return of the *jus circa sacra* to a State that will practise abstention in religious matters, and which will in this way allow religions to coexist instead of getting dangerously involved with each other: the capacity of a tolerant State to integrate under its own relation the relations of different communities as such, in such a way that the latter are adjusted

---

[10] *TP* VII, 26; CWS II, 558.

[11] See the remark by Moreau, concerning 'what happens when a people loses its state identity, by dispersion or conquest': 'It is remarkable that nobody else in early moder- nity posed the question in this way. One dealt with the right of the conqueror, not the identity of the vanquished. But Spinoza was principally interested in this problem of identity, which is one of the blind spots of the theory of the contract' (Moreau 1994: 461–2).

[12] *TTP* III, end; CWS II, 124. See also Letter 33 from Oldenburg: 'Here there is a rumor on everyone's lips that the Israelites, who have been scattered for more than two thousand years, will return to their Native Land. Few here believe this, though many desire it. Please tell your friend what you hear and think about this' (*Ep.* XXXIII [from Oldenburg]; CWS II, 24).

to one another without having to be dissolved (a sanctuary-State and longer an imperial one: this is the entire opposition between Spain and the United Provinces[13]).

What is the point of the *Political Treatise*? The only historical opportunities, for Spinoza, seem tied to political births, to the conquest of independence: from this point of view, the movements of decline are compensated for in History by the lateral processes of absorption and secession. These are not however opportunities for the present. In the end, we have only a hint: the coincidence of the presumed final stage of the decline – monarchy and invasion (if not annexation)[14] – and of Holland's new situation at the moment when Spinoza was working on the *Political Treatise*. In order to understand what this suggests, we must return to the initial question: what is a free multitude?

The People that Does Not Fear Death (Praise for the Ancient Hebrews)

Let us take the Hebrew people as our point of departure, leaving it to others to contest dominant contemporary interpretations. Is the theocratic regime, as Alexandre Matheron says, in fact a regime confined to barbarism and sadness? We have underscored the enigmatic transmutation of obedience into freedom suggested by the *Theologico-Political Treatise*. This idea is far from being allusive and secondary. Spinoza remarks that Moses played upon fear, but even more upon hope: he counted on the Hebrews behaving in a way that was *sponte*, 'spontaneous', 'of their own accord', 'voluntarily', 'of themselves'.[15] This remark is followed by a first sketch of the general political theory drawn from the analysis of the Jewish regime: Spinoza opposes democracy – in which, he says, there is no longer any sense in talking of obedience, since the laws are the object of a common consent – to absolute monarchy, which implies that everyone 'hangs on the words of the ruler'.[16] Faced with this alternative, the Hebraic regime seems unclassifiable: it seems to participate in both categories.

---

[13] *TTP* XIX; CWS II, 332–44. See the French problem of Jansenism and above all of Calvinism.

[14] Caught in the mire, figuratively and literally (the opening of canal locks interrupted the advance of French troops), the affair was not settled until a year after Spinoza's death, by the Peace of Nijmegen.

[15] *TTP* V, 20; CWS II, 144.

[16] *TTP* V, 25; CWS II, 144–5.

But let us go further. To give primacy to hope over fear is not merely the preference of the Spinozist educator, but is rather a wholly Mosaic sixth sense or intuition: on the one hand, the Hebrews did not allow themselves to be led by intimidation alone, *because of their disobedience* (which appears here in its paradoxically positive role: the final freedom of the slave or the terrorised subject, as we have said); on the other hand, in the case of war the Hebrews demonstrated *virtus*, for they did not fight solely out of the fear of torture. It is only from this point of view that religion gains its sense, because it inspires in the people a joyful passion, a love devoted at once to country and to God. In this way, the Hebrews became capable of 'suffering death rather than living under foreign rule'.[17] This love of country has an underside or counterpart: an equal hatred of the foreigner. That the latter in turn becomes a motivation is obvious; nevertheless, it remains true that the love is primary, and that without a positive devotion such hatred would have no reason for being. In the Hebrews, the hatred of the foreigner follows structurally from the type of love they experienced, tied to the belief in their singular election.

In each case it is this 'nature' acquired by laws and customs[18] that defines an affirmative behaviour when faced with the risk of war: death rather than submission. Is this conduct suicidal? It is remarkable that this question, which goes back to Plato (*Apology*), does not even arise as a problem in Spinoza's eyes: he interprets it as a victory over the fear of death. We must admit that the Hebrews, 'accustomed to the superstitions of the Egyptians, and worn out by the most wretched bondage'[19] (to our knowledge, Spinoza calls them 'childish' but never 'barbarous'), here displayed an extraordinary step forward. Spinoza sees in History only a single people comparable to the Hebrews: the Macedonians, who stood up to Alexander, 'too enlightened' to believe in his divinity. Their resistance shows that 'only men who are complete barbarians allow themselves to be deceived so openly and to turn from subjects to slaves, of no use to themselves' (and then there follows, by contrast, the line about the monarchist doctrine of divine right, cited above).[20]

To be of use to themselves: this definition, which is opposed to slavery, is applied to the Hebrews as well. Insisting on their bravery (*virtus*) in combat, on two separate occasions Spinoza pays homage to what he calls *libertas*

---

[17] *TTP* V, 28 (CWS II, 145); and XVII, 76 (CWS II, 313).
[18] *TTP* XVII, 76–7 (CWS II, 314); and XVII, 93–4 (CWS II, 317).
[19] *TTP* II, 46; CWS II, 107.
[20] *TTP* XVII, 24–5; CWS II, 301 (comparison with the Hebrews); and XVII, 68; CWS II, 311–12 (the awakening of the Macedonians).

militum concivium, 'the freedom of soldiers who are fellow citizens'.[21] What is characteristic of such an army, based on military service and not on the recruitment of mercenaries, is, on the one hand, that they fight only for the freedom of the State and the glory of God, and not for the glory of leaders;[22] and, on the other hand, that they go to war 'only for the sake of peace, and to protect freedom' (*bellum propter pacem et ad tuendam libertatem*).[23] Generally speaking, the Hebrews only had leaders during wartime: after Joshua, named by Moses, the army no longer had a permanent leader, which is what inspired Spinoza to make the vertiginous comparison between the kind of confederation that united the tribes without a supreme leader during the period of the Judges, and the present-day confederation of the United Provinces.[24]

The *Political Treatise* would later multiply *a posteriori* the safeguards against the militaro-monarchical danger, concretised by the restoration of the Stadtholder and the new status of General Captain and General Admiral for Life obtained by the Prince of Orange in the wake of the French invasion; it would also underscore the danger of a standing army. Then it would no longer be the glorious Hebrew people that Spinoza would compare with the Dutch, but rather the Roman people, who were its very antithesis and never knew *how to form* their State: while they were just as disobedient as the Hebrews, the Romans never learned, as the Hebrews did, the discipline that makes peoples free.[25] From the Etruscan period in which they only formed a

[21] *TTP* XVII, 67; *CWS* II, 311.
[22] *TTP* XVII, 69; *CWS* II, 312.
[23] *TTP* XVII, 75; *CWS* II, 313.
[24] *TTP* XVII, 52–4; *CWS* II, 307–8.
[25] The fall of the Roman Republic was due to the ambiguity of the regime: the conflict between senatorial aristocracy and the latent monarchism of military leaders, then the tyrannical collapse after the establishment of the Principate (three emperors in the year 69 alone, etc.). Spinoza brushes off Polybius, who saw the superiority of the Roman constitution in its adept mixture of the three canonical political forms, and thought that its equilibrium, having selected the best parts from each of these three forms, enabled the Romans to escape, up to a certain point, the fatal cycle of regimes (*The Histories* VI, 3 [Polybius 2010: 372]). [See also *The Histories* VI, 18 (Polybius 2010: 384–5). – GM.] Here is what Spinoza has to say about the harmony of a mixed constitution: 'But in Rome the Tribunes of the plebians were permanent, yet they couldn't suppress the power of a Scipio. Moreover, they had to refer what they judged to be salutary to the Senate for decision. Often the Senate frustrated them, so that the plebians favored more the [Tribune] the Senators feared less. In addition, the authority of the Tribunes against the Patricians was defended by the support of the plebians. Whenever they called upon the plebians, they seemed to promote sedition rather than convene a Council' (*TP* X, 3; *CWS* II, 598). Chapter XVIII of the *Theologico-Political*

'rebellious and infamous' people, to that of Augustus in which they remained 'barbarous' enough to accept the ritual of apotheosis, there is no trace to be found of a civilising process (we will see shortly that it is appropriate to nuance this judgment somewhat).[26]

To be of use to themselves: outside of the institution of military service, it is the equal division of the land that replaces the desire for desertion, in the hearts of the Hebrews, with the *ratio utilitatis quae omnium humanarum robur et vita est*, that is, the 'principle of advantage, the mainstay and life of all human actions'.[27] And if it is true that Mosaic discipline was based on a mixture of fear and hope, the primacy of hope is confirmed by the reference to the Hebrews' joy, *laetitia*, in festivals celebrated three times a year as part of their ritual life.[28] Thus there is nothing surprising about the fact that Spinoza could speak of a *libertas humani imperii*, 'freedom of a human

---

Treatise lays out a daring summary – in hardly a dozen lines – of the whole of Roman history. Spinoza adopts the traditional division into three periods, but his manner of defining them is original: 1. A precarious monarchy that did not manage to create the habits or morals that would stabilise it (three of the six kings were assassinated), and deprived of the characteristics of absolutism, since the right of election belonged to the people. 2. An extremely easy revolution, that of Brutus, celebrated by Machiavelli, whose circumstances corresponded to what the *Political Treatise* says could not but provoke a popular uprising (Sextus' rape of Lucretia), but which led to an Aristocracy (many tyrants in place of one, Spinoza says mockingly), a period in which the people was able to be maintained only through expedients, war externally and poverty internally. 3. Finally a monarchy, disguised under another name (principate, empire). In short, from the last Tarquin to Augustus, only the name of the regime changed, just as in England the new king Cromwell was baptised 'Lord Protector'. Better still – we might add – the monarchical form was strengthened, since its power became absolute (hereditary). Spinoza himself thus draws the parallel between contemporary absolutism and Augustus' absolutism. This summary has two stunning features: 1. Spinoza minimises the major fact – which Machiavelli emphasises – of the rise of the plebes. 2. Not a word is spoken of the famous republican constitution, and the *libertas* that the Romans already opposed to *regnum*, as does Spinoza, counts for nothing (on this point, see Martin 1994: 106; Scipio, in particular, was accused of *regnum* by Cato. On the Scipio-Cato debate in relation to Spinoza, see our remarks below). Unlike Machiavelli, for whom the incessant conflicts between the plebs and the patriciate were proof of the health and freedom of the political body (Machiavelli in fact developed the very modern idea that freedom only exists in a state of tension; see *Discourses on Livy* I, 4 [Machiavelli 1998: 16–17]), Spinoza developed a pessimistic interpretation of the republican period.

[26] *TTP* XVIII, 35; CWS II, 330–1 (primitive period) and XVIII, 21; CWS II, 300 (Augustus). Moreau underscores this: see Moreau 1994: 439, n. 3.

[27] *TTP* XVII, 84; CWS II, 315.

[28] *TTP* XVII, 88–90; CWS II, 316.

State',[29] which deserves to be thought together with the 'human life' proper to the 'free multitude' in the *Political Treatise*. The freedom of the Hebrews was certainly independence in relation to the foreigner, but this independence was only a consequence or property of the form that, thanks to Moses, they knew to give to their laws and mores, and which made them turn toward life rather than toward death.

We cannot therefore agree with Alexandre Matheron's judgment about theocracy, which seems to us to contradict the Spinozist evaluation of the regime, and to rest on an arbitrary deduction: 'A Theocracy, no doubt, would make it possible to avoid decline; but it would only manage to do so by preventing civilisation from developing: it organises barbarism in such a way that makes it unsurpassable.'[30] For without a doubt Spinoza saw in the Hebrew people equipped with Mosaic institutions a model of the free multitude, the progressive elevation of a child people from the state of initial barbarism (the freedom of the emancipated slave) to that of civilisation. And one must not get so turned around as to forget that Spinoza judged this regime to be so laudable that it was worth raising the question of its *imitation*.[31] To be sure, theocracy is a regime that amuses and scandalises us at the same time: a mixture of superstition and totalitarianism, it seems. But following Spinoza's example, we must approach it as dispassionately as possible, casting upon it the cold gaze of comprehension. Of course, theocracy is a fiction, but that is not at all the problem: rather the problem is one of collective education, or of the passage to civilisation, that is, to a social human life. For good reason, the idea of collective education horrifies us today. But Spinoza's final judgment is precisely: *imitabilis, sed non imitandum*. Pragmatically, Spinoza never criticises the fictive character of theocracy; he only says that it is suitable just for a small people closed in on itself, and not for human beings to whom it is vital 'to have dealings with others'.[32]

---

[29] *TTP* XVII, 69; CWS II, 312. Translation modified. ['Si haec itaque militum concivium libertas humani imperii principes, qui soli totam laudem victoriarum usurpare solent, retinet, multo magis Hebraeorum principes coërcere debuit, quorum milites non pro Principis, sed pro Dei gloria pugnabant, & solo Dei responso accepto proelium committebant'. Curley (CWS II, 312), Silverthorne and Israel (Spinoza 2007: 221), and Appuhn (Spinoza 1965: 290) all read 'humani imperii' as modifying 'principes', and so render the beginning of the sentence as *the freedom of citizen soldiers* providing checks on the *leaders of the human state*. – GM.]

[30] Matheron 1969: 461. This judgment is repeated by Étienne Balibar, who for his part sees only barbarism and sadness in the Hebrew state (Balibar 1998: 46–7).

[31] *TTP* XVII, 114–15 and XVIII, 1–3; CWS II, 322–3.

[32] *TTP* XVIII, 2; CWS II, 323.

Thus we remain in this aporia, bound to the ultimately historically impotent plea in chapter XX for freedom of thought and expression. Is that Spinoza's final word?

Combat and Freedom in the *Political Treatise* (VII, 22)

The stunning paragraph 22 of chapter VII of the *Political Treatise* is rarely if ever discussed.[33] Probably this is because it establishes a rather disturbing relationship between war and freedom. The passage ceaselessly reminds us that the civil state has peace as its object, and that the characteristic of royal mystification is to dissociate peace from freedom by promoting a simulacrum of peace that approximates the state of nature (the solitude of terrorised human beings). In the analysis of the monarchical regime, Spinoza thus attaches the greatest importance to banishing the military threat, and this is why he recommends conscription, in such a way that leaders are chosen only during wartime, have a mandate to lead for only one year, and cannot be considered for the position again.[34] Not only does he repeat in substance the steps taken by Moses, but his remarks far exceed the framework of the establishment of a constitutional monarchy, since here there reappears, just as in the Jewish theocracy, the opposition of the peaceful and free democratic pole (which makes war only for the sake of peace) and the militaro-monarchistic pole (which has an interest only in war), where we rediscover the macabre oscillation of Batavian sovereignty.[35] Now Spinoza adds the following digression:

> But we've said that the military are not to receive regular payments. For the army's greatest reward is freedom. In the state of nature each person tries to defend himself as much as he can, simply for the sake of freedom. No one expects any other reward for excellence in fighting than that he should be his own [master]. Now in the civil state all the citizens collectively ought to be considered as just like (*perinde, ac*) a man in the state of nature. So when they all fight for their state, they're looking out for themselves and devoting themselves to themselves. But the Counselors,

---

[33] The exception is Lucien Mugnier-Pollet (see Mugnier-Pollet 1976: 184–5), but all the same his analysis hardly grants this passage the interest that it deserves.

[34] *TP* VI, 10; CWS II, 535.

[35] *TP* VII, 5, 7, 12, 17; CWS II, 547–8, 549–50, 552–3. Mugnier-Pollet recalls that Johann de Witt believed it would be sufficient to struggle against the Stadtholder, whereas Spinoza judged that it would necessary to replace the standing army with a national one, comprised only of citizens (Mugnier-Pollet 1976: 184).

Judges, Officers, etc., are devoting themselves more to others than to themselves. So it's fair that they receive compensation for their service. Moreover, in war there can be no more honorable or greater incentive to victory than the image of freedom (*libertatis imago*). On the other hand, if only some of the citizens are assigned to military service, with the result that it's necessary to grant them regular pay, the King will necessarily give them greater recognition than the others (as we've shown in §12). Of course, these will be men who know only the arts of war, men who in peace are corrupted by extravagant living, because they have too much leisure, and men, finally, who because of their poverty think of nothing but plunder, civil discord, and wars. So we can say that a Monarchic state of this kind is really in a condition of war, that only the military enjoys freedom, and that the rest of the people are slaves.[36]

A hypothesis will guide our commentary here: is it not in the fight for independence that the multitude rediscovers the meaning of and taste for freedom?

This passage is the only one in the *Political Treatise* that treats the political body as an individual without qualification.[37] Is this by chance, or is it a sign that combat is the true ordeal of political individuation?

Following Machiavelli, Spinoza is receptive to the idea of decline tied to prolonged peace; peace delivers from us from fear, whence a passage from barbarism to civilisation and humanity, after which idleness wins out over action and vain competition wins out over virtuous emulation, and human beings fall back into slavery.[38] But peace remains an absolute objective for him, and unlike the Florentine thinker, he seeks the means for a *peaceful common activity*, and finds it, taking money into account, in the political stimulation of capitalist activity.[39]

But paragraph 22 of chapter VII invites us to reinterpret this cycle: is it the succession of war by peace that itself carries out the passage to civilisation and humanity? Or must we rather think that peace is engendered in struggle and the conquest of independence? Peace implies the free establish-

---

[36] *TP* VII, 22; CWS II, 554–5.
[37] The other occurrences are coupled with the adverb *veluti*: see *TP* III, 2, 5 (CWS II, 517–9) and VI, 1 (CWS II, 532).
[38] *TP* X, 4; CWS II, 598–9. On the double Machiavellian cycle, see Senellart 1989: 44, which cites a passage from the *Florentine Histories*: 'For virtue gives birth to quiet, quiet to leisure, leisure to disorder, disorder to ruin . . .' (*Florentine Histories* V, 1 [Machiavelli 1988: 185]).
[39] *TP* X, 6; CWS II, 599.

ment of a State, and not the slavery of a multitude dominated by another. Putting an end to fear presupposes knowing how to dominate it by defying death for something more than the mere maintenance of biological func- tions, to be delivered from the fear of death by the prevalence of a joyous desire – namely, freedom. This is the true departure from the mythical model of the contract: instead of human beings placed before the choice of the least bad (consenting to renounce the greater part of their natural right out of fear of solitude reinforced by that of supreme torture), the genesis of the State is totally different when it proceeds from a struggle for independence, whose spur is no longer fear but is necessarily hope.

Why necessarily hope? Might not one object that the difference is slight, and that subjected peoples only rise up through the fear of a still greater oppression? That schema is false, for casting off the yoke of the oppressor presupposes passing through the ordeal of death. The latter is absent from the totally irenic account of the original pact: no struggle, but a conven- tion; no defiance or succession, but the mutual rebirth of similar people being reinforced at the heart of a Nature that is certainly hostile, but not, strictly speaking, a dominator. Human beings do not need to combat in order to contract. The model of peace issuing from war was already present in the *Theologico-Political Treatise*: it was there in the flight from Egypt, and even in certain respects in the Revolution of 509. The difference is that, in the *Political Treatise*, this model is subordinated to that of the contract, as the example of the Aragonese demonstrates: first shake off the yoke, then choose a State form. For one does not depart from the state of nature, in Spinoza: one returns to it.

Such a schema clearly presupposes that the collective identity in a certain way precedes itself, within the heart of the oppressive State: all liberation is the reverse of a conquest, and any free multitude must have previously been enslaved, although perhaps it was free at its origin. The refusal of assimila- tion on both sides maintains a kind of latent State within a State, which is the condition of every colony (apart from the fundamental goal of peace and self-conservation, this is the reason why wars of conquest are condemnable, along with royal marriages implicating multiple States).

Let us return to VII, 22: everything thus happens as if union was never better achieved than in combat, and it is not wrong to say that citizens fight as if they were a single human being. But it is the collective striving for self- conservation, and not discipline, that is behind this: discipline seems instead in this regard to be the effect of the desire to work in combat collectively, the civil state returned to the heart of the preoccupations of human beings. Is it not that the collective *conatus* is formed or reformed in the ordeal of death, just like in the process described in the prologue of the *Treatise on the Emendation of the Intellect*? Indeed, we recognise here the vocabulary of the *conatus* (*quantum potest*).

Besides, this passage echoes the final notes of the *Ethics*: beatitude is virtue itself, and not its reward. For it is indeed a question here of an imma-nent reward of virtue (*virtutis praemium*), as a result of, it is true, a certain slide of meaning: there is quite a distance between the bravery of the soldier and the beatitude of the sage. Virtue and freedom are here that to which the multitude can aspire: to live from hope rather than from fear, to cultivate life without dreading death.[40] The multitude is educated in its fight for inde-pendence, which is a matter of conquering or maintaining it, and Combat, the immanent educator, is substituted in the *Political Treatise* for the mythi-cal or at least exceptional educator that Moses had been. By the same stroke, the model can no longer be theocratic but is democratic – democracy at least issues from war as a spontaneous convention preceding the explicit pact.[41]

Surprise: this is without question a Roman idea.

To say that 'the supreme reward of the army is freedom' does not simply mean that freedom is the *result* of war, or its outcome; or rather, the result must be understood as an immanent product, in the sense of Aristotelian *praxis*. The 'image of freedom' invoked by the text invites such an interpre-tation, and consequently a tight connection with the final proposition of the *Ethics*. No doubt the expression is open to two readings, one weak, the other strong. The weak reading: the image of freedom is the positive moti-vation that gives human beings the courage to do battle and to defy death (for the mere play of fear instead encourages one to submit or blindly flee: two equally suicidal behaviours). The strong reading: the image of freedom is never so present to the mind of human beings as in resistance or defence. It is here that the political body as such emerges or surfaces.

---

[40] This mode of life is moreover the one most favourable for the development of reason: see *Ethics* IV, App. XXV and XXXI; CWS I, 592–3.

[41] One might be tempted to object that, in the case of the Hebrews, it was the educa-tion through hope that disposed them toward warlike bravery and not the reverse. However: 1. War and education are in fact contemporaneous, and the hypothesis of their complementarity does not appear to be unreasonable. 2. It was the disobedience of the Hebrews that led Moses to choose to deal with them with hope rather than fear (his success as an educator was tied to his intuitions about collective tendencies). This disobedience, recall, was not natural (*TTP* XVII, 93; CWS II, 317); consequently, it arises either from 'malformed' institutions, and the corresponding *habitus*, or from enslaved *habitus*, taking into account the irreducible resistance of individual existence as such.

Can we not then imagine that, in the Dutch context of internal struggles at once social and religious, Spinoza saw the last chance for a renewal of the Dutch community with itself by means of a new fight for independence in the face of the French invaders? That he might have thought that collective struggle was the ultimate factor capable of subverting the Orangist restoration by giving rise to a new democratic *habitus*? We are familiar with those wars that for the powerful are occasions for distracting the social body with the divisions that they sustain, by reviving national passion. But that would not be an objection here, insofar as it is clear that Spinoza constantly opposes two kinds of war to one another: wars for glory, the suicidal expedient of royal absolutism, which keeps the multitude at bay by making use of mercenaries, or rather which manages the 'superstition' of human beings 'so that they will fight for slavery as they would for their survival';[42] and wars for the civil state or for freedom, in which citizen-soldiers, *in combat itself*, learn or relearn to 'look after themselves'. The war for independence or resistance is a process that by its very logic saps the bases of domination and slavery; even in the case of an already formed multitude – tyranny is anyway not really a form – we must suppose that it does not push back against the invader without at least tendentially reappropriating sovereignty. What matters is whether the tyrant conserves its power at the end of the day: the victory obtained is not its own, and it must henceforth make concessions based on the new *experience* of its subjects. This kind of war, and not the colonial kind, can be called civilising (a term, it is true, that is somewhat anachronistic).

We can perhaps draw out the theoretical formula for that *positive collective amnesia* whose problem we posed in the Introduction: war – not of conquest or colonisation, but of independence or the defence of that independence, which recreates conditions that are the exact inverse of those in which the salvation of the State, entrusted to a general, amounts to a transfer toward tyranny. The immanent reward of war, or warlike virtue, is no doubt freedom, but we have to account for the ambivalence here: what is this freedom if not the civil state itself in action, human beings never uniting except when in supreme danger (the nation at risk), the virtue consisting in *public* acts? The freedom acquired in combat is at once national independence and the experience of citizenship.

This issue perhaps leads to a more complex evaluation of the relationship between Spinoza and Roman civilisation. For does not this *virtus bellica* whose immanent reward is liberty come from Rome, through Machiavelli?

---

[42] *TTP* Praef., 10; CWS II, 68.

Spinoza did not think much, as we have said, of that people that never knew how to provide itself institutions capable of making reign anything other than war, internally or externally, or a false peace, *pax romana*, namely that *concordia* that Augustus demanded as one of the virtues of the prince.[43] However, one feels that he is quite close, in his conception of war and peace, of warlike virtue and the status of leaders, in his very mistrust with regard to the new, to the position of Cato the Elder in the conflict that opposed him to Scipio Africanus.

Cato was the man who led the struggle against the growing prestige of a general who multiplied military victories, and who he perceived as a threat to the institutions of the Republic. First of all, Scipio did not believe for a moment that a vote coming from the comitia could go to a talented military leader, whereas Cato responded, by contrast, not that the talent for leading an army would be found in the first to come along, but that a military campaign is always a collective task, and that rules and discipline matter as much as personal value (here one imagines the fiction of the reign of one alone, according to Spinoza). Secondly, Cato was opposed to war for war's sake, he did not see any salvation of Rome in conquest, and he even often expressed himself in favour of the freedom of peoples (same motif in Spinoza). Thirdly, Cato advised the return to the old austerity of customs, to the figure of the virtuous and anonymous citizen-soldier, in which he saw the origin of Roman superiority (like Spinoza's conservatism, but Spinoza's is without nostalgia, turned toward a foundation that has not yet taken place, but which perhaps implies a virtue drawn from combat).[44] Yet, while Cato may have prevailed, Spinoza retains from the conflict only Scipio's famous insolence toward the tribunes:[45] it was Scipio who represented the tendency that was victorious in the long run. One will note, and this is no doubt not by chance, that the military chief whose virtue Spinoza praises is Hannibal.[46] Cato dreamt of a Republic whose reality he himself projected into the past, but which for Spinoza, judging by the distressing picture he paints of the whole of Roman history, never existed. Spinoza is not far from being the Dutch Cato, but unlike the latter he drew on the most progressive forces, and this is perhaps why, instead of a Pyrrhic victory, his temporary defeat rang the death knell for royal absolutism and signalled the rise of 'popular regimes'.[47]

---

[43] See Martin 1994: 458. (Appian spoke of 'concord through monarchy', etc.)
[44] See Grimal 1975: 201–13.
[45] *TP* X, 3; *CWS* II, 598.
[46] *TP* V, 3; *CWS* II, 529–30.
[47] *TP* VI, 4; *CWS* II, 533.

At the beginning we posed the problem of the nature of Spinoza's distinctive 'conservatism'. Here at the end, there is hardly any relationship between Catonian conservatism, a dreamlike and objectless memory, and its Spinozist repetition – a *constituent* conservatism, devoted entirely to the unprecedented. For it is not what presently exists that can conserve itself: no more the Roman Republic of old, with the supposed equilibrium of its mixed constitution, than the new Republic of the United Provinces, with its bipolar institutions. *It is not a matter of conserving what exists, but of making exist what conserves itself.* Revolution has no impact that is not ruinous, because it is like a 'conclusion without premises': a transformation only in dreams. The first sense of 'conserve', by contrast, is being aware of a *given*, which is also to say: of causes that fade away only in dreams. For in a profound way it is a matter of setting out again from the cause in general, in order, thanks to favourable historical conditions, to transmute it or render it 'adequate': to reconnect with the collective striving for conservation, from the point of view of constitution. That is why there is necessarily a second, surprising sense of 'conserve': *to create.*

Pierre Macherey and François Zourabichvili on
Spinoza's Paradoxical Conservatism

This exchange took place on 4 February 2004, at a meeting of 'La philosophie au sens large', a study group led by Pierre Macherey that met weekly from 2000 to 2010.

Pierre Macherey

Of the two works devoted to Spinoza that François Zourabichvili published simultaneously with PUF in 2002, *Spinoza, une physique de la pensée* and *Spinoza's Paradoxical Conservatism*, the latter seems to raise the more delicate and intriguing problems. That is why we have looked at it with a view toward opening up a discussion about Zourabichvili's singular reading of Spinoza, a reading, let us be clear from the start, whose singularity makes it all the more stimulating. This book is subtitled 'Childhood and Royalty', which immediately provides a glimpse into the vertiginous rapprochements that take place in it. It is essentially composed of three studies, of which the first, which principally concerns the practice of philosophy, is dedicated to the theme of ethical transition that carries out the passage from ignorance to wisdom and from servitude to freedom; the second is dedicated to the theme of the child and the gaze, at once intimate and distant, stunned and yet comprehending, and at the very least interested, that the philosopher casts over it; and the third is dedicated to absolute monarchy, the form of organisation of power that was tending toward dominance in Europe at the time that Spinoza elaborated his political reflections, and which provided him, polemically, with a concrete target. At first glance, these three objects of reflection are quite removed from one another, and the move to bring them together is not an obvious one; yet it is their confrontation that, as we will see, provides Zourabichvili's work its content; the work exploits them by reflecting them in one another, with a view toward going back over the whole of Spinoza's philosophy, tying its threads together otherwise, in a way that escapes, or at least contorts, the properly doctrinal effects that have primarily been imposed upon it when the work is considered head-on, and which makes it possible to freely reconstruct its necessity by desystematising it.

Now, whether this is an editorial oversight or a deliberate choice by the author, neither of these works mentions the fact that François Zourabichvili was already known for his little book *Deleuze: A Philosophy of the Event*, published in 1994 in the PUF collection 'Philosophies',[1] which, in spite of its short length, or perhaps thanks to the concentration required by its restrained form, is one of the best introductions currently available to Deleuze's thought, grasped from a particular angle which makes it possible to resurvey it as a whole by casting it in a new light. In the book that concerns us today, Deleuze is hardly cited (only three times, and in a very marginal way), and it would be quite inappropriate to claim that Zourabichvili positions his reading of Spinoza as a direct extension of what Deleuze had done for the philosopher, to whom he assigns a special fate and an innovative perspective, which enabled him to incorporate Spinoza into the development of his own reflection as a philosopher and not merely as a historian of philosophy. For that would be to say that, rereading Spinoza through Deleuze, Zourabichvili at the same time provides the means to reread Deleuze through Spinoza, which is not at all his objective. It nevertheless remains true that his Deleuzian upbringing is not foreign to the approach that he proposes concerning Spinoza's work, and which perhaps helps explain certain of its peculiarities.

First of all, it clarifies the method, which can be applied to the qualifier that appears in the title of the work, and which recurs frequently, on all sorts of occasions, throughout the text: this method is 'paradoxical', in the sense that it leads to examining Spinoza's philosophy from the point of view of what constitutes, in a decentred way, one of its difficulties, namely the question of transformation or metamorphosis; whereas this question, in fact, only comes up in certain margins of his argumentation, which makes it strange and disconcerting to focus attention on it and to treat it as something that reveals the most profound preoccupations implicit in Spinoza's approach. Analogously, Deleuze had proposed to reread Spinoza in light of the question of expression, with a view toward developing a reading of this author that is in every sense of the term 'expressionist', whereas the substantive *expressio* is never found in his writing, and a category like expressionism, which comes from the history of art and which makes sense to apply to a painter

[1] [Zourabichvili 2012.]

like Francis Bacon, does not seem to have anything to do with Spinoza, this classical and precisely post-Cartesian philosopher. However, this does not prevent it – and this is one of the goals of the operation, also paradoxical, that Deleuze carries out – from revealing that Spinoza's rationalism, reread in light of the problematic of expression, which clarifies it laterally, turns out to have curious and unnoticed aspects, miles apart from the dogmatic theoreticism so often imputed to this thought, which, from Deleuze's point of view, strips it of its true content, and above all of its intensity. The history of philosophy, as it is ordinarily done, is not in the habit of performing paradoxical readings, and even instinctively turns away from them, which leads it to sanitise the thought of philosophers, which it leads into conventional, immediately identifiable and categorisable configurations, which is the best way to clear away what is living in them, and often, thanks to their disconcerting aspects, leads to embarrassment and even constitutes an obstacle to their communication.

On the other hand, there is on the side of the content a difficulty that this method carries, in treating something that also brings us back to an inspiration that one could call Deleuzian. Transversal to the three studies gathered together in Zourabichvili's work is an interrogation into the conditions of change: the personal change that is implied by the passage from the state of the child to the adult state, relived on another level by the reasonable human being that philosophy leads to that sovereign form of emancipation that is the free life, defined as the transition to a greater perfection, which makes the benefits of virtue coincide with the fact of practising it; and, in the final occurrence of this schema, change on the plane of collective existence, where the vagaries of politics lead to a renegotiation, for better or for worse, of the social link, in a form that is often that of rupture, on the basis of violence and renunciation, as Spinoza already saw first-hand in 1672. It is thus a matter, to summarise, of three situations involving change: education, conversion, and revolution. The problem, which is ultimately quite classical, that runs through these figures of change, and provides their treatment a common ground, is the following: is a philosophy of necessity like Spinoza's, generally placed under the header of 'substantialism', or as Renouvier said a 'philosophy of things',[2] in any position to think becoming, a becoming the possibility of whose foundations appear to be nullified by

---

[2] [I have not been able to locate this precise formulation either in *Manuel de philosophie moderne* or in *Les dilmmes de la métaphysique pure*, though both involve extended discussions of Spinoza's philosophy that accord with this description. See Renouvier 1842: 235–66; Renouvier 1901: 33–5, 61–3, 77–80, 226 and following, etc. – GM.]

closing up everything that exists, in the cold and implacable gaze of reason, in a rigid grid in which each thing has, from all eternity, its fixed place, and in which consequently nothing can change? This calls into question the ethical project at its core, which at first glance is difficult to reconcile with a necessitarian approach. It is not hard to see that this question of becoming would be crucial for what Deleuze called 'practical philosophy', which does not propose to develop an imperious view on a world of frozen things but seeks concretely and effectively to take part in the movement of their transformation which, on a concrete plane, consists in their alteration. Now it is important to see that behind this problem of change, there is another, still more fundamental one, which is that of the status of negation: can there be change without there also being discontinuity, that is to say the pure and simple annulment of a prior state by that which succeeds it and takes its place? The possibility that things would change, fundamentally required by a practical philosophy, which would above all be a philosophy of the event and of duration, brings to the fore the consideration of what happens rather than the state of things – does this imply the reinscription of negativity at the heart of being, as in the dialectical vision of the world advanced by Hegel? Or rather, and this is the option that Deleuze was led to adopt via his Bergsonised Nietzscheanism, must one on the contrary come to think change without negation, as a process that is positive from end to end, literally a 'creative evolution' expressing a vital dynamic that rejects any mediation of death, because from its point of view death is always an external accident, or a waning of the movement, and not an internal motor of the transformations of the real? Reduced to its basic principle, the idea defended by Deleuze concerning Spinoza is that the latter provides precisely the means to think change without negation, and thus as a vital process in which death plays no active role of the kind invoked by the formula 'if the grain dies'[3] – which is, incidentally, a way of indirectly saying that Hegel was right when he explained, in the *Lectures on the Philosophy of History*, that Spinoza 'does not do justice to the negative',[4] and even that he does it wrong. The key to Spinozism would then be furnished by its refusal of the negative, of which the three problems of the conversion of the sage, the mat-

---

[3] [*Si le grain ne meurt* was the title of André Gide's autobiography (Gide 2001). The phrase is a reference to John 12:24: 'Very truly, I tell you, unless a grain of wheat falls into the earth and dies, it remains just a single grain; but if it dies, it bears much fruit' (*NRSV*, 1903). – GM.]

[4] [This seems to be a paraphrase of the following: 'the moment of the negative is what is lacking and deficient in this one, rigid, motionless substantiality' (Hegel 1990: 161). – GM.]

uration of the child, and the resistance to the abuses of absolute monarchy, in the very particular ways in which Spinoza treats them, furnish concrete illustrations. It is in light of this problem of negativity that we must thus now take up the content of the three studies gathered together in Zourabichvili's work, so as to see how they resolve the problem thereby raised: the problem of the possibility of a change that would not involve a negative self-relation.

The first study, dedicated to the traditional schema of conversion, develops to the letter the thematic that we have just invoked, which justifies why it comes first – as though it provided a kind of model solution to the general problem of change, a solution that would then only need to be transposed into other domains of investigation.

The central idea accentuated in this study is that of perfection, which makes it possible to overcome the apparent opposition between ignorance and wisdom, in such a way, Zourabichvili writes, that the ethical journey presents 'all the traits of a transformation but without being one',[5] that is to say, without being, in the crude sense of the word 'transformation', the change of one form into another form to which it bears a specific difference. In fact, this is a point to which Spinoza ceaselessly returns; for the human being, ameliorating its condition in no way signifies a change in nature, but still and always '*perseverare in suum esse quantum in se est*', according to the canonical formula of the *conatus*.

In the passages of the *Short Treatise* (II, 22 and 26) examined first, this point brings us back to the paradox of learning that lay at the heart of the Platonic doctrine of recollection: at bottom, one never learns what one does not already know, according to the positive disposition of a confirmation or a coming to awareness, and not in the negative figure of an abandonment or renunciation. What is it to become wise or a sage? It is to return to a primary if not anterior stage, in the sense of a stage in which one found oneself first of all naturally immersed, like the fish that, without being aware of it, lives in the water that constitutes its element and which for this reason turns out to be incorporated in its constitution. A wisdom that would prescribe the necessity of changing one's nature in order to be liberated would be doomed to failure, in the same way that a fish who sought to attain a better life by living outside its element, and so ceasing to lead a life conforming to its nature as a fish, would be condemned to die, acting against itself – through ignorance, of course, for it is clear for Spinoza that no being, not even a fish, could consciously want its own destruction for itself. The aspiration

---

[5] [Above, 31.]

to change, in the sense of radically becoming other, involving a negative relation to oneself, is the symptom par excellence of an inadequate knowledge, of the kind that one might form when finding oneself in a desperate situation, which leads one to reproduce mentally the conditions that made this situation desperate, to the point of making one lose one's head in the immersion, which, concretely, makes one lose all hope of getting out of it. That is the reason why it is vain to act based on negation, and to think that by exploiting it one might pull off a positive change taking the form of an amelioration.

It is precisely this manner of seeing things that is narrated in the prologue of the *Treatise on the Emendation of the Intellect*, of which Zourabichvili, following Pierre-François Moreau (who dedicated the whole first part of his *Spinoza: L'expérience et l'éternité* to it[6]), presents a detailed analysis, going over its stages step-by-step. The subject of the experience relayed in this text, an experience which is that of an initiation into philosophy, finds themselves from the start precisely in an arduous situation of uncertainty which makes them see things in a literally depressing light, because it presents the problem that confronts them, that of leaving their present state of existential malaise, as insoluble. And it is only by rectifying this manner of seeing things little by little, that is, by posing the problem that they must resolve, that they discover that the idea of a change of state is in reality void of content, and that it is rather by returning to the root of their desire to change, which reveals a participation in the eternity in which their being finds its substantial principle, that they have a very slight chance, the only one they really have, of satisfying it, by reformulating it, and by discovering, in Zourabichvili's terms, that the 'mind thus discovers the true good in its striving to find it'.[7] Only then can the alternative formulated in the verse by Ovid that Spinoza likes to cite be overcome: *video meliora proboque, deteriora sequor*, which, in other words, means this: it is insofar as the good for which one searches is presented as an external good, and not as an immanent good, which one already possesses although under conditions that render its possession incomplete, that it is by the same token rendered inaccessible, so that all the moves that one makes in order to approach it instead lead to turning away from it.

One can see in this analysis an anticipation of the lesson that Spinoza would draw out in the very last proposition of the *Ethics* (V, 42): virtue has no other result, no other benefit, than that which is drawn from its

---

6 [See Moreau 1994.]
7 [Above, 63.]

very practice, which constitutes its immanent aim. That is to say that it is vain to seek to draw from the practice of virtue rewards fallen from heaven, which would guarantee the possibility of leading another life, in the sense of a wholly other life, possibly taking the form of a life after life; for such an aspiration really demonstrates nothing other than the fact that one is not virtuous, the essential problem not being that of understanding what virtue makes come to be, that is, what it procures as palpable benefits, but rather understanding the conditions making it possible to become virtuous in practice – which is the fundamental difficulty confronting a philosophy like Spinoza's if it is to be a practical philosophy, that is, above all, a philosophy which has no value other than what is gained in its practice, in which it finds itself engaged from the start.

The paradox at the heart of such a practical philosophy is perfectly summarised by the words that Nietzsche puts in Zarathustra's mouth: 'Become who you are!'[8] (implying: and not someone or something other). What is required by the calling to wisdom, insofar as the latter does not take on an illusory form, is not to cease to be what one is, or to start being so less, but just the opposite: to be what one is even more, by sinking deeper into what constitutes the very source of one's being, that is, in Spinoza's language, God, though a practice of union and not one of rupture. This is what allows us to understand how Spinoza could manage to resolve the traditional contradiction between freedom and necessity: it is because one is plunged in servitude that one suffers necessity as a constraint from which one wants to be delivered, whereas true freedom consists in going back into the regime of necessity to the maximum, and to integrate oneself there in such a way that this necessity is no longer suffered as a constraint, but is felt as being consubstantial with the one who experiences it in a way that is no longer negative but positive, by accepting it because one understands it, which is something completely different than suffering it blindly.

Let us remark moreover that the paradox of this becoming which is not a transformation is something that confronts every minimally attentive reader of Spinoza's work: the *Ethics* proposes to them a journey whose endpoint is opening up the prospect of apprehending things from the point of view of knowledge of the third kind, by which one attains this union with God, or *amor intellectualis Dei*, which is the final word of wisdom; but it is clear that the practice of knowledge of the third kind is already required when this journey begins. When, at the beginning of the first sentence of his book, Spinoza declares: *per causam sui intelligo . . .*, the practice of the intellection

---

[8] [*Thus Spoke Zarathustra* IV, 'The Honey Sacrifice' (Nietzsche 2006: 192).]

of essences or the intuitive science proper to this final form of knowledge is implicitly put into play, though its secret is not revealed until the end of the book, which comes to an end there where one must begin. Taking up the metaphor of the element from the rereading of the *Short Treatise* with which we began, the intellection of the true nature of things is like the element in which all our knowledges natively swim, including those that are false, since Spinoza provocatively affirms that 'All ideas, insofar as they are related to God, are true'[9] – all, that is, including those that are false in us because we perceive them inadequately, which does not prevent them from being necessary in their own way, which makes them into ideal truths [*vraies idées*] for lack of being true ideas [*idées vraies*]. This is why reading Spinoza's *Ethics*, unlike for example what happens when one follows a book like Descartes' *Meditations*, is in fact to embark on a regressive and not a progressive journey, because one really departs from the end, which it presupposes is acquired, the truth ultimately consisting in nothing else, from a dynamic and not a static point of view, than the striving that one performs with a view toward reaching it, a striving by which one makes oneself more and more conscious of this truth that was already there from the start.

The points that we have just summarily invoked, and which are luminously developed in the first part of Zourabichvili's work, do not present any difficulty. They can be considered as granting access to the profound spirit of Spinoza's philosophy. That is why they cannot provide us with a starting-point for discussion.

Can the same be said for the second study, which is dedicated to the education of the child? Let us say first of all that we will raise two kinds of questions on this issue: on the one hand, does the manner in which Zourabichvili presents Spinoza's point of view on childhood conform with the admittedly scant suggestions provided by the texts concerning this subject? And on the other hand, is the problematic of change involved in the treatment of this question really the same one that was at stake concerning the preceding theme of the conversion toward wisdom? On these two points, we will refrain from answering in the negative, and will content ourselves with remarking that at the end of the analysis that Zourabichvili devotes to them there remains an uncertainty, which justifies our raising them for discussion.

First of all, we take it as a given that Spinoza took very seriously the problem posed by the child, a being that is by definition immature, and as though incomplete, which the scholastics traditionally presented as a being

---

[9] [*Ethics* II, 32; CWS I, 472.]

in potentia, which is characterised as defective in relation to what they lack, in the manner of an incomplete nature, deprived of form, a nature which is thus not one except from the point of view of what its becoming promises it, when it will have passed from potentiality to actuality, which amounts to projecting onto the child the model of the adult of which it offers a dimin-ished, reduced, and in this way inadequate representation. A philosophy like Spinoza's, which refuses in principle any explanation by way of final causes, can only have extreme reservations about such a way of seeing things through their end, and such a recurrent point of view which inverts the real relation of succession between cause and effect. The whole question is thus of knowing whether this reservation led conversely to seeing the child as a being that is not defective but complete in itself, whose existence is as such open to a positive evaluation, which, like the representation that would prevail at the end of the eighteenth century when the modern image of the child would be put in place, would treat it as a being with a nature in its own right, with its own characteristics, a specific form, giving rise to a science called child psychology, a form requiring its own educational process that could not be ignored if it was to have any real chance of success, and which cannot be reduced to mechanical training of the kind that one imposes on animals in order to force them to change their behaviour from top to bottom.

It should immediately be noted that the examination of this problem is overdetermined, and as it were compromised, by the fact that, whenever Spinoza focused on the child, he was led irresistibly to project onto its nature the figure of the adult who remained a child, or who had become one again through some accident. Childhood might very well be a state that persists all throughout organic life, the existence of a child's mind in an apparently adult body constituting a case that might be much less rare than one ima-gines, and which might even be a convenient illustration of the common human condition, in which one encounters innumerable examples of adult children or child adults – which makes one despair of humanity's ability to ameliorate itself, to make progress, that is, to really and irreversibly pass into the adult state, which perhaps is something that is reserved only for some exceptional beings, among whom the sage would certainly figure, but for which there are simply no guarantees.

Zourabichvili goes quite far in this direction, and takes many risks in how he treats this problem. He presents Spinoza as the philosopher who was permanently haunted by the problem of education, and even goes as far as supposing that, if Spinoza had lived longer, he might have followed up the *Ethics* with a treatise on education (he raises this hypothesis twice, on page 106 and around 154, above), which amounts to interpreting the *Ethics* as an anticipation of or preparation for this treatise on education. In other words, the question of childhood does not simply constitute one object or theme among others to which the new form of philosophical thought that Spinoza developed is applied, but is rather, at the very heart of his philosophical reflection, the motivating principle that led to the establishment of an unprecedented figure of philosophical thought: 'childhood, finally placed back on its feet'[10] and stripped of its disparaging image, which turns it into a kind of sickness, an image of which Gabriel Metsu's painting *The Sick Child*, a stunning profane translation of the traditional theme of the *pietà*, furnishes a touching illustration; childhood would be the speculative paradigm of eth-ical life and of the obstacles, but also the promises, involved in its develop-mental dynamic, insofar as the latter follows an open trajectory, whose end is in no way prefigured in its beginning, as was the case in the Aristotelian schema of the passage from potentiality to actuality.

But what is this childhood 'placed back on its feet'? Zourabichvili clarifies that it is not a matter, for Spinoza, of inverting the negative image of the child, which still prevailed in Descartes (attested to by his lamenting the 'prejudices of childhood', as children are unable to resist the influence of ignorant nannies), and substituting for it the hypostatised representation of a childhood miraculously granted exceptional powers, making it into a model of a life that is free, innocent, and pure, which would be offered up to the free human being as a model to be imitated, and not simply as a stimu-lating theme for reflection. On this point, Zourabichvili is perfectly clear: an authentic thought of development is one that refuses to see in the child an autonomous norm of which the adult would be the completed figure by set-ting itself up in opposition to it. Being in development, the child by this very fact turns out to be in a mobile and uncertain situation that keeps it caught between joy and sadness, between hope and fear, activity and passivity, and even, quite concretely, life and death, given the significance of infant mor-tality in the seventeenth century. This is why it is impossible, and certainly detrimental, to consider the child as a state in the proper sense of the word, that is as a system seeking the conditions of its stabilisation, a stabilisa-tion that, in the case of the child, can only be obtained under precarious conditions, which need ceaselessly to be renegotiated: in Metsu's painting, Zourabichvili sees precisely an invocation of this fragility that expresses the 'gap between *conamur* and *patitur*'.[11] This is why the child is certainly inca-pable of conserving itself without external aid, in relation to which it is in a

---

[10] [Above, 111.]
[11] [Above, 126.]

receptive position; but this still does not make it into a slave in miniature, such that the one in charge of maintaining and educating it could manipulate it like a plaything with a view toward fashioning it in its own image.

Commenting on the scholium to Proposition 39 of Part V of the *Ethics*, Zourabichvili consequently explains that Spinoza's project is to 'make childhood and even *infancy* the common condition of human beings, and the point of view from which one must set out again in order finally to grasp a true ethical discourse'.[12] By 'true ethical discourse' one must understand not a moralising discourse that deals with norms of behaviour in a language of needing to be, which is as such external to the concrete reality of these behaviours, but the programme proper to an authentic practical philosophy that is not merely a philosophy of or about practice, a philosophy for practice, but a philosophy that arises from practice, and which is thus really engaged in its movement and at no point dissociated from it, and which it reflects without taking any distance from it. But practice, which is precisely the possibility of change, whose outcome is by definition uncertain, for nothing guarantees its success, unfolds between two poles: on the one hand passivity, open to the intervention of external causes; on the other hand activity, which, through the vagaries of occasions and encounters, continues to affirm, come hell or high water, the irrepressible need to persevere in one's being, and above all the need to persevere in being, that is to say, to continue to exist, under conditions of maximal viability – viable thus meaning: pointed in the direction of an amelioration, a reinforcement, and thereby protected from stagnation. In this way Zourabichvili is led to affirm, at the end of the study devoted to the theme of childhood: 'The relationship to childhood became the veridical ordeal of a philosophy that meant to grant no validity to the idea of privation, and which triumphed in this ordeal by rectifying the image of childhood, by appropriating it as the best illustration of itself. The child grasped in its becoming, at the end of the *Ethics*, is the very image, the unique, definitive image, conforming to the understanding, of becoming-philosopher.'[13] And he concludes that with this 'there is, for the first time in philosophy, an *active* gaze upon children'.[14]

One might ask whether this is not to give Spinoza too much credit: if the latter, rather audaciously for his era, was confronted with the problem of childhood, to which he never ceased to return, this is not necessarily because he had its solution at his disposal, a solution that would be the key

---

[12] [Above, 113.]
[13] [Above, 164.]
[14] [Above, 164.]

to his whole philosophical enterprise. To attribute to him a clear and positive viewpoint on the difficult problem of the child, whereas the cultural environment in which it arose obscured its terms – one could say the same about the problem of women, which, in every sense of the word, arrested [arrêté] Spinoza – is this not, by virtue of a revealing act of faith, to give credence to the representation of an exceptional philosopher who, thanks to his state of grace, was miraculously spared the prejudices of his time? One could maintain the opposite, on the basis of the collection of passages where this question is raised: that the image of childhood that emerges in Spinoza's remarks is not so clear and affirmative as Zourabichvili's reading makes it out to be, and rather constitutes an indicator of the problems that the philosopher needed to confront in order to advance toward the solution of this problem, which was in no way guaranteed success, as the fact of managing to pose a problem in no way presupposes the ability to resolve it.

On the other hand, is it really justified to line up the two problems of ethical transition and education in a perspective that invokes the philosophies of progress elaborated in the nineteenth century? What is becoming an adult for Spinoza? It is to gain the means of incorporating oneself into communitarian life: and for this, one must first of all learn to obey, that is, to conform one's external actions to rules acceptable for everyone, a necessity from which the sage, even if they are convinced of the relative character of these rules, cannot excuse themselves. It was in this way, for example, that Moses set up and imposed, via a Machiavellian ruse, the project of political pedagogy that he judged appropriate given the nature of his people. But access to true wisdom presupposes an approach of a completely different order, which cultivates the capacity to think for oneself, so as to manage to follow only one's own laws. What do we gain by presenting this perfection by interpreting it in terms of an education of the kind that is necessary in order for the child to learn to become an adult? Of course, it is not a question of opposing these two processes, which must be pursued in a parallel way; but this still does not authorise us to align their two trajectories, which obey distinct objectives; and this makes it debatable to bring them together under the abstract category of change.

The third study clarifies the broad outlines of Spinoza's political philosophy in a very interesting way, by interpreting it as a response to the factual problem represented in his time by the extension of the model of absolute monarchy to the majority of European countries, of which Louis XIV provides the example par excellence. It was precisely the monarchy of Louis XIV that took the lead in the crusade against the Batavian Free Republic, that very particular political experiment conducted in Holland between 1650 and 1672, a regime of assemblies that was in fact an aristocracy of elite merchants, in whose favour Spinoza explicitly spoke in the 1670 *Theologico-Political Treatise*, two years before the experiment was put to a definitive end by the conjunction of the foreign military invasion and a popular uprising of the masses issuing from the agrarian Provinces of the North against the urban bourgeoisie of the South. In a strikingly convincing way, Zourabichvili explains that this absolute monarchy could, from Spinoza's point of view, only be an aberration, properly speaking a chimera, whose principle rests on the artificial annihilation of any natural identity on the plane of the political body, according to the baroque principle of transformation and of the mobility of forms; this is why absolute monarchy exemplifies a kind of politics of the imaginary, devoid of any actual content, and which represents a sort of triumph of the negative when it comes to regulating human affairs, founded upon transcendence and arbitrariness. When Descartes represents God on the model of the monarch who decrees the laws of their royalty at will, he remains a prisoner of this non-philosophical model, which Spinoza by contrast denounced, not only in his positive politics, but above all in his reform of philosophy, in both cases following the same programme, whose fundamental principle is furnished by the idea of resistance. That is why, in his struggle against absolute monarchy on the plane of ideas, one rediscovers, according to Zourabichvili, the same demand to put an end to the negative that also characterises the way in which Spinoza conceives of ethical conversion and the education of children.

This way of presenting Spinoza's political philosophy sheds powerful light on certain issues in an innovative manner. But it nevertheless encounters the following difficulty: it foregrounds the question of the form of the political regime, a form of which absolute monarchy would be a perversion, whereas one of the originalities of Spinoza's political reflection is that, in opposition to the dominant tendency, it tends to push this problem of political form to the background, which it does by focusing attention first and foremost on the conditions of the formation of public spirit that provides political life its real foundation. In relation to this foundation, the formal modalities of the organisation of power constitute a sort of circumstantial garment which comes to cover it up after the fact, and which the work of philosophical thought must strip away in order to rediscover, upstream of this, the authentic bases of human solidarity, which are not juridical conditions in the sense of constitutional law [*droit*]. When Spinoza affirms, in philosophy, a preference for democracy, this is not the end result of a comparison of the diverse forms of monarchical, aristocratic, and democratic organisations of political power that enables one to evaluate their respective advantages and inconveniences; instead, he estimates that this question is subsidiary to that of the foundation of sovereignty which, from his point of view, no matter the juridical constitution that regulates the particular modalities of the social pact, and no matter the institutional figure donned by the sovereign authority, is essentially democratic – even if this democratic demand, which anyway can never be completely satisfied, unless we are to fall into the utopia of an ideal republic of minds, is realised according to the circumstances in highly unequal degrees of intensity. Whence the claim, which at first glance is very surprising, which Spinoza defends, and which he never abandons – it is this claim that radically distinguishes his position from that of Hobbes – according to which all political organisation, no matter its form, is tendentially democratic, in the sense that collective life responds to a certain number of fundamental common aspirations, to a most often unconscious desire to live together, in the absence of which it would not be viable. From this point of view, even monarchy (but not absolute monarchy) is, for Spinoza, a democracy that is unaware of itself, and which one must try to render more conscious of itself; and, if it so happens that, for conjunctural reasons, this political form is imposed on a people, in such a way that it would be dangerous to organise its disappearance by violent means, for one never knows what the outcome of revolution will be, the only thing that remains reasonable to consider is to rearrange it in order to ameliorate it, to make it come as close as possible to the democracy that it bears in its heart without being aware of it, which amounts to attenuating its risks of degenerating into tyranny. This is why, Spinoza explains, the best or least bad monarchies are still those in which the king is old and tired, and for this reason disinclined to start and conduct wars of conquest that make it dangerous for its own people and for others. And the right to revolt, which one must make use of only extremely rarely, as its effects can turn out to be devastating for everyone, is legitimate only in the extreme cases where the degeneration of a political form has doomed it to abuses that damage its democratic principle to the point of running the risk of this principle's destruction, by turning the members of the collectivity against one another: then, and only then, is it permissible to revolt, and it is even the case that one must do so, with a view toward recovering the basis of civil life, against the backdrop of the passions and a minimum of reason, by searching, without any triumphalism, for compromises that need to be ceaselessly renegotiated; for the idea of an unfailingly guaranteed social pact, whose results could be taken as given for all time, is to be rejected, as a pious vow foreign to the real life of civil communities, which can only damage their development, and quite simply their survival.

The idea of a revitalisation of social life, which supposes a turn back in the direction of its foundations, incontestably presents an analogy with the solution that Spinoza proposes for the problems of ethical conversion, which is also a return to the substantial origins of life, in its corporeal as well as mental aspects; and from this point of view, the concept of change, and more precisely of a change that would not be a transformation, but one that, however paradoxical this may appear, happens through conservation, might play the role of a common notion, and enable us to renew some of Spinoza's lines of reasoning. But still, this is a matter of two very different problems, since the one concerns the regulation of the interior life of the individual, and the other concerns interindividual relations, which cannot be subject to the same type of laws, on pain of degrading them and making it impossible to rationally comprehend them. Are the problems of political reform closer to those that are dealt with by educational pedagogy? One might say so, if one buys into the image of a child people, which Spinoza seems in fact to apply to the history of the Hebrews, as Hegel would do to the Greek aesthetic moment of the development of universal Spirit; but it is dangerous to consider all peoples on this model, and to present education as the universal panacea for all forms of political crisis. And this is why, once again, one might be reticent about assimilating these problems under one schema which would be that of a becoming purged of the motor of negativity, which would have the result of making Spinoza the philosopher who is saved from any compromise with the dialectic, and who would be the anti-dialectical thinker par excellence.

For lack of time, we will limit our presentation of François Zourabichvili's work, whose detailed analyses are passionate, to these very general considerations. To read a philosopher like Spinoza is no doubt not an easy undertaking, or one whose success is guaranteed; the reading that Zourabichvili proposes draws its principal merit from the risks it takes by interrogating this philosophy from brand new angles, which in turn authorises us to interrogate it by putting its assumptions to the test. It is by following this path that one has any chance of making progress in the knowledge of a philosophy whose possibilities we have certainly not exhausted, and which, since its dominant tonality is chiaroscuro, seizes our attention above all through its enigmas and paradoxes.

François Zourabichvili

Pierre Macherey presents my book from the perspective of the problem of negation. Not only does he admirably pose this problem (and it is proper to recall here his great book *Hegel or Spinoza*, published some twenty-five years ago, since my own work on Spinoza – or at least so I hope – bears its traces), but he goes directly to what is most important for me, and of which I have never been so clearly aware until the debate he has staged here today, not even during the definitive writing of the book.

What I find striking in Spinoza is the tension between, on the one hand, the assessment of transformation, that nature is nothing other than a perpetual lawful reshuffling of finite forms, and, on the other hand, how it correlates desire and form, which implies the impossibility that transformation would be desired, the contradiction of the expression 'to transform oneself' [*se transformer*]. All the great polemics that he launches against his time and the thought of his time – on personal identity, the Cartesian doctrine of the creation of eternal truths, alchemy, royal absolutism's taste for baroque metamorphosis, revolution – raise the question of transformation.

Beyond that, or perhaps falling short of the impossibility formulated by a 'negative self-relation' (Macherey), which is in some way opposed in advance to the Hegelian dialectic and its avatars, Spinoza combats the Christian theme of fallen nature, which amounts to placing the negative in being. My idea was the following: if Spinoza's challenge was to propose a philosophy that had no place for the category of *privation*, then childhood would need to constitute a sort of specific ordeal for him. In fact, if one refuses to give childhood a negative definition (not walking, not speaking, not reasoning), is one not condemned to hypostatise it like an essence apart, and to tend to interpret becoming-adult as a transformation in the strict sense? The impossible collision, in the scholium to *Ethics* V, 39, of the schema of progression and the schema of transformation, seems to bear the trace of this dilemma, which Aristotelianism hid beneath a third, perhaps chimerical schema, that of perfection, or in other words actualisation.

Spinoza's stunning originality here was to refuse both options back-to-back, by seeing them as two sides of one and the same chimera, that of the *adult child*. In both cases, we are given the complete human being: either one obtains it by the mere actualisation of a form *in potentia* (the child is only an adult in miniature), or else one attains it at the cost of an implausible change of essence and of species. It seems to me that this is enough to toss an interesting stone into the pool of our pedagogical prejudices: the two boundaries of the spectre of the relationships to childhood are even today the ideal of an always more premature maturation (the newborn is intellectually a small adult and morally a pre-adolescent), and the nostalgic myth of a golden age to be saved from all anticipated destruction (the child 'in its world'). The exception would be found with Vygotsky – but it is precisely the case that his whole psychopedagogy is inspired by Spinoza. This double illusion, Spinoza says, comes from the fact that we reason starting with a perfect human being that we take as given in advance, in full possession of its reason and its freedom, on the model of Adam before the Fall. The state of childhood then appears to us as the expression of a vice of our nature. In short, we do not know how to think childhood as a 'natural and necessary thing'.[15]

Once we arrive at this point, it no longer suffices to correct our conception of childhood: it is the trajectory of human life as a whole that demands to be reconsidered from the point of view of childhood. And this is why I maintain that childhood works at the end of the *Ethics* like a great all-encompassing or recapitulative image: just look at the scholium to V, 39. Macherey objects that the development by which the child is led little by little to the adult stage and ethical reform are two different changes. This is true in certain regards, and notably so when it comes to the present state of child development (it is not me, to be clear, who ascribes an educative project to Spinoza – it is he himself who says in the *Treatise on the Emendation of the Intellect* that 'attention must be paid to Moral Philosophy and to Instruction concerning the Education of children'[16]). For according to Spinoza, does not ethics logically converge, at some point, with the demand for a 'natural and necessary' view on childhood? What the scholium to V, 39 tells us, and which follows from the claim that 'the Mind and the Body are one and the same thing, which is conceived now under the attribute of Thought, now under the attribute of Extension'[17] (if the scholium to V, 39 does not explicitly refer to any prior statement, it is because in its way it recapitulates the whole *Ethics*), is that the separation of the development of the capacities of the body and of the mind's access to higher kinds of knowledge is only an abstraction.

One might ask whether Spinoza succeeded in producing this thought without the idea of privation, as he wished. Before giving an answer, I must say that I fully agree with Macherey in his concern not to give too much credit to Spinoza, not to dream up an unconditioned system that would overcome 'by its state of grace' the questions that its epoch knew neither

---

[15] *Ethics* V, 6 Schol.; CWS I, 600.
[16] *TdIE* 15; CWS I, 11.
[17] *Ethics* III, 2 Schol.; CWS I, 494.

how to pose nor resolve (the temptation, present in all epochs, of a religious usage of Spinoza – and the scandal-mongers suggest that his style lends itself to this).

As for the new gaze cast upon children, the Dutch exception of the seventeenth century seems well-attested by the best historians, as much from the medical point of view as the pictorial (one must here distinguish between the genre of painting in which children appear and the painting that, in an unprecedented way, takes the child in its naturality as its object).

If it is a matter of conceptual means, it seems to me, in view of the conditions of the problem, that the schema of perfection could no more suit Spinoza than transformation, even if its content were modified. In fact, as power is always actual in Spinoza, the increase of the power to act can no longer be thought as an actualisation. As Spinoza himself indicates elsewhere, it is only in relation to models whose legitimacy is merely pragmatic that we can retain the schema of perfection.[18] And it is clear that he is fine with this pragmatic usage, and that he does not offer us the means of another logic. He had however sought one, since the increase of the power to act is not only a gradual process, but involves a moment of rupture or conversion. In fact, it is possible to answer the question: how does Spinoza think this rupture, if he abandons the schema of actualisation? He thinks it as a reorganisation of the relations to self and to the other: to pass from the alienation from oneself in the other, to the genetic reinscription of the self in a greater whole, Nature, of which the other is also a part (this is the object of the first study of my book). This even enables us to see that there is no contradiction in posing, on the one hand, the permanence of a certain quantity of power, and speaking, on the other hand, of the increase and diminution of the power to act. So perhaps it is on this side of things that one must search for the sketch of a new schema of change.

The question of childhood would deserve a longer debate, and I understand Macherey's scruple concerning education, and about its relationships with ethics and politics. I would just like to clarify two things.

First of all, the problem whose terms I have just recalled does not enable us to attribute to Spinoza the idea that 'childhood might very well be a state that persists all throughout organic life, the existence of a child's mind in an apparently adult body constituting a case that might be much less rare than one imagines'. Actually, beyond the fact that this would be in contradiction with the scholium to V, 39 (the correlation of the body and the

---

[18] *Ethics* IV, Praef. (CWS I, 543–6).

mind of childhood), it is necessary to distinguish *pueritia* from the typically adult *puerilitas* that is at stake everywhere in the *Theologico-Political Treatise*. No doubt, for Spinoza, the majority of adults are in one sense children who have not grown up; one must however at the same time grasp that they are no longer children. The common run of people – the *vulgus* – is in this way the incarnation, precarious by definition, of the chimera of the adult child (is this not the inevitable outcome of the two illusory pedagogical options invoked earlier – precocity/heterogeneity?). This is why it gives rise to the Adamic nostalgia of preachers, and the resentment therein.

Furthermore, the distinction between *pueritia* and *puerilitas* – which is not an interpretive overreach, since it is required by Spinoza's own problematic – implies the redoubling of the concept of impotence. Spinoza, it cannot be denied, invokes the state of impotence of the child and of the ordinary adult, that is to say the incapacity to undertake the process of cultivation on one's own. But this cannot be the same state: the child is *barely powerful*, so little powerful that it needs assistance in order to be conserved; as for the ordinary adult, we are dealing with a definitively alienated power. The desire of the child oscillates, and is essentially imitative (its body is 'continually, as it were, in a state of equilibrium'[19]); it is not invested in the pursuit of privileged objects. The infantile adult, by contrast, lives under the sway of obsession, of fixation: it tends toward the cardinal figures of the drunk, the miser, the ambitious, and the lustful. One must thus conclude that there are two antithetical ways of extending childhood throughout the whole of life: to impose one's infantilism on oneself and others, and to work on leaving childhood behind. It is in this sense that the ethical trajectory is grasped at the end of the *Ethics* in the rectified image of the child who has grown up, against the chimera of the adult child. Then childhood is no longer properly speaking an age, but rather a regime of existence: no longer a state or a world that one wallows in, but the vital orientation of one who knows that it is natural and necessary to be born ignorant and dependent, and that, properly understood, perseverance in what one is (not in being in general) is one and the same thing as emancipation.

The second clarification concerns the relationship between education and politics. I did not want to confuse them (and it would have been embarrassing to do so, after the century that has just passed). I agree completely with Macherey when he remarks that 'it is dangerous . . . to present education as the universal panacea for all forms of political crisis'. In fact, the end of my book goes in the other direction, by posing the problem of the free

---

[19] *Ethics* III, 32 Schol.; CWS I, 513.

multitude. Macherey is right to recall that the foundation of sovereignty, in Spinoza, is essentially democratic (for my part I formulate this by saying that, in the *Political Treatise*, the freedom-servitude couplet works originally from within the concept of the multitude, far from being applied to it after the fact; so that there is not in Spinoza the concept of the multitude in general, but a concept or a problem of the 'free multitude'). However, I do not see the problematic of political forms being relegated to the background: instead, I see it being reorganised in an unprecedented way, which notably takes into account the concrete question of militant intervention into its conditions, which are never those of a virgin sociality. It is true that Spinoza focuses 'attention first and foremost on the conditions of the formation of public spirit that provides political life its real foundation', but I do not see any incompatibility here, because he remains profoundly faithful to the Ciceronian couplet of 'laws and mores': no laws without mores, nor mores without laws. Spinoza transposes into the political field the ontological problem of the conservation of form (all things considered, incidentally, it is not quite right to speak of a transposition here, as politics is one of the dimensions of the conservation of human beings in their being, as Part IV of the *Ethics* shows). His diagnostic is that historical regimes, with some very rare exceptions, are malformed. Whence this glimmer at the heart of pessimism: royal absolutism triumphs, and what looms at the end of the splendours of Versailles is an apathy analogous to that of Turkish society (it is incredible to recall that, during the same years, the young Leibniz saw in Louis XIV a possible slayer of infidels, and pushed him to direct his energy toward Egypt and the Holy Land, rather than Amsterdam); but at the same time, this regime piles up chimeras and is not viable as such. This is why the formula of his conservatism is so strangely compatible with insurrection: what exists is malformed, there can be no question of conserving it; the health of a collectivity lies in the establishment of a form capable of conserving itself. But how is this intervention possible? One will immediately say that Spinoza turns in a circle: he addresses himself, one will say, to 'free multitudes', where the problem to be resolved is thus already virtually resolved; tough luck – one might be tempted to add – for those who are enslaved, who are the only ones for whom the problem arises. In truth, one must take seriously the situations that Spinoza describes: these multitudes acquired freedom in a struggle for independence (and such was precisely the situation of the United Provinces at the time of Spinoza's writing of the *Political Treatise*, a militant book if ever there was one).

I thus came to the case of the ancient Hebrew people, analysed in the *Theologico-Political Treatise*: only there were education and politics tied

together. I re-examined this analysis because it seemed to me that commentators simplified the problem, by reckoning that the book's judgment on
this regime was negative. In reality, Spinoza's judgment was complex, as his
conclusion testifies: *imitabilis, sed non imitandum*. This is because the theocratic regime, he tells us, can be suitable only for a people closed in on itself,
contracted into its singular identity, and not for a people in open commerce
with the world (obviously he has in mind Holland, the theocratic aims of
Calvinism, and the biblical image of the child people that the Dutch liked
to apply to themselves). One might say that there is a tension between two
models: Moses the educator, and the collective war for independence. But if
one looks at it correctly, the tension is found at the very heart of the analysis
of the Hebrew regime, and in the end Spinoza only bets on the second model.

There remain two fundamental questions: on the one hand, education –
as Macherey himself underscores – includes in itself a political dimension
('to gain the means of incorporating oneself into communitarian life . . . one
must first of all learn to obey, that is, to conform one's external actions to
rules acceptable for everyone'); on the other hand, it is not the same as the
process of ethical reform. Let us thus try to better pose the problem:

1. Education and politics would be mixed up in illusory theocracy, but no
    more would they remain external to one another (there would be no
    private education).
2. Education corresponds to the first step of ethical reform, in which one
    is given 'rules of true life', in which in sum each is invited to make an
    educator of themselves under the guidance of the educator Spinoza
    (see, for example, the scholium to *Ethics* V, 10 – and in a general way
    the expression *ex ducto rationis*).
3. What justifies the very structure of education, that is, the relation of
    a master and a disciple so that the one conducts the other until the
    point when they conduct themselves, is a native impotence, in other
    words the initial disequilibrium between individual power and the
    power of external causes, the overwhelming domination of these latter
    (and there again, one passes from the child to the infantile adult when
    this overwhelming domination has become incurable by virtue of the
    obsessional fixation of desire: the reader of the *Ethics* is thought to be a
    large child, but not yet the troublesome chimera of the childish adult –
    as some of Spinoza's correspondents revealed themselves to be). Let us
    specify, in passing, that obedience is less the object of education than
    its condition, and consequently its limit – which constitutes the whole
    paradox of primary education, or of what today we call childcare.

4. The relationship of education to politics is confirmed by the fact that
   its first principle, in Spinoza, is to orient the disciple toward the search
   for the good rather than toward the flight from evil, which is precisely
   the criteria that distinguishes the free multitude from the servile multitude. Better, this cleavage intersects with that of the rectified image
   of childhood and the chimera of the adult child: the right orientation
   is thus decisive in order for ethics to have a chance.

With these remarks I do not pretend to close a debate that is organised
around a set of true questions. The debate remains open, and I would even
say it remains so by its nature, since the approach of my book aimed less to
establish the supposedly univocal meaning of Spinozist doctrine (on this
point, I adhere completely to what Macherey says about the interpretation
of texts in Avec Spinoza[20]), than to look in it for weapons in order to dis-
place certain contemporary concerns – on condition, of course, of respect
for the letter of the text and the historical plausibility of the interpretations
adopted. Such a debate constitutes the very life of a book, it is the proof of its
existence, and I extend my gratitude to Pierre Macherey for having known
how to *expose* mine, in every sense.

[20] [See Macherey 1992.]

Works Cited

I. Benedict de Spinoza

(1925), *Opera* (4 vols), ed. Carl Gebhardt, Heidelberg: Carl Winter.

(1951), *A Theologico-Political Treatise* and *A Political Treatise*, trans. R. H. M. Elwes, New York: Dover.

(1965), *Œuvres de Spinoza II: Traité théologico-politique*, trans. Charles Appuhn, Paris: Garnier-Flammarion.

(1985–2016), *The Collected Works of Spinoza* (2 vols), trans. and ed. Edwin Curley, Princeton: Princeton University Press.

(1986), *Korte Verhandelig/Breve trattato*, trans. Filippo Mignini, L'Aquila: Japadre.

(1988), *Éthique*, trans. Bernard Pautrat, Paris: Éditions Seuil.

(1992), *Traité de la réforme de l'entendement*, trans. Bernard Rousset, Paris: Vrin.

(1994), *Traité de la réforme de l'entendement*, trans. Alexandre Koyré, Paris: Vrin.

(2007), *Theological-Political Treatise*, ed. Jonathan Israel, trans. Michael Silverthorne and Jonathan Israel, New York: Cambridge University Press.

II. Works by Other Authors

Aillaud, Gilles (1987), *Vermeer et Spinoza*, Paris: Christian Bourgeois.

Alpers, Svetlana (1983), *The Art of Describing: Dutch Art in the Seventeenth Century*, Chicago: University of Chicago Press.

Aquinas, Thomas (1923), *Saint Thomas Aquinas' Exposition of Aristotle's Treatise on the Heavens*, trans. Pierre Conway and F. R. Larcher, New York: Oxford Clarendon.

Aquinas, Thomas (1957), *On the Truth of the Catholic Faith: Summa Contra*

Gentiles, Book Four: Salvation, trans. Charles J. O'Neil, New York: Image Books.

Aquinas, Thomas (1964), *Commentary on the Nicomachean Ethics*, trans. C. I. Litzinger, Chicago: Henry Regnery Company.

Aquinas, Thomas (1981), *Summa Theologiae*, trans. Fathers of the English Dominican Province, Westminster: Christian Classics.

Ariès, Philippe (1973), *L'enfant et la vie familiale sous l'Ancien Régime*, Paris: Éditions de Seuil.

Aristotle (2004), *Nicomachean Ethics*, trans. and ed. Roger Crisp, New York: Cambridge University Press.

Augustine (2006), *Confessions and Enchiridion*, trans. and ed. Albert Cook Outler, Louisville: Westminster John Knox Press.

Babel, Isaac (2002), *The Red Cavalry Stories*, in *The Complete Works of Isaac Babel*, ed. Nathalie Babel, trans. Peter Constantine, New York: W. W. Norton Company.

Bacon, Francis (1985), *The Essays*, ed. John Pitcher, New York: Penguin.

Bacon, Francis (2000), *The New Organon*, ed. Lisa Jardine and Michael Silverthorne, New York: Cambridge University Press.

Balibar, Étienne (1994), *Masses, Classes, Ideas: Studies on Politics and Philosophy Before and After Marx*, trans. James Swenson, New York: Routledge.

Balibar, Étienne (1998), *Spinoza and Politics*, trans. Peter Snowdon, London: Verso.

Beaussant, Philippe (1981), *Versailles, Opéra*, Paris: Gallimard.

Bodin, Jean (2010), *On Sovereignty*, trans. and ed. Julian H. Franklin, New York: Cambridge University Press.

Borges, Jorge Luis (1964), *Labyrinths: Selected Stories & Other Writings*, ed. Donald A. Yates and James E. Irby, New York: New Directions.

Borges, Jorge Luis (1981), *Borges, A Reader: A Selection from the Writings of Jorge Luis Borges*, ed. Emir Rodriguez Monegal and Alastair Reid, New York: Dutton.

Boss, Gilbert (1982), *L'enseignement de Spinoza. Commentaire du 'Court traité'*, Paris: Éditions de Grand Midi.

Bossuet, Jacques-Bénigne (1997), *Sermons et oraisons funèbres*, Paris: Le Seuil.

Bove, Laurent (1996), *La Stratégie du conatus. Affirmation et résistance chez Spinoza*, Paris: Vrin.

Brunschvicg, Léon (1971), *Spinoza et ses contemporains*, Paris: PUF.

Calvin, John (2006), *Institutes of the Christian Religion, Volume 1*, ed. John T. McNeill, trans. Ford Lewis Battles, Louisville: Westminster John Knox Press.

Carrère, Emmanuel (2007), *Un roman russe*, Paris: POL.

Colerus (1954), *La vie de B. de Spinoza*, in Spinoza, *Œuvres complètes*, Paris: Gallimard.

Coogan, Michael D. (ed.) (2018), *The New Oxford Annotated Bible: New Revised Standard Version, With The Apocrypha*, associate eds. Marc Z. Brettler, Carol A. Newsom, and Pheme Perkins, Fourth Edition, New York: Oxford University Press.

Copenhaver, Brian (ed.) (1992), *Hermetica: The Greek Corpus Hermeticum and the Latin Asclepius in a New English Translation*, New York: Cambridge University Press.

Cornette, Joël (1998), 'Le palais du plus grand roi du monde', in *Les Collections de l'Histoire, no. 2: Versailles, le pouvoir de la pierre*.

Delbos, Victor (1893), *Le problème moral dans la philosophie de Spinoza et dans l'histoire du spinozisme*, Paris: Félix Alcan.

Deleuze, Gilles (1988), *Spinoza: Practical Philosophy*, trans. Robert Hurley, San Francisco: City Lights Books.

Deleuze, Gilles (2001), *Difference and Repetition*, trans. Paul Patton, London: Continuum.

Deleuze, Gilles (2005), *Expressionism in Philosophy: Spinoza*, trans. Martin Joughin, New York: Zone Books.

Deleuze, Gilles and Félix Guattari (1987), *A Thousand Plateaus*, trans. Brian Massumi, Minneapolis: University of Minnesota Press.

Deleuze, Gilles and Félix Guattari (1994), *What Is Philosophy?*, trans. Hugh Tomlinson and Graham Burchell, New York: Columbia University Press.

Descartes, René (1964–76), *Œuvres de Descartes* (12 vols), ed. Charles Adam and Paul Tannery, Paris: Vrin.

Descartes, René (1994–95), *The Philosophical Writings of Descartes* (3 vols), trans. and ed. John Cottingham, Robert Stoothoff, and Dugald Murdoch, Cambridge: Cambridge University Press.

Descartes, René (2004), *The World and Other Writings*, trans. and ed. Stephen Gaukroger, New York: Cambridge University Press.

Doré, Joseph (ed.) (1979), *Dictionairre de théologie chrétienne, vol. 1, les grands thèmes de la foi*, Paris: Desclée.

Erasmus, Desiderius (2015), *The Praise of Folly*, trans. Hoyt Hopewell Hudson, Princeton: Princeton University Press.

Ernout, Alfred and Antoinette Meillet (2001), *Dictionnaire étymologique de la langue latine. Histoire des mots*, Geneva: Klincksieck.

Fatio, Olivier (ed.) (1986), *Confessions et catéchismes de la foi réformée*, Geneva: Labor et Fides.

Fénelon, François (1831), *A Treatise on the Education of Daughters*, Boston: Perkins & Marvin.

Fénelon, François (1983–97), *Œuvres* (2 vols), Paris: Gallimard.

Foucault, Michel (2005), *The Hermeneutics of the Subject: Lectures at the Collège de France, 1981–82*, trans. Graham Burchell, ed. Frédéric Gros, New York: Palgrave Macmillan.

Friedmann, Georges (1975), *Leibniz et Spinoza*, Paris: Gallimard.

Giancotti, Emilia (1985), 'La teoria dell'assolutismo in Hobbes e Spinoza', *Studia Spinozana*, vol. 1, Würzburg: Könighausen & Neumann.

Gide, André (2001), *If It Die . . . An Autobiography*, trans. Dorothy Bussy, New York: Vintage.

Gilson, Étienne (2002), *Thomism*, trans. Laurence K. Shook and Armand Maurer, Toronto: Pontifical Institute of Mediaeval Studies.

Grimal, Pierre (1975), *Le siècle des Scipions*, Paris: Aubier.

Gueroult, Martial (1968), *Spinoza, 1: Dieu*, Paris: Aubier.

Gueroult, Martial (1974), *Spinoza, 2: L'âme*, Paris: Aubier.

Hegel, G. W. F. (1990), *Lectures on the History of Philosophy: The Lectures of 1825–1826, Volume III: Medieval and Modern Philosophy*, ed. R. F. Brown, trans. R. F. Brown and J. M. Stewart with the assistance of H. S. Harris, Berkeley: University of California Press.

Hermes Trismegistus (1579), *Le Pimandre de Mercure Trismegiste*, Bordeaux: S. Millanges.

Hobbes, Thomas (1998), *On the Citizen*, trans. and ed. Richard Tuck and Michael Silverthorne, New York: Cambridge University Press.

Hobbes, Thomas (2012), *Leviathan* (3 vols), ed. Noel Malcom, Clarendon: Oxford University Press.

Huan, Gabriel (1914), *Le Dieu de Spinoza*, Paris: Félix Alcan.

Hubert, Christiane (1995), *Les premières refutations de Spinoza. Aubert de Versé, Wittich, Lamy*, Paris: PUF.

Jacopin, Paul and Jacqueline Langres (1996), *Érasme. Humanisme et langage*, Paris: PUF.

James, William (1992), *Writings 1878–1899*, ed. Gerald Myers, New York: Library of America.

Jeanneret, Michel (1998), *Perpetuum mobile. Métamorphoses des corps et des oeuvres de Vinci à Montaigne*, Paris: Macula.

Jolibert, Bernard (1981), *L'enfance au XVIIe siècle*, Paris: Vrin.

Kant, Immanuel (1998), *Critique of Pure Reason*, trans. and ed. Paul Guyer and Allen W. Wood, New York: Cambridge University Press.

Kant, Immanuel (2006), *Anthropology from a Pragmatic Point of View*, trans. and ed. Robert B. Louden, New York: Cambridge University Press.

Kantorowicz, Ernst H. (2016), *The King's Two Bodies*, Princeton: Princeton University Press.

Lachièze-Rey, Pierre (1950), *Les origins cartésiennes du Dieu de Spinoza*, Paris: Vrin.

Lacour-Gayet, Georges (1923), *L'éducation politique de Louis XIV*, Paris: Hachette.

Lampert, Jay (2006), *Deleuze and Guattari's Philosophy of History*, New York: Continuum.

Lebrun, François (1967), *Le XXIIe siècle*, Paris: Librairie Armand Colin.

Lebrun, François (1995), *Se soigner autrefois. Médecins, saints et sorciers aux XVIIe et XVIIIe siècles*, Paris: Éditions du Seuil.

Leibniz, G. W. (1967), *The Leibniz–Arnauld Correspondence*, trans. and ed. H. T. Mason, Manchester: Manchester University Press.

Leibniz, G.W. (1989), *Philosophical Papers and Letters*, trans. and ed. Leroy E. Loemker, Second Edition, Boston: Kluwer Academic Publishers.

Lett, Didier (1988), 'L'enfance: *aetas infirma, aetas infima*', *Médiévales* 15: 85–95.

Locke, John (1997), *An Essay Concerning Human Understanding*, ed. Roger Woolhouse, New York: Penguin.

Locke, John (2003), *Two Treatises of Government*, ed. Peter Laslett, New York: Cambridge University Press.

Lucas, Jean Maximillien (1954), *La vie de Spinoza par un de ses disciples*, in Spinoza, *Œuvres complètes*, Paris: Gallimard.

Lucretius (2001), *On the Nature of Things*, trans. Martin Ferguson Smith, Indianapolis: Hackett.

Macherey, Pierre (1992), *Avec Spinoza: Études sur la doctrine et l'histoire du spinozisme*, Paris: PUF.

Macherey, Pierre (1994–98), *Introduction à l'Éthique de Spinoza* (5 vols), Paris: PUF.

Macherey, Pierre (2000), 'Spinoza est-il moniste?', in *Spinoza: Puissance et ontology*, ed. Myriam Revault d'Allonnes and Hadi Rizk, Paris: Éditions Kimé.

Macherey, Pierre (2011), *Hegel or Spinoza*, trans. Susan Ruddick, Minneapolis: University of Minnesota Press.

Machiavelli, Niccolò (1988), *Florentine Histories*, trans. Laura F. Banfield and Harvey C. Mansfield, Jr., Princeton: Princeton University Press.

Machiavelli, Niccolò (1998), *Discourses on Livy*, trans. Harvey C. Mansfield and Nathan Tarcov, Chicago: University of Chicago Press.

Malebranche, Nicolas (1997a) *Dialogues on Metaphysics and on Religion*, ed. Nicholas Jolley, trans. David Scott, New York: Cambridge.

Malebranche, Nicolas (1997b), *The Search after Truth*, trans. and ed. Thomas M. Lennon and Paul J. Olscamp, New York: Cambridge University Press.

Martin, Paul M. (1994), *L'idée de royauté à Rome*, vol. 2, Clermont-Ferrand: Adosa.

Matheron, Alexandre (1969), *Individu et communauté chez Spinoza*, Paris: Minuit.

Matheron, Alexandre (1971), *Le Christ et le salut des ignorants chez Spinoza*, Paris: Aubier Montaigne.

Matheron, Alexandre (2020), 'Is the State, according to Spinoza, an Individual in Spinoza's Sense?', in *Politics, Ontology and Knowledge in Spinoza*, ed. Filippo Del Lucchese, David Maruzzella, and Gil Morejón, trans. David Maruzzella and Gil Morejón, Edinburgh: Edinburgh University Press.

Mead, G. R. S. (1906), *Thrice-Greatest Hermes, Volume 3*, London: The Theosophical Press.

Michael-Matsas, Savvas (2016), 'A Utopia of Innocence: Revolution in Deleuze and Guattari', *Deleuze and Guattari Studies* 10:3: 289–300.

Montaigne, Michel de (1993), *Essays*, trans. J. M. Cohen, New York: Penguin.

Moreau, Pierre-François (1994), *Spinoza: L'expérience et l'éternité*, Paris: PUF.

Moreau, Pierre-François (1979), 'Éthique et psychiatrie', in *Psychiatrie et Éthique*, ed. Guy Maurani, Privat: Toulouse.

Mugnier-Pollet, Lucien (1976), *La philosophie politique de Spinoza*, Paris: Vrin.

Nail, Thomas (2012), *Returning to Revolution: Deleuze, Guattari, and Zapatismo*, Edinburgh: Edinburgh University Press.

Naudé, Gabriel (1988), *Considérations politiques sur les coups d'État*, with Louis Marin, *Pour une théorie baroque de l'action politique*, Paris: Éditions de Paris.

Negri, Antonio (1991), *The Savage Anomaly: The Power of Spinoza's Metaphysics and Politics*, trans. Michael Hardt, Minneapolis: University of Minnesota Press.

Néraudau, Jean-Pierre (1986), *L'Olympe du Roi-Soleil. Mythologie et ideologie royale au Grand Siècle*, Paris: Belles Lettres.

Néraudau, Jean-Pierre (1997), *Introduction aux Amours d'Ovide*, Paris: Belles Lettres.

Nietzsche, Friedrich (1996), *Selected Letters of Friedrich Nietzsche*, trans. and ed. Christopher Middleton, Indianapolis: Hackett.

Nietzsche, Friedrich (2002), *Beyond Good and Evil*, ed. Rolf-Peter Horstmann and Judith Norman, trans. Judith Norman, New York: Cambridge University Press.

Nietzsche, Friedrich (2006), *Thus Spoke Zarathustra: A Book for All and None*, ed. Adrian Del Caro and Robert B. Pippin, trans. Adrian Del Caro, New York: Cambridge University Press.

Parker, Jack H. (1975), *Juan Perez de Montalván*, Boston: Twayne Publishers.

Pascal, Blaise (2004), *Pensées*, trans. and ed. Roger Ariew, Indianapolis: Hackett.

Pfersmann, Otto (1988), 'Spinoza et l'anthropologie du savoir', in *Spinoza, science et religion*, ed. Renée Bouveresse, Paris: Vrin.

Plato (1997), *Complete Works*, ed. John Cooper and D. S. Hutchinson, Indianapolis: Hackett.

Polybius (2010), *The Histories*, trans. Robin Waterfield, New York: Oxford University Press.

Préposiet, Jean (1967), *Spinoza et la liberté des hommes*, Paris: Gallimard.

Ramond, Charles (1995), *Qualité et quantité dans la philosophie de Spinoza*, Paris: PUF.

Ravà, Adolfo (1933), 'La pedagogia di Spinoza', in *Septimana spinozana*, The Hague: Nijhoff.

Renouvier, Charles (1842), *Manuel de philosophie moderne*, Paris: Paulin.

Renouvier, Charles (1901), *Les dilemmes de la métaphysique pure*, Paris: Félix Alcan.

Rodis-Lewis, Geneviève (2000), *L'oeuvre de Descartes*, Paris: Vrin.

Schama, Simon (1988), *The Embarrassment of Riches: An Interpretation of Dutch Culture in the Golden Age*, Berkeley: University of California Press.

Schuhl, Maxime (1964), 'Sur l'enfance d'une Infante', in *Mélanges Alexandre Koyré*, vol. 2, Paris: Hermann.

Senellart, Michel (1989), *Machiavélisme et raison d'État*, Paris: PUF.

Smith, Daniel W. (2012), *Essays on Deleuze*, Edinburgh: Edinburgh University Press.

Swift, Jonathan (2005), *Gulliver's Travels*, ed. Claude Rawson and Ian Higgins, New York: Oxford World's Classics.

Terence (2006), *The Comedies*, trans. and ed. Peter Brown, New York: Oxford University Press.

Tschirnhaus, Ehrenfried Walter von (1980), *Médecine de l'esprit*, trans. J.-P. Wurtz, Strasbourg-Paris: Ophrys.

Vernière, Paul (1951), *Spinoza et la pensée française avant la revolution*, Paris: PUF.

Vertron, Guyonnet de (1686), *Le Nouveau Panthéon, ou le rapport des divinités du paganism, des héros de l'Antiquité et des Princes surnommées grands aux vertus et aux actions de Louis-Le-Grand*, Paris.

Vygotsky, Lev (1996), 'Igri I iéio rol'v psikhitchieskom razvitii riébionka', *Voprossy psikhologuii* 6.

Vygotsky, Lev (1997), *Educational Psychology*, trans. Robert Silverman, Boca Raton: St. Lucie Press.

Wolfson, Harry Austryn (1934), *The Philosophy of Spinoza*, Cambridge, MA: Harvard University Press.

Zourabichvili, François (2002), *Spinoza. Une physique de la pensée*, Paris: PUF.

Zourabichvili, François (2011), *La littéralité et autres essais sur l'art*, ed. Anne Sauvagnargues, Paris: PUF.

Zourabichvili, François (2012), *Deleuze: A Philosophy of the Event*, together with *The Vocabulary of Deleuze*, trans. Kieran Aarons, ed. Gregg Lambert and Daniel W. Smith, Edinburgh: Edinburgh University Press.

Zumthor, Paul (1960), *La vie quotidienne en Hollande au temps de Rembrandt*, Paris: Hachette.

Index

EU Authorised Representative:

Easy Access System Europe Mustamäe tee 50, 10621 Tallinn, Estonia

gpsr.requests@easproject.com

Printed and bound by CPI Group (UK) Ltd, Croydon, CR0 4YY

08/07/2025

01913184-0009